Teaching Human Rights in Literary and Cultural Studies

Modern Language Association of America
Options for Teaching

For a complete listing of titles,
see the last pages of this book.

Teaching Human Rights in Literary and Cultural Studies

Edited by
Alexandra Schultheis Moore
and
Elizabeth Swanson Goldberg

The Modern Language Association of America
New York 2015

Library of Congress Cataloging-in-Publication Data
Teaching human rights in literary and cultural studies / edited by Alexandra Schultheis Moore and Elizabeth Swanson Goldberg.
pages cm. — (Options for teaching ; 38)
Summary: "Offers pedagogical techniques and syllabus suggestions for incorporating human rights issues into the college classroom. Includes information on legal imperialism; Universal Declaration of Human Rights; *testimonio*; gender; feminism; female genital mutilation; remembrance; social justice; torture; postcolonialism; loss; trauma; economic rights; law; sexuality; the other; racism; cultural encounters; composition; prisons" — Provided by publisher.
Includes bibliographical references and index.
ISBN 978-1-60329-215-3 (hardback) —
ISBN 978-1-60329-216-0 (paper) —
ISBN 978-1-60329-217-7 (EPUB) —
ISBN 978-1-60329-218-4 (Kindle)
1. Law and literature—Study and teaching—United States. 2. Human rights—Study and teaching—United States. 3. Human rights in literature—Study and teaching—United States. I. Moore, Alexandra Schultheis, editor. II. Goldberg, Elizabeth Swanson, 1966– , editor.
KF277.L38T427 2015
323.071—dc23 2015019339

Options for Teaching 38
ISSN 1079-2562

Cover illustration of the paperback and electronic editions:
Sin Miedo de Cruzar la Puesta Roja, by Claudia Bernardi. 2007. Fresco on paper. Snite Museum of Art, University of Notre Dame. © Claudia Bernardi

Published by The Modern Language Association of America
85 Broad Street, suite 500, New York, NY 10004-2434
www.mla.org

For Chloë, Samantha, and Marcelle

Contents

Marjorie Agosín

Foreword

When the editors invited me to write this brief foreword for *Teaching Human Rights in Literary and Cultural Studies*, I felt both humbled and privileged to be able to contribute to this vibrant collection of essays. At the same time I had an enormous curiosity about the ways in which the editors organized the subject matter and invited academics to participate in this collection.

The teaching of human rights through the prisms of literature, film, and the visual arts is one of the most challenging as well as vital tasks in which we can engage as academics. A fundamental question is always asked: How do we educate for social change? That is, how do we engage our students to be involved in their communities and in the world, and what is the role of the academy as a secure place to foster activism and scholarship?

Each of the carefully selected essays in this collection addresses with authenticity and brilliance how and why we teach human rights through the aesthetic representation of language and how we teach unspeakable subjects such as torture and censorship through artistic texts. In other words, how do we humanize through the arts a deeply dehumanized world? The contributors bring a deep knowledge of the subject to a multiplicity of topics—from the framework of empirical ethics in the essay by Kimberly Nance, to the rights outside Western nations and their relation to colonial powers, to rights in translation, to a more philosophical aspect such as the one addressed by Crystal Parikh and Nicholas Matlin in "Human Rights and the Tautology of Human Being." Each essay is a world in itself as well as a window to other worlds occupied by disciplines such as law, philosophy, and exile studies.

This collection is extraordinary and will be central to the rich and ever changing curriculum on the teaching of human rights. It is not a manual that gives us a mandate on how to teach within the human rights context but rather a collection that deeply inspires each one of us to rethink engagingly and creatively how the framework of literature and human rights engages with other disciplines such as feminist studies, thoroughly explored in the essay of Eve Wiederhold, or rhetoric, as in the essay by Belinda Walzer. All the essays engage with the ways in which we teach and speak about human rights and literature, fully rethinking and expanding on the cultural and aesthetic politics of human rights discourse and how this discourse is fluid, never rigid. It is hybrid and motivated by the existential challenges of who we are in the world as civilians and in the classroom as teachers. It asks how we can cultivate a depleted humanity, as defined by Martha Nussbaum and as addressed by Ryan Omizo and Wendy S. Hesford in their essay, as well as how the powers of the imagination function in the construction of narratives of trauma and displacement across borders and national identities.

The essays in this volume, beautifully crafted, allow us to believe that the literature of human rights is an essential pedagogical project, a labor of commitment and tenacity that brings the reader into the textual and imaginative powers of human rights literature. In this volume, the concepts of social justice and activism are not empty rhetorical questions; rather, the authors genuinely explore ways to transform the reader and his or her community into human rights bridges and ways to teach so that human rights literature ultimately will inspire others to act.

To experience empathy is to call attention to the diversity of human experience under the prism of human rights, including such phenomena as violence, censorship, displacement, and exile. Thus this collection does not act as a tool for convincing us or others that human rights matter; instead it shows us that the pedagogical quest of teaching the literature of human rights is a crucial debate in and outside the classroom and is an essential part of a humanistic education. The possibility of finding parallels among popular fiction, cinema, visual studies, and human rights is evident in each of these essays, as well as in the myriad narratives related in the literature of human rights.

The essays in this volume are thoughtful and inspiring, reflective, and abundant in possibilities of critical thinking. They are intellectually honest and provide a tapestry of readings from around the world, from slavery to freedom. As I read them, I feel I am aiming toward the possibility of living in a more diaphanous world, a world where the darkness of everyday and governmental violence is not so overpowering, a world where personal narratives are in dialogue with the historical. This collection offers the possibility of empathic thinking as well as the path to hope through art. It is a text that inspires and calls to action, but, even more, it empowers the academic community to engage in meaningful and transformative work. Each essay reminds me of a lighthouse, always shining in a dark and vast world.

Alexandra Schultheis Moore
and Elizabeth Swanson Goldberg

Introduction: Charting New Courses: Teaching Human Rights in Literary and Cultural Studies

This volume speaks to the proliferation of courses oriented toward human rights across the humanities in higher education, to the wide range of teachers who are drawn to this subject matter, as well as to the broad scope of the subject itself. When we bring human rights to the forefront of our reading practices, specific rights histories, concepts, paradoxes, and promises rise to the surface of a text. We share with our contributors the assumption that human rights discourses and practices, however fraught and contested, have vital potential that can only be realized through a robust understanding of human rights cultures. Literary and rhetorical scholarship and pedagogies geared toward human rights analyze how texts help create or diminish cultures of human rights and imagine the forms and substances such cultures might take. The contributors to this volume present conceptual frames, textual suggestions, and assignments to make human rights a central focus of teaching in literary and cultural studies. These approaches take as their purview both the wide span of content, examining how literary and cultural texts thematize human rights events (and thus the relation of aesthetic texts to historical context), and the deep focus on form, considering how literary artists use language, structure, and genre to represent human rights claims or to tell human rights stories. In addition, the essays address the affective and ethical demands that human rights content, especially in aesthetic presentation, makes on students and teachers. In these ways, the essays use the frame of human rights to speak to the fullest possible understanding of the analytic, contextual, emotional, and ethical dimensions of teaching in literature and cultural studies.

As the discourse of human rights becomes more prevalent, its scope changes from a specific body of laws and legal traditions to a correlative for social justice. In this volume, we define human rights in relation to the historical antecedents and legacies of the Universal Declaration of Human Rights of 1948 and its attendant debates and legal instruments. Contributors also draw attention to the kinds of stories of violation that this normative frame of human rights forecloses. The challenge remains to place rights in philosophical, political, and historical contexts without positing normative human rights as the inevitable, teleological product of those contexts. Whether one begins in the classical tradition, with Antigone's decision to defy Creon and bury her brother, thus grounding ethical duty beyond the laws of the state, or with complex narrative strategies of testimony and rights claims, as in Mary Shelley's *Frankenstein*, written just two decades after the Haitian Revolution and the French Declaration of the Rights of Man and of the Citizen, or at another legal-literary nexus, the choice may illuminate core components of imagining, defining, claiming, and contesting rights. Micheline Ishay reminds us, "where one locates the beginning of a history tends to privilege a particular worldview" ("Human Rights" xxii). Mindful of that danger, we nonetheless find great value in placing human rights in histories that illuminate, as Lynn Hunt and Julie Stone Peters have shown, how the individual human rights subject, the nation-state, global capitalism, and particular literary forms and genres have emerged in tandem. For teachers who approach human rights in literary and cultural studies from thematic, formal, or generic standpoints, understanding the evolution of normative human rights can underscore it at once as founded on particular assumptions that literary forms and genres may illuminate and as subject to change.

A significant challenge in teaching this field is its inherent interdisciplinarity. For human rights to frame a reading practice, its objects—the texts scholars study—must be situated in historical, legal, philosophical, and of course literary or rhetorical contexts. To help meet the challenges of that interdisciplinarity, we offer this volume as a sourcebook of approaches and best practices rooted in and organized according to the following topics: Issues and Definitions; Historical and Geographic Orientations; Bearing Wrongs, Reading Rights, Engendering Responsibility; and Classroom Contexts. A final section on resources points the reader toward further readings in history, criticism, theory, and literary and visual studies and provides a chronology of human rights legal documents. The field of human rights and literary and cultural studies has been nothing if not inventive in its approaches to synthesizing areas that diverge as much as they overlap and has built as much in theory, pedagogy, and practice on the resulting tensions, paradoxes, and gaps as it does on the harmonies. We hope the essays collected here will open new ground for pedagogical innovation.

Issues and Definitions

This section provides an overview of foundational issues in the human rights and literature classroom, including the status of literature, the question of the human being who is legible within rights discourse, the mutually "enabling fictions" of literature and the law (Slaughter, *Human Rights, Inc.* 45), and the limitations of normative human rights in a global context.

Arguably, most any literary text can be read and taught through the lens of human rights, in the sense that most texts reference the human, with the attendant vulnerabilities, connections, contexts, and conflicts that make up the field of the human in human rights. Most texts can be read philosophically for their depictions of the kinds of ethos that can ground the legal apparatus of the rights regime—or the lack thereof—and many often-taught literary texts are situated in historical contexts that constitute important instances in the evolution of human rights in their modern incarnation: the foundation and expansion of empires, encounters between European immigrants and Native Americans or between imperialists and indigenous populations in the places they colonized, the experience of revolution (political, economic, and industrial), the transatlantic slave trade, the American Civil War, the abolitionist movement, Reconstruction, the Spanish-American War, anticolonial emancipation and nationalist movements, minority rights movements of the 1960s through the 1990s, the post-9/11 moment. Whether reading the human or historical trauma, human rights as a mode of reception benefits from explicit links between literary representation and rights-speak, whether in the form of the person with legal standing, a political document, a relevant law, or key forms of rights discourse such as the human rights report or testimony. The essays in this section work against the argument that literature provides a useful vehicle for human rights, particularly in literature's ability to generate a humanitarian sensibility toward an other. Instead, these essays underscore how close readings of literary and narrative form can reveal the deep structures of violation with respect to rights and their representation.

Significantly, the interdiscipline of human rights and literature is driven by a productive tension since demands for legal certainty in the form of human rights claims often emerge out of narrative and historical ambiguity. The work of recognizing such claims in all their complexity is one of the most crucial—and underaddressed—preconditions for interrupting the toxic cycle of violations that endangers peace everywhere. In the developing context of international testimonial forums such as the International Criminal Court, the International Criminal Tribunals for Rwanda and the former Yugoslavia, and the Special Court for Sierra Leone, the location of agency in stories that have historically been marginalized or silenced—both voice and control over stories are central to postcolonial literary projects—introduces an alternative over time to more brutal methods of asserting identity and control. When students learn to read for and understand the histories and powers behind such loci of agency, they also learn to consider their own relation to the production and consumption of human rights stories.

The limits to cognitive truth regimes and the consequences of their imposition have been well demonstrated in the context of human rights stories, particularly the *testimonio*. Despite the survivor's struggle to find language sufficient for telling the experience of atrocity, the primary question posed to modern testimonials in a human rights context often has more to do with veracity than with form; as the controversy surrounding the *testimonio* of Rigoberta Menchú Tum has shown, veracity is a deciding factor in the construction and reception of such texts. One task of the instructor when examining the human rights narrative in the classroom is to situate such prioritization of factual veracity in the epistemological tenets of individualist Western notions, contexts, and applications of truth-value and the narrative forms that have accompanied them into being.

This task carries over to the teacher's examination of the ways in which human rights discourse, like any discourse, can evacuate or abrogate its intended meaning. Indeed, the language of human rights can be shown repeatedly, consistently, to be "used to justify their violation" (McClennen and Slaughter 2). Teachers in human rights and literature classrooms, as many of our contributors here note, must present human rights through the scope of their own doubled optic: as a discourse and practice of social justice and as a vehicle or alibi for militaristic neo-imperialism. Taking up that challenge in the classroom requires that, in Gayatri Spivak's words,

> the redressing work of Human Rights . . . be supplemented by an education that can continue to make unstable the presupposition that the reasonable righting of wrongs is inevitably the manifest destiny of groups—unevenly class-divided, embracing North and South—that remain posed to right them; and that, among the receiving groups, wrongs will inevitably proliferate with unsurprising regularity. ("Righting Wrongs" 530)

Spivak's understanding of the untenable fixity of groups marked as "righters" of wrongs and "receivers" of wrongs extends to the classroom, which Spivak cautions can easily become the site of a misguided sense of noblesse oblige on the part of privileged students learning about the suffering of others, elsewhere. At its best, and alternatively, the imaginative work involved in reading narratives of human rights calls for the student-reader, human rights worker, or theorist to reflect on his or her own position in the structural causes of human rights conditions as integral to formulating an ethical response to an other.

Historical and Geographic Orientations

We address historical and geographic orientations because questions of geopolitical and historical location traditionally frame both literary studies as well as critiques of human rights. Central to rights discourse and analysis of its imaginative and aesthetic counterparts in political and intellectual history are the emergence of the individual as the bearer of rights within and against the state; the importance of ideas of human dignity and natural law in justifying rights; the search for universalizable or, in Domna Stanton's important formulation, generalizable rights ("Top Down"); the question of inseparability versus a hierarchy of rights; the locus of rights in specific juridical-political institutions; and the relatively recent development of collective rights (so-called third generation rights, after civil and political and then economic, social, and cultural rights). Different historical moments bring these features of human rights discourse and practice into high relief. In this volume, Sarah Winter provides an overview of rights' historical development—from classical Greek and Roman philosophers' and playwrights' articulations of the desire for a universal set of principles based on natural law that supersede those of the state, to colonial-era considerations of who counts as human within human rights (one thinks of the Valladolid Debate of 1550–51, for instance), to abolition as a human rights claim within the context of liberal philosophy, to, finally, more modern and contemporary formulations. As Winter argues, undertaking such a genealogy necessitates careful attention to how concepts of the human, dignity, and justice are articulated in vocabularies that may lack explicit reference to human rights. Instructors may find different aspects of that history helpful not only for a deeper understanding of normative rights discourses but also for a rigorous critique of them at specific historical moments (including our own).

Placing rights in historical context also facilitates denaturalized readings of them, as both teachers and students may come to see rights discourses as selective choices or inventions made among diverse possibilities in particular circumstances. An intellectual history provides one framework for such comparisons, allowing instructors to explore the wider cultural and political context surrounding a particular event or situation. The other essays in this section complement this process of denaturalized readings, taking as their points of departure different geopolitical perspectives—examining rights in the African, European, Asian, Latin American, and post-9/11 United States contexts, although their individual assignments and choices of texts exceed any single course description—for teaching human rights representations. These perspectives open up traditional categories of literary studies that are organized by nation and period to alternative transnational and transhistorical perspectives on rights; they also turn attention back to the problems that arise from translation in reading local claims and transnational discourses simultaneously.

Bearing Wrongs, Reading Rights, Engendering Responsibility

Courses in human rights in literary and cultural studies are frequently organized thematically according to a particular form or genre or to a particular violation. The essays in this section address such approaches by foregrounding the embodiment of violations, in conjunction with responses in the rights cycle (i.e., violence, witnessing, resistance, and reconciliation or justice or mourning), in specific classroom practices and contexts. The essays take up issues of economic rights, women's rights, sexual rights, torture, and postconflict transitional justice, with particular attention to the ways in which violence is borne in the body, psyche, and polity. At the same time, this litany of categories of abuse or rights is merely suggestive of the wide scope of the field, and the specific assignments theorized and described, from close reading to building sociopolitical context to cultivating students' "response-ability" (to borrow from Kelly Oliver [5]) to the choice of texts, could be used across the spectrum of human rights and literature courses.

Reading within and across discourse communities, particularly those constructed by the text in relation to those within the classroom, demands attention to imagination—specifically, the ability to imagine others, the lives of others, and, now especially, the other as human. The range of the serious play of imagination depends, in turn, on strategies of representation. This notion of representation may take multiple forms: for instance, how people are represented—in a broad sense, the meanings that are attached to their beings in the world—in their communities and beyond as friend or enemy, aggressor or victim, beneficiary or bystander; how texts convey affect and emotion, especially across historical and cultural differences; the problems of representing human rights cases in the context of the international community such that action is initiated or change occurs; and the very specific criteria for legal standing established in forums for address or redress of human rights violations such as the International Criminal Court, various tribunals or truth and reconciliation commissions in global contexts, or local courts such as the Gacaca, in postgenocide Rwanda. Inasmuch as it scrutinizes the production of meaning through the descriptive, narrated, and dialogic elements of character, plot, setting, theme, and symbol or image—in short, through the same elements of story that form the basis of human rights testimonies—literary studies is a proving ground for interrogating and understanding the complexities of representation in the global information age.

Regardless of the forms they take, representations of human rights violations are often grounded in notions of collective or individual identity. Literary studies, particularly in the wake of the postmodern, multicultural, postcolonial, and feminist movements of the latter half of the twentieth century, offers tools to understand and counter violence as a response to identity difference, illuminating the production and the effects of power and oppression based on identity. Such theories analyze identity as socially and culturally contingent rather than essential, shifting rather than stable, multiple rather than singular in its loyalties and identifications—and, as our contributors demonstrate, these theories can productively be applied to global human rights problems past and present in the classroom. Rather than reify the distance between an ostensibly safe and secure world and the chaotic, violent world of the text, or between readers and the subjects of global human rights literature, teachers can direct students' attention to their location vis-à-vis the text to expose deeper structural conditions that underlie violations either to link reader and text or to make the politics of literary production and consumption available for scrutiny.

In addition, the essays in this section explore literary and cultural texts as a necessary supplement to the language of law and the state. Aesthetic forms and strategies may gesture toward truths that languish outside the systems of language and its attempts at representability, toward those truths that can find expression only, paradoxically, in the silences, aporias, and gaps of meaning and locution that have been so well documented by scholars of trauma studies. In her essay "The Testamentary Whimper," Avital Ronell explores the function of philosophy and literature in responding to the problem of inarticulability put forth by Jean-François Lyotard that "a wrong . . . is a damage accompanied by the loss of the means to prove the damage" (qtd. in Ronell 489). Human rights as a mode of literary reception might indeed supplement the work that Ronell demands of philosophical thought, that it "come up with a link to the feeling-tone of the unaccounted for, and offer privileged protection to the unaccountable refugees of cognitive regimens" (495). If not protection, this way of reading literarily at least creates a critical and pedagogical space for the extraordinary modes of expression necessitated by the extreme experience of atrocity; at the same time, it demands analysis of the material and ideological ramifications of those expressions.

Classroom Contexts

The essays in this section take up specific pedagogical challenges and methods, including negotiating student expectations in the classroom, teaching human rights and visual rhetoric, codisciplinary teaching, service learning, and a common read program. Whereas some readers may be drawn to essays according to these individual pedagogical approaches, others may find the specific textual examples inspirational or informative in designing their own syllabi based on different pedagogical criteria. These essays focus on particular classroom practices, but they work in conjunction with essays throughout the volume to provide a broad overview of course materials and assignments for teaching human rights in a literary and cultural context.

As Belinda Walzer reminds readers in her essay, "Rhetorical Approaches to Teaching Human Rights: The Pedagogy of *Speak Truth to Power*," normative human rights contains a pedagogical imperative. In the words of the preamble to the Universal Declaration of Human Rights, "Every individual and every organ of society, keeping this Declaration constantly in mind, shall strive by teaching and education to promote respect for these rights and freedoms and by progressive measures, national and international, to secure their universal and effective recognition and observance" ("Universal Declaration"). This urging implies that human rights as concept and practice has self-evident value. Although our contributors share a deep concern with issues of social justice and present the ways in which human rights discourse frames such issues more broadly, they also promote a critical approach to reading and writing rights. Instead of automatically promoting human rights, the pedagogies discussed in this section and throughout the volume emphasize how a course oriented toward human rights can facilitate students' more rigorous understandings of their place in the world and in relation to rights discourses. Across the different classroom contexts discussed in this section, the authors collectively embrace active learning in which students develop not only academic skills and content knowledge but also, and as important, come to see themselves as cultural knowledge producers and global citizens.

As with each section in this book, the range of pedagogies represented here is by no means exhaustive. We contend, however, that the issues addressed in this section apply broadly to courses in human rights and literary and cultural studies, whether offered in traditional or nontraditional formats and institutional settings.

Strategies for Using This Volume

In *Teaching Human Rights in Literary and Cultural Studies*, contributors focus heavily on the role of the reader in the triangulated nexus of author-artist, reader-viewer-student, and text-referent-other. They note that in this twenty-first-century moment of interactive technologies, interdisciplinary methodologies, and the myriad virtual and real global contact zones they engender, students are loathe to leave behind the problems raised by the texts, ancient or contemporary, upon concluding their readings, and the contributors believe that the energy generated in such pedagogical encounters ought not to be ignored, denied, downplayed, or condescended to but rather ought to be engaged with intellectual rigor and integrity. This common thread runs throughout the volume, making possible many different strategies—determined by the choice of literary and cultural texts, style of pedagogy, or thematic focus—for using the volume. In organizing the essays, we begin with the broadest concerns that form the foundation for teaching human rights in literary studies and then adhere to the categories through which individual courses are often organized and positioned in language and literary studies departments.

Instructors who are new to the field of human rights and to human rights as a literary approach may find it helpful to begin with this introduction and then the final section, on resources, to get a sense of the critical terrain, a chronology of primary human rights instruments, and various online pedagogical resources. The first essays in part 2, "Historical and Geographic Orientations," and part 4, "Classroom Contexts," by Sarah Winter and Kimberly A. Nance, respectively, also serve to frame key historical and pedagogical dimensions of human rights in the humanities classroom.

We recommend the first essay in the volume, Greg Mullins's extraordinarily thoughtful introduction to the field, to all readers, new and experienced, who want a fresh perspective on why teachers teach and how what seem at first to be losses in the classroom—in students' thinking about rights and literature—can become sources of creative, generative learning. Our collection bookends Mullins's essay with one by Megan Sweeney, who also reminds us of the privilege of literary reading and how it can connect students to the larger world. The three essays that complete part 1, "Issues and Definitions," provide rich conceptual pedagogical approaches to questions of who counts as human in human rights, whether human rights' legal framework is inherently imperialistic, and how human rights relates to other religious and cultural systems.

Our hope is that instructors will find many different ways of using the volume, from teaching a particular text, violation, or historical period to considering overarching theoretical arguments that might inform ways of reading human rights in literature and visual culture across institutional divisions.

Part I

Issues and Definitions

Introduction to Part 1

We begin with conceptual issues at the heart of the pedagogy of human rights in literary and cultural studies: definitions of the human, manifestations of law and the state, and the challenge of nurturing affective, analytic, and contextualized approaches to textual representations of difficult subjects. Questions about who can claim rights and whether rights can be understood outside specific legal and cultural frameworks will arise, we suspect, in any course on human rights and aesthetic representation. Greg Mullins provides a generous welcome to the field, examining the place of literature within a curriculum that addresses human rights and defining what may be our most widely shared objectives as teachers: "opening public conversation and debate about the role that human rights language plays in historical and contemporary political and cultural formations." A notable component of these courses is loss—loss of faith in rights, in people, and in literature. Mullins outlines strategies for transforming the loss that is "a constitutive feature of human rights" into a catalyst for student creativity and learning.

The following two essays take up the conceptualization of the human and the law. In "Human Rights and the Tautology of Human Being," Crystal Parikh and Nicholas Matlin focus on the ambiguous locus of rights: the space between the human being whose inherent dignity provides an oft-cited rationale for rights and the legal person who can claim them. Understanding rights as the shaper of the human, rather than the human as an a priori subject who claims rights, delineates an important role for inquiry in the humanities. It is through reading literarily, the authors argue, that one can begin to trace the contours of this concept of the human.

A second foundational question for the field is how to present the paradoxical status of law and the state. Within most human rights law, the state is both its guarantor (in and of itself or as a signatory to international conventions) as well as its object (as perpetrator of violations). This paradox is multiplied when rights discourse is used in postcolonial or neo-imperial contexts. Elizabeth Anker, in "'The Language of the Criminal': Teaching the Legal Imperialism Debate," presents pedagogical strategies and textual suggestions for balancing the critical analysis of rights, especially in relation to the intertwining of human rights projects with forms of aid and intervention that often have neo-imperial overtones, alongside an acknowledgment of their usefulness.

The different ways of understanding the human subject as well as the "legal imperialism debate" necessitate an examination of alternatives to human rights from other philosophical and cultural traditions. We conclude this section with the essay "Human Rights Cultures and Traditions: Beyond the Post-/Colonial and the West" to provide an overview of three alternatives, drawn from scholarship on Islamic, Buddhist, and indigenous approaches to human rights. In addition, we discuss several course readers that address these issues and three distinct pedagogical approaches to reading rights in a comparative cultural context.

The essays in this section also include specific case studies of recommended texts for classroom use and questions for class discussion that speak directly to other essays in the volume (one could imagine groupings, for instance, determined by literary field, conceptual approach, or specific pedagogy).

Greg A. Mullins

Losses of Human Rights in the Literature Classroom

Over the past decade I have taught a number of courses on literature and human rights, and they have been among the most rewarding experiences of my career. The response from students has been enthusiastic, and graduates have told me that their work in my course stimulated them not only to think but also to act in new ways. Here I share some thoughts about what is to be gained by teaching literature in relation to human rights and vice versa, but I focus on the losses of teaching human rights and literature. Human rights violations involve loss by definition: loss of rights, loss of respect of rights, or loss of homes, livelihood, liberty, loved ones—even loss of life. If the study of human rights includes the study of human rights violations, loss will be a presence in the classroom. And in my experience, students also experience loss in that classroom.

Some of my students are drawn to study human rights and literature because they are curious about human rights and because they enjoy literature. They enrolled, they tell me, because they believed the pleasure of reading fiction would make it easier to learn about human rights. Among these students I've noticed a remarkable loss of interest in literature, registered primarily in their choice of final projects: they pursue individual research on a human rights topic, rather than squarely examine the literary engagements with human rights that introduced them to that topic. In this pattern, the urgency of a particular variety of human rights violation displaces literature, the place of the literary, or the attraction to literature (pleasure, perhaps?) that brought the student to my classroom.

Another group of students (and many students fall into both groups) are drawn to the course by the promise of human rights. They tell me they want to learn about solutions to a wide range of social and political problems and about the human rights promise to defend and protect the weak from the abuses of the powerful. They want to know how human rights accomplish this work, and very often students tell me that they also want to accomplish such work in their lives. Very few students in this profile understand human rights as law, policy, or technique before enrolling; they primarily understand human rights as a slogan or very loosely as an expression of moral rightness. My course asks them to understand the aspirations of human rights as well as their obstacles and deficiencies. Many students who admire human rights as an ideal are disappointed by human rights realities—so much so that some turn away entirely from human rights. For these students, gaining knowledge of rights can speed a loss of confidence in them.

In addition to the grief that attends many varieties of human rights violations, these are the two losses that primarily intrigue me: the loss of interest in literature and the loss of faith in rights. We could dismiss the first case as an instance of professionalization: students abandon amateur (pleasurable) reading practices for inquiry into "serious" topics. We could dismiss the second case as a necessary loss of innocence. The conventional view is that both varieties of loss are inevitable and even healthy; they are the preconditions for professional and intellectual advancement.

I do not intend to overturn this conventional view; in fact, I see a great deal of value in helping undergraduates shed layers of naïveté about human rights, literature, and a great many other topics. I do, however, wish to sharpen our understanding of the extent to which loss is a constitutive element of the human rights project, and to suggest that we may wish to teach loss in a systematic way.

The contexts of my teaching experience have undoubtedly influenced my views. I have taught as a visitor at Wesleyan University and at Mount Holyoke College and more permanently at the Evergreen State College. The two private liberal arts colleges attract students who are conventionally understood, on the basis of elite high school training, to be especially well prepared for college, and the human rights seminar I taught at both schools attracted English majors. Evergreen is a public liberal arts college in which students design their own majors; there are no departments, and my students have a wide range of disciplinary training. Differences among the three colleges are, however, less important than the fact that their liberal arts missions emphasize creative and critical inquiry rather than preprofessional training. I have never been asked to teach human rights professionals (or, for that matter, preprofessionals). To the extent that I am a human rights educator my responsibility lies not with imparting a technical mastery of human rights law but rather with opening public conversation and debate about the role that human rights language plays in historical and contemporary political and cultural formations. In the undergraduate liberal arts classroom I don't teach human rights to promote them but rather to promote critical thinking about language, text, narrative, culture, power, and responsibility.

I should mention that I admire human rights. In my view, the language of human rights provides an insufficient but much needed set of tools that can be used to create a more fair and just world. But I do not tell my students I hold this view until well into the term, and I do not structure a syllabus that is designed to encourage them to agree with me. On the contrary, my syllabus challenges students to make their own assessment of human rights, and I invite them to critique human rights both as theory and as practice. Doubtless my preference to refrain from rallying for human rights contributes to the loss of confidence in rights that my students frequently express. At the same time, I provide texts that help students argue in favor of human rights, and I encourage them to offer reasoned replies to the many available critiques of rights.

My course tends to attract students who are predisposed to admire the language of human rights but who have little technical knowledge of them. In the initial weeks of the term I provide definitions of rights and historical and cultural contexts for the rise of human rights regimes following World War II. Students typically express their first disillusionment with human rights after this basic overview, for they had hoped or assumed that the promises of the Universal Declaration of Human Rights were readily enforceable. From the outset, therefore, the classroom is a site of loss—and this loss is a necessary precondition for a knowledgeable discussion of human rights.

In presenting texts that define the history, promise, and pitfalls of human rights, I attempt to make the ideological positions of those texts transparent. I stage a variety of ideological starting points by, for example, assigning Michael Ignatieff's defense of human rights and Wendy Brown's critique of Ignatieff. I ask students to scrutinize the assumptions and agendas that shape the theorists we read in the remainder of the term—and we read quite a range of them. I typically assign four or five novels and a great deal of theory and criticism, and I organize the reading around thematic units. These units emphasize the narrative and rhetorical structure of many aspects of human rights work and the capacity or incapacity of literature to deepen our understanding of human rights as both theory and practice. My syllabi have included units on the narrative work of witness, testimony, and denial; on the emotional work of literature and human rights (especially anger, sorrow, compassion, and empathy); on human rights investigations and literary memorializations; on the various and often conflictual ways that fiction, law, and political struggle place claims on truth; on cultural specificity and universal rights; and on the ethical claims that permeate all these areas of inquiry. Over the years I have assigned literary texts that advance these interrelated areas of focus, including Dorothy Allison, *Bastard Out of Carolina*; Ivan Ângelo, *The Celebration*; Dionne Brand, *In Another Place, Not Here*; Gil Cuadros, *City of God*; Edwidge Danticat, *The Dew Breaker*; Antjie Krog, *Country of My Skull*; Herman Melville, *Benito Cereno*; Toni Morrison, *Paradise*; Michael Ondaatje, *Anil's Ghost*; and Alicia Partnoy, *The Little School.*

As this list suggests, I draw on both literature that offers representations of "classic" human rights concerns such as disappearance and torture and literature that invites students to consider wider contexts for the narrative, cultural, and political interweavings of literature and human rights. I teach texts from the United States alongside those from other nations to frustrate the notion that human rights are merely a problem elsewhere in the world, and I emphasize the interdependence of civil and political rights and economic and social rights. By the end of my course, students have advanced their foundational understanding of human rights to the point where they appreciate many of the paradoxes and dilemmas that human rights professionals face in their work; students have also developed a sophisticated understanding of how narrative can be deployed by fiction writers as well as by states, nongovernmental organizations, activists, and scholars to build worlds of meaning.

Training students to read human rights instruments closely is enormously helpful in developing these critical skills. For example, pairing the Convention against Torture (CAT) with the United States' endorsement of it ("U.S. Reservations") provides students an opportunity to perceive the struggles involved in legally defining *torture*—a term they intuitively understand to have a much broader meaning than human rights law allows. Both these documents present traces of their political histories even as they imagine the conditions of efforts to prevent or prosecute torture. Also useful are assigned readings that make use of the legal definition of torture for their own purposes, such as John Yoo's "Torture Memos" and any of a number of fund-raising appeals or action alerts from Amnesty International. Asking students to read such a set of texts exposes the ideological fault lines that inform debate about contentious issues such as torture; more important, such an assignment underscores how and why various human rights actors assemble certain words in specific frames to advance their aims. The aims of a work of fiction are typically more complex. In a unit on torture, I might assign Partnoy's *The Little School*, J. M. Coetzee's *Waiting for the Barbarians*, or Danticat's *The Dew Breaker*. Any one of these texts is as concerned with torture's resistance to representation as it is with the exploration of a language capable of encountering it. Literary texts are, in this sense, richer than some of the legal or activist texts I might assign alongside a novel, and through them students acquire the capacity to judge the merits of a text's argument and the merits of its narrative achievement. Paradox, irony, and metaphor might expose the tensions or hidden agendas of legal texts while mobilizing the narrative force of a literary text. The point is not to teach students to read disparate texts blandly but rather to help them analyze how a range of writers (literary artists, human rights workers, and state functionaries) use narrative arts and rhetorical forms to unfold the discourse of human rights.

Along the way, students frequently lose confidence in human rights when they discover any of the following: international enforcement mechanisms of human rights standards are very weak; human rights and humanitarianism are not infrequently promoted by states or groups with colonial and imperial agendas; rights, instead of trumping politics, are politics; public shaming of rights violators often does not leverage respect for rights; human rights has become an industry, and NGOs often operate with narrow (and sometimes self-serving) agendas; denial of violations is often more powerful than witness or testimony; and reading literature sometimes fosters compassion, but compassion does not always foster positive action. In addition, when we study atrocities such as slavery, genocide, torture, or ethnic cleansing, students often lose faith in humanity itself. This material can be severely depressing, especially when I teach it in the long, gray winters of the Pacific Northwest. Mindful of the severity of the topics, I alternate relatively heavy weeks with relatively optimistic weeks and include examples of success stories. My intention is not to discredit human rights practices but rather to provide students with a realistic appreciation of human rights obstacles, as well as to invite them to examine their ideological assumptions about rights. Losing confidence in rights may well be a sign of a student's reflecting deeply on the foundations of his or her idealism or liberalism. Through self-reflection, students learn to challenge any initial assumptions and eventually build a stronger foundation for their work.

One could argue that these aims could be achieved without introducing literature into the human rights curriculum. Indeed, I could devise an inquiry into the usefulness and effectiveness of human rights practices without reference to literature or other cultural practices. But literary and cultural analysis permits a broad view of the uses and abuses of human rights frameworks. We understand ourselves to live in the "age of rights" not merely because rights are enunciated in formative declarations and national constitutions but also because rights talk is so widely diffused in nontechnical usage. How often do you hear someone declare, "I have my rights!" without being able to name those rights in legal terms, let alone being able to explain what remedies may be available when specific rights are violated? Rights talk forms a crucial dimension of the political unconscious in the United States, as it does in many other societies, with variations. Cultural expression opens a window onto this political unconscious, and cultural analysis allows us to expand our understanding of how and why the contemporary period is an "age of rights." We could as well investigate the relation that film, music, the visual arts, and so forth have to rights talk, but literature is especially helpful insofar as it invites analysis of rhetoric, language, and narrative form, and these modes of analysis illuminate both the technical and the nontechnical uses of human rights.

State actors such as investigators and prosecutors and nonstate actors such as NGOs and activists are more likely to employ the technical language of international human rights law than are poets or novelists, who might well pepper their imaginative works with aspirations and sentiment. Technical and nontechnical usages, however, reinforce rather than contradict each other. Aspiration and sentiment carry weight in the court of public opinion and in courts of law; oral arguments as well as judicial decisions shape narratives no less attuned to audience than those in poems and novels. Moreover, both state and nonstate human rights actors are skilled in pitching human rights in nontechnical terms to reach certain audiences. Committees and congresses spend decades hammering out the language that defines, for example, the right of women to access bank loans and credit without suffering gender discrimination, as in the Convention on the Elimination of All Forms of Discrimination against Women (CEDAW; art. 13.b). Human rights workers will ground their advocacy work in the specific language of such conventions but will quickly abandon specificity when a more generalized appeal to equality will better serve the purpose. Studying human rights in and through literature might illuminate a discrete instance of human rights law, but it is more likely to enlarge our capacity to understand how and why rights claims gain force in and through cultures of rights.

I first began to think seriously about human rights, literature, and culture when, as a graduate student, I interned with the International Gay and Lesbian Human Rights Commission (IGLHRC). I responded to the call for interns with about as much knowledge of human rights as my undergraduate students typically bring to my classroom. I too had grown up understanding human rights as a slogan rather than as a legal, ideological, or political framework. I was in favor of human rights merely because I was in favor of justice, and I assumed that the work I did would advance progressive social and political change.

I realized, however, that to work effectively for IGLHRC I had to quickly shed my preconceptions and acquire a professional knowledge of rights. I studied those international declarations and covenants that form the backbone of international human rights law and learned which mechanisms and channels the United Nations and regional bodies have created to funnel human rights initiatives. As I learned both the history of how human rights came to be an internationally recognized language of law and politics and how various political actors make use of that language to advance their aims, I came to deeply appreciate the intellectual work that professionals at IGLHRC had accomplished to pursue their mission. This organization was one of the leading pioneers in articulating how and why human rights protections must be understood with specific reference to sexual and gender minorities and with specific reference to one's HIV status. Before initiating education, advocacy, or program work, the organization needed to articulate in the clearest possible terms how and why sexual and gender rights matter and how and why they form part of the tapestry of human rights.

Among the most prominent criticisms of sexual and gender rights is the argument that human rights claims made with reference to gender and sexuality quickly become a form of cultural imperialism. Branches of this critique often assert that normative gender roles and normative heterosexual practices are moral concerns of a given society. This argument presents gender and sexual diversity as a problem to be "solved" through moral sanction and normative gender roles and heterosexuality as deserving of human rights protection insofar as they are features of cultural tradition and religious belief. Any human rights effort on behalf of sexual or gender minorities is, in this argument, characterized as an effort orchestrated by "outsiders" to impose nontraditional meanings on gender and sexuality—hence the charge of cultural imperialism. The burden lies on human rights advocates to establish their relation to both overt and covert imperial relations of power. They must resist wearing the blinders of moral righteousness and see clearly how specific forms of human rights practice operate through culture toward specific political ends.

During the 1990s (when I was in graduate school) queer theory and postcolonial theory were erupting in the academy, and I was steeped in the emerging theoretical debates about sexual and gender identity, race and racial identity, essences versus social constructions, social norms and normativity, the discursive production of empire and orientalism, and so forth. When I began my internship for IGLHRC, I was immediately impressed that the staff and board members were thinking along lines very close to those in the emerging scholarship and that they had crafted precise and thoughtful policies that reflected the best thinking on the cultural diversity of sexual and gender expressions. I was also delighted to learn that the kind of scholarship I was pursuing in an English department resonated with the practical needs of a human rights organization. When teaching today, I reserve the story of my trajectory into human rights work for a week when my students are seeking some uplift: amid all the losses in the classroom, it is invigorating to acknowledge the gains offered by the study of literature and theory.

As it turns out, the English department where I received my graduate training was an ideal place to have learned why the conceptual tools developed in queer and postcolonial theory corresponded with the needs of IGLHRC. The study of literature advanced my own understanding of culture and the multifarious ways that power is exercised through culture. In my ongoing teaching and research, I continue to believe that the trajectories of literature and human rights cross most productively at the axis of culture. For example, I encourage students to read literature closely so that they might attend to the ways that aesthetic Culture with a capital *C* is produced in and through a complex relationship with the lowercased culture of human rights. Sexual and gender rights are far from the only varieties of human rights that demand precise thinking about culture, universality, power, and politics, and literature offers much more than a mere illustration of human rights practices. Cultural study of human rights and literature in and through each other advances our capacity to understand how they mutually produce and reproduce meaning.

The recent surge of interest in human rights by students and faculty members in literature departments—usefully signaled by the essays in this volume—is itself part of an expansion in the culture and cultural politics of human rights. As scholars, we are all participants in forming this expanding culture, even while we are engulfed by its expansion in ways we may not fully understand. It is well worth our time to allow room for reflection on the conscious motivations that bring us to this work and on what is to be gained by pursuing it. At the same time, we have much to learn from analyzing the wider currents that have propelled human rights and literature into common waters. A great deal of work remains to be done, including improving our analysis of why and how the work is unfolding.

The publications and pedagogies cited throughout the essays in this volume offer vibrant examples of how much we have collectively gained from crossing scholarship in literature and human rights in recent years. In my classroom, I have witnessed extraordinary levels of student engagement with the texts and ideas at this intersection. Student interest and engagement is an index of the extent to which literature pulses with the language and frameworks of rights. Given the readily apparent gains of this collective enterprise, I have been surprised over the past decade to witness so much loss in the classroom. I have come to understand that loss is a constitutive feature of human rights—not only because violations of rights involve loss at so many levels but also because human rights ideals often promise more than can be achieved. I have also come to believe that I have a responsibility to anticipate the varieties of loss my students are likely to express in my classroom and to structure the course in ways that allow space for those losses to become part of our intellectual labor. Anticipating these losses is made all the easier since I keenly remember entering human rights work with much the same naïveté and commitments my students bring to the classroom.

I offer three strategies for engaging the losses of human rights in the literature classroom. The first, and perhaps the most important, is to acknowledge loss where and when it appears—in the very constitution and imagination of human rights, to be sure, but also in the traumas, griefs, and wrongs represented in the literary texts we read. Readers respond to texts in startlingly differentiated ways; one person's tender tale of sorrow is another person's overwrought melodrama. Classroom discussion of the emotional experience of reading brings these differences to the surface and provides an excellent opportunity to underscore variability in the emotional dimensions of rights and rights appeals. Moreover, this individuated discussion of one's personal emotional response to human rights violations invites reflection on one's own assessment of or allegiance to human rights language. In other words, it provides another avenue toward opening the question of whether or why one might have confidence in human rights. Teaching ideologies of rights (and ideological critiques of rights) is another valuable route toward this question, but asking students to consider how the sorrows of human rights might lead them to lose faith in human rights regimes acknowledges a common classroom dynamic and places it squarely on the table for analysis.

Analysis, then, is my second strategy for dealing with the losses of human rights. I provide students with vocabulary and opportunities to pursue this analysis. One especially helpful essay to assign in this context is Judith Butler's "Violence, Mourning, Politics," a chapter from her book *Precarious Life* (19–49). Butler usefully suggests that we think of the structure of grief and the structure of desire in and through each other. Both bind us to others in a condition of sociality through which we at once find ourselves and lose ourselves. In this account, loss is not merely something that often happens around human rights; loss is part of the human connectivity that human rights language attempts to express. "Despite our differences in location and history," Butler writes, "my guess is that it is possible to appeal to a 'we,' for all of us have some notion of what it is to have lost somebody. Loss has made a tenuous 'we' of us all" (20). Butler's essay frames loss as productive of human sociality, mutuality, and responsibility and thus gives students a conceptual model for analyzing the generative potential in their personal experience of grief and mourning. Moreover, the essay models a mode of building confidence in humanity while remaining fully cognizant of the insufficiencies of human rights. To stake rights claims under the law, Butler suggests, "we have to present ourselves as bounded beings—distinct, recognizable, delineated, subjects before the law, a community defined by some shared features" (24). The language of law and rights, however, "does not do justice to passion and grief and rage, all of which tear us from ourselves, bind us to others, transport us, undo us, implicate us in lives that are not our own" (25). Students, among the many interpretations they may offer of this essay, are likely to comment on the confidence Butler expresses in discovering human mutuality precisely in the aftermath of political violence.

My third strategy for structuring the function of loss in the classroom is to avoid excessive structure. In my experience, loss ebbs and flows. I cannot, as an instructor, predict which of my students might lose or gain confidence in rights or literature or when or what that loss or gain means to a student. Moreover, human rights are messy. Even their tidiest articulations—in the Universal Declaration and in other covenants negotiated by the United Nations—expose discord, contradiction, and opacity. The attempts by states, activist organizations, and individuals to realize human rights promises are replete with misunderstanding, unanticipated outcomes, and work left undone. Loss is also part of this disorder, and a certain amount of its unruliness needs to breathe in the classroom. Loss is part of the daily life of human rights professionals and part of the mix of the creative chaos of the human rights field. In many circumstances, loss may well be the catalyst that propels thought and action. Many students may follow a trajectory much like my own, in which I lost an amateur's enthusiasm for the rightness of rights as the first step toward specialized knowledge and a well-grounded, carefully wrought and rigorous assessment of the use and abuse of rights frameworks. A learning environment that acknowledges loss, provides tools to analyze it, and permits loss to ebb and flow can leverage its chaos to foster student creativity.

The leap from loss to creativity explains what first appeared to me as a puzzle when I began teaching literature and human rights. A great many students express a loss of confidence in rights and a great love of literature. But when I invite them to devise a capstone research project on any topic, most prefer to investigate a specific human rights topic, and very few prefer to investigate a literary work or literature's engagements with human rights, even among students who demonstrate a deep affinity for literary language and who are intellectually alive to the human rights interventions offered by fiction. When I began teaching these courses I was surprised by students' readiness to set literature aside, even if temporarily. But now I view it as a creative and generative response to the other varieties of loss they encounter in the course. Students' loss of interest in literature is a demonstration of a new measure of responsibility—a responsibility to know at greater length and depth a particular human rights issue. Loss, in these cases, pays off. Especially in the context of a liberal arts college that asks that I prepare students to think critically and creatively about the world and to bring knowledge to bear on real-world problems, I measure the success of my human rights and literature course not through the students' affirmation of either human rights or literature but rather through the depth of their engagement and the responsibility they assume to advance knowledge, critique, and creative work in the world.

Crystal Parikh and Nicholas Matlin

Human Rights and the Tautology of Human Being

Even the most keen of students find themselves at a loss when faced with the human rights scholar Jack Donnelly's tenet that "Human rights are, literally, the rights that one has simply because one is a human being" ([2003] 10). Framed as a tautology, this definition proves troubling because, as Donnelly himself acknowledges, it offers no ultimate justification or authority (whether God's law or natural law) by which rights are guaranteed. In other words, "human rights have no foundation" (18). This definition of human rights evokes a host of further troubling questions: How is *human being* to be defined? Who is to be charged with enforcing human rights? How does one know what constitutes the essential rights necessary to the human?[1]

In this essay (which emerged from a graduate course in literary studies on human rights and cultural politics), we propose an ethical pedagogy that provides students with an understanding of the (potential) productivity and efficacy of human rights principles and discourse. A humanities perspective engages the seemingly problematic tautology of human rights and moves beyond a strict binary of natural and positive law to see such a tautology as other or more than a paralyzing problem. Although the subject of human rights continues to be addressed primarily by the social sciences (law and political science in particular), we contend that literary studies models a form of critique by which to interrogate and reconceptualize the stakes and subjects of human rights politics. As such, we have structured this essay, on the one hand, to describe the theoretical principles and applications at stake in such an enterprise and, on the other, to sketch out (through a reading of Kazuo Ishiguro's novel *Never Let Me Go*) the contours of a course for advanced students that illuminates how literary approaches can contribute to students' understanding of the discourses, problems, and politics of human rights.

Sovereignty and Vulnerability

Before turning to the specific interventions that we have found theorists making in human rights scholarship, we find it helpful to elaborate the central conceptual bind endemic to the formulation of contemporary human rights, which was most famously and astutely articulated by Hannah Arendt in her classic essay "The Decline of the Nation-State and the End of the Rights of Man." Arendt's essay serves as a fitting departure point for classroom discussion and analysis, because, in critiquing the state's role as the guarantor of basic human rights, she gestures toward the possibility of a rights regime that is not tethered exclusively to national sovereignty. As Arendt insists, the claim that rights are located in individual human subjects contradicts the political autonomy and legal authority granted to states as sovereign units in a regime of international law and politics that is often described as the Westphalian state system. As she further observes, since the French Revolution, the question of human rights has been imbricated in that of national emancipation, such that "only the emancipated sovereignty of the people, of one's own people, seemed to be able to insure them" (370). Thus, although the "rights of man" were supposed to be independent of all governments, "it turned out that the moment human beings lacked their own government and had to fall back upon their minimum rights, no authority was left to protect them and no institution was willing to guarantee them" (370). Accordingly, civil rights always conceptually supersede human rights, assuming that "all human beings were citizens of some kind of political community" (372).

The seemingly stable totality of the nation-state system renders those excluded from such community an "unfortunate *exception* to an otherwise sane and normal rule" (342; emphasis added). The subjects of human rights, Arendt laments, exist as a problem of nonrecognition: "no law exists for them" (375). Besides being subject to indiscriminate police action, whatever liberties or privileges the stateless do enjoy, they enjoy out of charity and not as a right (376). The loss of recognition before the law amounts to a loss of the "right to have rights," rendering the stateless "nothing but human" (380). The stateless exist in a zone of pure vulnerability or pure humanity that is abhorred because it threatens public life, political order, and conceptions of national belonging: "the dark background of mere givenness, the background formed by our unchangeable and unique nature, breaks into the political scene as the alien which in its all too obvious difference reminds us of the limitations of human activities—which are identical with the limitations of human equality" (382).

It can be valuable, however, for students to see that the vulnerability of being human that so worries Arendt has more recently become the point of departure for social theorists such as Bryan Turner and Judith Butler, who imagine alternative forms of political community by striving to traverse the positivist limits of political philosophy and the social sciences. A factor of the embodiment of being human, vulnerability registers the body's openness to the world and to injury and loss. Vulnerability makes visible social dependency and connectedness (B. Turner 25–28) and hence affords us the insight that "there are others out there on whom my life depends, people I do not know and may never know. This fundamental dependency on anonymous others is not a condition I can will away" (Butler xii). Contrary to the liberal assumptions of many students, individuation and autonomy are thus "an accomplishment, not a presupposition, and certainly no guarantee" (Butler 27). All forms of autonomous life remain haunted by dependency on "the primary others who are past for me . . . [but who] live on in the fiber of the boundary that contains me (one meaning of 'incorporation')" and who return us to "the fundamental sociality of embodied life" (28).[2]

As Butler insists, vulnerability is not, in and of itself, an experience of deprivation, abandonment, suffering, or violence, and, as Turner delineates, it has provided the basis for social and political solidarity. Institutions, rites, and rights all function to nurture and protect human existence (Butler 31; B. Turner 28–29). Yet such conventions are precarious, and as the traditional social arrangements that offered some protection to human life have become denaturalized and deinstitutionalized—and therefore less reliable and more open to negotiation—human rights abuses destroy, or at least endanger, the conditions that make "embodiment, enselfment, and emplacement" possible (B. Turner 27). Contemporary forms of state sovereignty are essentially attempts to transcend the constitutive violability of human existence (Butler xiv). As a counterpoint, human rights pose a political project that affords recognition to the shared experience of bodily vulnerability. Human rights politics constructs the human as a historical-political subject:

> [W]hen a vulnerability *is* recognized, that recognition has the power to change the meaning and structure of the vulnerability itself. In this sense, if vulnerability is one precondition for humanization, and humanization takes place differently through variable norms of recognition, then it follows that vulnerability is fundamentally dependent on existing norms of recognition if it is to be attributed to any human subject. (Butler 43)

A human rights project founded on embodied vulnerability thus returns students to the tautology with which we began, where human rights are "the rights that one has simply because one is a human being." Donnelly argues that the source of human rights relates to neither natural needs nor an ordained spiritual order. Rather, he contends, human rights *create* a type of person posited in a moral vision (14). Instead of a presocial given, human nature is a social project, and individuals are created as political subjects, as free and equal rights-bearing citizens, through discursive (social, legal, political) practices (15–16) or through Butler's "variable norms of recognition" that human rights principles can elaborate. Again, human rights and the subjects to whom they are granted have no foundation but rather come into being through consensus or social decision (Donnelly [2003] 18–21).

Such a model of human rights politics can demonstrate for students of cultural theory, literary studies, and the humanities the crucial role that these fields play with respect to denaturalizing, historicizing, and transfiguring the concept of being human as it relates to human rights. By emphasizing the performative power of language, a literary approach to human rights provides insight into how variable norms of recognition are socially and culturally produced. That is, by probing the possibilities and pitfalls of human rights from within literary or cultural texts, students can trace and critique the historical transformations and radical reinscriptions of the human form. Conventional approaches to literature and human rights describe the value of, in Richard Rorty's words, a "sentimental education," wherein shared emotions provide the basis for progressive change and humanitarian intervention depends on eliciting the assent of "powerful people" and a "leisure class" who consume human rights narratives (413). In contrast, we emphasize the disarming, and even estranging, ethics in which the literary instructs us, a mode of reading by which to recognize others who are coming to rights.

"The Likes of Us" and "Everyone Else"

Joseph Slaughter's *Human Rights, Inc.* is especially instructive for students of literature in terms of the cultural forms by which the human subject has taken its place. The tautology that defines the problem of human nature and human rights does not, for Slaughter, simply express a "paralyzed logic" but instead indicates "the site where culture-bound knowledge confronts its own limits and turns back on itself" (78). Human rights law, he explains, constitutes a hybrid of natural law (which describes rights as existing in a state of nature, before any social relations) and positive law (which views rights and obligations as granted by authoritative power, namely the state) (63).[3] For Slaughter, the tautology of human rights actually functions as a "transitive figure" for the positivization of natural law (68). The tautological structure also posits a telos, where human rights regimes are to create the very subject that they are designed to serve. This positivization requires a "human rights plot of personality development [that] emerges as a plot of incorporation—a plot of the development of a human person and personality capable of occupying the place of the 'human'" (79). The "person" (a legal term that becomes operative in place of "the human") who inhabits international human rights discourses is, according to Slaughter, the same subject of the bildungsroman genre (perhaps the most familiar of genres for literature students) such that the two make up "consubstantial," "mutually enabling fictions" about modern human existence (4). Bereft of a supernatural or superhuman sovereign who designates the forms of life that qualify for personhood, the bildungsroman acts as "a cultural surrogate for the missing warrant and executive sanction of human rights law" and offers "an especially important ally in naturalizing the positive norms of human rights" (85).

Because it takes both the human being and the state as its subject—and because the state is conceived as both a predator and a manifestation of the "People's will" (114)—the bildungsroman strives to center the once marginal bourgeois individual as the national citizen, such that what was a particularly situated subject ascends to the status of a (new) universal (20). Likewise, human rights law channels rebellious political impulses into socially acceptable, individual claims on the state (91). Both the bildungsroman and human rights law hence share a "pacific spirit," providing for their subjects reformist plots as alternatives to revolutionary politics (115). The coming-of-age narrative reconciles the unruly individual to the demands for social conformity by offering a plot of development and incorporation in which the "subject being incorporated becomes responsible retroactively for the figurative act of incorporation itself, and thereby for both fate and the state" (104). The plot of incorporation that structures both law and literature "conceives of harmonious human personality development (*Bildung*) simultaneously as an *unfolding* of an individual's latent humanity in its encounter with the structures of the social world and as an *enfolding* of the individual within and by those structures" (101).

Nevertheless, it is important to emphasize to students that human rights discourse imagines a political terrain other than that of Westphalian citizenship; it creates and naturalizes the "world citizen" that does not (yet) exist in institutional practice (30). In its "world novel" instantiations, the bildungsroman likewise locates its human person in "an international literary public that is emerging (we like to think) in advance of the administrative structures and social formations that such a sphere ordinarily serves" (33). If their practical enforcement remains elusive, human rights have garnered the force of "extrajuridical" common sense by way of their own articulation (82). They enact the transitive grammar and proleptic temporality of "narrative aspirationalism," looking forward to a time "when the human person will have become positively the human person it ostensibly already is by natural right" (26).

Close readings in the classroom of any number of novels from world literature might bear out this perspective. We offer Ishiguro's *Never Let Me Go*, a novel of speculative fiction, as a case study and suggest that its provocative expression and limning of Slaughter's thesis reimagines the subject of human rights in a way that then alters our reading of other, extraliterary scenes of sociality. In Ishiguro's dystopian portrait of a Britain that parallels our own reality, human clones are raised to provide donor organs to "normals" until the donors "complete" (a telling euphemism for their deaths). Written from the perspective of Kathy H., *Never Let Me Go* recounts the childhood education and friendships that develop at Hailsham, an experimental boarding school for donor clones. The nature of Kathy and her classmates' existence, however, is only gradually revealed to the reader.

The plot turns on the revelation made to an adult Kathy (now a "carer" who tends to other donors before beginning her own series of donations) by her former educators. Encouraged by their teachers to create works of art, the students at Hailsham wonder at the mysterious process by which a regular visitor, known simply as Madame, chooses and leaves with selected pieces of their work. As an adult, Kathy pursues a rumor that Madame's selections qualified (a few) clones for special treatment and the deferral of their services as donors. Upon locating Madame and the school's former headmistress, however, Kathy learns instead that the work had previously been exhibited to a public audience to secure for Hailsham students the exceptionally benevolent treatment (in contrast to the degraded conditions in which other clones in England were raised) that they had already received. In other words, the donors are afforded no categorical right to life, family, bodily integrity, or self-determination, no matter the evidence of their humanity as creative beings. Because they are not recognized as incorporated persons in the first place, Hailsham students had enjoyed humane treatment only as a form of charity.

Recalling her drive back to the donor center after this confrontation, Kathy imagines her world as spatially distinct from that of the "normals":

> We'd occasionally encounter other headlights, and then I'd get the feeling they belonged to other carers, driving home alone, or maybe like me, with a donor beside them. I realized, of course, that *other people* used these roads; but that night, it seemed to me that these dark byways of the country existed just for *the likes of us*, while the big glittering motorways with their huge signs and super cafés were for *everyone else*. (272–73; our emphasis)

The "normals" occupy a parallel realm to that of Kathy and her community of fellow clones. Carers and donors travel on the same roads as those individuals from whom they are copied and to whom they will donate their organs. Nevertheless, they remain inhibited from entering the sphere of legal personhood that these other individuals occupy. Despite being exact genetic replicas of human persons, Kathy and her friends remain radically and unalterably different from the "normals" they seem to resemble. By virtue of their orphaned upbringing, categorically eradicated fertility, and curtailed agency in their own futures, their lives are governed by the private rules, conditions, and trajectories imposed on them as future donors.

As Slaughter shows, the concept of the "person" is radically sundered from that of the "human": "From the point of view of the law, 'person' is a technical term designating a 'right-and-duty bearing unit'; it has no necessary relation to the human being since it merely names something that has been endowed with the capacity to 'enjoy . . . the protections of the law and of the forces of the law.'" As such, "'person' is the rhetorical vehicle through which the law personifies (or incorporates) the human as a creature capable of bearing its rights" (58). In its apparent banality and casualness, Kathy's narration normalizes the world of the text for the reader. Of course, students will recognize that this narrative scripting identifies her story—and by extension, Ishiguro's novel—as by no means "the idealist *Bildungsroman*" that incorporates "the problematic individual into the rights and responsibilities of citizenship, and thereby legitimat[es] the democratic institutes of the emergent rights-based nation-state" (Slaughter 94). Rather, Ishiguro's novel is a morph of the genre, incorporating the problematic individual into the responsibilities of their given roles as nonpersons. Ishiguro does not allow "the likes of us" and "everyone else" to interact: whereas "everyone else" is a subject of the state, Kathy and her friends remain embedded within a privatized corporate zone separate from yet implicated in the maintenance of the larger state of the "other people."

Ishiguro's juxtaposition of the two spatially and socially segregated worlds positions the text as an allegory for neoliberal disenfranchisement. Although we do not (yet) live in a world where cloned organ donors programmatically give their lives to ensure the longevity of "normal" people, we do live in one sustained by what the anthropologists Jean Comaroff and John Comaroff call "illicit zombie workers," on whose attenuated and exploited existence we depend for a range of goods. Consumers for the most part remain distanced from the producers, much as the "normals" remain conspicuously offstage throughout Ishiguro's narrative. In their South African case studies, Comaroff and Comaroff depict how this disconnect engenders beliefs in occult economies, which govern zombie existence:

> Long-standing notions of witchcraft (*boloi*) have come to embrace zombie-making, the brutal reduction of others . . . to instruments of production; to insensible beings stored, like tools, in sheds, cupboards, or oil drums at the homes of their creators. In a world of flextime employment, it is even said that some people are made into "part-time zombies," whose exhaustion in the morning speaks of an unwitting nocturnal mission, of involuntary toil on the night shift. (787)

Although a connection between Comaroff and Comaroff's description of zombies and Ishiguro's portrayal of clones might seem far-fetched, a literary approach demonstrates that a perverse type of incorporation occurs in both cases.

As scholars of neoliberalism have observed, global capitalism has expanded the "citizenship gap," where the insecurity of claims to rights for those who are displaced as refugees and migrants accompanies the decreased capacity of citizens to control participation in state processes (Brysk 10–11). Globalized states "introduce new threats and provide declining opportunities to citizens, while increasing numbers of residents who lack citizenship claims" (14). Moreover, Saskia Sassen explains that economic citizenship and the right to (economic) rights have become located in markets, rather than in individuals or citizens (138). As such, global capital markets are enabled to discipline governments, not simply as a matter of money purchasing influence, but as an embedded logic in global capital, which requires of states economic policy objectives that unabashedly instrumentalize human life in the name of development (141).

Like the zombie workers, Kathy and her fellow donors are brutally reduced to their constitutive parts to maintain the world of the "normals"; they only become "incorporated" into sovereign political society when their organs are "incorporated" into the bodies of the legal persons that the law recognizes. Thus when donors "complete," it is not *they* who are "completed"; indeed, they have been rendered radically and unsustainably incomplete. Their deaths instead complete the personhood of "normals" who, increasingly impervious to the bodily vulnerability that defines human existence, seem paradoxically on the verge of a *post*human existence. Reading backward, we see that Kathy's vision of the schematic separation of the two worlds is exposed as exactly what it is: a dream. Indeed, the world of the clones is intimately "incorporated" into the world of the "normals." But although self-representation allows for humanness, humanness does not ensure rights. Instead, Kathy and the other clones must exist within this liminal realm, caught uneasily between humanity and personhood.

Yet, as this passage also shows, for a brief moment ("that night"), the articulated memory and "feeling" related by Kathy allow her to subtly claim the obscure "dark byways of the country" for herself and her fellow carers and donors. In so doing, she relegates "everybody else" to the "big glittering motorways with their huge signs and super cafés." Kathy's restrained and subtle assertion of equality constitutes a partial version of what Jacques Rancière calls the staging of "dissensus" in his essay "Who Is the Subject of the Rights of Man?" (304).[4] Kathy's narration shows that "the border separating bare life and political life [can] not be so clearly drawn" (Rancière 303). Rancière conceives of human rights subjects as discursive elements of "dissensus," who disturb any self-apparent recognition of personhood. In a move that might seem to literature students at first glance to be a perverse negation (not unlike Ishiguro's perverse incorporation), Rancière ultimately intensifies Donnelly's tautological formulation of human rights by surmising that the subjects of the "rights of man" are "those who have not the rights that they have and have the rights that they have not" (302). In a careful response to Arendt's concept of bare (human) life (and to Giorgio Agamben's famous elaboration of it in *Homo Sacer*), Rancière describes the subject of human rights as one who is coming to rights, such that the subject of human rights is the "process of subjectivization" (302). In laying claim to the name of the human, the rightless become something different from what they were and, concomitantly, reconfigure the political collectivities that have refused to hear them and rendered them speechless in the first place. The human is not essentially bare life deprived of all political capacity but instead names precisely the possibility that those who are thought not to be capable of political speech in fact enact the equality denied to them.

Inserting themselves as a division or dissensus in the political common sense, the subjects of human rights make visible just how unstable the referent for the "demos" ("the people," or Kathy's "everyone else") is. Consensual strategies manage political conflicts to do away with such instability.[5] Dissensus, in contrast, always poses the possibility of an other('s) perspective and claim—one that unsettles the ordered "state" of political community (Rancière 304–05). The force of human rights "lies in the back-and-forth movement between the first inscription of the right and the dissensual stage on which it is put to test" (305). There is no permanent subject to whom rights "belong"; rather, there is a political process by which subjects come to human rights or to being human through their performative speech, the iterative acts to which literary study is especially attuned.[6] In demonstrating that they can enact the rights denied to them, the putative subjects of rights demonstrate that they have arrived as the subject of those rights. Kathy's depiction of the realm of the "normals" as parallel with that of the clones momentarily puts "two worlds in one and the same world" (Rancière 304). Even so, this is a fleeting "opening of an interval for political subjectivization," only illuminated briefly in the recollection of a series of headlight beams (304). It thus remains essential to remind students that there is nothing guaranteed or exhaustive about the dissensus of human rights politics; those who have gained recognition might be returned to the zone of unimaginability from which they arrived and which remains constitutive of political consensus.

Moreover, the right to speech, which is at once the right to rights and the right to life, is hardly natural. It must be cultivated through an ethical pedagogy, in which learning to be silent allows for the arrival of the other, who announces himself or herself by saying something new and "strange" to the community (Lyotard, "Other's Rights" 184–85). This ethical reception of the other not only marks the limits of a critical politics that prizes unity, transparency, and ready intelligibility but also poses the pedagogical project for the teaching of human rights and literature. Approaching human rights from the perspective of literary studies can teach us to recognize those moments when something new and strange has issued from the (human) vulnerability of embodied existence. By acknowledging the discipline's own contributions to the constitution of the human, humanities students might forego trying to locate the pregiven human subject and its sovereign author (Cheah 3, 10). Instead, our close reading of the tautological development of the human demonstrates how humanity is not opposed to inhumanity. Rather, human existence is given up by inhuman conditions and practices, and the borderline between humanity and inhumanity is continually indeterminate and shifting (230). Literary and cultural studies can afford to treat the central tautological paradox of human rights not "as a shameful limitation of human rights discourse and practice" but as the productive possibility of new cultural norms that attend to other forms of being human (Slaughter, *Human Rights* 13).

Notes

1. These questions have formed the basis for Human Rights and Cultural Politics, a graduate course in the Department of English and the American Studies Program at New York University.

2. Butler's explication of *incorporation* draws on her extensive engagement with psychoanalytic theory throughout much of her prior work and, as such, offers a theoretical inflection to the term that differs from Slaughter's discussion of the incorporation of the subject before the law. Nevertheless, insofar as Butler and Slaughter both address the constitution of the human as formed through social and cultural processes of recognition, we can take their interest in incorporation as resonant for identical modern subjectivities.

3. The Universal Declaration of Human Rights, for example, describes rights as both the basis for freedom and an achievement gained through the enactment of freedom (Slaughter, *Human Rights* 63–64).

4. For example, in revolutionary France, Rancière notes, "equal-born women were not equal citizens. They could neither vote nor be elected" (303). Yet Olympe de Gouges asserted that, "if women are entitled to go to the scaffold, they are entitled to go to the assembly" (qtd. in 303). Rancière continues, "If, under the guillotine, they were as equal, so to speak, 'as men,' they had the right to the whole of equality, including the equal participation to political life" (303–04).

5. Indeed, consensus does away with politics by aiming to establish "the identity of law and fact" (Rancière 306).

6. Although the point is certainly arguable, some theorists, such as Butler, find intimation of this "performative freedom" in Arendt's own formulation of political community. Butler sees, in the second half of "The Decline of the Nation-State," Arendt "re-declaring" the rights of man, attempting to "reanimate" the political promise there: "'Declaring' becomes an important rhetorical movement, since it is the very freedom of expression for which it calls or, rather, it is the very call of freedom. Freedom cannot pre-exist this call . . . but can only exist in its exercise" (Butler and Spivak 49).

Elizabeth S. Anker

Teaching the Legal Imperialism Debate over Human Rights

In a geopolitical era characterized by unprecedented globalization, human rights have become the world's primary idiom for approaching international social justice. Human rights have represented, in large part, a success story, working not only to combat egregious and exceptional rights violations but also to eradicate systemic suffering and abuse. While virtually no region of the world has been immune to crises in human rights, the postcolonial nation-state has witnessed some of the late twentieth century's most protracted offenses, at the same time as it has fallen victim to deep patterns of economic disenfranchisement under late capitalism. In turn, the postcolonial world has increasingly become a primary object of human rights discourse, as well as of humanitarianism writ large, meaning that human rights activism is often synonymous with regimes of foreign aid and development. As such, respect for human rights within the postcolonial nation-state is commonly read in the West as a benchmark for a country's relative degree of civilizational progress and advancement.

Thus configured as "gifts from the West to the rest," human rights, although they remain salutary in many contexts, have aims and ideals that are far from neutral or cost-free when imposed on postcolonial cultures and societies. On the one hand, rights discourse commonly animates neo-imperialist tropes and presumptions, casting the postcolonial as a chronically backward, regressive, and violence-prone space while applauding the West for its paternalistic beneficence. On the other hand, to the extent that human rights campaigns are intertwined with other mechanisms of Western charity and aid, rights in practice can come with countless preconditions attached, so that they often reinforce existing geopolitical relations of power, dominance, and dependence.

Despite the many liabilities that have accompanied the globalization of rights, most students initially regard human rights as unambiguous and uncomplicated goods, their views thus mirroring the international legitimacy that rights have acquired. As a consequence, one of the greatest challenges in teaching a course on human rights and literature (or, for that matter, on human rights as a political and cultural construct) surrounds what one might call the legal and cultural imperialism debate over rights. An instructor is almost guaranteed to confront students who are highly averse, if not outright resistant, to the notion that human rights should present cause for suspicion. And precisely because many students are defensive about rights—often due to praiseworthy and even legitimate impulses—I have found that a pedagogy that requires students to challenge human rights demands unusual circumspection. An instructor must preserve a delicate balance between interrogating rights and encouraging students to keep broad considerations of social justice as a frame of reference. This essay outlines a series of techniques that I have employed in teaching, contextualizing, and introducing the imperialism debate, which I apply to two textual examples.

Framing the Debate

First, in constructing a syllabus on human rights and literature, I begin the term with texts and authors that work to verify most students' predilections about the positive achievements obtained in the name of human rights. We start out by examining narratives about human rights that attest to the world's urgent and overwhelming need for them, registering both their effectiveness as a discourse and their innumerable accomplishments. A syllabus might begin with an introductory unit on the Holocaust, framed by a text such as Primo Levi's *Survival in Auschwitz*. Indeed, Levi's memoir stages an extended appeal for human rights, implicitly endorsing the definition of the human that the Universal Declaration of Human Rights

(UDHR) promulgates as it catalogs the many injuries and harms that Levi sustains in a concentration camp.

Alternatively, in a course focused on human rights in the postcolonial world, a syllabus might begin with a range of problematics that would independently confirm the necessity of human rights for redressing injustice. Possible units and literary texts include women's rights (Nawal El Saadawi's *Woman at Point Zero* or Tsitsi Dangarembga's *Nervous Conditions*), genocide (Edwidge Danticat's *The Farming of Bones*), torture (J. M. Coetzee's *Waiting for the Barbarians* or Michael Ondaatje's *Anil's Ghost*), or political restitution and reconciliation (Coetzee's *Disgrace* or Ariel Dorfman's *Death and the Maiden*). Each of the foregoing examples, while attesting to the world's vital need for human rights, simultaneously exposes crucial limitations besetting rights in their operations as adjudicatory and truth-producing instruments. Whether by pointing to the oversights of truth commissions (Coetzee [*Disgrace*] and Dorfman), the politically volatile project of humanitarian fact-finding (Ondaatje), or how a trial forces a victim to replay their injury (Coetzee [*Disgrace*] and Saadawi), each of these texts at once evinces wariness about human rights and vigorously champions them. In this way, they can communicate to students why one might be ambivalent about what rights entail, even before the question of the neo-imperialism of human rights is explicitly introduced.

On a separate level, debates about human rights' cultural and legal imperialism need to be situated within a history of colonization and empire. Especially if students lack a background in postcolonial studies, an instructor must provide a miniseminar on the legacy and varied permutations of imperialism, along with the many discursive codes and motifs that have legitimated it. Before students can evaluate the rhetoric of human rights critically, they must be able to emplace contemporary humanitarianism within a long trajectory of similar "civilizing" interventions. A brief unit with excerpts from Edward Said's *Orientalism*, David Spurr's *The Rhetoric of Empire*, and Graham Huggan's *The Postcolonial Exotic* can help attune students to the genealogy of the field of discourse within which rights talk directly participates, allowing them to identify parallels between human rights and other rhetorical technologies of domination. Such a framing will allow them to understand how, in projecting derogatory stereotypes onto the postcolonial world, the language of human rights becomes a basis for its disempowerment. By constructing the postcolonial as a region of incurable need, lack, and dependency, human rights discourse justifies American and European intrusion, even while that interference masquerades as generosity and self-sacrifice. Moreover, by relating rights talk to nineteenth-century apologias for colonialism, an instructor can encourage students to comprehend how it becomes both self-serving and self-congratulatory. One teaching strategy might involve asking students to find examples of contemporary popular or political appeals to human rights that are problematic for precisely such reasons.

Finally, when we as a class do, at last, overtly address the cultural-imperialism complaint about human rights, I make sure that such an allegation is first articulated by literary or cultural texts. A syllabus might look to a wide range of writers to illumine the many ambivalences that trouble the truth claims of human rights. For a nonfictional example, Jamaica Kincaid's *A Small Place* offers an extended polemic against the indenture of the contemporary Caribbean to the tourist industry that, along the way, demonstrates how manipulations of the rule of law work to condone Western malfeasance. Alternatively, certain human rights best sellers, such as any of Khaled Hosseini's novels, provide case studies that disclose how popular fiction both exoticizes the non-Western world and promotes coercive Western intervention within its crises. The liabilities of the best-seller genre become especially striking to students when paired on a syllabus with Tony Kushner's play *Homebody/Kabul*, which conducts a lengthy and involved satire of the self-indulgent and consumer-based "armchair activism" fashionably marketed at the Western women's book club circuit.

This essay, however, discusses in some depth two texts that have worked especially well for me in the classroom as platforms for debating the many layers of discursive imperialism that regulate the international circulation of human rights. Zana Briski and Ross Kauffman's *Born into Brothels* is a highly acclaimed documentary about successful activism on behalf of the children of prostitutes living in a brothel in Kolkata (Calcutta); the Somali author Nurrudin Farah's novel *Gifts* presents a fictional meditation on the politics of foreign aid in the midst of the 1980s famine in East Africa. Taken together, these two very different texts illustrate how even the best-intentioned human rights activism and reportage fall prone to various representational pitfalls. As such, they reveal why human rights narration faces something of a double bind. To incite public and popular interest, it must mobilize compelling images of urgent suffering and abuse, yet those very images inevitably demean the victims, portraying them as immature, helpless, and underdeveloped—in short, as less than fully human.

Before moving on to examine these two texts, let me offer a caveat. Introducing students to the question of human rights' cultural imperialism unquestionably cultivates their suspicious reading and viewing practices; nevertheless, pedagogy should not lose sight of the many laudatory endeavors that continue to occur under the auspices of human rights. Indeed, in my estimation, a course on human rights and literature would be a failure were it merely aimed at producing a new generation of human rights skeptics. Rather, an instructor should frame the imperialism debate as presenting proponents of human rights with a problem or dilemma. As a doubled or dualistic discourse, human rights function both as a vital language of resistance and as a means to disenfranchise the postcolonial world. Correspondingly, the human rights classroom should assume a doubled agenda, charting a cautious equilibrium between critique and affirmation. In this sense, pedagogy should maintain an unflagging commitment to awakening students to the protracted suffering of formerly colonized peoples, as well as to the need to assume social and political responsibility for redressing that marginalization, especially as it relates to the long history of neo-imperial policy. By emphasizing how human rights are polluted by their inevitable complicity with Western economic and other geopolitical interests, pedagogy can expose human rights as compromised and limited tools—but tools that nonetheless remain enormously potent and efficacious. Such an approach to human rights divulges to students their own implication within contemporary structures of power. I had one such moment when I last taught Kincaid's *A Small Place*. As one student put it, in response to the text, "I feel like my own lifestyle contributes to the violation of people's human rights." But teaching students self-scrutiny by no means culminates with defeat; rather, it can paradoxically serve, in the end, to enliven their appetites for social justice and fidelity to the very humanist aims that constitute the broader ethos of human rights.

The Human Rights Exotic

Briski and Kauffman's *Born into Brothels*, winner of the 2005 Academy Award for Best Documentary, exemplifies nonfictional human rights activism that is meritorious in its aims yet inadvertently relies on the problematic descriptive codes that frequently govern popular narratives of postcolonial abuses of human rights. In the light of this tension, it serves exceptionally well to demonstrate the dilemmas encountered within even estimable attempts to represent postcolonial crisis to a Western audience. The film follows the photographer Briski's efforts to raise funds for the children of prostitutes growing up in a Calcutta red-light district, although it approaches Briski's activism as well as its own documentary project relatively uncritically. Initially intending to produce a short-term exposé on the brothels, Briski becomes attached to the disadvantaged youth and expands her agenda to teach photography to the impoverished and neglected children. The documentary chronicles the gradual process of the children's education as well as the many cultural and societal impediments to Briski's endeavor, along the way configuring the postcolonial state in terms of epidemic chaos and disorder. Yet, as the children become skilled in photography, they are simultaneously inculcated into other, interrelated norms. To mark this implicit Westernization, the film's narrative concludes with the auctioning of the children's photographs at Sotheby's, an institutional imprimatur that signifies their successful acquisition of recognized standards of aesthetic sophistication and taste. Since the children's photographs make up large portions of the film's footage, this tactic in and of itself provides fuel for debate in the classroom. Students might, while they inquire into the costs of such a device, ask why the photographs work especially well to arouse the viewer's coextensive outrage and sympathy. Although the photographs lend authority to and thereby humanize the children, they primarily depict the squalid, depressed living conditions of the brothels, aestheticizing postcolonial tragedy to incite Western concern.

Despite this tendency, *Born into Brothels* has met with a relative dearth of criticism. Moreover, its acclaim has subsequently been parlayed into the not-for-profit organization Kids with Cameras, which continues to sponsor the children's education as well as other projects around the world, relying for funding both on donations and on sales of the children's artwork, including a signed limited-edition portfolio of their photographs priced at a hefty $10,000. In many respects, the organization epitomizes effective and self-aware human rights consciousness- and fund-raising. Its success as a venue for activism, moreover, has increasingly been pitched as a pedagogical opportunity. Indeed, the Kids with Cameras Web site offers a freely downloadable, seventy-six-page guide, Born into Brothels *Curriculum Companion*, that overtly frames the film as a morality tale both legitimating the philosophy subtending human rights and demonstrating the essence of "Personal and Collective Responsibility," as its first instructional unit is titled. To evaluate the reception of the film, students might be encouraged to spend time browsing the organization's Web site before class, noting what is commendable versus objectionable about its strategies.

As a whole, the Kids with Cameras Web site, in terms of its advertisement of the film and expectations about the Western donor-viewer, compels students to confront hard questions about the politics of "armchair activism," wherein even praiseworthy efforts become commodified in ways that effectively turn the plight of sex workers into fodder for Western coffee table art. An instructor might challenge students by asking whether the marketing of the prostitutes' suffering justifies fund-raising on behalf of their children. Likewise, students might be pressed to examine why the packaging of the children's photographs has been fruitful in the first place—namely, what Western consumerist desires and anxieties does it indirectly work to satisfy? Overall, the film helps reveal the double bind, or catch-22, troubling much human rights work. That is, successful human rights activism depends on what can only be described as the exploitation of the underlying injuries that it purports to redress. When coffee table books, T-shirts, and other such artifacts serve as tokens of the individual consumer's financial support of a given cause, humanitarianism becomes an insignia of cultural capital and distinction for the Western donor—to state things cynically, essentially transforming liberal guilt into a fashion statement.

Born into Brothels, moreover, deploys a number of the neo-imperialist presumptions often accompanying human rights discourse. The brothels are portrayed as sites of sordidness, filth, and fear, emblematized by the rats the camera lingers over as the film's spoken narrative begins. This squalor is projected onto the Indian nation at large. As Gour, one of the children, angrily informs us, "People here live in chaos. . . . Nobody lives as filthily as they do in our country." Juxtaposed with the brothel's misery are the perfect innocence and purity of the children. Makau Mutua has described how human rights discourse relies on the polarized terms of savages, victims, and saviors ("Savages"), and while the children are absolute victims, the film constructs their mothers as unconscionable savages. The camera frequently follows the prostitutes as they apply makeup, solicit clients, violently curse at the children (saying things like "you fucking cunt," as the film translates into English), and otherwise manifest ignorance and superstition. In one especially calculated sequence, a young girl, Puja, narrates how her father tried to sell her as a baby—a story told against footage of a male toddler, naked from the waist down, who is restrained from wandering by a heavy, metal, linked chain. The young girl's brief narrative concludes with a commentary on her future that displays knowing foresight: "I fear that I might become like them."

At the same time as the film figures the postcolonial world through the Manichaean polarities of iconic victimhood and savage cruelty, Briski and her Western viewers and donors assume the role of saviors. Not only does photography yield the "restorative power of art," as the Kids with Cameras Web site prophesies, but the humanitarian is figured as something of a present-day *mission civilisatrice*. By thus legitimating Western intervention in the Global South, the film further verifies the fiction of its viewers' cultural superiority. The Calcutta children are shown to be helpless to overcome their oppression without Western guidance and other aid. As Briski pleads, attesting to the children's dependence on such foreign assistance, "The children ask me for help, and they ask me for it all the time. And it's heartbreaking; there's so little I can do." As much as the film apologizes for paternalistic Western breaches of the sovereignty of the postcolonial state, students might contemplate other contemporary instances where humanitarian evangelism both obscures and justifies what are in truth opportunistic political aims.

Beyond how the film mobilizes a tropology of Third World depravity and arrested development, the "education" Briski offers is by no means neutral, instead imparting overwhelmingly liberal humanist values. It is not merely a mechanical or practical training in the skills of photography that Briski bequeaths to the children; rather, her education cultivates a highly particularized regime of aesthetic taste. Students might inquire into whether those standards are in fact Western, as well as how they contravene the conventions of the wider brothel community. For instance, the kinds of aesthetic merit that Briski commends require the children to transgress the brothel's norms about privacy to capture "bold" images. Even more, artistic production is construed as foremost an exercise in individualist self-fashioning, or *Bildung*, confirmed by the children's frequent meditations on what education will allow them to become. Beyond subscribing to the myth of the enlightened self's uniqueness of personality, the film endorses the cult of male genius, as one child, Avijit, is singled out as exceptionally talented and increasingly becomes the narrative's protagonist. Its trajectory culminates with his entrance into distinctively cosmopolitan norms, which are materialized in his trip to Amsterdam to participate in a World Press Photo children's convention, an international congress of youth from around the world who come as their country's representatives, staging something like the model United Nations of child photographers. This celebration of photography as inherently democratic is further premised on a series of interrelated slippages: although the medium of photography is applauded as naturally equalizing, it is in fact a pricey one that, moreover, inducts the children into a stratifying game of distinction and taste. As the young girl Shanti tells us, "In the photo class, I like to do the selection thing, 'I like this one, I like that.'" While the children thus adopt a hierarchy of aesthetic worth, we as viewers are tempted to equate cultural refinement with moral character, as the film encourages us to anxiously search for indicia that the kids will avoid their parents' lassitude.

This interpretation has played up my own reluctance about the film, deliberately casting it in a negative light for somewhat polemical purposes. I do so to underscore the types of debates that it might allow an instructor to stage within the classroom. Students tend to respond to the film in polarized ways. On the one hand, I have found that some vigorously resist the foregoing complaints, instead defending the film as an instance of salutary consciousness-raising and socially engaged documentary art. And, indeed, *Born into Brothels* has been a noteworthy fund-raising success. Likewise, it is unquestionably a moving testament to the transformative work of art, and it ultimately depicts the children as reflective, self-aware agents of their own futures, capable of transcending the disabling conditions of the brothels. But on the other hand, many students do become quite exercised about its biases, condemning it as little more than a glaring case of postcolonial exoticism masquerading as humanitarian goodwill. In teaching *Born into Brothels*, I therefore allow the film to engender such heated disagreement, although I ultimately frame that controversy as one afflicting much contemporary human rights activism. In other words, the tensions that the film inspires in the classroom illumine deep and impassable questions about the discourse of human rights—namely, whether it is even possible to talk effectively and persuasively about postcolonial abuses of human rights to a Western audience without using either neo-orientalist constructions of the Third World or self-congratulatory myths of Western superiority.

The Politics of Third World Aid

My second textual example, Farah's novel *Gifts*, works extremely well in dialogue with *Born into Brothels*. In effect, Farah evokes and interrogates a number of the pejorative stereotypes about postcoloniality that are submerged within yet motivate the film. Whereas *Born into Brothels* manifests paternalism that is sincere and even construed as praiseworthy, *Gifts* articulates a sustained critique of precisely such a posture. Pairing the two texts on a syllabus, then, allows students to envision how postcolonial literature might write back to and thereby challenge the insidious discursive codes that animate many popular accounts of human rights. Overall, Farah's *Gifts* offers a complex meditation on the geopolitical economy of foreign aid and the logic of development, demonstrating through its plot why no humanitarian bequest is neutral or innocent. While, on the surface, it is a love story about the middle-aged, twice-divorced Duniya and the accidental circumstances that afford her a new relationship, Duniya's story is both encased within and conspicuously allegorizes the politics of Western aid during the East African famine of the mid-1980s. Beyond this love story's tangential relation to matters of international governance, Farah employs dual strategies to conspicuously enact a layered critique of Western opportunism and postcolonial dependency. First, Duniya's predicament in a patriarchal culture mirrors that of the postcolonial African nation-state, being compelled to rely on aid and other "gifts" from the West. As such, Duniya's circumstances recurrently inspire the novel's other characters to meditate on the social status of the gift and how it indebts its recipients. Second, interspersed within and bookending the novel's individual chapters are excerpts from alleged media reports that editorialize on and venture different explanations for the depleted African infrastructure that precipitates the famine, as well as the foreign donations intended to replenish it.

These excerpts exhibit and implicitly parody an array of the characteristic motifs of imperialist discourse, highlighting for students the obstructionism rife within the idiom of human rights and commonly maneuvered by the Western media. They fixate on the dollar amount of the aid bequests, exposing the tyranny of numbers and the extent to which mathematical vastness obscures the individual lives it purports to quantify. By juxtaposing numerical abstraction with the particular lives *Gifts* emplots, the novel foregrounds the disconnect between Western reportage and postcolonial reality. The media proffers a range of different diagnoses for the famine and the atrophy it induces, and these overdetermined explanations collectively reveal the internally divided codes that govern neo-imperial constructions of the postcolonial. Some reports mystify the famine's causes by blaming it on the negligence and prodigality of the African people, for instance by citing a history of deforestation and nonconservationist practices (87), whereas others project that profligacy onto the African landscape, figuring it as a site of disease and infestation ridden with a "plague" of "pests" (9). Other briefs, however, give the lie to such stereotypically demeaning accounts and indict Western interference for having exacerbated the crisis. One clip censures the "policies of Western creditor nations" for not merely turning a blind eye to but fully sanctioning the widespread starvation (33). Moreover, other excerpts cynically impugn the entire philosophy of Third World aid as merely one tactic in a contemporary European power play, providing a means for both "the strengthening of relations" between allies and "creating future generations of potential consumers" or for perpetuating Western global economic dominance (99, 197). All the while, the novel satirizes the very kind of "armchair activism" advocated by *Born into Brothels*, poking fun at the popular gimmick of marketing charity as a fashion statement. A number of its Somali characters are depicted wearing Band Aid or UNICEF T-shirts, and one media clip relates the celebrity Liv Ullman's trip to monitor the African famine (51–52). Such references invite students to contemplate what Farah would think of the efforts of *Born into Brothels* and Kids with Cameras, asking whether they would equally become objects of his fiction's critique.

Embedded within and contextualized by such news reports is *Gifts*'s relatively straightforward though magic realist plot. Its narrative charts Duniya's romance and engagement to a wealthy Somali, Bosaaso, who has recently returned after living in the United States. Throughout, Duniya's plight parallels that of the African nation-state vis-à-vis its foreign donors. As a woman, Duniya is reluctant to accept charity and assistance, fearing that it will be construed to mark her lack of autonomy and inability to support her small family. Farah's characters explicitly liken her circumstances to those of Africa, "[b]ecause unasked-for generosity has a way of making one feel obliged, trapped in a labyrinth of dependence. . . . [H]aven't we in the Third World lost our self-reliance and pride because of so-called aid we unquestioningly receive from the so-called First World?" (22). The plot stages several scenes in which Duniya and her three children evade forms of generosity that either require their displays of excessive gratitude (111) or, in Duniya's words, "take me for granted, as a woman" (92). Duniya is acutely aware that few gifts are innocent; rather, most bind the recipient to the donor, demand favors in return, and legitimate the donor's exercise of discipline and control. Gift giving, and by extension humanitarianism, is thereby cast as a calculated ploy that entraps the postcolonial nation-state in cycles of indentured servitude, perpetuating a subservience that justifies continued Western interference.

Students might examine the novel's commentary on the politics of foreign aid from a range of directions. Tracing the implications of the novel's analogy between Duniya and the postcolonial nation-state might guide class discussion, as students map the ways that Duniya's predicament enacts such a commentary. For instance, an instructor might ask whether it is not incidental, first, that the novel's protagonist is a woman and, moreover, that her suitor, Bosaaso, has been Westernized. In this way, applying the novel's many levels of dialogue to *Born into Brothels*, a class might debate why, in both texts, human rights discourse necessarily feminizes and infantilizes its postcolonial victims. What does this gendering of foreign aid illumine, and how does it work to authorize the expectations underwriting human rights? Why must the objects of Western beneficence be almost exclusively women and children? And, from Duniya's perspective, why does her gender render her especially vulnerable and subject to manipulation?

Much as it parodies the paternalism guiding Western humanitarianism, *Gifts* derides the West's patronizing tendency to play mediator to political conflict in the non-Western world. When Duniya and her sister-in-law experience a disagreement, Duniya complains of such interference: "I've learned to be suspicious of men presenting themselves as peacemakers between women . . . when they, the men, are the cause of the quarrel, the initiators of the enmity and rivalry between women-folk" (120). Akin to how patriarchy presumes women to be insufficiently reasoned to negotiate their own interests, international conflict resolution protocols construct the postcolonial nation-state as irrational, obstreperous, and unable to self-determine—once again, in need of Western mentoring and intervention. This ruse driving humanitarian policy, however, masks the root causes of postcolonial discord and crisis. As *Gifts* suggests, much upheaval in the postcolonial world stems directly from the legacy of imperialism, rather than from a regressive postcolonial tendency toward disorder and chaos.

At the same time that it critiques the politics of foreign aid, *Gifts* contrasts Somali norms surrounding gift giving with those originating in the West. In doing so, it problematizes Western models of exchange, raising complex questions about whether human rights and other forms of humanitarianism both subsidize and rely on global capital. As Duniya fears the predatory expectations that accompany gifts, so Western aid typically comes with arbitrarily defined "strings attached" that depend on preadjudicated yet biased measures of fair equivalence (48). Such an insidious logic of quid pro quo is articulated in particular by the European expatriate Ingrid, who bequeaths her used china set to Bosaaso and his first wife on her departure from Somalia. While Ingrid defines the exchange as a "gift," she nonetheless requires a large sum in payment (47). Ingrid's usury disguised as generosity reveals how the language of humanitarianism obscures the imbalanced and not-bargained-for prerequisites that precede its allocation and that, in actuality, compromise its status as genuine charity. By reducing human interdependence to cost-benefit analysis, Western formulations of the gift mutually indenture people to each other not as members of a community but as atomistic and self-interested individuals, thereby impoverishing human affairs. Students might be prompted to assemble a list of the kinds of gift giving that *Gifts* implicitly indicts, asking why the novel excoriates them. An especially ambitious classroom might supplement such a discussion with excerpts from Karl Marx's *On the Jewish Question*, inquiring whether human rights—like the gifts condemned in the novel—are naturally prone to encourage egoistic behavior at the expense of collectivist social practices.

While *Gifts* exposes how Western patterns of gift giving deplete the resources of the African nation-state, it also gestures toward alternative modalities of generosity that instead might enrich the fabric of social life. Bosaaso discounts the European Ingrid's self-serving calculus by citing a Somali proverb that contains a competing formulation of the gift: "He who distributes the offerings of fortune receives little as his personal share" (49). This opposing mind-set construes charity as predicated not on expectations of perfect equivalence but instead as unrequited and incalculable. The novel similarly celebrates gifts that involve a private, unpublicized act, rebuking the self-congratulatory impetus motivating much Western aid. As the narrative cautions, "[W]hy devalue the significance of [an] act by mentioning it in public?" (126), it suggests that aid ultimately confirming the self-image of the donor trivializes and debases the meaning of charity. Overall, *Gifts* points to an alternative framework for humanitarianism that is not invested in the axiomatics of self-interested entitlement, meaning that it cannot be adequately explained through the dual idioms of either capitalist exchange or human rights. In turn, it is not accidental that its narrative culminates with Duniya's encounter with love, a transaction that transcends the quantifying logic of profit and equivalence, participating in a murkier economy of reciprocity and self-sacrifice.

Students might also debate what commentary the novel undertakes through its concluding image, in which Duniya not only is reunited with her brother but consents to Bosaaso's marriage proposal. Do these new relationships merely enmesh Duniya in the circuits of paternalistic control against which she otherwise rebels? Or do they augur a new mode of social belonging that renders obsolete her self-protective defensiveness? By ending with a vision of the restoration of the collective, does the novel applaud the obligations exerted by the community, reconfiguring them not as threats to the self-determining individual but rather as productive of social meaning? Through considering such questions, students might contemplate opposing structures of ethical responsibility and civic engagement that diverge from neoliberal formulations of human rights and the capitalist underpinnings of humanitarian aid. Such a point of entry into the cultural imperialism debate thereby compels students to ask about the epistemic rupture enacted by human rights—that is, how the globalization of human rights potentially enfeebles local cultural practices and registers of belonging.

In sum, one of the most vexing issues confronting human rights from a non-Western vantage is the question of cultural imperialism. This issue, moreover, is an especially thorny one to introduce within the humanities classroom, in that it requires subverting many students' preexisting views that human rights are unqualified social and political goods. As such, the cultural imperialism debate concretizes the dual agenda that pedagogy must assume: that is, pedagogy must expose the liabilities that compromise rights as they migrate to the non-Western world while also affirming an unyielding commitment to the broader humanist ideals that rights embody. In the end, although it compels students to confront the biases that inform their own worldviews, my experience in teaching this debate is that students, at the same time, discover a renewed appreciation for the demands of global social justice. Indeed, these fraught quandaries facing human rights are destined to afflict almost any highly popular and effective legal and political term of art. For this reason, they urge students to contemplate the necessary work performed by literature and other arts as a supplement to the law, disclosing how the literary or artistic imagination might register complexity and paradox otherwise elided within legal and political discourse.

Alexandra Schultheis Moore
and Elizabeth Swanson Goldberg

Human Rights Cultures and Traditions: Beyond the Post-/Colonial and West

For all its universalist aspirations, one of the most tenacious critiques of human rights since its modern incarnation in international customary law has been its cultural boundedness or, better put, its cultural imperialism. This position was forcefully articulated before the United Nations had even voted to adopt the Universal Declaration of Human Rights, when the Executive Board of the American Anthropological Association submitted the "Statement on Human Rights" to the UN Commission on Human Rights, which famously asked, "How can the proposed Declaration be applicable to all human beings, and not be a statement of rights conceived only in terms of the values prevalent in countries of Western Europe and America?" (539).

Since then, the debate about the legitimacy of the universal rights system outside the Western and Western postcolonial context has raged, and continues to rage, first in the shape of the dichotomy between cultural relativism and universal values and then through the deconstruction of that dichotomy, with perhaps a brittle truce having emerged in the early twenty-first century based on practices that, as Sally Engle Merry puts it, "bring human rights home, adapting them to local contexts and systems of meaning" (72). While the chapters in this volume adhere to a relatively strict definition of human rights as those that fall under the purview of international human rights and humanitarian law and its institutions (rather than encompassing all social justice issues), we offer this essay as a brief overview of some traditions outside the West and its former colonies that share philosophical or legal foundations with what has become the modern international human rights system. To do so, we frame a comparative context that takes into consideration the concept of and justification for rights (minimum protections and human needs; source, origin, or authoritative guarantee of rights); their form (legal and discursive); and the human being or the legal person who can claim them. Central to human rights as such are the pivotal role of the state vis-à-vis the individual (and, more recently, the collective) and the question of the universality of rights concepts and discourses versus their translatability into particular cultural contexts. We focus on these problems in addressing select non-Western and nonpostcolonial traditions, in particular those of Muslims, Buddhists, and indigenous peoples. We conclude with a look at several prominent course readers alongside theoretical perspectives to teaching alternative or comparative approaches to human rights in literary and cultural studies.

On Rights in Global Contexts

Both legal and literary scholars articulate a broad range of approaches to address the differences between the normative international human rights regime and frameworks that lie outside the West (with the exception of indigenous movements) and its former colonies. In *Human Rights: A Political and Cultural Critique*, Makau Mutua builds on long-standing claims that human rights cannot escape its Eurocentric origins and biases. His chapter "Human Rights as a Metaphor" provides an excellent critique for undergraduate and graduate students of the "grand narrative" of savages-victims-saviors that, he argues, defines normative discourses of rights and produces a troublingly limited vision of a "good society" (10, 13). Through the prism of savages-victims-saviors, too often non-Western or Third World individuals and governments appear savage, their populations abject victims, and an ostensibly "civilized" West the savior in a narrative that is complicit with Western colonial and neocolonial objectives. Mutua's critique offers students tools for reading the paradoxes characterizing increasingly widespread humanitarian appeals—for instance, the international nongovernmental organization Invisible Children's campaign Kony 2012. This campaign was highly successful in raising global awareness about the war criminal Joseph Kony. As of November 2014, there have been nearly one hundred million hits on the campaign's *YouTube* site; the International Criminal Court at the Hague wants Kony for his involvement in the atrocities the Lord's Resistance Army committed against Ugandan civilians; and, among the indirect outcomes that could arguably be linked with the campaign, the United States has issued Congressional resolutions condemning Kony and the Lord's Resistance Army in March 2012 and is supporting a new five-thousand-person African Union force, headquartered in South Sudan, dedicated to locating and arresting Kony. Still, the campaign's rhetorical address and imagery depend on a rigid separation of good and evil that recapitulates the Manichean racism of European imperialism in Africa and Asia and call for an international military-humanitarian intervention highly questionable in terms of international human rights norms and outcomes, let alone in terms of questions of global justice. Perhaps the fullest expression of this position came from Teju Cole, first in a series of six tweets that started with the blunt assertion "From Sachs to Kristof to Invisible Children to TED, the fastest growth industry in the US is the White Savior Industrial Complex" and ended by claiming, "I deeply respect American sentimentality, the way one respects a wounded hippo. You must keep an eye on it, for you know it is deadly." Cole built on the framework of these tweets in a widely circulated feature essay in the *Atlantic*; other major media outlets, such as the *New York Times*, considered the role of social media in human rights activism ("Fighting"). As the work of many scholars has shown, global human rights and humanitarian campaigns too often continue to rehearse such harmful divisions, which in turn reinforce the very power structures that inform the global distribution of rights and safety (see, e.g., Hesford). To those of us teaching and learning in the Global North, Mutua's work encourages us to ask, in the words of Gayatri Spivak, what it might mean to read with "a suspension of the conviction that I am necessarily better, I am necessarily indispensable, I am necessarily the one to right wrongs, I am necessarily the end product for which history happened" ("Righting Wrongs" 532).

By comparison, in *Human Rights in Cross-Cultural Perspectives*, Abdullahi Ahmed An-Na'im argues for a cross-cultural approach to human rights that draws on the "internal discourse" of the different cultures engaged (4). Rather than emphasize fixed cultural particularities, An-Na'im, while "sensitive to the needs of internal authenticity and legitimacy" (5), nonetheless seeks to identify shared conceptions of dignity and human nature across cultures that might form the basis for a "universal cultural legitimacy" of human rights (433). For many, that goal is either unreachable or requires untenable compromises, yet we suggest that it may be helpful as a reading practice if reformulated as a contingent cultural legitimacy—in other words, a recognition of those instances in which human suffering and its amelioration become legible both within a cultural epistemology or ethical framework and within international human rights norms, albeit in different registers (what John Rawls referred to as an "overlapping consensus").

We begin with the subject of Islam, acknowledging the fundamental tensions between its dominant, text-based norms and the tenets of the modern human rights regime, while also exploring the areas in which some Muslim beliefs and practices may find harmony with philosophies and policies of human rights. We follow An-Naʿim's lead in locating our study of human rights in the context of the people identifying with a cultural or religious tradition (e.g., Muslims) rather than in the name of the tradition (Islam). As An-Naʿim shares, "I prefer to focus on believers to emphasize our responsibility and ability to change ourselves and transform our understanding and practice of our religious beliefs, instead of invoking abstract doctrines of religion for which we may not feel personally responsible, or believe we can change" (*Muslims* 1).

Determining an area of overlapping consensus between text-based Muslim norms and the demands of international human rights requires working through both epistemological and temporal discontinuities. The ethical and legal precepts of Islam are embodied in the shari'a, in general the religious law of Islam but more particularly the interpretation of divine revelation offered through the teachings of the Qur'an and the collection of Muhammad's statements and actions, called the Sunna, as they set forth religious and ethical principles to guide the everyday lives of Muslim people. In terms of epistemological origins for rights claims, all duties and rights in the Islamic context are derived from the authority of Allah, a point that is fundamentally at odds with the international human rights system's identification of the source of human rights in the inherent dignity of the human as a human, untethered to any divine, natural, or human authority. Still, there may be room for consensus in the precept of dignity, as Heiner Bielefeldt notes in "Muslim Voices in the Human Rights Debate," an excellent overview of the relation of a range of Islamic perspectives to the international human rights system:

> [M]odern Muslim thinkers place a great deal of emphasis on human dignity as an essential part of the Qur'anic teaching. For instance, they invoke the idea of each human's vocation as God's deputy on earth (Sura 2:30); they cite Sura 17:70 which says that God has honored the children of Adam; and they point out that, according to Sura 33:72, God has bestowed a special trust upon humankind, elevating the human person above all cosmic power. (608)

While the idea of dignity here is still linked with recognition from God, these suras can provide a path for practicing Muslims to avoid having to choose between their religion and human rights.

As An-Na'im points out, shari'a represents the interpretation and elaboration of the Qur'an and the Sunna, as well as "their supplementation through other sources by the founding Muslim jurists of the eighth and ninth centuries CE—the second and third centuries of Islam" (*Muslims* 43). Given the length of time between the original revelation of God's word to Muhammad in the Qur'an (610–632 CE) and the codification of the Sunna and the relevant suras in the Qur'an as shari'a law, there is, in An-Na'im's view, room for ongoing interpretation of the shari'a in modern contexts, just as instructions for ethical and religious practice were originally interpreted from the Qur'an and the Sunna by Muslim jurists operating centuries after (and in a different location: Medina as opposed to Mecca) the death of the Prophet. In his argument, An-Na'im makes room for a reform of Islam (which he grounds in the methodology of the Sudanese thinker Mahmoud Mohamed Taha), particularly in the areas of treatment of women and religious minorities, as well as freedom of religion and the use of corporal punishments, which he identifies as "problematic from a human rights point of view" (29). An-Na'im's body of work questions the dominant, text-based view of shari'a, which holds that tenets including the unequal treatment of women or the use of punishments such as stoning or removing a limb set forth in the seventh and eighth centuries must be upheld today. A parallel body of feminist thinkers calling for such reform includes Asra Nomani, *Standing Alone in Mecca: An American Woman's Struggle for the Soul of Islam*; Fatema Mernissi, *Islam and Democracy: Fear of the Modern World*; and Amina Wadud, *Qur'an and Woman: Reading the Sacred Text from a Woman's Perspective.*

Of course, there are many different expressions and practices of Islam for many different communities of Muslim people, and teachers of literature and human rights will likely locate their readings in particular texts set in particular places and times in order not to impose an idea of cultural or religious homogeneity or fixity. Leila Ahmed, in her seminal memoir, *A Border Passage: From Cairo to America—A Woman's Journey*, spends a great deal of time exploring what it means to be a Muslim woman growing up in Egypt and negotiating her faith as it came to her not from what she calls the "official Islam" of the men in her family and community but rather from women's understandings, which "[were] an essential part of how [all the women of the house] made sense of and understood their own lives" (121). This Islam was less textual and more lived, according to Ahmed, who describes it as a "way of being in the world" passed on more by example than by "elaborate sets of injunctions or threats or decrees or dictates as to what we should do and be and believe" (121). This was surely a woman's Islam, passed from mother to daughter to daughter, and the suras that were emphasized were expansive and life affirming: "[My mother] quoted to me the verse in the Quran that she believed summed up the essence of Islam: 'He who kills one being . . . kills all of humanity, and he who revives, or gives life to, one being revives all of humanity'" (122).

This sura contains one of the most foundational injunctions of all the monotheistic religious traditions—and of the Universal Declaration of Human Rights: the proscription against killing and its converse, the right to life. There is, of course, significant overlap between the tenets of Islam, both as set forth in the Qur'an and in the lived experience of Muslims, and the principles of international human rights. Attempts at codifying such overlap have been made in several documents, including the Universal Islamic Declaration of Human Rights (UIDHR) and the Cairo Declaration on Human Rights in Islam (CDHRI). The latter, unanimously adopted by the Organisation of Islamic Cooperation, has not been accepted by the United Nations Human Rights Committee and indeed was strongly criticized in a statement to the United Nations Commission on Human Rights from Adama Dieng, the esteemed Senegalese jurist and then secretary general of the International Commission of Jurists. Dieng's criticisms—along with those from many others around the world—focused mainly on the ways in which the CDHRI, "under cover of Shari'a Law," confirmed discrimination against non-Muslims and women as well as the "legitimacy of practices, such as corporal punishment, which attack the integrity and dignity of the human being" (qtd. in "Effective Functioning" 3). A comprehensive overview of Islamic human rights documents and conventions can be found in Ann Elizabeth Mayer's *Islam and Human Rights: Tradition and Politics.* Like Dieng, Mayer finds that "hybrid" human rights documents such as the CDHRI can be used by rulers of Muslim states to oppress their people—in the name of Islam.

Indeed, many Muslim thinkers have concluded that it may not be human rights as philosophy or practice so much as the form of the nation-state that is the most troublesome Western import for Muslim states. As An-Naʿim argues, "The proponents of a so-called Islamic state in the modern context seek to use the institutions and powers of the state, as constituted by European colonialism and continued after independence, to regulate individual behavior and social relations in ways selected by the ruling elites" (*Islam* 7). Highlighting the ways in which oppression is perpetrated by corrupt rulers through the adoption and manipulation of the state form using Islam as a cover leaves more room for Muslim people to reconcile international human rights norms with the religious and cultural practices governing their everyday lives.

Buddhists and Human Rights

An-Naʿim's approach, especially when we emphasize the potential of contingent cultural legitimacy, may be particularly useful in teasing out the stakes for different constituencies represented in and consuming the growing body of world literature of human rights. Another example, drawn from a Buddhist context, is the Canadian author and activist Karen Connelly's *The Lizard Cage*, a critically acclaimed novel about a prisoner of conscience tortured by the Burmese government. The protagonist, Teza, pursues two forms of resistance to his circumstances. On the one level, the novel emphasizes the efficacy of his journal (and its journey across national borders) and of writing as resistance more generally as an expression of the liberal subject's transnational claim to rights. This theme underscores the link between literature and the law inasmuch as "a human rights abuse is characterized as an infringement on the modern subject's ability to narrate her story" (Slaughter, "Narration," par. 8). As a corollary, this formulation also implies that to tell one's story is (necessary) to make a claim for rights. On another level, Teza's perhaps more radical action is his growing practice of meditation within Theravada Buddhism, whose beliefs and institutions are claimed by both the authoritarian government and its critics. Teza's extreme asceticism at once evinces an alternative conception of the subject to the autonomous, bounded individual in rights discourse and, in leading to his death, places him literally beyond the reach of normative human rights. Outside the scope of human rights but not without moral significance and political effect, his individual and interiorized practice charts a path toward alleviating his suffering, understanding his relationship to others both near and far, and influencing his immediate community. In terms of contingent cultural legitimacy, the novel asks readers to consider how claims on behalf of prisoners of conscience and against torture, for example, might be imagined through different conceptions of selfhood and through means other than international law and humanitarianism.

An understanding of Teza's resistance through Buddhism is enhanced by historical and sociopolitical material on the role of Buddhism in maintaining the legitimacy of the ruling party as well as of that party's most vehement detractors, including the Nobel Peace Prize recipient and parliament member Daw Aung San Suu Kyi (see Suu Kyi; Gravers). Suu Kyi's landmark essay "Freedom from Fear" in particular offers a compelling argument for a revolution of the spirit to spur the fight against corruption and to ward against the ills of desire, ignorance, fear, and animosity (echoing the core afflictions according to Buddhist philosophy: ignorance, attachment, and aversion). In addition to Suu Kyi's 1990 speech, "Freedom from Fear," which connects political and spiritual causes in ways that parallel Teza's meditative practice, students can benefit from the debate over the concept, form, and justification for rights in the collection *Buddhism and Human Rights*, edited by Damien Keown, Charles Prebish, and Wayne Husted (see, in particular, the essays by Inada; Keown; Ihara; Junger; and Garfield). Scholars debate whether the dynamic, contingent, unbounded self in Buddhism can easily stand in for the liberal, autonomous individual in rights philosophy; whether Buddhism's attention to duties and compassion within dharma (and its laws of cause and effect) can be equated with rights as an individual possession; and whether Buddhism's emphasis on shared suffering and vulnerability can substitute for the roles of dignity and natural law in justifying human rights. But, in place of the argument over whether there is "a transcendent ground for human rights in Buddhism" (Keown 34), Tenzin Gyatso, the fourteenth Dalai Lama of Tibet and the world's foremost Buddhist spokesperson, has issued his own declaration, "Human Rights and Universal Responsibility." Invoking the familiar rhetoric of rights and freedoms, he calls for compassion to ease human suffering on a small, shared planet, thereby combining metaphysical and material arguments.

Indigenous Peoples and Human Rights

Although we have been focusing on alternatives to human rights as a set of norms, institutions, and practices, the development of so-called third generation or collective rights, notably in the 2007 United Nations adoption of the Declaration on the Rights of Indigenous Peoples, also asks us to consider how human rights are changing and evolving. Ronald Niezen looks at intersections of indigenous (as a "fragile legal concept," self-identification, and strategy within [4]) social justice movements and normative human rights in the United Nations' increasing engagement with indigenous peoples and their claims (and vice versa). Looking predominantly at the ways in which people mobilize for rights and for justice, as opposed to epistemological differences in theorizing these concepts, he points to the struggle for rights as one in which indigenous movements are increasingly engaged using the discourses and institutions of the human rights regime, notwithstanding the intrinsic paradoxes, first, between the statist mechanisms of human rights and indigenous claims that challenge state authority (136) and, second, between a legal system that favors an individualist understanding of the "person" and bids for collective claims (140–41). At the same time, he highlights the compromises such efforts require, as indigenous claims to self-determination clash with the state mechanisms through which rights are recognized and adjudicated and as appeals to individual rights often dovetail with earlier colonizing rationales for interference in these same communities (133). Unpacking these paradoxes in the classroom necessitates close reading in and against the grain of both normative human rights frameworks and the local systems of meaning in the text. Such readings may bring into high relief the ways in which bureaucratization and state juridical norms and institutions are not outside indigenous cultural identity but continually shape, though do not determine, its expression. A dialogic reading between literary texts and the relevant legal documents also allows students to trace specific changes in legal theory or, more broadly, to understand human rights less as a set of fixed principles than as a fluid set of commitments, policies, and procedures flowing from local and global sociopolitical contexts.

Also important to consider are arguments that reading alternative approaches to human rights solely in terms of the debate over individualism versus collectivity can elide the specific oppression faced, for example, by indigenous women as well as the ways in which they articulate their own resistance to that oppression. Shannon Speed, in her analysis of women in the Zapatista movement, for instance, highlights "indigenous women's refusal to accept formulations of rights [individual or collective] that limit them to one aspect of their experience" and addresses their pursuit of multiple, contingent forms of resistance (241). This example, like the discussion of Islam above, underscores the fallacy of reading human rights in terms of an either-or choice between normative rights and its others by paying close attention to simultaneous claims for justice articulated in different registers.

Resources

For instructors who are looking for wide-ranging source materials on the intellectual development of human rights and its alternatives in religious and other philosophical belief systems, and for the possibility of comparing these perspectives, several readers are available. Patrick Hayden's *The Philosophy of Human Rights*, arranged historically, includes writings of major philosophers as well as core documents. Each entry begins with a brief paragraph that describes the salient human rights contribution of the text and concludes with questions for discussion. A short section on non-Western perspectives features excerpts from Confucian, Buddhist, Islamic, and Akan (West African) moral and ethical systems. Micheline R. Ishay's *The Human Rights Reader: Major Political Essays, Speeches, and Documents from Ancient Times to the Present* is more ambitious. Structured by historical-philosophical eras (ancient times, liberalism and the Enlightenment, socialism and industrialization, the era of decolonization and self-determination, and contemporary globalization), the volume includes contributions from Buddhist, Hindu, and Muslim philosophers and legal discourses. Within each historical section, Ishay has organized the material thematically, juxtaposing, for instance, Plato, Confucius, and Asoka's writings on justice, war, and peace. This approach allows for a comparative discussion of the topic at hand; it does so, however, at the expense of a more focused understanding of any single contributor, whose excerpted writings may lie in multiple sections of the book. Indigenous perspectives receive little attention in either Hayden or Ishay. Most comprehensive is Thomas Cushman's *Handbook of Human Rights*, which includes critiques and analyses of human rights from several religious, philosophical, geographic, and cultural perspectives. Sections on world religious traditions and human rights and on geographies of rights, in addition to other essays on communitarian and anthropological approaches, will be of particular interest to those looking for concise, cutting-edge essays to frame the problem of ascribing universality to human rights in specific contexts.

The historical trajectory of these readers (excluding Cushman's, which is organized thematically) can make human rights appear to be the teleological conclusion of moral thought. Ishay works against this tendency in short essays for each section that emphasize the political milieu and competing interests structuring the debate over rights at key historical moments. Each section also ends with texts that take up the explicit question, Human rights for whom?, underscoring the partial and contested nature of human rights. Although these readers will not satisfy those looking for in-depth treatment of non-Western and nonpostcolonial alternatives to human rights, they do open up questions of how and why human rights predominate in specific contexts. The comparative approach also enables rich classroom discussions of how normative human rights discourse emerges from particular understandings of the relation of the individual to the community and to the state.

Instructors looking for more commentary and analysis of the fundamental relation of the individual to the collective in different religions may find the first part of Irene Bloom, J. Paul Martin, and Wayne L. Proudfoot's *Religious Diversity and Human Rights* especially useful. Drawing on some of the same primary source materials provided in the readers, the critical essays in this collection provide much greater discussion of the evolution and implications of foundational human rights concepts, including the self vis-à-vis the community, rights versus duties (both of the individual and of specific social groups), compassion versus responsibility, and issues ranging from private property to voting guarantees to the structure of the family in various major religions. When paired with literary texts from these different traditions, the essays can help explain how a particular religious moral framework may render human rights immaterial or vital to the context at hand.

Finally, we point toward strategies such as the one pursued by Carol Gluck and Anna Lowenhaupt Tsing in *Words in Motion: Toward a Global Lexicon*. Although it is not about human rights per se, the book includes entries on words such as *security*, *custom*, *injury*, and *terrorism*, each written by a different scholar and located in a discrete context, that "track [how the terms] cross cultural borders and become embedded in social and political practices, changing their impact and their meaning as they go" (3). In the entry on *injury*, for example, Lydia H. Liu traces the term's meanings from nineteenth-century British trade and trade treaties in India and China to show "how the discourses of injury produced and *smuggled* words, meanings, and psychic energies across languages in the service of imperial objectives" (201). Her analysis illuminates how the legal meaning of injury produced subjects and claims that lie at the core of "the political structure of suffering in the modern world" and, thus, the international legal frames, including human rights, used to address that suffering (213). Beyond their specific, contextual insights, the essays in this book model an investigative close-reading practice that steers away from either universality or cultural particularity and toward the ever-changing circumstances in which the suffering of human wrongs is translated and transfigured among different groups. We find this practice to be emblematic of the movement toward contingent cultural legitimacy that we advocate in theorizing and teaching cross-cultural approaches to human rights in the twenty-first century.

Part II

Historical and Geographic Orientations

Introduction to Part 2

Many language and literature departments are organized according to geographic region and, within a region, historical eras, and the essays in this section speak directly to teachers approaching human rights from those perspectives. These contributions also take up two of the central challenges to the purported universality of human rights: the antecedents and historical development of human rights and how literary studies transports and translates rights across different national or cultural contexts.

Sarah Winter's examination of rights discourse before the Universal Declaration of Human Rights in 1948 emphasizes the need for "extensive interpretation, documentation, and retrospective insight [about] what kinds of arguments and representations from the past might or should count as relevant to human rights." She begins with Frederick Douglass and the abolition of slavery as arguably the first modern human rights campaign. Tracing abolitionist arguments about justice, dignity, and the human back in time through classical and Enlightenment philosophies of natural law and human nature, she also notes critiques of those genealogies from literary (Slaughter) and historical (Moyn) perspectives. Winter's essay provides a valuable overview not only of key literary and philosophical texts in the history of rights but also of how its foundational concepts have changed over time.

Our next two contributors demonstrate that "not only are human rights everywhere, they are on the move" (McClennen and Slaughter 3). As human rights literatures migrate into classrooms across national borders, both the rights discourses and literatures undergo a worlding that may produce a provisional sense of the universality of rights as well as a clearer understanding of where translation fails. Ira Dworkin shares his experience teaching African American literature in Egypt (in the milieu of the Arab Spring), noting that to read such literature within a human rights frame, as opposed to solely in the context of United States civil rights, is to "locate [African American literature] on the literary map of human rights." Manav Ratti argues against the "rights machine" that homogenizes diverse experience under the umbrella concepts of rights, violence, and suffering. Looking at the impossibility of international discourses of rights to translate fully in the South Asian context of Michael Ondaatje's novel *Anil's Ghost* (set in Sri Lanka) as well as in classroom discussion of human rights in China, he underscores the importance of pedagogical attention to the "geographies of intellectual labor" (borrowing from Sunder Rajan) as well as the "labors of intellectual geography."

The next essay focuses on Latin American storytelling and *testimonio* in literatures and films, although the essay's insights about the relation of ethics and aesthetics—of how we teach and respond to human rights content through literary and cinematic narratives—pertain to Latin American literature as a whole. Sophia McClennen argues for exposing students to a range of human rights storytelling genres to hone their analytic skills in comparing "representational strategies and politically engaged art." Her pedagogical questions ask students to pay particular attention to the risks of representation and its inevitable partiality (and thus trauma or violence) toward the experience at its core. McClennen's discussion of three key texts—Rigoberta Menchú's *testimonio*, the film *La historia oficial*, and Ariel Dorfman's play *Death and the Maiden*—reflects on how different forms can draw forth responses from the reader that range from recognition to identification.

We conclude this section with Eve Wiederhold's examination of the film *The Visitor* in the context of post-9/11 United States. Wiederhold investigates the question of the purported universality of human rights in relation to the figure of the illegal immigrant (particularly in a climate of fear). As opposed to critiques of universality from philosophical or sociopolitical perspectives, she argues for a feminist materialist rhetorical approach to the relation of language and political judgment to unveil the otherwise hidden judgments of character and deservedness that often subtend human rights talk.

Each of these contributions examines literature and film taught frequently in courses oriented toward human rights. The authors' diverse approaches to the history and circulation of human rights in literature and culture probe the concepts of justice, rights, dignity, and the human with which all such courses must wrestle.

Sarah Winter

On the History of Human Rights before 1948

In the *Narrative of the Life of Frederick Douglass, an American Slave, Written by Himself* (1845), Frederick Douglass describes his feelings of "great insecurity and loneliness" on arriving in New York after his escape from slavery, "without home or friends—without money or credit—wanting shelter, and no one to give it—wanting bread, and no money to buy it, . . . pursued by merciless men-hunters, and in total darkness as to what to do, where to go, or where to stay,—perfectly helpless both as to the means of defence and means of escape" (69–70). To the reader of his *Narrative*, Douglass suggests, "let him be placed in this most trying situation,—the situation in which I was placed,—then, and not till then, will he fully appreciate the hardships of, and know how to sympathize with, the toil-worn and whip-scarred fugitive slave" (69–70). Douglass's catalog of deprivations and injustices could be translated directly into the basic civil rights already enshrined in the United States Constitution's Bill of Rights but denied to slaves, such as "the right of the people to be secure in their persons," as stipulated in the Fourth Amendment. Douglass's powerful depiction of the fugitive slave's plight might even be interpreted as envisioning rights that would be formulated in the 1948 United Nations Universal Declaration of Human Rights (UDHR), such as the abolition of slavery (art. 4) and the rights to security of the person and equal protection of the law (arts. 3, 6, 7, 9), to freedom of movement (art. 13), to access to food and shelter (art. 25), and to work (art. 23).[1] Making such connections, however, raises the question of what kinds of historical contexts and arguments are required to read Douglass's *Narrative* in a human rights frame. Do human rights as they are understood today have a history before the adoption by the United Nations General Assembly on 10 December 1948 of the UDHR? Could the history of human rights be a universal one, involving a project to chart a difficult, unlikely, and unfinished development extending across centuries and cultures? If modern ideas of human rights are instead distinctive and new, what kinds of continuities might exist with earlier conceptions of the human, justice, or the protections and obligations to others entailed in membership in a polity? What kinds of ruptures with past conceptions of the human were required to articulate human rights as both a project "imagining the world as it did not yet exist" and a set of international laws (Lauren 38)? In surveying possible approaches to answering these questions, this essay also introduces an ongoing debate in human rights scholarship.

A strong case can be made that abolitionism was the first modern international human rights movement. A context for reading Douglass's account of the fugitive slave's plight as an articulation of human rights claims appears in other more explicit references to the human rights of slaves by Douglass as well as by other British and American abolitionists, including Olaudah Equiano—who may have been one of the first writers to use the phrase in his *Interesting Narrative of the Life of Olaudah Equiano, or Gustavus Vassa, the African* (1789)—Thomas Clarkson, Harriet Beecher Stowe, and Charles Sumner.[2] The many debates during the extended period of international political agitation for the abolition of slavery beginning in the eighteenth century played an important role in formulating ideas of human rights and modeling the forms of political advocacy—such as boycotts, investigations publicizing abuses, and the formation of pressure groups and peaceful campaigns for political action—that have been effective in subsequent human rights movements. Eighteenth- and nineteenth-century abolitionists' crusades for the human rights of slaves were often inspired by religious commitments as well as explicitly articulated theories of morality, politics, international law, and jurisprudence (see Baucom; Blackburn, *American Crucible* and "Reclaiming Human Rights"; C. Brown; D. Davis; and Drescher). Robin Blackburn has recently argued that George Wallace's chapter on slavery in *A System of the*

Principles of the Laws of Scotland (1760) includes "the first clear statement that Atlantic slavery was incompatible with what could surely be described as a human right" ("Reclaiming" 132). Asserting the illegality of slavery, Wallace writes that "every one of those unfortunate men, who are pretended to be slaves, has a right to be declared free, for he never lost his liberty, he could not lose it; his prince had no power to dispose of him. Of course the sale [that made him a slave] was *ipso jure* void. This right he carries around with him, and he is entitled everywhere to get it declared" (qtd. in Blackburn, *American Crucible* 146–47).

The idea that a right to natural liberty could apply to slaves, its scope narrowed to English law, would also appear a few years after Wallace's text in the first volume of the influential jurist William Blackstone's *Commentaries on the Laws of England* (1765): "And this spirit of liberty is so deeply implanted in our constitution, and rooted even in our very soil, that a slave or a negro, the moment he lands in England, falls under the protection of the laws, and with regard to all natural rights becomes *eo instanti* a freeman" (qtd. in Shyllon 59).[3] Blackstone qualified this statement in subsequent editions of his *Commentaries*, but it still became a rallying point for British abolitionists who were campaigning to have the English courts declare slavery and the slave trade illegal (see Shyllon 55–81). In a recent study, Jenny S. Martinez has also linked abolitionism to the emergence of international human rights law, focusing on measures adopted to enforce more than twenty international treaties banning the slave trade after the abolition of the slave trade in Britain in 1807 (12–13). These measures included the establishment in 1820 of "mixed commission" courts located in Freetown, Sierra Leone; Havana, Cuba; Rio de Janeiro, Brazil; and Suriname (6). Presiding over these courts were international panels of British, Dutch, Spanish, and Portuguese judges who ruled on the disposition of captured slave ships and their cargo of seized Africans (34–35; 68–70).

In considering the history of human rights before the eighteenth century, scholarly discussion tends to shift into studies of the philosophy of natural law. Such investigations look to histories of the categories of rights, international law, and the human. The writings on natural law of such ancient and medieval philosophers as Plato, Aristotle, Cicero, and Thomas Aquinas also appear in anthologies devoted to the origins of human rights because of these philosophers' alignment of human reason and morality with the order that pervades nature and the cosmos. Such a coherent and hierarchical order, whether natural or divine, founds justice as both a human virtue and a system of eternal laws (see Hayden). Sixteenth- and seventeenth-century political philosophers such as Hugo Grotius, Thomas Hobbes, and John Locke formulated secularized conceptions of natural law that became foundational for modern formulations of political rights and international law in the eighteenth century, particularly in the contexts of the American and French Revolutions. Grotius argued that natural rights derived directly from human reason (Hayden 4), but his separation of the principle of jurisdiction from the right of property helped justify the expropriation of territory and resources accompanying European colonial expansion (Tuck 104–08). Hobbes and Locke took different positions on the question of what constituted a legitimate sovereign political authority—Hobbes arguing for an absolute sovereign and Locke for the right of citizens to dissolve a tyrannical government—but both defined rights in relation to the human person's natural equality and liberty, capacity for reason, proprietary relation to nature and the self, and capacity to consent to government in a foundational contractual relation with a sovereign power.

The Lockean theory of natural rights takes on a more ambiguous character in the context of the history of the abolition of slavery as an early human rights struggle. In chapter 4 of his *Second Treatise of Government* (pub. 1689, dated 1690), Locke equates enslavement with conquest in war, arguing that "no Man can, by agreement, pass over to another that which he hath not in himself, a Power over his own Life" (284–85); he also rules out a child's inheritance of his parent's condition as a slave (393; Glausser 206). Locke's lucrative personal investments during the 1670s in two slave-trading companies and his likely participation in the drafting of the Fundamental Constitutions of Carolina, which included a clause stating that "every freeman of Carolina shall have absolute power and authority over his negro slave of what opinion or religion soever" (qtd. in Glausser 205), however, suggest that Locke viewed the enslavement of Africans as compatible with a colonial constitution affording broad religious tolerance.[4]

The writings of the Enlightenment philosophers Jean-Jacques Rousseau, who condemned slavery as antithetical to the natural rights of humanity in book 1 of *Du contrat social, ou Principes du droit politique* (*Of the Social Contract; or, Principles of Political Right*, 1762), and Immanuel Kant were also influential in delineating how natural rights underpin human equality and liberty, the just treatment of others in society, and citizenship. Kant's "categorical imperative," defined in his *Grundlegung zur*

Metaphysik der Sitten (*Grounding for the Metaphysics of Morals*; 1785) as the idea that right actions should be motivated only by a good will and the obligation to uphold a universal law or form of justice, has been identified as an important precursor to the human rights concept of human dignity, since it implies that all persons should be treated "as ends in themselves and not merely as means to other ends" (Hayden 109; see also Slaughter, *Human Rights* 18).

On more detailed investigation, however, these Enlightenment philosophers' writings also present complexities that invite further debate on the implications of European political theories for the history of human rights. For example, the famous argument in Locke's *Second Treatise of Government* that the consent of the governed is essential to political legitimacy strongly influenced conceptions of the rights of citizens adopted in the United States Declaration of Independence (1776), a document that in turn influenced the French National Assembly's Déclaration des droits de l'homme et du citoyen (Declaration of the Rights of Man and of the Citizen; 1789) (Hunt 113–30). In his treatise on epistemology, *An Essay concerning Human Understanding* (1689), Locke links rights to the "human person," which he argues should be understood as a "Forensick [*sic*] Term appropriating Actions and their Merit; and so belongs only to intelligent Agents capable of a Law, and Happiness and Misery" (346). Thus for Locke, legal rights belong by definition not to an abstract category of the human but to persons insofar as their actions conform to a social and legal order and entail consequences. Locke also denies that a clear definition of the human species exists in nature: "Wherein then, would I gladly know, consists the precise and *unmovable Boundaries* of that *Species* [Man]? 'Tis plain, if we examine, there is *no* such thing *made by Nature*, and established by Her amongst Men" (454). Modern theories of inherent human rights as an endowment from birth, as articulated in article 1 of the UDHR, would not find unambiguous support in Locke's writings, if such inherence is understood to imply a species-level definition of humanity.

Since Plato's *Republic*, Greek tragedy has provided both an influential model and a counterexample for philosophers' definitions of justice and the human. When considered as works of literature that formed a central part of the classical education of educated men (and some women) from the Renaissance through the nineteenth century, Greek tragic dramas of the fifth century BCE also become relevant to teaching the history of the category of the human, although discussions of the modern notion of rights in relation to ancient works would involve an anachronism that should be acknowledged openly. In Sophocles's tragedy *Ajax*, for example, the goddess Athena invites her favorite, Odysseus, to spy on the deluded Ajax, whom she has driven to madness in punishment for his defiance of the gods. Gathering up the carcasses of goats and cattle outside his tent during the siege of Troy, Ajax believes that he has killed the commanders of the Achaean army in revenge for the dishonor he suffered when they awarded the armor of the slain Achilles to Odysseus. "Do you see, Odysseus, how great is the power of the gods?" Athena asks. "What man was found to be more farsighted than this one, or better at doing what occasion required?" But Odysseus cannot share in the goddess's triumph: "I pity him in his misery, though he is my enemy, not thinking of his fate, but my own; because I see that all of us who live are nothing but ghosts, or a fleeting shadow" (44, lines 118–120, 121–26; 45). Odysseus's response defines humanity as being mortal, creating a human bond through pity that counteracts both his personal enmity toward Ajax and the superiority of being and power represented by divinity that motivates Athena's retribution.

Euripides's *Hecuba* creates a context for a discussion of the history of claims for the humanity of the slave through its focus on the fate of Hecuba, queen of the Trojans, who has been enslaved by the Achaeans after the fall of Troy. In the final section of the play, Hecuba attempts to convince Agamemnon to permit her to take vengeance against Polymestor, a former Trojan ally, for the murder of her youngest son, Polydorus, whom Polymestor had promised to shelter and protect. Calling on Agamemnon to respect the laws of the gods, which "uphold clear distinctions between unjust and just," Hecuba pleads, "Pity me, and having stepped back like a painter, behold me and examine such troubles as I have. I was queen, but now I am your slave, once lucky in children, now I am at once old and childless, cityless, alone, most wretched of mortals" (376, lines 799–805, 806–11; *Hecuba* [2006] 66; trans. modified). Hecuba defines her slave status (also evoking for us the stateless status of the modern refugee) in ways strikingly similar to Douglass's description of the fugitive slave. While Douglass seeks his readers' sympathy and outlines the rights of citizenship that the fugitive American slave lacks, through Hecuba's persona, Euripides's play also imagines its effects on the spectator. To understand her situation, Hecuba suggests, one must view it at a certain distance, the way a painter steps back and examines an image before resuming work on it (*hôs grapheys t' apostatheis*; [1984] 376, line 807). This evocation of the dispassionate but interested regard of the artist or craftsman seems analogous to Douglass's text's insistence on addressing how his sympathetic reader, or a spectator at an abolitionist meeting, should respond when encountering a slave's testimony. The solicitations of pity expressed by the characters of ancient tragedy and the sympathy that Douglass's text seeks to evoke attempt temporarily to overcome the distance of experience and status between parties to the encounter, but at the same time they call attention to the necessity of such distance instead of seeking to cancel it out.[5] Modern human rights claims similarly require awareness of the complexity of articulation, response, and redress in relation to human rights violations as encounters involving not just the temporary overcoming of differences between victims and those able to offer aid or reparation but the acknowledgment of the permanence of such differences. The historical gap between ancient slavery in the Athenian polis and nineteenth-century American slavery can be both investigated and bridged, with due attention to historical and linguistic specificity, in classroom discussions of human rights and literature by examining the grounds of the claim to justice in each text and the way they all self-reflexively solicit attention to artistic and literary creation and the dynamics of reading, witnessing, or spectatorship.

Plato's and Aristotle's writings are also cited by human rights scholars in discussions of the history of natural law and slavery. In an influential study, Gregory Vlastos argues that Plato's "views about slavery, state, man, and the world, all illustrate a single hierarchic pattern":

> [T]he key to the pattern is in his idea of *logos* with all the implications of a dualist epistemology. The slave lacks *logos*; so does the multitude in the state, the body in man, and material necessity in the universe. Left to itself each of these would be disorderly and vicious in the sense of that untranslatably Greek word, *hybris.* Order is imposed upon them, by a benevolent superior: master, guardian, mind, demiurge. . . . The common title to authority is the possession of *logos.* In such an intellectual scheme slavery is "natural," in perfect harmony with one's notions about the nature of the world and of man. (303)

Vlastos contends further that in book 1 of the *Politics*, Aristotle shows consistency with Plato in providing a "metaphysical sanction" that aligns the naturalness of slavery with "a pattern that pervades all nature," quoting the *Politics* (1254a 29–32; 302): "because in every composite thing, where a plurality of parts, whether continuous or discrete, is combined to make a single common whole, there is always found a ruling and a subject factor, and this characteristic of living things is present in them as an outcome of the whole of nature (*ek tês apasês physeôs*)" (Vlastos 302).[6]

Vlastos's analysis draws our attention to the ways that Hecuba, though a slave, undeniably still possesses *logos*, defined as articulate and reasoned speech. (In the context of human rights, one should also note the restrictive nature of this definition of *logos*, which could exclude children and persons with certain intellectual disabilities.) Douglass's *Narrative* also constitutes a declaration, with all its modern political connotations, of the slave's capacity for *logos*. If abolitionism is one of the first modern human rights movements, it can be argued that modern notions of rights were attached to the slave after an extended history involving the contributions of drama, rhetoric, philosophy, political theory, autobiographical narrative, and other forms of writing, performance, and art, through which the slave's *logos* became a recognizable proof of his or her humanity and equality. By bringing these texts that are remote in time into dialogue, a human rights frame adds a new emphasis to the observation that discussions of justice and freedom in the Western philosophical and literary traditions have been built with remarkable consistency around the antithesis between the rational, rights-bearing, and eloquent human person or citizen and the alternatively passive or rebelliously articulate figure of the slave (see also Buck-Morss; DuBois).

Behind Douglass's representative *logos* as an American slave is also a history of political revolutions, including the Haitian Revolution (1789–1804; see Ghachem). In *Inventing Human Rights: A History*, Lynn Hunt links the emergence of human rights to the strategic use of Enlightenment natural rights theories to justify the American and French Revolutions. Also highly influential were the writings of Thomas Paine, who used the expression "human rights" in *The Rights of Man* (1791) (Lauren 20).[7] Hunt points out that because human rights were codified in the late eighteenth century in documents called declarations, which imply a claim toward or even seizure of political sovereignty, their political logic extended to groups who initially were not included in the more limited category of man or citizen and who did not have political rights, such as the rights of "those without property or of religious minorities" (133), as well as of slaves, Jews, and women (146–75). When based in this universalizing logic, "[r]ights questions thus revealed a tendency to cascade" (147). Hunt further argues that the eighteenth-century sentimental novel was pivotal to the formulation of human rights because its epistolary form and focus on emotional connection taught readers to empathize with characters who modeled the emerging cultural value of the individual, autonomous subject, endowed with universal human rights (35–69). She also points to such eighteenth-century criminal law reforms as the abolition of judicial torture in France as a further development through which "the traditional framework of pain and personhood fell apart, to be replaced, bit by bit, by a new framework, in which individuals owned their bodies, had rights to their separateness and to bodily inviolability, and recognized in other people the same passions, sentiments, and sympathies as in themselves," even across differences of race, gender, and social position (112).

Johannes Morsink, while drawing attention to the Holocaust as an event immediately preceding and instigating the formulation of the 1948 UDHR (*Universal Declaration* 36–91), has also argued that the drafters of the UDHR adapted from the Enlightenment natural rights tradition the idea that human rights are inherent in human beings from their birth (*Inherent Human Rights* 24), as expressed in the preamble: "Whereas recognition of the inherent dignity and of the equal and inalienable rights of all members of the human family is the foundation of freedom, justice and peace in the world, [and] Whereas disregard and contempt for human rights have resulted in barbarous acts which have outraged the conscience of mankind" ("Universal Declaration"). According to Morsink, this "metaphysics of simple inherence" is linked to the "epistemic universality" of human rights—their understandability as "moral truths" to human beings across cultures, based not on a pregiven definition of what human rights are but rather "because of the kind of creatures we know human beings to be" (*Inherent Human Rights* 25–26). This moral intuition, which "speaks in a universal voice" (105), is activated within individuals as "an appeal to the conscience of humanity" in response to atrocities (104). A self-conscious connection with Enlightenment notions of inherent rights also appears in the title change that was voted by the 1948 drafters from the original "International Bill of Rights" to "Universal Declaration of Human Rights." Morsink suggests that this revision "shifted the attention from the international delegations that did the proclaiming to the peoples of the world being addressed," so that "the term 'universal' in the title of the document captures both the metaphysical and the epistemological universalities that make up the doctrine of inherence" (57).

Paul Gordon Lauren and Patrick Hayden have also supported the argument that human rights were imagined and articulated before the issuance of official declarations and charters, pointing to a wide-ranging and inclusive array of possible sources and traditions, including the moral teachings of all the world religions as well as writings by philosophers, political economists, politicians, and activists from several cultural traditions and historical periods. Lauren gives a central role in forging human rights to the political, ethical, and religious commitments and compassion of individuals and nongovernmental organizations, using as an illustration the pathbreaking, worldwide abolitionist movement (38–45). For Lauren, an important historical criterion for the emergence of human rights lies in the international dimensions of particular initiatives—that, in Stanley Hoffmann's phrase, they represent "duties beyond borders" (qtd. in Lauren 9)—and their translation into international treaties, global movements, and nongovernmental humanitarian organizations. Such human rights activism seeks not only to achieve the humanitarian goal of alleviating human suffering but also to take responsibility and mobilize actions to solve problems not recognized or addressed by governments. A salient example for Lauren is the role of the Swiss businessman J. Henry Dunant in drawing attention to the suffering of wounded soldiers through the publication of his memoir, *Un souvenir de Solferino* (1862). In the memoir, Dunant recounted his witnessing of the scenes of carnage in the aftermath of the battle of Solferino in June 1859. Dunant's writings and activism spurred the organization of the Geneva International Conference of 1863 that resulted in the founding of the International Committee of the Red Cross, which would take on the task of caring for wounded soldiers and later civilians displaced by war, ultimately contributing to the development of humanitarian law relating to armed conflict (Lauren 58–63; see also Barnett). Lauren also observes that human rights initiatives tend to stem from periods of political and social conflict or revolution allowing "significant shifts of power, the testing of political institutions by disruption or chaos, or even violence and destruction to provide opportunities for serious reassessment and significant change" (39–40). Important historical contexts for human rights would also include labor movements beginning in the nineteenth century (94–95), as well as movements for racial equality and civil rights (96–97), women's and children's rights (254–55), and decolonization and the self-determination of newly independent colonies (239–45; see also R. Burke).

Scholars working in the humanities are accustomed to thinking of such categories as "the human," "humanity," and "rights" as historically and culturally determined and thus may question the idea of inherent human rights insofar as it suggests a kind of essentialism or lacks historical specificity.[8] The concept of humanity or the human as considered in the frame of inherent human rights, in turn, seems to imply a species-level definition or a normative legal or political approach based in morality or the obligations that human beings have toward other living beings. In the context of human rights, however, such obligations often entail a responsibility to prevent extreme bodily harm, such as torture, or to hold perpetrators accountable for such violations, thus drawing the notion of humanity as a category of embodiment automatically into the orbit of physical and biological vulnerability. Human rights seem to become attached to human bodies only belatedly, or as a promise of a future, utopian world system of justice, but rarely at the opportune moment to prevent abuses, violations, rapes, or killings. Jack Donnelly theorizes human rights historically as emerging from the "moral hazard presented by the modern state" through its ability to "operate relatively free of the moral constraints of custom" but with "far greater administrative and technological reach" ([1989] 105–06), but he also points out that "[r]ights are actually put to use, and thus important enough to talk about, only when they are at issue, when their enjoyment is questioned, threatened, or denied" ([2003] 8). Morsink, from his different moral intuitionist perspective, nevertheless comes to a similar conclusion: "Each basic human right has its own justification, one that is discovered when that particular right is violated in some gross way" (*Inherent Human Rights* 108). It is perhaps this sort of recognition of violation that Douglass seeks to evoke from his readers by pushing beyond the representational limitations of the generic conventions of sentimentalism, both inciting the reader to sympathize with the fugitive slave's human emotions and insisting on the impossibility that the slave's deprivation could be understood by the rights-endowed citizen. Douglass's feelings can, by implication, be shared most directly by a fellow human being without regard to status, even if he or she cannot fully grasp the experience of the "whip-scarred fugitive slave" ([1997] 69–70). Such an abstract figure of the vulnerable human without qualities could nevertheless appear monstrous to a critic of the "rights of man and citizen" such as Edmund Burke, who in his *Reflections on the Revolution in France* (1790) terms the so-called principles proclaimed by the French revolutionaries as "barbarous philosophies . . . void of solid wisdom" and "laws . . . supported only by their own terrors" (171).

Whereas Lauren, Morsink, and Hunt see the continuity of human rights with Enlightenment concepts of equality and natural rights and suggest that their recognition expresses a moral awareness or psychological capacity for empathy common to all human beings (Hunt 33, 210–12), Samuel Moyn has argued that international human rights are significantly different from the political rights envisioned by the French and American revolutionaries, as well as from the civil rights demanded by nineteenth-century abolitionists and the nationalist agendas of the communist and anticolonial movements of the 1950s and 1960s. Earlier notions of rights, according to Moyn, were articulated in the context of revolutionary changes to the governments of nation-states and not, as in human rights, to protect individuals across borders, often from abuses of state power (12–14). Questioning what he terms the "celebratory attitude" of many historians of human rights and dismissing the "myth" that the UDHR was framed as a strong response to the Holocaust (5, 6), Moyn argues that human rights only became widely accepted in the 1970s in response to the failure of other utopian political movements that still represented "fidelity to the state" (85).

Joseph R. Slaughter provides an equally critical account of the "banalization of human rights" that has accompanied their growing acceptance after 1948, arguing that "the discursive victory of human rights" now supports conditions through which "increasingly systematic, corporate, and institutional" violations of rights are committed in the name of protecting such rights through so-called humanitarian interventions (*Human Rights* 2). Slaughter's analytic approach to questioning the universality of the categories invoked by the UDHR focuses on the role of the bildungsroman as a central model for the idea of the full potential and dignity of the human personality articulated by the UDHR's drafters. Slaughter contends that the UDHR's preamble's invocation of the "human person" as the subject of human rights enacted a "subtle displacement of the human being" that in its subsequent effects "all but eliminated 'human' as a substantive noun from the text of human rights law, as a proper grammatical subject of universal human rights" (18–19). This "incorporation" of the "human person" functions as the "human's legal representation" in international human rights law (22–23). This "human person" is nevertheless also naturalized as the real, developmental human personality, recognizable from the bildungsroman tradition, that human rights culture aspires to promote and protect (23–24). Thus according to Slaughter, one should consider

> both hegemonic international human rights and the *Bildungsroman* as necessary but suspicious vehicles, not because they naturalize a monadic, self-sufficient Enlightenment individualism (which is more sociable than most critiques admit) but because of the historically narrow, generic universalism and the residual nationalism of the forms they conscript to project a new universal, international citizen-subjectivity. (33)

Slaughter's history also shows how the bildungsroman as a genre embraced and modified by postcolonial writers continues to play a central role in formulating, promoting, and questioning both definitions of the human and contemporary human rights values and legal regimes.

How do these compelling debates over the history of human rights, sketched briefly here, become relevant to teaching literature in a human rights frame? As I have begun to show, investigating the possible histories of human rights in different textual and cultural traditions often requires assembling historical and textual evidence about the history of the category of the human and what attributes have been included in or excluded from it, what constitutes the moral and ethical treatment of others, and how to define justice, rights, the human person, and human dignity. Definitions for these terms become particularly significant when reading texts written before the late eighteenth century, which may seem to develop such themes but often lack explicit references to human rights. Understanding human rights in historical context, therefore, involves determining through extensive interpretation, documentation, and retrospective insight what kinds of arguments and representations from the past might or should count as relevant to human rights. Such interpretive work could also include drawing attention to the inadequacy of certain categories, such as individual rights, as distinctively modern formations derived from Western political systems that have been strongly criticized for their histories of systemic and often legalized inequalities.[9]

Reading literary, autobiographical, and theoretical works in relation to possible histories of human rights often involves tracing imaginative representations of the argument that certain political, social, and civil rights that have been attached only to privileged persons must be reconceptualized as universal so that they can be claimed by minorities and stigmatized or subordinated groups. These arguments, however, are often made through stories about individuals, supporting the Enlightenment claim that human rights are attached to individual persons. Historically, defining universal human rights also entails putting particular pressure on categories defined according to inclusion or exclusion, such as one's belonging to a particular nation, race, gender, or religion. Human rights readings of literature can therefore focus on specific scenes that perform the conceptual transfer of a stigmatized group from exclusion to inclusion—that is, such scenes offer a basis for an individual belonging to a group traditionally excluded from political or social participation to be included within categories of natural rights, equality, or universal humanity. In the process, certain positive qualities that were attached to a dominant group as well as negative qualities made salient to marginalize a subordinate group may also become universalized to humanity. For example, in contesting Edmund Burke's critique of the rights of man in *A Vindication of the Rights of Woman* (1792), Mary Wollstonecraft also addresses the conceptual problem of universal humanity, but this time in relation to sex:

> [I]f [women] be really capable of acting like rational creatures, let them not be treated like slaves; or, like the brutes who are dependent on the reason of man, when they associate with him; but cultivate their minds, give them the salutary, sublime curb of principle, and let them attain conscious dignity by feeling themselves only dependent on God. Teach them, in common with man, to submit to necessity, instead of giving, to render them more pleasing, a sex to morals. (120–21)

Wollstonecraft attempts to transfer the valuation of certain moral qualities associated with men—dignity, rationality, adherence to principle—by showing that they belong to women as well, but in doing so she also makes these qualities universally human, part of the "natural rights of mankind" and thus foundations for the equality of the sexes (88). In this way, she also associates sex (or gender)—an attribute that forms the basis of the differential and prejudiced treatment of women—with more general human capacities. Sex (or gender) therefore becomes a universal human category, while reason, morality, and dignity also become universal attributes of humanity. Within the logic of Wollstonecraft's argument, then, one can see the kind of redefinition that, in moving the concept of sex into the domain of the universal human and the domain of the rights of man, also articulates rights of humanity. At the same time, Wollstonecraft still refers to the figure of the slave as a negative counterexample to represent the human being deprived of rights. Within the frame of the history of human rights, such redefinitions are not so much to be celebrated as interrogated.[10]

In focusing on classical Greek, British, and American texts, I have only begun to map the terrain of further research on the history of human rights concepts across languages and national and international traditions.[11] Discussing the possible relevance of texts from earlier periods to the history of human rights does not imply that the emergence of human rights was historically inevitable but rather provides an approach for investigating the genealogies of the values and claims embodied in official articulations such as the UDHR, which was not framed as a complete rupture with the past. Because long-standing injustices persist and new violations continue to occur despite the widespread recognition of human rights after 1948, attention to past conceptualizations of the human, human dignity, and rights, along with their differences from and discontinuities with the present, remains important for understanding both significant breakthroughs and failures in conceiving, ratifying, and upholding political and legal requirements for justice and human equality.

Notes

My work in the history of human rights and my teaching of literature and human rights have benefitted greatly from interactions with colleagues and visiting scholars in a faculty study group on narrative forms and human rights sponsored by the University of Connecticut Human Rights Institute's Research Program on Humanitarianism.

1. On African Americans' efforts after World War II to gain recognition by the newly founded United Nations of the systematic violations of their human rights in the United States, see Anderson.

2. For such references to violations of slaves' "human rights" see Olaudah Equiano, *The Interesting Narrative of the Life of Olaudah Equiano, or Gustavus Vassa, The African, Written by Himself* (1789), chs. 2 and 6; Thomas Clarkson, *The History of the Rise, Progress, and Accomplishment of the Abolition of Slavery* (1808) (486); Frederick Douglass, *Narrative of the Life of Frederick Douglass, An American Slave* (1845), ch. 7; and Harriet Beecher Stowe, *Uncle Tom's Cabin* (1852), ch. 19. In his final speech before the United States Senate in 1866 during the drafting of the Fourteenth Amendment to the Constitution, Sumner, the senator from Massachusetts, stated, "From the beginning of our history, the country has been afflicted with compromise [with slavery]. It is by compromise that human rights have been abandoned" (qtd. in Foreman 33). References to the human rights of slaves during this early- to mid-nineteenth-century period did not automatically entail the abolition of slavery, however; in an 1806 speech before the United States Congress, President Thomas Jefferson supported the abolition of the slave trade to "withdraw the citizens of the United States from all further participation in those violations of human rights which have been so long continued on the unoffending inhabitants of Africa" (qtd. in Martinez 17).

3. Blackstone may be echoing Locke's assertion in the opening sentence of the first of his *Two Treatises of Government* (1690): "Slavery is so vile and miserable an Estate of Man, and so directly opposite to the generous Temper and Courage of our Nation; that 'tis hardly to be conceived, that an Englishman, much less a Gentleman, should plead for't" (141). Here, however, Locke refers to slavery in a political sense as an unjust subordination to an autocratic power in the context of his refutation of Robert Filmer's *Patriarcha: or the Natural Power of Kings* (1680).

4. For details of Locke's investments in the Royal African Company, a slave-trading venture, and the Bahamas Adventurers, a company established to support the expansion of Bahamas plantations (which depended on slave labor), as

well as an account of his likely participation in drafting the Carolina constitutions, see Glausser 200–04. Locke also served as the secretary of the Lords Proprietors of Carolina from 1668 to 1675 and concurrently as one of eleven members of the Council of Trade and Plantations (Bernasconi and Mann 89). The import of Locke's connections to slave holding for his political theory has been the subject of significant debate (Glausser; Bernasconi and Mann).

5. Two different Greek verbs are translated into English as "to pity" in the passages I have quoted from Sophocles's *Ajax* and Euripides's *Hecuba*: *epoiktirô* (*Ajax* 44) can also be translated as "to have compassion on" whereas *aideomai* (*Hecuba* [1984] 376), a term that was used in Attic law, can also mean "to pardon." A sense of hierarchy is absent in the first term and present in the second, but both indicate a general human vulnerability to reversal and suffering intrinsic to mortality and antithetical to the immortality of the gods, thus voicing a central theme of tragedy. Douglass's idea of sympathy posits a relation of human equality as a basis for the rights of citizenship that he claimed for emancipated slaves throughout his abolitionist writings and oratory. For two recent useful discussions of differences in definition among *sympathy*, *empathy*, and *altruism*, terms that come up frequently in discussions of emotional response to witnessing or reporting on human rights violations, see Greiner; Keen.

6. Vlastos endorses a translation by H. Rackham, reading the Greek phrase *ek tês apasês physeôs* in the broadest terms as referring to "the whole of nature," or the entire natural order (302). A translation by T. A. Sinclair and T. J. Saunders seems to mitigate the metaphysical connection that Vlastos draws by making the phrase refer more specifically to the internal organization of living organisms (Aristotle 512). Such a translation does not, however, contradict Aristotle's statement on the naturalness of hierarchical relations: "That one should command and another obey is both necessary and expedient" (1254a 21–22; 512). Though he does not discuss Plato and Aristotle in relation to human rights, Vlastos does connect the contradictions and injustices inherent in a democratic Athenian polis based in a slave system to later arguments concerning the incompatibility of slavery and democracy (303–04).

7. For a conceptual analysis of human rights within eighteenth-century writings in English, with a particular focus on Paine's works, see De Bolla.

8. For a recent report on some reservations about human rights research in the humanities, see Harpham.

9. This critique of the modern concept of rights is fundamental to historical and cross-cultural considerations of human rights but too complex to be treated here. Slaughter traces one dominant strand to Burke, Marx, and Arendt (*Human Rights* 12–13).

10. For a further account of similar literary transactions of human rights, see Winter.

11. For a wide-ranging collection of essays analyzing definitions of human rights in cross-cultural historical perspective, see An-Na'im, *Human Rights*. See also, in this volume, Moore and Goldberg, "Human Rights Cultures."

Ira Dworkin

Mapping African American Literature and Human Rights

> All the nations that signed the charter of the UN came up with the Declaration of Human Rights and anyone who classifies his grievances under the label of "human rights" violations, those grievances can then be brought into the United Nations and be discussed by people all over the world. For as long as you call it "civil rights" your only allies can be the people in the next community, many of whom are responsible for your grievance. But when you call it "human rights" it becomes international. And then you can take your troubles to the World Court. You can take them before the world. And anybody anywhere on this earth can become your ally. (Malcolm X [el-Hajj Malik el-Shabazz] 180–81)

When I first began teaching in the Department of English and Comparative Literature at the American University in Cairo (AUC) in 2008, I was assigned the course Literature and Human Rights. As the department's Americanist and a specialist in African American literature—a tradition with a long commitment to social justice—it was a logical and welcome assignment, even as it was one that was new to me. My initial question was where to locate the United States on the literary map of human rights. Human rights seemed vaguely international—something that would more likely be part of a world tradition than a national one. Then I recalled Malcolm X's insistence that the African American freedom movement be considered a struggle for human rather than civil rights and saw it as a way of conceptualizing the role African American literature could occupy in a course on literature and human rights.

Given this context, it should not be surprising that I immediately turned to antebellum slave narratives, in particular *Narrative of the Life of Frederick Douglass, an American Slave*, which, like many other classics of the genre, considers the relation of literacy and liberation in a manner that demonstrates the connection between writing and human rights. The process of reframing canonical texts like Frederick Douglass's in the way suggested by Malcolm X has been facilitated by the experience of teaching in Egypt, where, for most students, African American writing is not part of their national literary heritage in the same way it is (or at least should be) for students in the United States. In particular, at AUC, the experience of the Egyptian students—multilingual and relatively well-informed, generally well-to-do, and commonly well-traveled—with the American course materials differs greatly from that of students in the United States, who often encounter world literatures from and about places that appear nowhere else in the school curriculum (and whose languages are rarely taught). It is important for students, wherever they are, to be reminded that human rights is not only an issue in the so-called Third World or some other ill-defined place "out there" and that they must be encouraged to attend to the local as well as the global.

By placing this dialectic at its forefront, the course sought to create a map of human rights that would include both the local and the foreign. To do so, I later developed a community-based learning (CBL) project to complement the American readings. A collaborative initiative with a local nongovernmental organization that actively works with young adults on human rights issues brought Egyptian writers across a range of media—from poets to bloggers to graphic novelists—into public conversations about the relation of literature and human rights in contemporary Cairo. As impressive as the students' final projects were, some of them did find the work occasionally overwhelming, in part because of the seemingly different tracks they were expected to pursue—for example, reading Douglass for class discussion while preparing for an interview with a young Egyptian writer. The connections between the many (though not exclusively) African American texts we discussed in class and the extraordinarily rich local literary scene to which my students introduced me proved difficult to articulate in the classroom, where the assignments required intersections as concrete as those articulated by one of the class texts—William Gardner Smith's nearly forgotten novel *The Stone Face*, which foregrounds connections between African Americans and the Arab world.

The Stone Face follows Simeon Brown, an African American writer living in Paris during the Algerian revolution, and climaxes with the October 1961 police massacre in Paris of Algerian protestors. The novel reveals that colonial violence is not the exclusive province of the colonies. The brutality takes place at home and abroad, and Simeon comes to recognize the similarity between the racist brutality he experienced in Philadelphia and what his Algerian friends experience in Paris. Through a series of flashbacks, Simeon locates his experiences on a world map of human rights violations, displacing the possibility of any exclusively national narrative. As a result, for students experiencing both an African American tradition and a contemporary Egyptian scene all under one banner, human rights could emerge as a potentially coherent field or discourse.

Egypt's contributions to a discourse about human rights have come to the forefront of global consciousness thanks to the Egyptian Revolution of 25 January 2011. The goals of the protestors in Midan Tahrir were (and remain at the time of this writing) broad democratic changes, which enabled their national movement to reverberate internationally. The capacity of Egyptian youth to create space for a discourse about human rights within the larger body politic suggests new possibilities for pedagogy that my colleagues and students in Egypt are already beginning to articulate (in ways my past teaching could hardly anticipate). As a result, this chapter remains, much like the revolution itself, necessarily provisional. The question Brian Edwards asks in his 2009 introduction to a collection of contemporary Egyptian writing—"What is left after one has confronted an authoritarian state in the streets and shouted *Enough!?*"—remains as prescient as it is unresolved (132).

In writing of the role played by literature in the Egyptian and Tunisian revolutions, Sharif Elmusa explains:

> Language under authoritarian regimes rusts, turns dull, loses its edge and luster. Revolution restores to words their truthfulness, meaning, even magic. The first word of the revolution was "The people want to bring down the regime." It is the people who want, not the ruler. The declarative statement is economical, uses the active verb, and announces the expiry of the old order. It is in itself an act, a performance.

Like Edwards's question, the literary performance of politics that Elmusa describes has long-standing roots in the African American tradition where, as Eduardo Cadava explains, a "conviction in the relation between literary performance and politics" is central to Douglass's famous oration "What to the Slave Is the Fourth of July?" and his 1845 *Narrative* (1560). Douglass, for example, uses writing to measure his suffering, as when he explains, "My feet have been so cracked with the frost, that the pen with which I am writing might be laid in the gashes" ([2014] 37). His self-consciousness of his identity as an author marks the ways that he has overcome dehumanization and rhetorically binds together the course's titular dyad. Douglass does more than simply describe a human rights violation; he writes about writing about human rights. Douglass's reflective gestures draw, Cadava argues, on Mary Shelley's *Frankenstein*, which shares many themes with the *Narrative*: "language, self-hood, genealogy, freedom, rebellion, violence, creation, racism, rights, and the question of what it means to be human" in the entangled legal and philosophical senses (1560). While Douglass's pen serves as the measuring stick of his physical suffering, his prose—like the music, poetry, humor, and visual art of Midan Tahrir—reclaims the humanity that a brutal system sought to deny.

Despite the importance of abolition as an antecedent tradition, the discourse of human rights remains a modern one whose most immediate roots, as Malcolm X understood, are in the 1948 Universal Declaration of Human Rights. As a result, if the only African American literary texts in the curriculum are slave narratives (or modern works about slavery), human rights violations within United States borders may seem to be fixed in a distant past. Similarly, in the twenty-first century, discussions around the United States and human rights are less likely to turn to the African American experience, as they may have during Malcolm X's lifetime, than they are to violations at Guantánamo, Abu Ghraib, and unmappable sites of extraordinary rendition. While these locations urgently deserve as much critical scrutiny as possible, they all place abuses by the United States outside the country's physical borders.

To make this point, Colin Dayan describes how a 2006 United States Supreme Court decision allowing Pennsylvania to prohibit inmate access to reading materials was overshadowed by the court's decision the very next day, in *Hamdan v. Rumsfeld*, granting habeas corpus protection to Guantánamo detainees. *Hamdan* overshadowed the Pennsylvania decision and in the process placed the violation of prisoner's rights outside the United States. Dayan draws parallels to Douglass's *Narrative* to point out how such human rights violations within the United States are part of a domestic regime that remains invisible despite essential connections between the actions at home and abroad. As Amy Kaplan notes in her 2003 presidential address to the American Studies Association, "the draconian changes . . . in the prison system within the U.S.—the use of solitary confinement and sensory deprivation, for example—circulate across international borders to make this penal regime in Guantánamo possible" (14). The "interconnections" that Kaplan traces "between the domestic and the foreign" (7; admittedly problematic terms) are the kinds of things that can be emphasized by a novel like Smith's, which not only compares the African American and Algerian struggles but also links France's colonial regime to the occident.

The often ignored United States domestic prison regime, which is the subject of a substantial body of literary work (including autobiographies by Angela Davis, George Jackson, Assata Shakur, and Malcolm X that draw on the slave narrative tradition), can play an important role in classes in literature and human rights.[1] Social scientific analyses of the United States prison system regularly make the point that Malcolm X made by framing the crisis through international comparison. As Glenn C. Loury summarizes in *Race, Incarceration, and American Values*:

> According to a 2005 report of the International Centre for Prison Studies in London, the United States—with one-twentieth of the world's population—houses one-quarter of the world's inmates. The US incarceration rate (now at 714 prisoners per 100,000 residents) is almost 40 per cent greater than the nearest competitors (the Bahamas, Belarus, and Russia). Other industrial democracies, some with significant crime problems of their own, are much less punitive: The US incarceration rate is 6.2 times that of Canada, 7.8 times that of France, and 12.3 times that of Japan. (4–5)

Loury's analysis is intriguing rhetorically because he introduces the statistics through international comparison, firmly locating the crisis in global terms before offering stark data on domestic racial disparities; indeed, this internationalization precedes even a survey of the staggering absolute numbers. By presenting the prison crisis as a matter of global importance, Loury follows Malcolm X's paradigm.

United States Department of Justice figures for 2012 indicate that there were 2.3 million individuals incarcerated and 4.8 million adults under other forms of correctional supervision (probation or parole), to say nothing of the impact on the families, friends, and communities of those 7 million people ("Total U.S. Correctional Population"). The perspective of family members is the focus of another class reading, John Edgar Wideman's memoir *Brothers and Keepers*, in which the author grapples with the limits to what he can do on behalf of his incarcerated younger brother, Robby: "A thousand books would not reduce his sentence one day" (194). Wideman realizes that "[h]e was inside and I was outside," and with the publication of *Brothers and Keepers*, "Robby's story would be 'out there,' but he'd still be locked up. . . . Imprisonment profoundly alienated him from the finished product of our collaboration" (200). Where Douglass sees the pen as a foil to the experience of enslavement and the written word as a tool for abolition, Wideman confronts the impossibility that literature can change his brother's situation. Douglass and Wideman make up part of a tradition that is struggling with the relation, to borrow from Cadava, of "literary performance and politics."

In his preface to a twentieth-anniversary edition of *Brothers and Keepers*, Wideman is still struggling to articulate the social value of his literary work:

> I write to hear myself think, to remind myself I own a voice with the power to construct a version of what my senses experience. With words I can make something of my world, no matter how private or subjective or useless to anyone else on the planet that making turns out to be. I use words to rattle the bars of my cage. To remind myself the cage is there. Remind myself I don't like it. (xvi)

Wideman's first-person discussion of his "cage" marks his relationship to his brother, which, like asha bandele's relationship to her husband in *The Prisoner's Wife*, serves as a critical reminder that a prison's walls confine far more people than they can physically contain. Wideman explains his position: "For better or worse, I carry around a prison inside myself. I'm connected as intimately to its walls and bars as I am to my brother" (xv). While it may seem natural for Wideman to empathize with a younger sibling, his self-reflective journey provides a model for reading and teaching human rights. As Susan Sontag explains in *Regarding the Pain of Others*:

> So far as we feel sympathy, we feel we are not accomplices to what caused the suffering. Our sympathy proclaims our innocence as well as our impotence. To that extent, it can be (for all our good intentions) an impertinent—if not an inappropriate—response. To set aside the

> sympathy we extend to others beset by war and murderous politics for a reflection on how our privileges are located on the same map as their suffering, and may—in ways we might prefer not to imagine—be linked to their suffering. (102–03)

Wideman similarly elaborates on the relation of literature and human rights:

> Neither writing a book nor reading one grants a free pass from th[e] encompassing reality [of one's own complicity]. Reading and writing may seem to offer temporary immunity . . . , but the privilege to step aside and enjoy the opportunity to consume a book, a candy bar, a movie, a Mercedes, or to enjoy leisure time or obtain a formal education—all of these "freedoms" are purchased by vast injustices visited upon others. (xv)

Both Sontag and Wideman caution against sympathy, preferring instead a self-critical position that recognizes that there are no safe spaces from which to read—or write.

Their common vision, shared by Malcolm X, is a by-product of a human rights map where neither a prison wall nor a state border can insulate a person from what is happening on the other side. Still, such boundaries may veil many things, creating illusions that pose real challenges. How, for example, do writers or teachers make a group of people who do not feel directly threatened by a human rights violation identify with those who are? For instance, the racial disparity in the incarcerated population in the United States serves as a linchpin in the widespread acceptance of the prison system, because it allows a majority of white United States citizens to believe that incarceration will not happen to them or to those around them. Loury reflects:

> Suppose we had to stop thinking of us and them. What social rules would we pick if we actually thought that they could be us? I expect that we would still pick some set of punishment institutions to contain bad behavior and protect society. But wouldn't we pick arrangements that respected the humanity of each individual and of those they are connected to through bonds of social and psychic affiliation? If any one of us had a real chance of being one of those faces looking up from the bottom of the well—of being the least among us—then how would we talk publicly about those who break our laws? (30–31)

Consider the commonplace question posed to those considered liberal on criminal justice issues, a crude variation of which was famously put to the

United States presidential candidate Michael Dukakis in a 1988 debate: if someone attacked your loved one, how would you want that person punished?[2] One could just as easily ask a parallel question, which did not come up in the debate: if a loved one was accused (justly or not) of doing something wrong, how would you want to see your loved one punished? The question asked, much more than the answer given, reveals a great deal about how one imagines one's relation to the criminal justice system and human rights.

Perhaps, therefore, Simeon Brown is quick to identify with the Algerian victims of police brutality because he easily imagines himself in their situation. From the moment Simeon sees an Arab man being beaten by the police, the domestic and the foreign are fused in his mind. Toward the end of the novel, Simeon finds himself caught up in the 17 October 1961 demonstration in Paris when the police killed hundreds of peaceful Algerian protestors. His expressions of solidarity are consistent with what Moustafa Bayoumi describes as a "strong and dedicated cultural politics . . . within the African-American tradition that seeks an alliance with the rest of the world, including its Arab and Muslim corners."[3] This tradition of cultural politics is part of what makes African American texts so germane to the teaching of literature and human rights, particularly in an Egyptian educational context.

After the massacre and his brief subsequent detention, Simeon resolves to return to the United States to renew his commitment to the civil rights movement because every country has its Algerians, and "America's Algerians were back there" (210). Significantly, Smith's novel, published in 1963, bore public witness to these historical events at a time when they were not officially acknowledged, telling a story that the French authorities did not want in the public record.[4] While there are more recent works that can serve as classroom companions to the novel—Philip Brooks and Alan Hayling's documentary film *Drowning by Bullets* and the 2008 English translation of Leïla Sebbar's novel, *The Seine Was Red: Paris, October 1961*—Smith's novel remains an important exemplar of an author "rattling the bars of his cage."

Within the novel, it is no coincidence that Simeon is a journalist and his closest Algerian friend, Ahmed, is an aspiring, if pessimistic, correspondent for whom writing "seems so useless when so many people are dying" (84). Among the novel's African American expatriate community in Paris, the accomplished James Benson abandoned his craft for journalism after moving to Paris: "Ain't gonna be no more books. I ain't got nothing more to say to them people. Said all I got to say" (31). And "Joey the Drunk" had been working on his "*bitch* of a novel" for years when he dies suddenly (135). Though not all Simeon's compatriots abroad share his interest in the Algerian struggle, they are grappling with the relation of literary performance and politics in different ways that collectively embody the vexed role of writing at a time of crisis.

Even among the African American expatriate community, there are no outsiders in Smith's Paris, only people whose illusions of such are ultimately shattered (usually violently). Though set in France, *The Stone Face* creates a map of human rights that places Paris beside Philadelphia, Algeria beside France, France beside the United States, the colony beside the colonizer, the South beside the North. Out of this process, African American literature emerges in the classroom as world literature, and the Third World becomes less an exotic site of human rights abuse than a part of a map that is contiguous with the rest of the world, reflecting an internationalism that runs throughout African American literary history. This framework, to quote Malcolm X, allows African American literature to "be discussed by people all over the world."

In the Egyptian context, such a class suggests a particular kind of transnational inquiry, which allows students to look at the multidimensionality of the United States and understand the ways that human rights are neither exclusively local nor exclusively foreign. At the same time, it is encouraging to see college students in the United States developing new interest in the Arab and Muslim worlds, as indicated by the increased popularity of study-abroad programs in the region (Conlin). That interest, however, must not supplant careful attention to human rights violations in the United States, from slavery to incarceration and beyond. Whether or not students study abroad, African American texts on human rights that engage the region can be tools for exploring these bridges. One lesson for students in the United States is that human rights violations are not only "out there" but also at home in places that, as Loury reminds us, most people do not have to see. At its best, literature tells stories that can make all these sites visible.

Notes

1. See James's *The New Abolitionists: (Neo)Slave Narratives and Contemporary Prison Writings* and Davis's introduction to her edition of Douglass's *Narrative*. For resources on teaching the prison industrial complex, see the special issue of *Radical Teacher* dedicated to the topic (Agid, Bennett, and Drabinski).

2. The CNN anchor Bernard Shaw asked this question at the opening of the 13 October 1988 presidential debate, held at the University of California, Los Angeles. For a transcript of the debate, see Woolley and Peters.

3. Other novels in that tradition include Sam Greenlee's *Baghdad Blues* (1976), which Bayoumi also discusses, and David Du Bois's . . . *And Bid Him Sing* (1974). For more on Du Bois, see Feldman.

4. The French government did not commemorate the events of October 1961 until 2001. For details on the historical debate, see House and MacMaster 6–10; their *Paris 1961* is the most comprehensive English-language source on the subject.

Manav Ratti

Representing China and Asia: Translating Outside in the Rights Machine

Who's afraid of China? Where do recent events—WikiLeaks' publishing cables from the United States that claimed the Chinese were hacking Google, Tibet's being again in flames in 2008 and reporting nearly one hundred self-immolations, the artificially controlled yuan's being featured in international trade debates—leave university instructors and students wishing to teach and learn about human rights and China? The three examples above are only some instances of China's mediated and polarizing images on the world stage. In this essay, I discuss some of the rewards, practices, and challenges of teaching the idea of human rights and China.

The context for the teaching I discuss in this article is a graduate seminar I offered in the Department of English and Comparative Literary Studies at Warwick University, for the master of arts in translation studies. I taught a ten-week interdisciplinary seminar entitled Issues of Representation: Between Literature and the World, which met once a week for a two-hour session. Under the rubric of translation studies, I interpreted translation in its broadest sense, to include cultural translation. I wanted students to appreciate how concepts travel across languages, literatures, and cultures, especially how those concepts become modified, contested, adapted, and appropriated. The overarching aim in the seminar was for students to have some exposure to the various relations between literature and the world. To satisfy degree requirements for the MA, students could choose from among a range of required and optional courses, including courses on cultural transfer and difference, research methods, literary translation, and the theory and practice of translation studies. I began my course with an introduction to the linguistic, cultural, and semiotic theories of Ferdinand de Saussure, Stuart Hall, and Michel Foucault. The students then read works of postcolonial and anthropological theory by Edward Said, James Clifford, and Gayatri Spivak. They also read primary literary texts including Michael Ondaatje's *Anil's Ghost* and *The English Patient* (and saw the film adaptation) and Mahasweta Devi's "Pterodactyl, Puran Sahay, and Pirtha" (in the collection *Imaginary Maps*).

Seven students enrolled in the seminar: five from China, one from the United States, and one from the United Kingdom. Four graduate student auditors, from China, India, Malta, and Mauritius, sat in on the seminar's last meeting, described here.

Chinese human rights and *Anil's Ghost* were the topics of the final session of the seminar. Why this pairing? I had already assigned *Anil's Ghost* to our last meeting since the novel's deeply rich texture could allow for multiple understandings of the discourses we had examined throughout the course, on law, postcoloniality, human rights, diaspora, and anthropology, among others. In their midcourse feedback, students expressed an interest in discussing Chinese human rights, which then became a welcome, serendipitous point of connection with the established syllabus focusing on *Anil's Ghost.* By the last session, the preceding weeks of discussion had established a sense of familiarity and intellectual community in the seminar room, allowing students to articulate some of their own subject positions, both nationally and internationally, as reflected also in the thematic of diaspora in *Anil's Ghost.*

The protagonist, Anil, is diasporic, visiting Sri Lanka after years of working and studying in the United Kingdom and the United States. Her journey requires a certain humility, an openness to the difference and opacity that parts of Sri Lankan culture represent for her. As the novel progresses, there is a development in Anil's sensitivities to nuance, mood, and complexity. I hoped to duplicate this process and ethic among my students in the final session, to help them maintain an openness to learning and difference. In my discussion of *Anil's Ghost,* I narrated a brief history of postcolonial Sri Lanka, particularly as it led to the contemporary question of human rights. The events I highlighted included the 1956 Sinhala

Only Act and the watershed July 1983 violence in Jaffna and Colombo. I sought to keep a transnational perspective to help students understand patterns in human rights violations and to avoid any negative or positive biases of nationalism. I emphasized Ondaatje's writing from Canada and his reference to Guatemala at the beginning of the novel. The seminar discussion afterward also highlighted violence in Rwanda, through the topic of ethnicity. I hoped that such examples would offer the students the tool of cultural translation. How do Chinese issues compare with Sri Lankan ones? What does *minority rights* mean? How does that meaning alter according to national context? For the instructor working at the interstices of various student nationalities and various disciplines—literary studies, postcolonial studies, translation studies—the stakes demand a close sensitivity to the geographies of intellectual labor, since those geographies affect everyone in the classroom.

When Robert Young argues in *Postcolonialism: An Historical Introduction* that postcolonial cultural critique and theory find their origins in anticolonial thought and practice (67–69), could there be a similar historical transformative moment within the Euro-American academy with respect to the university-level disciplinarization of human rights? This question in turn could provoke reflections on the various advantages and problems of teaching human rights. Whether advantageous or problematic, among the assumptions constituting the idea and practice of human rights are the Western liberal democratic ideals of freedom of the self ("the human") and of freedom of access to information ("What are rights? my rights?"). But in Asia—across Sri Lanka and China—criticisms proliferate on the Eurocentrism of the idea of human rights and the selectivity of their implementation. Whose rights matter? What merits international attention?[1]

These are some of the questions that Ondaatje's novel has eloquently raised, provoking debates across at least South Asia, Canada, and Euro-America. *Anil's Ghost* became a springboard in the MA seminar's final session for the wider discussion of human rights in China. The diasporic situatedness that *Anil's Ghost* thematizes through its protagonist is one that became embodied by the Chinese students. Their distance from China and concomitant situatedness in the West positioned them to reflect on human rights as perceived both inside and outside China. My hope, which I directly stated, was that by reflecting on their international subject positions, the students would also be able to understand the challenges faced by Ondaatje and Anil. The first useful pedagogical lesson therefore was from an observer-participant position that allowed both the thematization of human rights and the self-conscious analysis of human rights as rights, highlighting that each of us in the classroom was implicated in the international dynamics of rights creation and legislation.

Theory: The Teaching Machine, the Rights Machine

Part of the context in which Spivak formulates her idea of "the teaching machine" is through her argument that Said's *Orientalism* was a study not of marginality or marginalization but of the "construction of an object, for investigation and control," leading to the study of colonial discourse wherein "the marginal can speak and be spoken, even spoken for" (*Outside* 56). She continues:

> As this material [on marginality] begins to be absorbed into the discipline, the long-established but supple, heterogeneous, and hierarchical power-lines of the institutional "dissemination of knowledge" continue to determine and overdetermine its conditions of representability. It is at this moment of infiltration or insertion, sufficiently under threat by the custodians of a fantasmatic high Western culture, that the greatest caution must be exercised. (56)

I would insert here teaching as an example of the "institutional 'dissemination of knowledge.'" An awareness of the right to rights can be considered as dissemination of a kind of knowledge. When those rights are about a part of the world that the instructor too embodies—by accident of birth, by upbringing, by filiation and affiliation—and when those rights become part of the discourse and are disseminated in yet another part of the world, then there is a subject position akin to being inside and outside the teaching machine. For example, how are China and Asia inserted into the Western discipline and the Western institution, and by whom? It is in this strict sense of separation and connection that I want to propose the idea of "the rights machine." Spivak states that "we [as teachers] are now involved in the construction of a new object of investigation—'the third world,' 'the marginal'—for institutional validation and certification" (56). Translating into the concept of rights: which geographic spaces get institutionally validated and certified?

Joseph Slaughter, building on the work of Hannah Arendt, Edmund Burke, and Karl Marx, presents a paradox constituting human rights, stating that they are "in practice if not in principle, not the natural rights of humans qua humans but the positive rights of citizens" (*Human Rights* 12). This paradox raises questions of nation and citizenship and the attendant questions of state sovereignty and international intervention, making the implementation of rights all the more challenging. In this context, Wendy Brown asks, "How might paradox gain political richness when it is understood as affirming the impossibility of justice in the present and as articulating the conditions and contours of justice in the future?" (qtd. in Slaughter, *Human Rights* 13). Literature can add to that process of political richness, by presenting several perspectives—contradictory, paradoxical, oppositional. It is the constitutively polyphonous space of literary representation that allows Slaughter to elegantly use the trope of literary personification to argue for "incorporation" into human rights:

> If literary personification produces a person who seems capable of responding to my call, incorporation is imagined to configure a person with self-consciousness who can recognize itself as capable of making and answering calls (even its own). . . . [T]he figurative act of human rights incorporation fulfills itself when the incorporated person acquires human rights literacy: the capacity to read itself and others as human rights persons, as creatures of dignity and bearers of international rights and responsibilities. (23)

Incorporation in the above sense is a potent concept. One could argue that this is the conceptual paradigm with which Anil enters Sri Lanka. By the end of the novel, however, that paradigm has been challenged: the Western rights regime is confronted by the irreducible difference represented by Sri Lanka. Incorporation can enable a dialogue, but it should also enable genuine recognition and acceptance of difference. The dangers in incorporation are that nations and regions such as China, Sri Lanka, Asia, or the West could be homogenized through a concept of "identitarianism," as some sort of stable, fixed, undifferentiated identities. Equally, difference could be negatively homogenized, as merely predictable reactionism. This alertness to the dangers of identitarianism and predictable reactionism should apply not just to nationalities and regions but also to disciplines, instructors, and students. Spivak again:

> To a London audience, academics and cultural workers, eager to hear a speech on cultural value, it is important that the speaker's [Spivak's] identity that afternoon was "Asian," with underclass *differentiations* out of sight. Unless we continue to nurse the platitudinous conviction that the masses are necessarily identical with 'the revolutionary van-

> guard,' or conversely that, stepping into the university, 'The truth has made us free,' we must attend to the possibility of such dissension, and their imbrication with the history and burden of names. Identitarianism can be as dangerous as it is powerful, and the radical teacher in the university can hope to work, however indirectly, toward controlling the dangers by making them visible. (*Outside* 54; emphasis mine)

Among the dangers of identitarianism for human rights pedagogy is the reduction and reification of teaching human rights as simply another mechanism for the West to "witness" the Third World (see Ratti, *Postsecular Imagination* and "Michael Ondaatje's *Anil's Ghost*"). Human rights university education, especially in locations where minority discourses and relations are particularly present, runs the risk of becoming reductive, reactionary, and essentializing. Postcolonial literature has gone through the same route. A single-semester course could cover Shakespeare, or it could be made to cover, separately or combined, the literatures of South Asia, the Caribbean, Latin America, and Africa. Such reduction and reification in human rights courses exemplify "the rights machine," because they can work to trivialize and stifle intellectuals into, in Spivak's formulation above, a burden of names (or appearances, under the category of "ethnicity"; e.g., consider the use of the phrase "people of color" in the United States today). Concurrent with such reductionism and reification there is of course serious scholarly work striving to expose the machine and the ongoing violence, epistemic and otherwise, of its regimes. The rights machine can negatively produce a solid, stable identity for rights education, such as "token minoritarianism," "the concern only of minorities," "the voice only of minorities." Such a machinating rights ideology contrasts, ironically, with the fact that the object of human rights is the irreducibly particular: a particular case, a particular legal instance on the heterogeneous stage of the global, accompanied by the paradigm of the universal human. Within such a context, the instructor must be acutely, ethically aware of maintaining objectivity—a cosmopolitan objectivity, as per human rights legislation—especially in a multicultural or multinational classroom. For the ethnic minority intellectual finding herself or himself simultaneously inside and outside such structures, self-vigilance could be one way of maintaining resistance to the always ready cadres of neo-orientalism. Attending to the geographies of intellectual labor—Where is the work being produced?—must also involve sensitivity to the labors of intellectual geography—Which nations are constructing our rights?[2]

The Exercise

In a mid-semester evaluation, one of the students from China stated that she had enjoyed the seminar devoted to Said and its discussions of *Orientalism* and *Culture and Imperialism*. The concepts especially from *Orientalism* had inspired her to reflect on the complex questions of human rights in China and their various representations—and misrepresentations—in the Western media. She stated that she and her Chinese classmates would enjoy discussing these ideas with the class, especially as a way of learning about specific perceptions among those outside China of China and its human rights issues.

Building on this expression of interest, I invited the group of Chinese students to collaborate and offer the other two students and the four auditors a presentation on human rights in China during our final session. They could focus on whatever points they wished, using the opportunity as a forum for sharing knowledge and experiences both among themselves and with their peers. My only formal requirement, to ensure a minimal academic standard, was that they produce a handout complete with references for future reading and research.

Among the issues and points included in the handout were the legal system of China; civil liberties; the treatment of ethnic minorities; legislative policies, such as the one-child policy; human rights issues, including Tibet and the impact of Falun Gong on political freedom; and areas for reform. This wide-ranging list of topics was impossible to discuss adequately in the two-hour seminar session, but I mention some of the topics to provide a glimpse into the imaginary of contemporary Chinese youth's ideas on perceptions of human rights inside and outside China. Especially striking in the seminar discussion was the coverage of the one-child policy. This topic also raised the question of sexual rights, particularly because four of the five Chinese students were women; almost all the other students enrolled in or auditing the seminar were also women. The students discussed examples of the policy's implementation—or, more interestingly, lack of implementation—among their peer groups and relatives. The Chinese students, especially the women, were keen to dispel any misunderstandings that the one-child policy applied uniformly across the nation. They emphasized that affluent families, especially within urban areas like Shanghai, were able to have several children by paying the relevant governmental fees. In my discussion of Sri Lankan politics, I had also raised the point of limited university places for Tamil students. This prompted the Chinese students to highlight the enormous competition for university places in China. Who gets access? How? Everyone in the room held a bachelor's degree—to use Slaughter's terms, we had all once been incorporated into the category of "undergraduate"—allowing us to reflect on the particular historical and national forces shaping such a privilege. With serious funding cuts across Euro-American universities, all students in the class appreciated that the problems of others were also their problems. I expressed my hope that such cross-cultural discussion would allow all the students to question the category of "the other." Was it a construct? Why or why not?

Lessons Learned, Part 1: Between Ideology and Knowledge

In a course devoted to examining the various issues and facets of representation—literary, translational, ideological, anthropological, political—here was a session that explicitly exemplified and problematized these themes in its structuring of the discussion of human rights across China, Sri Lanka, and the West. As the course instructor, and also as someone trained in postcolonial studies, I was keen not to place the Chinese students in the position of native informants, as if they were uncritical representatives with little to learn themselves of their culture. If instructors might be in a position of having to negotiate the role of native informancy, then students might also have to negotiate such a problematic position, especially those falling under the unchosen rubric "international student" (with its possible connotations of "overseas" or "foreign"). And with Euro-American universities seeking to internationalize (or globalize or diversify) their curricula, research profiles, faculty, and student bodies, would it not be a marker of success—within this institutional logic, as an achievement of global awareness—for every student to be considered an international student?

One Chinese student elected not to participate in the seminar discussion. She felt uninformed about human rights in China. More important, and demonstrating an astute understanding of Said's and Spivak's theories, she did not want to carry any burden of representation, resisting any role as native informant. She stated she may have felt more comfortable speaking had she better understood all seminar participants and their motivations, so that she could be sure there was an openness toward trying to understand China. In a sense, this student was vigilant of the nascent orientalism and of the capacity for orientalism, both within herself and her audience.

Although the Chinese students had knowledge that others in the seminar did not have, my pedagogical commitment throughout was to reinforce for seminar participants that we were all there to learn rather than simply or uncritically to supply and receive information. And another lesson thus emerged: respect students' positions to be either reticent or forthcoming, especially with such sensitive topics as sexual rights and ethnic identity. Throughout the discussion, I had also asked Chinese students whether they agreed or disagreed with their peers and had invited them to offer their own stories if they so wished.

To frame it within theoretical terms, such dialogue could be a modest form of what Spivak has termed "ethical singularity." By this Spivak means one-to-one encounters between people when they both inhabit normality (not a crisis), an engagement in which responses "flow from both sides," inspiring individuals to "reveal and reveal, [to] conceal nothing" ("Translator's Preface" xxv). Recognizing the impossibility of such a full ethical engagement, Spivak asserts that "ethics is the experience of the impossible." It is not that ethics themselves are impossible, but that the experience of the impossible or impossibility paradoxically becomes the impetus to continue further work: further engagement, further understanding. Would this not be an attractive pedagogical aim for university teachers?

I also taught Spivak's essay "The Politics of Translation" toward the end of the seminar (*Outside* 179–200). Spivak invites readers to assume solidarity with the so-called other, to learn his or her language, and then to assess whether such solidarity can still be maintained. To show the Chinese students respect for their linguistic integrity and difference, I invited them to demonstrate and explain the Cantonese or Mandarin characters for particular topics under discussion.

Our discussion of the one-child policy was particularly lively. All of us in the seminar room were aware of the English phrase "one-child policy." The Chinese students explained to us that the phrase 汁划生育政策 (*jìhuà shēngyù zhèngcè*) could be translated as "family-planning policy." Some government documents use the translation "birth control policy" (not to be confused with "birth control" in the contraceptive sense) since 生育 (*shēngyù*) can mean "to bear or to breed." But in the context of 汁划生育政策 (*jìhuà shēngyù zhèngcè*) the sense of "family" is stronger and more logical than "birth" since the policy's aim is to ensure the well-being of the family. Students mentioned that "one-child policy" is not used in English translations in China, because of the exceptions to having more than one child, and that the policy is open to continuing revisions as a reflection of national changes in China.

The differences between the English and Chinese versions were clear. For me, the English-language version that has become so normalized in Western discourses, in naming the number of children permitted, seems to emphasize the restrictions of communism in comparison with capitalism's "freedoms." The Chinese version showed me the influence of the state, by omitting any specific number and infusing the phrase with a kind of aspirational idealism based on the warm affective connotations of "family" and "birth." One of the Chinese students mentioned that the concept of "control" is not necessarily negative but could be interpreted to contain a benevolent intention, that the intelligent, compassionate state has its citizens' best interests at heart. This point allowed me to refer to the adult-child power relation formulated by Ashis Nandy in the context of colonialism in *The Intimate Enemy*: "[I]t has become obvious that the drive for mastery over men is not merely a by-product of a faulty political economy but also of a world view which believes in the absolute superiority of the human over the subhuman, the masculine over the feminine, the adult over the child, the historical over the ahistorical, and the modern or progressive over the traditional or the savage" (x). Both the English and Chinese linguistic expressions of limiting a family to one child showed the fingerprints of ideology, so that while the translation highlighted the differences—and the amplification of differences—between "us" and "them," the seminar process ultimately increased our solidarity as intellectuals, ones vigilant of ideology. That recognition of the aspirational idealism of intellectual solidarity per se reinforced my strongest pedagogical aim for the seminar, to help students appreciate how pedagogy and dialogue can increase knowledge, sensitivity, and awareness.

Lessons Learned, Part 2: How Not to Orientalize China and Asia

When discussing the teaching machine, Spivak cautions that perhaps "we are becoming complicitous in the perpetration of a 'new orientalism'" (*Outside* 56):

> It is not only that lines separate ethnic, gender, and class prejudice in the metropolitan countries from indigenous cooperation with neocolonialism outside, in the Third World proper. It is also that arguments from culturalism, multiculturalism, and ethnicity, however insular and heteromorphous they might seem from the great narratives of global financial control, can work to obscure such separations in interests of the production of a neocolonial discourse. (57)

Spivak wrote the above in 1993. The global finance-scape has of course changed dramatically since then, including since 2008. This is not to say that the drive to produce neocolonial discourses has witnessed a similarly radical reorientation. The drive has remained; the stakes are now different. With China's replacing Japan as the world's second-strongest economy, Western political and business leaders visiting China (and India) on trade missions, and the West and China's (and India's) increasing research collaborations and academic ties, the facts stand all the greater alongside any Manichaean neocolonizing representations of "the East."

Where is the academy left in this? And is there any coincidence now, on the world historical stage, between the politics of global discourse and this volume dedicated to encouraging academic dialogue on the teaching of human rights? Rey Chow might argue that this collection is yet another instance of Western demand for consuming politicized human rights, ones that are eagerly supplied by the non-West (19–23). One hears the long voice of Said: let us not reorientalize. And Spivak would add: be cautious.

Teaching toward the Field of Justice

Brown has asked, "[H]ow might the paradoxical elements of the struggle for rights in an emancipatory context articulate a field of justice beyond 'that which we cannot not want'?" (qtd. in Slaughter, *Human Rights* 13). By paradox, Brown signals the tension between the impossibility of justice in the present and the possibility of justice in the future. That possibility of justice exists as a field—I am compelled by the metaphor. The space represents a journey, a going to, a vision, a possibility. Does there not exist a similar inspiration in the quest for knowledge, that gaining knowledge will transform and empower student understanding, taking students to a future of greater sensitivity, openness, discernment, and empathy toward themselves, others, and the world? I have not intended any part of this chapter to serve as a report or fact-finding mission. It is a small gesture toward knowledge, toward assisting self-understanding, understanding students, and understanding some serious global challenges.

Notes

1. See especially Mahbubani.

2. For an excellent article on some of the political stakes at play in the location of the so-called Third World intellectual, see Sunder Rajan. I am indebted to Sunder Rajan's usage of the idea of the geographies of intellectual labor.

Sophia A. McClennen

Between Official Stories and Coerced Confessions: *Testimonio* and Storytelling in Latin America

The practice of human rights storytelling in Latin America has a vast and varied history. From Bartolomé de Las Casas, whose *Brevísima relación de la destrucción de las Indias* (1552; *A Brief Account of the Destruction of the Indies*) chronicled the abuse of the native populations, to Bernal Castillo, whose early "testimonial" attempted to challenge the account of the Mexican conquest offered by Hernán Cortés, the history of writing about Latin America offers a lesson in the distinct ways that cultural forms have been used to call attention to atrocity, abuses of power, and the violations of rights. Not only is the history of such writing in the region long, but it is also quite diverse. Practically every generic form and aesthetic strategy has been deployed in the service of finding the adequate means through which to mediate trauma, remember atrocity, and provoke activism.

To investigate the pedagogical advantages to teaching students to be aware of the connections between forms of storytelling and human rights, this essay focuses on three texts from three different genres that are frequently used in courses that cover human rights violations in Latin America: the Academy Award–winning film *La historia oficial* (*The Official Story*), the testimonial *Me llamo Rigoberta Menchú y así me nació la conciencia* (*I, Rigoberta Menchú*), and Ariel Dorfman's international hit play

La muerte y la doncella (*Death and the Maiden*). Each of these texts has played a significant and also controversial role in depicting human rights violations, and each uses a distinct mode of human rights storytelling. *The Official Story* was one of the first texts to represent the traumas of the Argentine Dirty War to an international audience, and its focus on illegal adoption and the struggles of the Mothers of the Plaza de Mayo had a substantial impact on human rights advocacy in Argentina, but its quasi-melodramatic form and its choice of a privileged middle-class protagonist could be considered problematic. *I, Rigoberta Menchú* is probably the most controversial case of human rights storytelling in the region. The text led to Rigoberta Menchú's receipt of the Nobel Peace Prize, interest in ending the assaults on the native Guatemalan population, and the boom of study in the literary form of *testimonio*. The later accusation by David Stoll that Menchú may not have been entirely factual in her account, at least not according to Western terms, led to sustained questioning of the ways that the testimonial form linked to ideas about the truth. Dorfman's play about a torture victim who confronts her torturer and violently forces him to confess is arguably the most internationally visible theatrical work in Latin American history: it has been staged in over thirty countries, and in 1993 there were fifty different productions of the play in Germany alone. Despite its international success, however, the play continues to provoke tension and resistance in local Chilean audiences. Of interest is the way that its open, ambiguous, complex form is read as meaningfully suggestive outside Chile but frustratingly direct within Chile. Looking at these texts together, this essay suggests that there is a distinct advantage to exposing students to a variety of human rights genres, since such a range can encourage them to reflect on the connections between representational strategies and politically engaged art.

Beyond questions of genre and human rights stories, this essay is principally interested in encouraging those who teach these texts to consider the ways that aesthetic concerns can often be overshadowed by ethical dilemmas. Human rights stories face a series of inevitable representational conflicts, not least of which is how to tell the story to an audience who may be unaware of an atrocity while simultaneously respecting the dignity of the victims or survivors. The crisis of legal, political, and civic representation at the heart of human rights violations dovetails with the crisis of symbolic representation at the heart of storytelling, offering us an opportunity to consider how ethics and aesthetics are necessarily intertwined.[1] Each of these texts emerges from a representational paradox, since telling a story to those unaware of a human rights violation requires a loss of specificity; that is, the urge to make these tragedies more broadly legible necessitates a loss of local legibility. And that loss, that story that is left untold, that detail that is omitted at the service of reaching a wider audience, will always be traumatic since it will always signify the limit of what stories can do in the struggle for human rights activism. Some representational violence is done at the service of representing violence, and this must be measured against the violence of those official histories that repress, deny, and omit these stories.

Thus the representation of human rights violations is always a vexed undertaking. It is both urgent and necessary, while also incomplete and inadequate. James Dawes explains in *That the World May Know* that human rights violations cause a crisis of representation: "How do we make comprehensible stories out of incomprehensible atrocities? And what are the ethical risks and obligations of doing so? For many humanitarian and human rights workers . . . storytelling is the very nature of their work" (1). Similarly, for many faculty members, human rights stories are the basis for beginning conversations with students about the history of human rights violations, their commitments to human rights, and their potential as activists, but such work needs to be accompanied by attention to aesthetic issues, representational politics, and the vexed human rights storytelling process. The analysis of these texts allows me to trace this complicated process through three cases that reveal different risks to the representational conflicts caused by human rights violations. Alongside these risks, though, these are each stories of considerable success. How does one reconcile these conflicting results? And what can our students learn from them? I conclude by suggesting that the teaching of human rights stories requires a balance of context and close reading, where stories are studied both for what they say and how they say it.

The Official Story

Luis Puenzo's *The Official Story* is as much a lesson in the representation of a tragic moment in Argentine history as it is in the complications of postdictatorship culture. On the one hand, the end of military rule in Argentina in 1983 brought with it an opening of cultural spaces and an urge to attend to trauma collectively as a wounded nation. But, on the other hand, the moment was also accompanied by the desire to reinvigorate a positive sense of national identity and project that image outward to an international audience. The desire to attend to the national need to mediate trauma through locally specific forms of storytelling was linked in complicated ways to a yearning to redefine Argentina to audiences and markets abroad. Tellingly, *The Official Story* was released during a moment of renewed state investment in cinema that caused Argentine film production to almost double in numbers, from approximately fifteen films per year during the military dictatorship (1976–83) to twenty to twenty-five films per year in the period directly following the return to democracy (1984–89). Tamara L. Falicov notes that the National Film Institute under the leadership of Manuel Antín sought to "mold the film industry into a public relations mechanism for the state" (123). A film that would appeal to an international audience, however, would invariably have problems finding a local audience, since in Argentina, as in many Latin American countries, working-class audiences prefer local-national cultural products and the middle and upper classes prefer imports (124).

Written to appeal to a "universalized" middle-class audience, *The Official Story* was the first Latin American film to win an Academy Award, and it shared the award for best actress in Cannes, leading to success at the box office in the United States and in Europe. It also enjoyed a sizable viewership in Argentina: 889,940 viewers in 1985 and 828,436 viewers upon its rerelease after winning the Academy Award (128). But its success at home and abroad points directly to its weaknesses. In portraying the tragedy of the military dictatorship through the figure of a middle-class woman and in the form of a Hollywood-style melodrama, the film glosses, or perhaps even represses, many crucial features of the story that it purports to tell.

The film takes place in Buenos Aires in March 1983, in the last days of the military dictatorship. It traces the coming to consciousness of Alicia, a high school history teacher, who is married to Roberto, a successful businessman. Together they have an adopted daughter, Gaby. Throughout the military regime, Alicia has remained unaware of the atrocities taking place daily in her country. What's more, she has spent these years teaching a narrow and reactionary view of official history to her students, punishing any who attempt to challenge her version of the past. In this sense, the character of Alicia is an ideal vehicle through which to explore issues of social ignorance, since the viewer acquires knowledge alongside the protagonist. The return from exile of Ana, a friend of Alicia; the provocations of a colleague, Benítez, who chastises her for being bourgeois and ignorant; and finally the intercession of Sara, whose photograph of her disappeared pregnant daughter as a young girl bears a striking resemblance to Alicia's adopted daughter—all combine to force Alicia to come to terms with the ways that her country has violated human rights and how she may have unwittingly participated in these violations.

As mentioned, the film's strengths in representing this crisis are precisely its weaknesses. Diegetically, the plot of the film, by centering on a middle-class woman who reluctantly becomes aware of human rights violations, favors the viewer's affective connection with Alicia rather than with those who directly suffered the violence of the dictatorship. The actual victims of the dictatorship all remain marginalized, undeveloped characters in the film. Audiences based in the United States, for the most part unaware of this history, thus find the character of Alicia nonthreatening, since her lack of knowledge absolves any sense of collective guilt about the violations committed by the Argentine military, which in reality were significantly aided by the United States. The power of this affective connection, though, is responsible for palliating a story that ostensibly should be far more difficult to watch.

In this sense, the film is less interested in representing the atrocities of the military regime and in giving voice to its victims than in provoking a complacent public to question their tacit complicity with state power. The story of Alicia is clearly not the story of the Dirty War, nor is it the story of the Mothers of the Plaza de Mayo, nor is it really the story of the children of the disappeared who were illegally adopted, although the film certainly nods to all these events and persons.[2] And it is not surprising that, given the film's box office success, critics would accuse the film of glossing the real story of the Dirty War in favor of a Hollywood-style melodrama. Emily Tomlinson notes that for some critics the film "soft focuses reality to opposite effect, air brushing out all shades, all shadows, distorting atrocity through a Vaseline-smeared lens" (218). Of interest is the way that the realist or melodrama aesthetic form of the film appears to complement the middle-class, intimate story. The conventional aesthetics, therefore, are directly linked to its nonconfrontational narrative. As Clara Kriger notes, the film "lacks a radical voice" both in terms of cinematic practices and in terms of plot (181).

Puenzo, however, was well aware of the advantages such an aesthetic approach would offer his project, deliberately using the format of "intimate, not political cinema" as a means of reaching an audience for whom a more experimental style would have been unappealing, if not inaccessible (qtd. in Kriger 181). From the view of human rights storytelling, then, the film offers critically engaged viewers the opportunity to seriously consider one of the central aesthetic dilemmas that art about atrocity consistently confronts. Should the story be simplified to appeal to a wider public? And what are the ethical risks involved with focusing on a figure like Alicia rather than on the victims, such as Gaby's mother? What is lost when a film seeks to represent human rights to a broad audience by avoiding the representation of human rights victims?

Moreover, as a teachable human rights text, *The Official Story* offers students an opportunity to engage with cinematic aesthetic modes through a form that on examination reveals a surprising degree of aesthetic complexity. Essays by both Tomlinson and Low Taylor have highlighted the ways that the film constructs a series of narrative images that offer significant symbolic power. In addition, the use of sound, especially Maria Elena Walsh's song "En el país de no me acuerdo" ("In the Country of I Don't Remember"), offers further layers of cinematic form for viewers to analyze. But perhaps the most productive source of cinematic analysis from the view of human rights can be found in the scene when Alicia hears the story of Ana's abduction, rape, and torture.

The scene takes place as the two women reunite and attempt to catch up on their lives since Ana left the country. It begins with the women laughing and reminiscing, with Alicia reading old letters from Ana that she has kept all these years. The scene intercuts with images of Roberto reading in bed, and the editing follows standard realist practices, with alternating images of the women. The scene abruptly shifts, though, in the moment when Alicia asks Ana why she left so suddenly and Ana responds by confessing the details of her abduction. The screen is then filled with close-ups and extreme close-ups of the two women in an uninterrupted long take that lasts over three minutes.[3] The long take produces an unsettling feeling in the viewer as the scene becomes increasingly more intense—both in terms of the story that Ana is uttering aloud for the first time and in terms of the way the camera tightly frames their anguished faces. Next, as Alicia asks Ana whether she ever reported her abduction, the montage quickly separates the faces of the two women, who are still held in tight close-up but are now shown alone in frame.

I would argue that this scene is the aesthetic moment in the film when melodrama meets fictionalized testimonial, thereby underscoring the fact that the melodrama that dominates the film is only one in a series of potential narrative modes, just as the focus on Alicia is not meant to eclipse the victims' stories. Perhaps more important, though, the complex ways that the film navigates between conventional storytelling and more subtle narrative forms facilitate productive classroom conversations about how mainstream cinema can participate meaningfully in public accounting of national atrocities. Of interest is the question of whether human rights stories can be served by a form like narrative cinema. When I teach the film, I often ask students to imagine how the story, and their appreciation of it, might change if it were a documentary or a gritty, independent film. Given that students generally respond very favorably and strongly to this film, it is useful to ask them to consider what would have changed if it had been aimed at a different audience or if it had been less smooth in its appearance. What would have been lost? What might have been gained?

I, Rigoberta Menchú

Of the Latin American human-rights-related texts taught in courses in United States universities, *I, Rigoberta Menchú* is probably the most well known. When the text first entered the United States academic scene in the 1980s it immediately participated in two key intellectual debates: that of canon reform, specifically in Stanford University's decision to alter its great books course, and that of subaltern studies, the critical theory that called for reassessing the ways that Western imperialist epistemologies have shaped our understanding of history and identity.[4]

Not only did *I, Rigoberta Menchú* demand reconsideration of the forms of writing that had hitherto been valued in United States classrooms, but its urgent and compelling story of human rights violations against the indigenous communities of Guatemala also added to the immediate impact of the work. It is not an understatement to say that Menchú's story played a substantial role in calling attention to the abuses her community was suffering at the hands of the Guatemalan government. The work immediately reached a wide international audience that then applied pressure to the Guatemalan government, and it also led to Menchú's receipt of the Nobel Peace Prize in 1992. Thus teaching the text as an interventionist human rights narrative allows students to understand the direct and immediate ways that cultural forms can influence politics.

The scandal that followed in 1999 with the publication of David Stoll's *Rigoberta Menchú and the Story of All Poor Guatemalans*, in which he charged that Menchú had not been entirely factual in her depiction of the circumstances of her family, provides readers with an opportunity to consider a series of issues central to human rights stories. Should human rights texts be principally sources of fact and documentation, or are they more properly vehicles for raising consciousness and developing empathy? And what are the standards of truth that are used to judge these works? If the story of Menchú is true in a collective sense, if not a personal one, and if she clearly positions herself as the voice for an entire people, then should her narrative be judged according to Western notions of the individual subject?[5] And what are the ethical consequences of obsessing over the veracity of her personal story at the expense of attending to the very real material violence of which she speaks?

In addition to the question of the representational ethics of human rights stories, the aesthetic form of this text deserves special attention. The work was heralded as an example of the testimonial, or *testimonio*, a textual form that links the personal story of one to the collective tragedies of a large disenfranchised group. Much has been written about the aesthetics of *testimonio*, and space does not permit a thorough engagement with the way that this textual form engages and dissents from traditional representative structures, both literary and political (see Gugelberger). Navigating this bibliography may, in fact, seem daunting for faculty members less aware of these debates. But for the purposes of teaching human rights literature, Menchú's text offers an opportunity to ask students to seriously consider how specific literary forms participate in the construction of political subjects. *Testimonio*—as a textual form that refuses to code subjects on individualistic Western terms and instead understands the individual as always, already part of a community—radically destabilizes dominant attitudes about the structures through which individuals acquire rights. In contrast to the bildungsroman, which Joseph Slaughter has identified as the literary form that helped develop the fully formed personality required by Enlightenment rights ideals (*Human Rights* 52), the *testimonio* refuses to function as the literary accomplice to an individualistic rights framework. And this radical reconceptualization of the role that stories can play in human rights thought demands much of Western readers who often find that texts like *I, Rigoberta Menchú* require them to reassess how they understand social conflict and ethical obligations. Thus, unlike the reader's affective connection to Alicia in *The Official Story*, *testimonio* seeks recognition of, rather than identification with, the marginalized subject.[6] Readers are not asked to view the world from Menchú's perspective, to be in her shoes so to speak, but instead to respect and recognize the value of her culture and the legitimacy of her claims to rights. As Zygmunt Bauman explains, "recognition of cultural variety is the beginning, not the end, of the matter; it is but a starting point for a long and perhaps tortuous, but in the end beneficial, *political process*" (136).

The text develops this connection between the reader and the testimonial witness in two ways: first, as Doris Sommer has noted, Menchú underscores the fact that she will not reveal all her secrets, that she does not abdicate the right to privacy by seeking civil and political rights. And second, the book, instead of beginning with sensationalist accounts of atrocities, begins slowly, with great attention to particular details of Menchú's community and how it lives. This is done to underscore the difference between her life and that of the reader and to claim the right to dignity, equality, and political representation within a context of difference. The claim to rights, then, combines a necessary space between the lived experiences of the reader and those of Menchú with a conviction that those differences cannot translate into unequal access to rights. Students, however, tend to find the opening of the book to be difficult and slow. Some have told me that the slowness led them to quit reading the book entirely. Thus, I position the book on my syllabus after working on a case study about the differences between fictional and nonfictional human rights stories. Before beginning Menchú's *testimonio*, we have already explored the different relation readers tend to have to such stories, and we have discussed the advantages and disadvantages inherent in a storytelling form that denies the reader standard forms of narrative pleasure and association. After the case study, we work on the question of whether they as readers have an ethical obligation to pay attention to the stories of those whose rights have been violated. We often have strong debates about whether the text should have begun with atrocities or by describing the life and daily practice of Menchú's community. How might that early information be fundamental to establishing her and her community as human beings deserving of rights and respect? By introducing the text this way, I often find that most students feel that the slow start is an essential part of the aesthetic project. Either way, though, the students have come to understand that the structure of the text plays a crucial role in establishing the subjectivity and humanity of those it depicts.

One of the key moments in *I, Rigoberta Menchú* that reveals the complicated connections between the speaking subject and the subject of rights can be found at the beginning of chapter 17, "Autodefensa en la aldea" ("Self-Defence in the Village"), when Menchú describes the process through which she became aware of the social structures that made it possible for fellow Guatemalans to deny her community rights and dignity. What is of interest in this passage is the way that Menchú balances a repeated use of the first person with a series of questions and revelations:

> ¿Qué quería decir explotación para mí? . . . Hubo un tiempo en que los ladinos dudaban que nosotros éramos gente. Que éramos una clase de animal. Todo eso llegué a clarificarlo en mí misma. (*Me llamo Rigoberta Menchú* 148–49)

> What did exploitation mean to me? . . . Apparently there was a time when the *ladinos* used to think we weren't a people at all, but a sort of animal. All this became clear to me. (*I, Rigoberta Menchú* 122–23)

The balance between her use of the first-person plural ("nosotros" ["us"]) and her use of the first-person singular to identify her individual thoughts exposes the process through which she personally became more fully aware of the way that her community collectively suffered. Aesthetically it also reveals how Menchú as an individual is always mindful of her larger collective identity, since even in the moment when she is most conscious of her break with former patterns of thought her agency is always socially mediated. She becomes aware of the repression of her community and then vows to convince her community to fight for its rights. It is directly after this passage that the reader learns details of the ways that Menchú worked with her village to fight back. Using all means available, the village is able to fend off a series of attacks by creating booby traps, guarding access to their homes, and hiding in the mountains.

Beyond the text's immediate intervention in a human rights crisis, its questioning of the role of truth in human rights narratives, and its development of the subject of rights, one of the most productive ways that the text can be used in the classroom oriented toward human rights is through analysis of how its formal aesthetics are directly linked to the human rights crises that it depicts. The text facilitates in-depth discussion of the ways that social struggles have given rise to new forms of communication. John Beverley, one of the foremost scholars of *testimonio*, asks:

> What happens when, as in the case of Western Europe since the Renaissance, there has been complicity with the rise of "literature" as a secular institution and the development of colonial and imperialist aggression against which many of these struggles are directed? Are there experiences in the world today that would be betrayed or misrepresented by the forms of literature as we know it? ("Margin" 23)

Analysis of the human rights storytelling practices of *I, Rigoberta Menchú* allows us to begin to consider how to answer these questions.

Death and the Maiden

After Chileans voted to oust Augusto Pinochet in 1988 and to elect Patricio Aylwin in 1989, Dorfman wrote his first play and his first postexile work, *Death and the Maiden* (see McClennen, "Torture" and *Ariel Dorfman*). Dorfman's play emerges out of a very concrete, local event: the establishment of the Chilean truth commission known as the Rettig Commission, which would only investigate the crimes of the dictatorship that had ended in death or the presumption of death. The commission was immediately understood as a compromise between the right and the left, since even though it would publicly account for the disappearances that resulted in death, there would be no arrests.

Dorfman keyed into the absence of the voices of the torture victims in the commission's mandate and used this gap as a way to investigate the complicated ways that states attempt to publicly transition from dictatorship by staging a highly intimate play where the characters are forced to debate these issues on personal terms. Dorfman explains in the afterword of the play that he felt that his work allowed for a public airing of many of the questions that Chileans were asking privately. But the key information Dorfman reveals in his afterword is that once these events began to shape his story they needed to take form as a play: "[I]t did not take me long to conclude that, rather than a novel, what needed to be written was a play" (145). Plays are the most public form of literature, and they require collaboration and collective reception, making the genre well suited to address collective crises. Theater has long been used to stage social conflicts, and it played a significant role in creating a public space for dissent during the Pinochet years. Thus reading *Death and the Maiden* within the context of human rights culture allows for an analysis of both the role that truth commissions play in performing a public accounting of the past and the way that theater serves as a public, communal form of art. It is useful, then, to preface this text on a syllabus with a section on truth commissions, especially the Chilean Rettig Commission. I usually spend one day on that background followed by another on the use of theater and other forms of public performance as forms of political intervention, especially in Latin America.

Death and the Maiden is arguably the most internationally significant play in Latin American history. Maya Jaggi writes that for "Carlos Fuentes, who deemed *Death and the Maiden* Sophoclean in its power and simplicity, no other play in Latin America has achieved its universal resonance." And yet, it was not considered a success when it premiered in Chile (Dorfman, *Muerte* 98).[7] Perhaps the lack of local success for the play was a consequence of its relative directness and local specificity within a postdictatorial cultural environment that was still largely accustomed to self-censorship and metaphorical forms of social critique. In fact, as Dawes explains in relation to human rights storytelling, it is often ironically the case that internationally successful texts that represent human rights violations are intolerable to the local audiences that they purportedly represent (*That the World* 182). Dorfman's experience as an exiled writer arguably complicated public reception of the play as well. Not only was his style more critically direct than that of other playwrights like Marco Antonio de la Parra, who had not left Chile during the dictatorship, but Dorfman's status as a postexile writer further distanced him from the public he hoped to address.

At the heart of the text are the questions of how one can ever know the truth of atrocity and what types of reparations are possible in communities that have suffered extreme forms of authoritarianism. In this way the play engages some of the issues in *The Official Story*, but where the film gently traces the coming to consciousness of Alicia, Dorfman's play creates a raw, intense space that marks everyone—the audience included—as responsible for the perpetuation of social violence, since widespread acts of torture and repression require varying degrees of participation and complicity. Given the way it implicates the audience, the text allows for productive debate about the ethical obligations of audience members who might not have any direct connection to the human rights violations depicted. The play means to disquiet the audience, but such a strategy is risky. When I teach this text I use it as an opportunity to debate the strengths and weaknesses of taking such a provocative position.

The play centers on three characters: Paulina, the torture survivor who has never told her story; Gerardo, her husband, who has just been named to a commission like the Rettig; and Roberto, a doctor, who may or may not be the man who tortured Paulina. When Gerardo gets a flat tire, Roberto gives him a lift to his home only to later return to the house after hearing that Gerardo has been named to the newly formed truth commission. Paulina immediately senses that Roberto is one of her former torturers; she ties him up and hatches a plan for a forced confession. Since she was blindfolded while detained, though, her evidence seems weak. Is she right about Roberto, or is she crazy? And what of Gerardo's commitment to the reconciliation process? Does he owe loyalty to his wife or to the commission's principles? Is Roberto guilty? And, if so, what should be his punishment?

Driven more by questions than by answers, the dialogue of the play emphasizes that it is precisely the exchange of words that both hinders and makes possible any form of reconciliation for atrocity. Moreover, torture and language are inextricably linked, since the body suffers pain to provoke speech. Can Roberto's forced confession be linked to the force Paulina endured at the hands of her torturers? And, if so, what are the hopes that words can help heal the nation? Is the truth of violence always, already violent? The play weaves these layered concerns for the possibilities for postdictatorial communication and recovery through an elaborate series of tensions over not only who has the right to speak and be heard in such an environment but also who has the right to pass judgment on what constitutes the truth when society has been structured by lies. Dorfman frames the linguistic question at the center of *Death and the Maiden* this way: "how do you reach the truth if lying has become a habit?" (146).

One of the key ways that Dorfman calls attention to these issues is through the use of repetition. Characters repeat phrases: Roberto has a habit of saying "la verdad la verdad" ("the real real truth") and "pocón" ("teensy weensy"). Characters also repeat the words just spoken by another:

GERARDO. Estás enferma.
PAULINA. No estoy enferma.
GERARDO. Estás enferma.
PAULINA. Entonces estoy enferma. (*Muerta* 39)

GERARDO. You're sick.
PAULINA. I'm not sick.
GERARDO. You're sick.
PAULINA. All right then, I'm sick. (*Death* 107)

And the last lines of the play repeat the opening, when Gerardo speaks first to Roberto and later to the audience about Paulina's ability to mix a strong drink. He says she "hace un piscosour que es de miedo" 'makes a margarita that will make your hair stand on end' (16, 83; 89, 143).

What is most important about this repetition is the use of the words "de miedo," translated into English as "make your hair stand on end," words that doubly signify because they can refer to a strong drink but also to torture. This layering and doubling of language asks the audience to sort out how repeated words signify differently according to the subject's position and interlocutor. What Dorfman hopes to suggest is that it is the words as well as the context of their utterance that enables us to approximate the truth. From the perspective of human rights literature, the play underscores the fact that the truths of human rights culture are often not the truths of truth commissions, even if they can be compatible. Moreover, its form as a theatrical work facilitates engagement with the ways that collective accounting for human rights violations requires dialogue that is both public and private.

Each of these texts allows for rich, sustained debate of the ways that cultural forms represent and reflect human rights issues, and the above analysis has only scratched the surface of their interpretive possibilities. Placing this array of texts together on a syllabus offers students the opportunity to reflect not only on differences of genre but also on the varied ways that different aesthetic practices produce different human-rights-related responses in the reader. What happens when a human rights text is easy to consume as in the case of *The Official Story*? when it refuses easy identification with the subjects of the story as in *I, Rigoberta Menchú*? when it implicates the audience as a tacit accomplice to human rights violations as in *Death and the Maiden*? After teaching these texts and their contexts, I spend one week in class on their comparison, asking students to compare the risk and rewards with their storytelling forms. We then discuss further comparative connections. It is worth noting, for instance, that each of these texts has a woman at the center of the story, allowing for an examination of the ways that gender issues can both displace and advance attention to the politics of rights. In addition to analysis of their comparative connections, their specific contexts of production, and the ways that they engaged in the human rights debates of their times, each of these texts also demands that readers consider the purpose of human rights stories. Should they raise awareness, develop empathy, incite intervention, restore memory, debate issues, offer alternative representations of claims contexts, or give a voice to the victims? And, given the monetary success and public recognition of these texts, what ethical dilemmas surround personal gain achieved through the suffering of others or even of oneself? What exactly is the function of the human rights story? And what differentiates human rights stories from stories writ large? Is the art of a human rights story compromised or eclipsed by the urgency of that which it depicts? Or is there an art to human rights art that is absent from other representational practices? What is the balance between testimonial exigency and enduring artistic communication? And are there representational obligations to the human rights story that are not shared by other forms of art? In the absence of any ready answers to these questions, the challenge that faces those of us who teach these texts lies in encouraging students to recognize that a permanent state of questioning should not lead to a paralyzing sense of political possibility.

Notes

Special thanks to John D. Riofrio for comments on an earlier version of this essay.

1. This topic is the subject of the special issue of *Comparative Literature Studies* that I edited with Joseph Slaughter, *Human Rights and Literary Form*. See esp. our introduction to the issue.

2. Tomlinson notes that in the specific moment of its release—almost immediately postdictatorship—the film was arguably far more ambitious in terms of plot than some of its later critics have recognized, especially with regard to the illegal adoptions of the children of the disappeared (226).

3. I am indebted to a former student, Jorge Trinchet, for first calling my attention to this long take.

4. For more details on the ways that this text participated in these debates see Pratt; Beverley, "What Happens."

5. These issues are taken up in great detail in Arturo Arias's edited volume *The Rigoberta Menchú Controversy*.

6. See McClennen, "Humanities," for more on the connection between recognition and human rights.

7. Dorfman states that the play had a mixed reception in Chile. It was successful in free showings but received very negative reviews and did not appeal to the Chilean theatergoing elite (*Muerte* 97). Idelber Avelar, who critiques the film version, writes that the play "was a resounding failure among the public that it had attempted, secretly and in bad faith, to translate and express, the Chilean population" (45). In contrast, Robert A. Morace provides a more subtle critique, recognizing that the play meant to "provoke, not please" and that where it failed was with the elites (136), not with what Avelar calls the "Chilean population."

Eve Wiederhold

Revisiting *The Visitor*: Rhetoric, Ethics, and Feminist Models of Interpretation

Friend or foe? And how to tell the difference? Such questions convey a way of seeing that would characterize encounters with unknown people as strange and potentially dangerous. In the context of human rights discourses, the impulse to see strangeness first implies a problem in need of a solution. That solution might include a declaration about the importance of human rights. Presumably, human rights exist. Recourse to those rights would seem to provide the method for resolving any quandary about how to regard the stranger, who, at the very least, should be afforded certain civil liberties, including the right to be heard before being dismissed.

But the promise to render everyone equal is built on a potentially disturbing premise: that the strange be converted into the familiar to enable recognition of another's worth. Indeed, liberal human rights discourses too often assume that the language of rights will translate transculturally and transhistorically, as if words simply convey what they mean and as if the relation of language use and social practices is knowable and controllable. Such a premise addresses neither who acts to convert whom to what kind of subject nor precisely how any act of transformation occurs. The idea that ethical interpretive methods are encoded within rights discourses implies that representations are neutral conduits, when they might instead be described as enculturated vehicles that shape how we both find and create meanings.

Teachers can promote critical scrutiny of the relation of language and political judgment by asking students to analyze Thomas McCarthy's 2008 film *The Visitor*, which tells the story about the twin experiences of friendship and alienation in the aftermath of September 11, 2001, a time when people in the United States were expected to fear the outsider. The title and plot raise the question of rights as a product of hospitality or as a priori to categories such as citizen or illegal immigrant. Using the film as a case study, I propose that teachers engage students in explorations of the language of human rights by deploying a rhetorical approach that incorporates elements of feminist materialism.

This approach engages a double analytic that allows for both the specific examination of the film text as well as metareflections about the ethics of conventional interpretive processes, particularly those associated with democratic inquiry. Because rhetoricians explore the discursive and visual networks through which meaning is made and assigned significance, a turn to rhetoric can contribute to reshaping conventional conceptions of how we evaluate and judge public representations of what constitutes a rights violation. A feminist-materialist rhetorical approach emphasizes that the interpretive act of converting the strange to the familiar is neither neutral nor generalizable. Interpretations emerge within situated, material contexts and are undertaken by people who have bodies, desires, and lived histories that will affect what they see and how they assign value to their observations. A feminist rhetorical analytic can give students a conceptual framework to use when contemplating how ideologies influence interpretive practices and why such contemplation matters to conceptions of how rights violations are identified and how, then, they might be adjudicated.

Ethos and Identity

The Visitor's main character, Walter Vale, is a sixty-two-year-old white professor and widower who seems to be living a bland life until he encounters a young couple inhabiting his apartment, a second home, in New York City. Walter spends most of his time in Connecticut, where he teaches. The couple, Tarek (from Syria) and Zainab (from Senegal), are in the United States illegally. Walter's helping hand allows them to stay in the United States and, in the process, form friendship and community. Walter and Tarek become drumming buddies and spend afternoons playing their instruments in the park until an unfortunate mix-up in the subway leads to Tarek's arrest and deportation. At the movie's end, Walter is alone but continues to play the drums in public and private settings. While it is possible to read this behavior as an indicator of his journey toward redemption, the meaning and significance of the film's final scenes are open to other interpretations.

Questions about visitation and identity arise when the film opens—the audience sees Walter from behind, peering out a window in a nicely appointed house, apparently waiting for someone to arrive. We do not know the circumstances of this visit or if Walter is excited or apprehensive about the meeting, but the visitor turns out to be benign enough—a seasoned piano teacher, Barbara Watson, who will be giving middle-aged Walter introductory lessons. That he has decided to take lessons at this point in his life says something about his character, although it is not clear why he has made this choice. He rejects Barbara's instruction and displays discomfort when adopting the role of a student.

Such a conclusion arises from our reading of the scene's characters—or, to use a key rhetorical term, their ethos. *Ethos* may be a familiar word to those students who have taken communication courses devoted to public speaking. The term, from Aristotle's *Rhetoric*, is one of three *pisteis*, or means of securing persuasion (the two others are *logos*, appeals to logic, and *pathos*, appeals to emotion). It describes the ways in which a speaker's character affects his or her ability to persuade audiences and is concerned with how audiences assign identities and then judgments to someone who is unknown. Ethos delineates methods for conferring authority and credibility. It is central to judgments about who should be heard.

Everyone deserves to be heard, yet only some voices carry, and those that do seem to convey an intrinsic power. This premise bespeaks a positivistic view of authority. Ostensibly, judgments of a speaker's character seem to emanate from a straightforward reading of a personal power that is communicable to audiences who have the ability to discern its presence or absence. Either a person is authoritative or is not. Either they possess charisma or do not. This, in turn, implies that audiences will inevitably share responses after noticing desirable qualities inhabiting the person being evaluated. Such conceptions of ethos effectively echo liberal discourses about human rights that posit rights as existent, eternal, and observable (although the right to claim rights is ostensibly inherent in each person).

Both perspectives presume that judgments of what exists follow a discernible order that can also be identified and referenced to explain how persuasion works. But this premise overlooks a crucial rhetorical element: audiences decide whether to listen to and identify with the one who speaks. This element of choice shifts considerations of where to locate language's authorizing power. It is not revealed but bestowed by audiences amenable to being persuaded in a given case. Further, assignations of credibility are not inevitable but influenced by what audiences believe has value.

Teachers can ask students to apply these precepts to readings of Walter and Barbara. Various enculturated narratives, including those that inform how to identify teachers and students, will have affected students' responses to the film's first scene. For example, what do students make of an older man having to take basic direction? Is his discomfort understandable? Does it matter that his teacher is an older white woman? What makes a teacher authoritative? What makes someone a good student? How might responses to these questions affect ways of determining whether Walter is a sympathetic character? How might readings of his character affect whether viewers are invested in his story?

Discussions about ethos can be expanded to address an important feature of a materialist rhetoric: the role that language plays in shaping conceptions of what we see. Indeed, judgments of a speaker's character will include judgments about the speaker's language choices as audiences draw inferences about the relation of the words a speaker uses and estimations of the person existing behind the words. As we listen, we form judgments about whether the speaker seems glib, evasive, honorable, deceptive, and so on, and then we factor those responses into our estimations of whether this person is trustworthy or even worthy of attention. Ethos, then, addresses the ways in which our judgments about a speaker's character are based on our evaluations of what the speaker says, underscoring how language use functions as a representation of character (see Schüssler Fiorenza 15).

There is a subtlety here that students will often miss: we tend to accord a positive view of someone's ethos when we approve of his or her linguistic behavior, as if language offers an outward manifestation of an inward state of being. Indeed, ethos describes that process where estimations of character get connected to what cannot be seen: our sense of the speaker's intentions. Contemporary rhetoricians such as Gerald Hauser formalize this point and explain how authority and an ascription of a "good ethos" gets conferred on speakers who exhibit what are called "practical virtues": *phronesis*, good sense or practical wisdom; *arête*, good moral character; and *eunoia*, good will toward the audience. Indeed, we see virtue in speakers whose language uses exhibit qualities we have been taught to hold in high esteem such as courage, temperance, generosity, magnanimity, magnificence (156). We tend to be open to the possibility of friendship and community when we approve of a speaker's mode of self-representation.

But several interpretive questions arise that can help teachers prompt students to rethink assumptions about who should earn respect and admiration (if not identification). Precisely how do abstract qualities of value get attached to specific language practices? Which language practices seem to exhibit something as amorphous as goodwill? And how might a regard for any particular way of speaking tell us less about what constitutes a practical virtue and more about the ways in which seeing virtue's signs has been culturally influenced? These questions can be posed by analyzing the dialogue that ends the film's first scene, after Walter finishes his lesson and walks Barbara to the door:

BARBARA. Next Tuesday at the same time?
WALTER. No. I don't think I'm going to continue our lessons.
BARBARA. Oh, no. Are you giving up?
WALTER. No.
Pause.
BARBARA. Oh. Okay. Well, good-bye.

Conventionally, we do not expect people to rebuff each other with such candor. Even if Walter planned to reject Barbara's tutelage, we might expect (prefer?) that he replace the blunt dismissal with a statement of ambiguity (e.g., "I'll need to check my schedule" or "I'll call you"). That Walter does not follow this protocol can prompt discussion about who he seems to be—an older man who is insensitive, honest, impatient, rude, admirable, cranky, and so on.

Barbara responds to Walter's statements with a candor of her own. As he begins to close the door, Barbara interrupts and says, "Mr. Vale? If I may ask, how many teachers have you had before me?"

WALTER. Four.
BARBARA. Well, for what it's worth, learning an instrument at your age is difficult. Especially if you don't possess a natural gift for it. I'm not saying this to be mean. But if you do decide to give up, I'd really like to buy your piano.
Walter registers a small expression of surprise.
WALTER. Okay.

Again, not the typical statement one might expect from a teacher, who convention would suggest should encourage all to strive to learn. Students can be asked to consider Barbara's motivations for her question and how they read Walter's response (i.e., even though she denies as much, is she trying to be mean?). They might also be asked to come up with a word to describe the kind of dialogue that has occurred and then to notice how their term (*honest*, *no-nonsense*, *cruel*, etc.) does not neutrally convey information but suggests an attitude about perceptions of the scene. When we name, we situate a given scene or person within a narrative context that then influences our interpretations of what has happened. We tell stories about what we see and then tend to forget that descriptions of our visions are not simply re-presented but involve our making choices about how to use the cultural terms made available to us. Those terms communicate ways of seeing that are inflected with beliefs, values, and assumptions about what should be. In this case, we might wonder about what Walter's response should be to the request for the piano. And what should be our own—what conclusions about ethos or character seem appropriate after this brusque encounter between people who never met before?

Ethos and Ethics

The idea that ethos demarcates an interpretive transaction may be complicated enough for students to grasp, and teachers may want to devote class time to analyzing how the act of assigning cultural categories to name people and situations can shape perceptions of what is at issue. But more can be said to facilitate explorations of the relation of discourse and judgments of character by bringing attention to the interplay between cultural ideologies and estimations of ethos.

If, as James Berlin points out, our experience of the world (including the experience of interpretation and judgment) is always mediated by the signifiers made available to name those experiences (78), then it becomes important to consider which terminology is available to describe the results of our acts of scrutiny. One reads character not by seeing what is but by mediating one's individual response with classificatory norms that precede and then influence one's judgment of character. Hence, when we ascribe named qualities to a person and assign a reading of an ethos, we have entered an interpretive domain that gives expression to the ways in which identity is not intrinsic but culturally positioned within an existing social structure.

Acknowledging our inevitable dependency on language alters the framework for thinking about how to account for ethical behavior. Rather than read ethics in terms of ascertaining innate character, ethos describes a way of seeing in relation to something else. Ethos is etymologically linked to the term *ethics*, and, in Elisabeth Schüssler Fiorenza's use of the term, it describes a disciplinary space that "expresses the way one lives. 'Ethos' in this spatial sense theorizes the 'positionality' inherent in rhetoric" (16)—a positioning that incorporates questions about how one is positioned by (or subjected to) the cultural terms that preexist our interpretive acts and then how one responds to those impositions. Schüssler Fiorenza continues, "Ethics can thus be understood not simply to encompass the formation and judgment of character, but also to include the production of a place that character can inhabit" (16). Hence, ethics would concern itself less with locating absolute rights and moral identities and more with considering which actions normative classifications make possible, in what contexts, and to what effects.

This emphasis on cultural positioning recalls "the ancient Greek sense of ethos as 'habit,' that is, as a pattern of social practice inseparable from social relations" (Con Davis and Gross 65). Habits influence the ways in which we assess where a character belongs and whether we think he or she belongs to a group that we have joined. We assess character not by knowing who a person is but by locating his or her ways of speaking within social contexts that we believe to exist and be recognizable. As Robert Con Davis and David Gross put it, "ethos [describes] a positioning within culture and always in relation to power" (66).

If we think of the ways in which discursive habits craft spaces of interpretation, the questions about what is just may be asked differently: not "is a speaker virtuous?" but "what rhetorical positions are made available to speakers to exhibit signs of virtue?" What kind of positioning enables a speaker to appear authoritative (or not)? How might representations act oppressively by establishing expectations of what should be—expectations about how speakers should behave linguistically to be perceived as a friend, or at least, nonthreatening? Must a speaker follow the norm—appear to be normal—to obtain a positive reading of character? A question of ethics is raised when we consider whether our willingness to identify emerges because the speaker (or text) affirms our habituated perspectives. If we identify because our normative sense has been affirmed, have we fulfilled our responsibilities as interlocutors? What is our interpretive ethos in such situations?

Two scenes from *The Visitor* can help students explore the complexities of this alternative rhetorical framework. The first involves the initial encounter between Walter and the couple occupying his apartment. Having been forced to attend an academic conference in New York, Walter arrives at his second abode, and it is clear that he has not been there for a while. On entering his home, he sees fresh flowers and lights turned on. As he walks down a dark hallway, he hears vague noises and sees a light shining through the bottom of a closed door. The scene feels somewhat threatening, but after pausing, Walter walks to the door, opens it, and finds a beautiful female stranger relaxing in a bubble bath. They share responses: both are startled. Zainab screams. Walter quickly closes the door and, in the hallway, rapidly apologizes and tells Zainab, "It's okay, I won't hurt you," while she demands to know who he is and what he's doing there.

Zainab speaks English, and so does Tarek, as we learn immediately after this exchange when, as Walter apologizes, he is grabbed from behind by Tarek, who yells, "What the fuck!," slams Walter into the wall, and shouts, "Did you touch her?" Since most United States citizens would likely identify with the homeowner who would feel violated on discovering strangers in his home, it is worth thinking about how the film crafts a space that allows for a sympathetic response to Tarek and Zainab. That they speak English (and French to each other—also significant when assigning identities) is important to dispelling at least one sense of strangeness for viewers in the United States (and for Walter) who consider English their primary language. An instant familiarity is established, and there is no need to engage in basic acts of translation when attempting to sort through the confusion of this encounter.

Further, while Tarek's aggressive response is literally threatening, the scene has familiar elements to it, enabling viewers to reference recognizable domesticity and gender narratives. The image of the woman taking a bath is certainly recognizable—a whole series of assumptions about that act will inform how Zainab's cultural location gets read. Tarek's response is also familiar, and, within the patriarchal codes that this culture continues to value, it would be possible to argue that in speaking his outrage, he behaves as he should. Walter and Tarek exchange mutual confusion, each asking, "Who are you?" and "What are you doing here?" Walter's keys are taken as evidence that he has some proprietary claim on the apartment space, and when Zainab tells Tarek (in French) that Walter probably called the police, the dynamics of power shift. Their fear of a police presence is clear, and they apologize for the confusion, declaring that they will leave immediately. They had been renting the apartment from someone named Ivan, and once this information is presented, the discourses of capitalism are invoked to sort through who can make what kinds of claims. That Tarek and Zainab are paying rent means that they are not squatters, a clarification that legitimizes one aspect of their outrage. But all three know that Walter's claims of ownership trump everything, putting Walter in the position to be benevolent and extend an invitation to them to stay, which he does.

This scene could have been played in any number of ways, but it provides a useful illustration of the point that one's ethos is evaluated in terms of cultural locations. Indeed, viewers may find their assessments of Walter changing after observing his responses to his visitors. He is inclined to kindness and generosity of spirit that is then rewarded as the movie progresses and his friendship with Tarek grows. It would be interesting to consider what alternative responses could have been engendered had the circumstances changed—had Zainab not been naked, vulnerable, eroticized in familiar ways, had neither she nor Tarek displayed rhetorical competence or offered reassurances of their "normalcy."

Here, then, is a place to apply rhetoric's doubled analytic. On the one hand, the scene of this initial encounter offers a wonderful representation of mutual fear overcome by a willingness to place trust in one another. The scene delivers a potentially clichéd but nonetheless poignant message about the ways in which we are all connected—we all love, fear, get hungry, seek shelter, are dependent on others. On the other hand, there is a danger of imposing normative frames onto readings of the people characterized in this scene. Must the one in the subordinate position prove—linguistically and otherwise—membership by exhibiting recognizable discursive habits? And without that proof, would citizens be in their rights to be wary?[1]

The second scene involves the moment and aftermath of Tarek's arrest. Following an afternoon of drumming, Walter and Tarek are late for a meeting with Zainab and hurry to the subway, awkwardly toting the drums, which do not maneuver through the turnstiles. Walter has no subway pass and Tarek offers his, swiping his card and allowing Walter to enter the turnstile first. After doing so, they trade the drums, Tarek swipes his card again, and, as he pushes through, the turnstile gets stuck, locking Tarek in its middle. He laughs and then jumps over the turnstile to gain entry. But he is quickly arrested by two NYPD officers who do not believe that he paid a fare and subsequently discover that he has no proper identification. While they grill Tarek about his identity, Walter tries to intervene by quietly saying, "C'mon, he paid," and then remarking that handcuffing Tarek is "unnecessary." The officer tells Walter to step back or risk arrest and advises him that he can make a statement at the station. At the end of the scene, Walter asks, "Where are you taking him?" and the officer replies, "Tenth precinct."

Back at the apartment, Walter breaks the news of Tarek's arrest to Zainab, and as she begins to panic, he calmly says, "It was just a misunderstanding. They said he would be released later tonight."

ZAINAB. How could this happen? He knows better! He would not do anything wrong!

WALTER. No, he didn't. He didn't. I'm sure it will be okay.

ZAINAB. No. It won't be okay.

WALTER. No, I went down to the precinct and made a statement.

ZAINAB. That doesn't matter! We are illegal! We are not citizens, and when they find out they're going to—

She interrupts herself, leaves for her room, and slams the door.

Here, teachers might point out how Walter assumes that discourses of reason will be able to sort through and clear up the confusion. Walter makes assumptions about where one may speak authoritatively "from a particular place in a social structure" (Jarratt and Reynolds 47–49). Walter has lived in a social space in which "the reasonable exchange of ideas" informs how cultural location is imagined. He relies on the discourses of liberal humanism that promise that reason, and the reasonable utterance, can be invoked to sort through misunderstandings. Walter fails to see that, as a member of the dominant class, he has choices that Tarek does not. In town to attend a conference that would advance knowledge, Walter is able to reject that life and happily embrace Tarek's tutelage and way of living. The film nicely dramatizes different social spaces—inside the conference hall, quiet, closed, constrained, where people speak in restrained narrative codes as members of an academic community versus the lively and free gathering in the park that ostensibly anyone may join. With Tarek's introduction, Walter is welcomed and seems to blossom in his new environment.

But Walter makes the mistake of thinking that because he can shift social spaces, everyone else can too. He reads his social-rhetorical position neutrally, as if social space (and by extension discursive space) exists equitably and universally. Just as he entered Tarek's musical world, so he believes Tarek will be able to negotiate the domains that value discourses of the law and reason. That this negotiation is not available to Tarek creates a different context for regarding Walter's faith in the reasonable rule of law. His assurances to Zainab, his belief that Tarek will be quickly released, and even his consultation with an immigration lawyer (that he kindly pays for) are at best naive. The question the film poses is, Should that ignorance be characterized differently? While Walter thrived under Tarek's instruction, he was unaware and apparently not that interested in learning about the precariousness of Tarek and Zainab's status. It is only after Tarek is arrested that he comes to learn that Zainab—as well as Tarek's mother—cannot visit him in detention because they too will be arrested immediately and automatically.

How such considerations affect readings of Walter's ethos is worth exploring, especially since film critics have described Walter as an everyman character. Should Walter have known about the risks facing Tarek and Zainab as they went about their daily lives? Should he be excused for not pursuing such inquiry? Has Walter's ignorance about the dangers facing people identified as "illegal" indicated a questionable self-absorption that is tantamount to an ethical lapse (despite his financial generosity)? Indeed, might one argue that his ignorance is partially responsible for what happened to Tarek? How do responses to these questions implicate the rest of the citizenry? Is it our (United States citizens') obligation to know and understand how social positionings have material consequences that disempower those identified as noncitizens?

By posing such questions, teachers can simultaneously ask students to consider how doing so shifts the context for interpreting rights discourses that would define ethical practices in terms of looking for evidence of abuses. Rather than seek clarity by delineating differences between rights and wrongs, discussions about interpretive ambiguities establish a different ethos of inquiry that calls for a perpetual exploration and evaluation of the ways in which personal interpretive habits encounter patterns of social practices promulgated by social institutions. This context of inquiry obliges a continual questioning of what constitutes an ethical practice instead of making the assumption that one must know what that is in advance. It encourages students to reconsider the consequences of the binary logic underwriting not only liberal discourses of human rights but also conventional conceptions of what it means to judge at all. And through such questioning, students can be asked to consider the possibility of devising different models of ethics that would engage interpretive practices that do not automatically reproduce those that are culturally sanctioned.

Institutions and Interpretive Obligations

By the end of the film, Tarek has been made to disappear. With no explanation, no warning, and no hearing, he is moved among detention centers and then deported. Or at least that is all that Walter is told. What should have happened to Tarek? What does he deserve and why?

Were we to rely on the positivistic logic informing liberal rights discourses, we might come to two contradictory conclusions. First, deporting Tarek was the wrong thing to do. He was a nice guy not looking for trouble. He desired to work and enjoy life just like any decent citizen. Second, whether or not Tarek is nice doesn't matter to the law, which he broke. Categorically, he is an illegal immigrant. (His mother failed to follow court-directed procedures.) It is within a nation's rights to protect its borders. Citizens have the right to be protected from invaders. Property owners have the right to have their property protected.

Being stuck in this irresolvable contradiction (one that drives contemporary public discussions of immigration policies) indicates how the invocation of natural rights will not necessarily resolve interpretive complexities. Indeed, liberal discourses that claim that rights exist and are self-evident can be inadequate to the act of judging ambiguity. Even language use is ambiguous. What kind of language should be used to communicate responses to Tarek's situation? Could any language communicate why a person might want to give him asylum after witnessing the harmonious beauty he helped create when sitting in the park playing his drums? Or how one might want to prevent any person from having to experience the dawning dread that emerges after his arrest, as it gradually becomes clear that Tarek's situation is hopeless, that the legal institution will have no interest in the particularities of his situation, that he and Zainab will probably never see each other again? Would those languages, if available, be authoritative and persuasive in a court of law?

In a feminist-materialist rhetorical framework, ethics is not described as a possession. Rhetorical analyses of power instead consider what kinds of spaces are produced for habitation. And in describing ethos as a process in which identities get assigned in relation to cultural contexts (that include language practices), ethos may be applied not only to people but also to institutions. How might we read the character—the ethical habits in relation to social contexts—of institutions that sanction the kinds of legal practices illustrated in *The Visitor*? How might we read the practice of making someone disappear in a context in which a sense of nationalism is presumed to be a virtue?

A feminist-materialist rhetorical ethics does not seek to resolve ethical quandaries by referencing knowledge of what is always true and right. Rather, it emphasizes that if we do not question how rights are rhetorically situated, we reproduce sites of power and potential injustices. We create the possibility of a social space in which those identified as illegal can be subjected to practices that carry legal authority even if the authorized response violates a sense of what seems right. Teachers can offer students a rhetorical rearticulation of what constitutes interpretation and inquiry by denaturalizing conventional discursive practices—by making them strange and allowing students both to see and to experience the idea that referencing the normative and familiar is not necessarily ethical.

When one is not authorized to speak, one effectively disappears, revealing a disparity between the promise of natural rights and contemporary practices. A feminist-materialist rhetorical ethics is important pedagogically because it offers an analytical framework for both identifying differences between language and social practices and contemplating their material consequences. Any text that depicts interpretive dilemmas can benefit from the kind of analysis undertaken here. Prompting students to rethink how they maneuver from perceptions of strangeness to identification can offer them alternative ways of seeing and talking about who belongs and who, by extension, does not.

Notes

This chapter is dedicated to the memory of Stephen B. Stallcup.

1. It is interesting to note that, unlike Tarek, Zainab never seems to trust Walter.

Part III

Bearing Wrongs, Reading Rights, Engendering Responsibility

Introduction to Part 3

Whereas many courses feature human rights content as a theme within traditional disciplinary categories such as nation, language, or literary period, others approach the material through genre, specific violations, or what we term the "human rights cycle": the discursive positions that emerge through human rights claims, whether through witnessing one's own or another's violation; resistance to atrocity; testimony; redress; and expressions of mourning, healing, or reconciliation. This section speaks to and about courses organized in relation to the human rights cycle, through a primary focus on the material grounds of egregious suffering—the violated body—and the discursive responses it engenders. The six essays here examine different positions within this cycle, from torture to witnessing to postconflict searches for justice and responsibility.

In her recent book *Fictions of Dignity*, Elizabeth Anker argues for a phenomenological approach to reading the embodied aspects of suffering human rights abuses as an antidote to the abstractions of liberalism that constitute the fundament of human rights. Postcolonial and feminist critiques of human rights also work assiduously to draw attention to the unequal abuses perpetrated on different kinds of bodies as well as the unequal claims afforded them. Uma Narayan, for example, offers a particularly compelling analysis of the different levels of both local and transnational response to domestic violence murders in the United States as compared with dowry murders in India (83–117). In concert with these kinds of theoretical approaches, the essays that follow in this section pay particular attention to the need to develop rich contexts for reading abuses on the body, "with the clear proviso," as Neville Hoad notes in his contribution, "that neither the novel nor the background reading are reducible to each other." Cultivating that "dialectical relation" can help students interrogate the gap between the relatively safe space of the classroom and the vulnerable world of the texts as they begin to craft their ethics as reader-witnesses.

We begin this section with Heather Hewett's analysis of how reading for intersectionality and reading for the body can illuminate violations of economic, social, and cultural rights (so-called second-generation rights) that often get little political or literary attention as opposed to civil and political (first-generation) rights. Hewett turns to Tsitsi Dangarembga's novel *Nervous Conditions* to demonstrate how the two-pronged reading strategy makes visible the thematic and structural connections among the novel's depiction of Rhodesian racism, British and Shona patriarchy, subsistence farming, colonial education, and bodily health.

The next four essays further emphasize the pedagogical challenges of balancing literary analysis with historical or sociopolitical context. Looking at United Nations documents, popular media, film, testimonial, and fiction, Jennifer Browdy de Hernandez provides several strategies for teaching the complex topic of female genital cutting or mutilation (FGM). While acknowledging the criticism leveled at international activists who seek to end the practice in various local communities (criticism of the ways in which human rights can become an alibi for both foreign intervention and the spectacularization of other women's bodies), she insists that literary and cultural studies can nonetheless generate an empathic solidarity that may form the seeds for transnational, transcultural collective action against FGM.

Hoad takes a more skeptical approach toward cultivating activism or future activists, focusing instead on teaching students to pair close textual readings with the construction of an archive of knowledge to enrich their understanding of the text at hand as well as their positions as readers. He layers his reading of a deceptively simple passage in Jude Dibia's novel *Walking with Shadows* with a comparison of antisodomy and other laws denying the rights of homosexuals in the United States and Nigeria to examine how human rights violations on the basis of sexual orientation are perpetuated and often egregiously and varyingly unacknowledged around the world.

Also stressing the need for close reading and providing a sample assignment that demonstrates the broad pedagogical implications of this task, Karen Bishop turns to literary and visual depictions of torture. As scholars and survivors have shown, torture as a category of violations pushes against the limits of representation, such that close attention to its narrativization, to the discursive form it takes, models an approach to understanding one's relation to the suffering of another. That approach begins by acknowledging its necessary incompleteness, the impossible project of knowing fully, yet it insists on the need "to begin to sound out the prolonged suffering that torture engenders."

For Brenda Carr Vellino, witness poetry and the poetry of transitional justice offers a particularly powerful "embodied form" for addressing the postconflict societies we all share as well as specific human rights violations. Drawing on Carolyn Forché's extraordinary analysis of the evidentiary quality of poetic language of atrocity (see, e.g., "Reading") as well as Roger Simon's theory of "remembrance/pedagogy," Vellino examines how the condensed and multisensory dimensions of poetry written in the aftermath of atrocity can create an "alternative memory archive" from which translocal conceptions of citizenship may emerge, particularly when the poetry is put in dialogue with other forms of remembrance.

The final essay in this section, by Susan Spearey, takes up the profound questions of witnessing and responsibility raised by Bishop and Vellino. Looking specifically at postconflict texts, Spearey theorizes a form of ethical engagement between instructor and students, among students, and between students and the texts they study in class. This method is modeled on Kelly Oliver's definition of "response-ability": the ethical relationship to another, enacted through witnessing, that not so much defines the other as determines the self.

From the "ears on the floor . . . pressed to the ground" in Forché's poem "The Colonel," set in El Salvador, to the tortured woman in Jessica Hagedorn's novel of the Philippines, *Dogeaters*, to the perhaps "softer" violations of dispossession and entrenched discrimination in colonial Rhodesia, the United States, or Nigeria, the texts discussed in this section represent a spectrum of corporeal (and psychological) suffering. The essays offer theoretical frameworks, textual pairings, discussion questions, and writing assignments that ask students to look, listen, feel, and think—not to approximate the suffering of an other nor to pity him or her but to understand the deep structure of violence and the embodied vulnerability we all share as precisely what a literary approach has to offer the study of human rights.

Heather Hewett

Linking Economic Justice and Women's Human Rights: Feminist Approaches for the Human Rights Literature Classroom

In the developing field of human rights and literature, literary critics have given far more attention to civil and political rights than to economic, social, and cultural rights—the so-called soft or aspirational rights (Goldberg, "Intimations" 103). Narratives that explore human rights violations incurred through genocide, torture, imprisonment, and state-led attacks on free expression are recognizably identified as texts that speak to the centrality of witness and testimony in the project of exposing state violence and claiming rights through narrating counterhistories. Yet creative texts that explore soft or second-generation rights, particularly economic rights, tend to remain underaddressed and undertaught in literary studies classrooms. In this essay, I suggest some ways to incorporate discussions about economic justice into the university classroom setting, using feminist theories and pedagogical approaches to literary texts.

Perhaps inadvertently, the reluctance to address economic rights in the classroom may partly reflect the long history of debate about the role of individual governments in guaranteeing access to second-generation rights. The economic rights named in the 1948 Universal Declaration of Human Rights (UDHR) constitute an understanding of human dignity that acknowledges the need for a certain level of material security and recognizes that governments must play a positive, active role in providing a baseline for this security. As a consequence, these rights continue to be debated and contested. Many question whether these rights are even realistic. Are these rights or ideals? What obligations and duties do nation-states have to guarantee citizens' access to these rights? What about nation-states that lack the economic resources for creating the social programs necessary for these rights? One can understand why many human rights activists and practitioners have prioritized civil and political rights, particularly in capitalist systems, where the redistribution of resources is often highly contested. If anything, political resistance to economic rights has increased during the last decades of the twentieth century and the first decade of the twenty-first century, a period characterized by hegemonic neoliberal economic policies and global recession. Many countries have cut basic social services and have retreated even further from these commitments; ideologically, economic rights rarely have a place at the table. It is no wonder that economic justice frequently receives short shrift in classes about literature and human rights.

But university classrooms do not have to replicate the outright rejection of economic rights. In fact, I argue that any curriculum attempting to introduce human rights literacy needs to include all generations of rights: first-generation civil and political rights; second-generation social, economic, and cultural rights; and third-generation collective and development rights. Framing discussions about economic rights with some of the relevant history can provide a context for why these rights are often overlooked as well as what the debates have been. In my experience as a professor in a liberal "blue state" in the United States, many students have never encountered the concept of economic rights in their education, although they possess at least a passing familiarity with political (and frequently partisan) debates about capitalism and socialism. As an educator, I want my students to become familiar with the broad range of rights named in the UDHR and to ask basic philosophical questions for themselves: how do they define human rights? Are human rights indivisible, as is often claimed by human right activists and practitioners, or can they be divided into groups and generations? What is human dignity, and what conditions are necessary for it? How can literature enable us to explore these questions?

Feminist pedagogical approaches and creative literature focusing on women's experiences can provide a productive avenue for opening up these discussions. Much feminist theory and writing explore the material and embodied conditions of women's lives, providing another way to understand how the absence of economic opportunity and material resources can disempower women. Literary analysis can enable students to work through the complex interconnections between different kinds of oppressions. Two strategies in particular—reading for intersectionality (understanding identity, social location, and subordination through the intersecting and codetermining axes of race, gender, and class, as well as other identitarian classifications) and reading for the body—can highlight the complexities of the material experiences of women's lives. This approach may be helpful in making the absence of specific rights more visible for First World students.

Here I look at a handful of creative texts by women that illuminate these connections. I focus in particular on the novel *Nervous Conditions*, by Tsitsi Dangarembga, which provides a rich meditation on the interconnections of material conditions, women's bodies, and the multilayered ways in which women experience oppression. Furthermore, Dangarembga's novel asks readers to develop alternative perspectives on both liberal feminism and human rights. Situating discussions about women's human rights in postcolonial and transnational contexts can create a framework for students to reexamine familiar ideas and reflect on their locations as readers. My goal is not to convince students of what feminism—or human rights—is or is not but rather to call attention to the existence of a diverse range of ideas, experiences, and agendas when we examine feminism (and human rights) globally. This interdisciplinary approach makes available some of the insights from feminists who identify as postcolonial or women of color (or both) and who have focused attention on the need to understand all differences, not just gender, within their historical and material contexts.

Historical and Political Contexts: Transnational Feminism and the Indivisibility of Rights

Article 22 of the UDHR establishes the scope of economic rights by stating that everyone "is entitled to realization, through national effort and international cooperation and in accordance with the organization and resources of each State, of the economic, social and cultural rights indispensable for his dignity and the free development of his personality" ("United Nations Universal Declaration"). Surrounding articles name specific rights: the right to own property (art. 17); the right to work—"to free choice of employment, to just and favorable conditions of work and to protection against unemployment"—the right to equal pay for equal work, the right to just and favorable remuneration, and the right to form and join trade unions (art. 23); the right to rest and leisure (art. 24); the right to "a standard of living adequate for the health and well-being of himself and of his family" and the right to "special care and assistance" for mothers and children (art. 25); and the right to education (art. 26). Article 25 elaborates on what is meant by an adequate standard of living: "food, clothing, housing and medical care and necessary social services, and the right to security in the event of unemployment, sickness, disability, widowhood, old age or other lack of livelihood in circumstances beyond his control."

Subsequent to the UDHR, the International Covenant on Civil and Political Rights and the International Covenant on Economic, Social and Cultural Rights, both adopted in 1966, revealed the fault lines between those countries that restricted rights to the civil and political realm and those that included or prioritized economic, social, and cultural rights (such as the right to health, education, and freedom from hunger). Manisha Desai puts it thus:

> Historically the West has supported the enforcement of the civil and political rights, for which member states have legal obligation, while the former Soviet Union and the Third World countries have been promoters of the economic and social rights for which there is very limited enforcement. It is these latter rights that have been used in the 1990s by the transnational women's movements to forge solidarities and demand accountability from their governments. (26)

Indeed, many feminists have argued that the exclusive focus on civil and political rights contributed to the failure to incorporate women's rights into human rights agendas. As Charlotte Bunch explains:

> Some important aspects of women's rights do fit into a civil liberties framework, but much of the abuse against women is part of a larger socio-economic web that entraps women, making them vulnerable to abuses which cannot be delineated as exclusively political or solely caused by states. The inclusion of "second generation" or socioeconomic human rights to food, shelter, and work—which are clearly delineated as part of the Universal Declaration of Human Rights—is vital to addressing women's concerns fully. ("Women's Rights" 488)

As Bunch makes clear, an understanding of gender and of women's rights has informed understandings of the interconnectedness, or indivisibility, of rights. This paradigm shift has largely occurred because of the work of the transnational women's movement, forged by feminists working across local, regional, and national borders over the past forty years. In particular, many women from the Third World or Global South, as well as many women of color worldwide, have prioritized a broad range of social and economic concerns, thus broadening and challenging mainstream articulations of liberal feminism in the First World or Global North.

This shift has not occurred without conflict. Reina Lewis and Sara Mills observe in their introduction to *Feminist Postcolonial Theory* that second-wave Anglo-American feminist theory tended to generalize "from Western middle-class women's experiences and developed a form of theorizing—'sisterhood is global'—which assumed that those white concerns were the concerns of women everywhere" (4). By contrast, the theorizing and activism of many feminists who identify as postcolonial or women of color (or both) advanced an intersectional understanding of identity that highlights how race is interlocking with gender. In the United States, these feminists include such figures as the authors of the Combahee River Collective Statement and Audre Lorde, bell hooks, Kimberlé Williams Crenshaw, and Patricia Hill Collins. As feminist thought has developed, theorists have come to understand gender as interlinked with several axes of identity, including race, class, caste, ethnicity, sexuality, religion, education, disability, age, and geographic location. This intersectional understanding of identity brings with it a parallel observation: oppressions are interlinked.

In the political arena, the challenge to mainstream liberal feminism in the First World or Global North began during the world conferences on women beginning in Mexico in 1975. As Aili Mari Tripp describes, tensions and conflict between feminists broke out during the 1980s, when women from the Third World or Global South tended "to focus on how women's problems were defined by global inequality, imperialism, and other political concerns that were not seen as gender-specific" (61). Tripp argues, however, that by the beginning of the twenty-first century, much of the transnational feminist movement had come together around a "rights-based approach" that merged "human rights issues and sustainable development concerns"—a consensus largely led by feminists from the Global South (63).

During this same period, the United States government has proven a reluctant and at times resistant participant in international conversations about human rights. To date, the United States has not signed several human rights treaties, including the International Covenant on Economic,

Social and Cultural Rights and the Convention on the Elimination of All Forms of Discrimination against Women. Beyond the United States, Tripp charges that the energies of many feminist "movements in the Global North have declined or become complacent or merely parochial" at the same time that activists in the Global South have "push[ed] new women's rights agendas" (73, 70). Perhaps as a consequence of these trends, not all students in the United States have considered how or under what circumstances human beings might have a right to food, health, or education or how these rights might be feminist issues. A broadened understanding of feminism frequently requires students to rethink how they may have defined feminism or how they may have viewed the framing of feminism by their peers or in the United States mass media.

Classes on literature and human rights provide a wonderful opportunity for introducing students to different perspectives on feminism and human rights. Two pedagogical strategies prove particularly effective when reading creative literature. The first is reading for intersectionality and then linking discussions about interlocking oppressions to the language of human rights. Bunch offers some insight into the powerful role that narrative can play:

> While indivisibility has not yet been realized in human rights practice, it reinforces what feminists have called intersectionality or the interrelatedness of factors like race, class, age, gender, and sexuality. A person's rights or experience of violation cannot often be divided out according to one of these factors alone, for how one experiences each of these is affected by the others. The everyday reality of this principle was reiterated in most of the testimonials presented in the hearings and tribunals organized by the Global Campaign for Women's Human Rights at the UN world conferences. As women told the story of how they were violated in one area of their lives such as domestic violence, it was evident how this was exacerbated by other factors such as race or their lack of economic or political rights in other areas. ("Women's Human Rights" 141–42)

Women's testimonials at these United Nations hearings helped make clear connections between different kinds of human rights violations. Like these women's testimonials, all narrative can dramatize theoretical concepts, making the lived, material conditions of women's lives accessible to outsiders, and can tug at the emotions of its audiences, providing another way of grasping the more theoretical and abstract concept of intersectionality.

A second effective pedagogical strategy is reading for the body. Here I draw on the reflections of Brenda Carr Vellino, who observes that "[b]ecause the body is freedom's limit, the site where violations are scored, marked, amplified, endured, and resisted, reading for the body is an essential strategy for a human rights pedagogy" ("Everything" 141). She clarifies that she is most concerned with the body "as an experiential entity," not as it is often made abstract by academic language (142). (She correctly points out that much theory can help us understand the body as both a physical entity and a constructed ideal, writing that "[t]wenty years of gender, queer, race, and postcolonial theory have variously foregrounded the body as a central category to each" [141–42].) Reading for the body in literature shows students how individual human beings suffer large-scale human rights abuses. As Vellino writes, the body "is the locus where social suffering registers daily as close as one's own skin and bones, within situations of insidious, domestic abuse and catastrophic political events on a global scale" (142). The body, in other words, can make visible a wide range of human rights abuses and oppressions. I would add that graphic descriptions of the body can also have an emotional, visceral effect on readers.

A range of creative works lend themselves to these two reading strategies and, either taught together or individually, can open up discussions about gender, economics, and women's human rights. With these questions in mind, I have successfully taught many of the following texts: Virginia Woolf's *A Room of One's Own*, Jamaica Kincaid's *Lucy*, Monica Ali's *Brick Lane*, Nawal El Saadawi's *Woman at Point Zero*, Nuruddin Farah's *Maps*, Buchi Emecheta's *The Joys of Motherhood*, and Tsitsi Dangarembga's *Nervous Conditions.* It is to this last novel that I now turn.

Case Study: Reading *Nervous Conditions*

Nervous Conditions, an accessible and, as Susan VanZanten Gallagher puts it, "highly teachable" novel, provides an entry point for discussions about the full spectrum of human rights as well as the ways in which this expanded notion of rights has informed feminist struggles globally (61). Dangarembga's novel, published in 1988, tells the coming-of-age story of Tambudzai (Tambu), a young Shona girl living in colonial Rhodesia in the 1960s and 1970s, the final years of white minority rule. As a novel that represents the victimhood and agency of African women in complex and moving ways, *Nervous Conditions* dramatizes the many connections of civil, political, and socioeconomic rights in the lives of its characters.

Its richly detailed and emotionally engaging narrative taps into students' inclinations toward (and in some cases, deeply felt connections with) gender justice at the same time that it locates these struggles in an unfamiliar context: rural Africa. Its careful attention to the rhythms and hardships of daily life in colonial Rhodesia provides opportunities for First World readers to consider how the experiences of subsistence-level existence can provide alternative ways of viewing the world. In addition, the aspirations and ambitions of the novel's narrator, who manages to attend school despite the relentless poverty that affects her family, resonates with the lives of students who are working-class or are the first in their family to attend college. Although Tambu's situation is clearly very different from that of most college students in the United States, I have found that students frequently identify and empathize with her determined upward trajectory.

The trick, as Lisa Eck perceptively observes, is to acknowledge that students identify with Tambu's struggle while helping them internalize the novel's complex critique of the "liberal individualism promoted by Western 'first wave' feminism" as well as the "related issue of liberalism's faith in linear progress, implicit in the form of the bildungsroman" (580). That is, *Nervous Conditions* requires readers to "balance liberal feminism . . . with a postcolonial critique" (593).[1] Yet this critique of feminism, while central to the novel, must compete with dominant United States cultural narratives about self-sufficiency, self-determination, and individual success; indeed, for some readers, fully acknowledging the novel's critique may feel threatening.

Thus for many students, the challenge of the novel lies in the way it requires readers to understand how it is, as Eck succinctly articulates, "both a bildungsroman and an antibildungsroman" (580). As a coming-of-age novel, the events of *Nervous Conditions* are narrated years later by Tambu, wise about the ways in which her youthful desires for a "clear-cut escape from poverty and subsistence farming" do not turn out to be so transparent (Creamer 351). The result is a complex unfolding of Tambu's struggle against oppressive Shona and colonial gender categories and her ultimate insight, through her reflective observations about her experience and about the lives of several women in her family, into how her upward trajectory is defined and contained by a racist, colonial system of education. As Joseph Slaughter observes, the narrative of *Nervous Conditions* demonstrates how the "idea and project of *Bildung* itself" is "sociohistorically contingent" and unavailable to a young Shona girl in colonial Rhodesia (*Human Rights* 216).

Recognizing that self-development through education may be foreclosed to some individuals might feel threatening to some students, particularly because it contradicts national narratives of the "American Dream." Yet critical self-reflection about the cultural work of this national narrative as well as its powerful utility—or unavailability—within individual lives not only can provide a powerful moment of educational growth but also is in keeping with the novel's inquiry. To this end, I have found Eck's in-class writing exercise, "Education, It's a Family Affair," quite useful (584–85). The assignment asks students to reflect on their own educational experiences and their locational identities and thus enables them to complicate the very powerful United States narrative that education always leads to success. Many of my students have explored alternative family realities in which this story did not always hold true. Another theme has emerged around socioeconomic class structures and the material constraints that prevented the attainment of an education, especially as students reflected on the experiences of their parents or grandparents. Ideally, this exercise produces an opportunity for increased self-awareness about the students' identification with Tambu's upward trajectory while also laying the groundwork for their appreciation of how her situation differs from their own.

Reading for Intersectionality and Reading for the Body

Thematically, *Nervous Conditions* explores the possibilities of resisting and overcoming oppression—an enduring theme in many human rights struggles, including minority rights and women's rights movements. As Tambu tells the reader in the beginning, "my story is . . . about my escape and Lucia's; about my mother's and Maiguru's entrapment; and about Nyasha's rebellion" (Dangarembga 1). As a result of these multiple stories—an expansion of the traditional single-character focus of the bildungsroman—the reader comes to understand both the varying social conditions faced by women as well as the similarities of their positions. With this strategy, Dangarembga circumvents what might be a tendency among some readers to read Tambu as standing for the "African Woman" or, indeed, for the "Third World Woman"— monolithic categories that, as Chandra Talpade Mohanty reminds us, frequently permeate Western feminist discussions about Third World women (49). Yet although *Nervous Conditions* suggests how greatly women's experiences vary, it simultaneously asserts that gender remains a common denominator for the oppression of women. As the young narrator reflects:

> The victimisation, I saw, was universal. It didn't depend on poverty, on lack of education or on tradition. It didn't depend on any of the things I had thought it depended on. Men took it everywhere with them. . . . But what I didn't like was the way all the conflicts came back to this question of femaleness. Femaleness as opposed to and inferior to maleness. (116)

The narrator's struggle with the "question of femaleness" provides an opportunity for Dangarembga to invoke powerful narratives about human emancipation and freedom. Indeed, the power of the novel lies in its nuanced sense of what it means to be liberated and its suggestion that emancipation may not invariably produce self-determined and empowered individuals; it can also lead to self-alienation and entrapment. Through its inclusion of other female characters, the novel suggests alternative possibilities that lie outside colonial education and the liberal humanist form of the bildungsroman, possibilities suggested by the strategies of the wise but formally uneducated Lucia as well as the hint (but only a hint) of collective action.

The novel engages in this exploration of freedom on the level of plot as well as of language. In discussions about *Nervous Conditions*, then, I push students to explore the nuances of what words such as *liberation*, *emancipation*, and *development* (all of which recur throughout the text) might mean. We further consider the variety of historical, political, religious, and cultural narratives that these words might signify, as well as how the novel interrogates these narratives. How have these words, used in the novel to refer to the individual trajectories of the characters, also been invoked by human rights struggles globally? How might these narratives, as well as the plot trajectories suggested by *entrapment*, *rebellion*, and *escape*, be influenced or determined by the impoverished material conditions the novel so carefully details? Do these words represent "exaggerated promises" and "inflated rhetoric" or, alternatively, utopic and visionary ideals (Slaughter, *Human Rights* 228)? How might *liberation* and *emancipation* differ from *development*, which not only signifies the personal development of the bildungsroman but also, as both Slaughter and Fawzia Mustafa argue, the socioeconomic project of development taken up by the international community? Identifying these larger narratives enables the class to situate the personal stories of Tambu and the women in her family within multiple discourses. These discourses can also help inform close textual readings of the novel's many scenes that provide glimpses (frequently missed by first-time readers) of the workings of colonialism and economic racism.

Close attention to these scenes reveals the many systemic and material obstacles standing between Tambu and her ability to write herself into a narrative of self-liberation. It is easy to understand how Tambu chafes against restrictive gender roles and gendered labor divisions; she makes this injustice clear to the reader, whose sympathy she gains through an appealing combination of honesty and determination, most of all her resolve to go to school—a human right frequently denied to girls. But the novel also dramatizes the many obstacles standing in the way of Tambu's attempt to garner resources for herself. In the United States, the cumulative effect of such details are easily categorized as *poverty*, a word so often used to describe Africa in the Western media that it seems to describe the naturalized, essential condition of the entire continent. But naming poverty as a direct result of the human systems of colonialism and patriarchy—for example, pointing out that the Rhodesian colonial government nullified Africans' economic human rights through the early-twentieth-century colonial land grab sanctified by the 1930 Land Apportionment Act—may enable students to better understand Tambu's poverty.

Likewise, the novel's sustained reflection on food suggests how hunger—or to use the language of rights, the obstruction of the human right to food—may also be understood as a consequence of colonialism and patriarchal cultural practices. *Nervous Conditions* furthermore makes clear how the right to food is gendered: women's reproductive labor (the "normal back-breaking routine" of fetching water, tending the fields, preparing food, and so on) does not translate into eating the same amount as men (156). Indeed, Tambu returns, again and again, to the question of a "fair division of labour" (12), while she simultaneously delineates the social hierarchy and how it is only the "patriarchy" (which includes men plus her aunt Tete Gladys) who eat meat (138). By contrast, while she and the other girls are performing household labor, they only eat breakfast once "everyone else had finished" (136); later in the day, they are so busy fetching water and doing laundry that they miss the "afternoon meal" (137).

Food not only preoccupies Tambu's consciousness but also, as many critics have observed, suffuses the language of the novel (Creamer; Hill; Wright; Bhana; Wixson; Thomas). Words related to food and eating—*crop*, *harvest*, *stomach*, *appetite*, *tongue*, *seeds*, *cultivate*, *digest*—become tropes for figuring the interrelated issues of education, colonialism, class, sexuality, women's bodies, consumption, nourishment, language, culture, and resistance. In groups or individually, students can identify passages that characterize the novel's different characters with descriptions of food and patterns of consumption:

Tambu grows her own mealies and controls the proceeds from their sale; she subsequently transforms physically from her "peasant self" to a "plump" young woman who menstruates once she leaves her family's subsistence-level existence (95, 97).

Nyasha forgets Shona and finds that her eating disorder is misunderstood by everyone around her, even though she herself comprehends that "it's more than just . . . a plateful of food" (190).

Mainini can't "stomach so much Englishness" in her children and stops eating (203).

Maiguru supplies her overflowing dining room table with British food and utensils.

Lucia is described as having "fecund appetites" (138).

Babamukuru is described as being seen by the missionaries as "cultivatable, in the way that land is, to yield harvests that sustain the cultivator" (19).

While in no way exhaustive, the above list begins to suggest the complexity of food and consumption in the novel. When students focus on particular characters and compare them, they gain a better sense of the novel's deep and profound connections between food cultivation, hunger, eating disorders, poverty, colonialism, gender, education, and culture. This enables students to view individual plot developments, most of all Nyasha's eating disorder, in a larger landscape.

Nyasha's story points to another dominant feminist narrative that can interrupt more complex readings of the novel: the narrative of accepting and controlling one's body. Many of my female (and, increasingly, male) students understand self-empowerment as a quest centered in their bodies, which includes the desire for full freedom to express themselves sexually as well as the desire to love their own imperfect, human bodies in a visual culture saturated by airbrushing, digital retouching, and plastic surgery. Indeed, the novel's dramatization of the concerns surrounding women's bodies and bodily integrity provides a powerful point of feminist connection between First World and Third World points of view. I suspect that many incoming college students anticipate a certain kind of liberation made possible through the "conjunction of a new intellectual identity with a transformed physical body," as Tambu experiences (Gallagher 63); those students who have struggled with eating disorders may also identify with Nyasha's struggle. In my experience, classroom discussions about these issues, in particular Nyasha's eating disorder, yield valuable insights. Students are quick to home in on the question of whether Nyasha's eating disorder represents a form of resistance or of internal colonization: as Derek Wright puts it, "her bulimia is fertile in ambivalence and contradiction, and has been seen both as a positive act of self-control and as a despairing, suicidal attempt to efface herself from an alienating environment" (16). Students also respond strongly to the ways that "the turf of [Nyasha's] body" becomes the arena of struggle with Babamukuru, her father, as her sexuality serves as the flashpoint culminating in a physical fight in which he accuses Nyasha of being a whore and hits her (Bahri, para. 4). Babamukuru's easy violation of his daughter's bodily integrity and his violent patrolling of her sexuality, driven by a quasi-Victorian ideology of female chastity, provides fodder for the young Tambu—as well as the reader—to reflect on the binaristic construction of femininity that affects all the women in her family. Many of my students recognize the binary of Madonna/whore as familiar (and still active) categories.

And yet, Tambu's and Nyasha's bodily struggles differ from those of a typical college student in the United States; the novel demonstrates how the cultural and historical realities of colonial Rhodesia create an environment of scarcity and poverty in which both characters' bodily struggles must be understood. A careful reading of *Nervous Conditions* requires us to silence, at least momentarily, the "noise" of dominant First World narratives about feminism and human rights. The strategies I have suggested—shifting the frame to enable students to escape the problems of a simplistic identification with Tambu based on liberal feminism and global sisterhood, highlighting the presence of powerful First World cultural narratives, and introducing concepts such as the interconnectedness of rights—can help all of us, both students and professors, in classrooms in the United States and elsewhere in the Global North read more attentively and critically. Once we still the noise of dominant First World narratives, we can hear how the novel so eloquently gives voice to women who are frequently not heard in political discussions of rights. The resulting chorus refutes hierarchical conceptions of rights and urges us to imagine a holistic vision of freedom and justice that incorporates the many dimensions of human identity and experience.

Notes

The author wishes to thank the Rutgers Institute for Research on Women for the opportunity to participate in its 2008–09 seminar The Culture of Rights / The Rights of Culture, out of which this essay emerged.

1. Scholars such as Linda Strong-Leek and Lindsay Pentolfe Aegerter identify this alternative perspective as "womanism." See also McWilliams; Shaw.

Jennifer Browdy de Hernandez

Engaging the Literature and Film of Female Genital Mutilation in the Undergraduate Classroom

Testimonials are ideal texts for teaching undergraduates about human rights. As personal narratives, testimonials convey the anguish and the urgency that survivors feel in bringing their story to the public. As collaborative texts, they also potentially model an effective form of political alliance that crosses all kinds of borders. They provide a bottom-up approach: we begin with an inside account of the personal experience of someone whose rights have been violated and then relate this individual story back to the larger human rights framework, as laid out in the United Nations Universal Declaration of Human Rights (UDHR). In my mid-level seminar Cross-Cultural Perspectives on Human Rights, we constantly move back and forth between the personal and the political, from the embodied experience of human rights violations to the more abstract framework by which these individual experiences can be contextualized and contested on a larger scale.

The testimonial genre, which first gained prominence in Latin America in the 1970s, is related to the earlier genre of slave narratives: both often result from a collaboration between a literate scribe and a survivor of atrocity who tells his or her story to effect political change. Although some contemporary testimonials are written by the testifiers themselves (e.g.,

Ismael Beah's *A Long Way Gone*, his account of being forced to serve as a child soldier in Sierra Leone), most testimonials are collaborative efforts that bring to the fore questions of alliance across typical boundaries of race, class, nationality, and so on. Such alliances can be politically fraught, as in one of the most famous and controversial Latin American *testimonios*, *I, Rigoberta Menchú*, in which the scribe, Elizabeth Burgos-Debray, embedded into the narrative "subtle but unmistakable gestures that . . . surreptitiously reinforce existing oppressor/oppressed hierarchies" (Browdy de Hernandez 163). While we need to be careful in the classroom to interrogate our own position vis-à-vis the text, as teachers we should aim to lead students in joining a circle of productive alliance with the testifiers.[1] As Allen Carey-Webb writes in his introduction to the anthology *Teaching and Testimony*:

> as a communicative act testimony aspires to human continuity, the establishment of justice, and the making of the future. Indeed, the very activity of testifying turns victims into survivors, witnesses into agents of change. Teaching testimony brings this transformational potential into the classroom. It stresses the power of language to recreate past experiences, foster new understanding, and enlarge the circle of witnesses. (7)

Teaching Transformation: Transcultural Classroom Dialogues, by Ana-Louise Keating, and *Understanding White Privilege: Creating Pathways to Authentic Relationships across Race*, by Frances Kendall, are particularly useful for analyzing and enacting alliances across difference. In addition, it is helpful to remind students that the genre of *testimonio* holds one of the foundational paradoxes of human rights: that such testimony may provide the speaker with a sense of empowerment simultaneously with a sense of further violation in describing and making public one's experience of atrocity.

In Cross-Cultural Perspectives on Human Rights, we spend the first two weeks on a brief historical overview of the theory of human rights, from the French, American, and Haitian Revolutions, to the nineteenth-century abolition and women's suffrage movements, to the mid-twentieth-century anticolonial struggles, to the American civil rights and women's rights movements. As we paint this history in broad strokes, we also consider each article of the UDHR and discuss the ways in which these provisions both respond to and push against specific historical and social situations. I ask each student to design a poster around one or two of the articles of the UDHR, which we hang up on the classroom wall, and these become frequent reference points as we move on to explore specific contexts of human rights violations. The issue that often resonates most strongly with my students is that of female genital mutilation (FGM). Testimonials by women who have survived FGM give students an opportunity to explore some of the thorniest challenges of cross-cultural communication and alliance that arise in transnational human rights advocacy, since the practice is so hotly contested both in local cultures that engage in genital cutting of girls and in the broader international community, particularly among medical professionals, human rights advocates, and global feminists.

A good place to start a discussion of FGM is with the term itself, since it has frequently been a site of argument. Opponents of the practice prefer the term *female genital mutilation*, which, they say, reflects the reality of what is done to a girl when she has her clitoris, and often her labia, removed in a ceremony that marks her transition to womanhood. Supporters of the practice often prefer the medicalized term *clitoridectomy* or the more neutral-sounding *female circumcision* or *female genital cutting*. The Inter-African Committee on Traditional Practices Affecting the Health of Women and Children, a nongovernmental organization affiliated with the United Nations and representing twenty-eight African countries, affirmed the use of the term *female genital mutilation* in its 2005 Bamako Declaration, arguing that "frank wording" was necessary "to confront the issue head on with . . . practicing communities" (qtd. in Levin, "Assaults" 4). Of course, there are also hundreds of other names for this practice in specific African languages and dialects to refer to removing all or part of a woman's clitoris, all or part of her labia, and sometimes, in the most severe forms of the practice, sewing up the vaginal opening to leave only a small hole for the outflow of urine and menstrual fluids.

Traditionally, and still frequently today, women perform this operation with razors or knives, in rural locations without access to anesthesia or antibiotics. It is not uncommon for girls to die of the hemorrhaging that can result, and it is quite common for women who have been cut to have ongoing problems with urination and menstruation, pain and bleeding during sexual intercourse, and severe complications in childbirth that can lead to newborn deformity and death. These chronic complications, affecting millions of girls and women annually throughout Africa and the African and Muslim diasporic populations, have led the World Health Organization to take a strong stand against FGM, arguing that the practice has no health benefits for girls and women.

A good overview of American, European, and African literary engagement with the topic of FGM is provided in the essay "Excision and African Literature: An Activist Annotated Bibliographical Excursion," by Pierrette Herzberger-Fofana, which traces the literary outlines of the abolition movement. Herzberger-Fofana also documents the backlash that has sprung up among traditionalists in African and Muslim communities who argue that to abandon the practice would be to accede to the cultural imperialism of the West, as well as among African women who may agree that the practice is harmful but resent Western feminists' sometimes self-righteous interventions and the tendency of the Western media to sensationalize FGM because it deals with women's sexual organs. Clearly, to lead a class of undergraduates into this territory is to wade into the heart of fiercely contested cultural issues that may at first seem to be far removed from the concerns of ordinary American students.

Fadumo Korn's *Born in the Big Rains*, like many other testimonials by women who have survived FGM and become advocates of ending the practice, provides a strong answer to the question of shared concern. Korn tells her life story "to win allies who support our common goal" of ending FGM (163). Very few Americans will be directly affected by the practice of FGM (though there is increasing evidence that African immigrants to the United States and Europe are continuing to have their daughters cut), but all opposed to the practice have the potential to become allies of the anti-FGM activists.

Here is where the human rights framework can provide a valuable reference point for students. Article 3 of the UDHR states unequivocally, "Everyone has the right to life, liberty and security of person." Article 2.f of the Convention on the Elimination of All Forms of Discrimination against Women (CEDAW) calls on states to "take all appropriate measures, including legislation, to modify or abolish existing laws, regulations, customs and practices which constitute discrimination against women," and article 24.3 of the Convention on the Rights of the Child (CRC) directs states to "take all effective and appropriate measures with a view to abolishing traditional practices prejudicial to the health of children." Article 19.1 of the CRC also insists that states "protect the child from all forms of physical or mental violence, injury or abuse."

No one reading the testimony of a survivor of the practice could fail to interpret FGM as a form of violence against children, although the question of how childhood is defined remains important. Here is how Khady

Koïta of Senegal describes what was done to her with a razor when she was seven years old:

> Two women caught and dragged me in. The one behind me grabbed my head and, with all the strength in her knees, crushed my shoulders to the ground; the other clutched my thighs to force the legs apart. . . . Using her fingers, the exciser grasps the clitoris and stretches that minute fragment of flesh as far as it will go. She then—if all goes well—whacks it off like a piece of zebu meat. Often, she can't hack it off in one go so she's obliged to saw. To this day, I can hear myself howling. (11)

While human rights conventions may be able to make global pronouncements about the violation of bodily integrity that this scenario represents, literary narrative possesses the unique power to awaken what Martha Nussbaum might refer to as "compassionate empathy," in which students are able to look through the eyes of the first-person testimonial narrator and walk a ways in her shoes. Nussbaum argues that identification with a sufferer is necessary to awaken the kind of compassionate empathy that drives human rights advocates to action:

> Equipped with her general conception of human flourishing, the spectator looks at a world in which people suffer hunger, disability, disease, slavery, through no fault of their own. She believes that goods such as food, health, citizenship, freedom, do matter. And yet she acknowledges, as well, that it is uncertain whether she herself will remain among the safe and privileged ones to whom such goods are stably guaranteed. She acknowledges that the lot of the beggar might be (or become) her own. This leads her to turn her thoughts outward, asking about society's general arrangement for the allocation of goods and resources. Given the uncertainty of life, she will be inclined, other things being equal, to want a society in which the lot of the worst off—of the poor, of people defeated in war, of women, of servants—is as good as it can be. Self-interest itself, via thought about shared vulnerabilities, promotes the selection of principles that raise society's floor. (*Upheavals* 320)

The joining of the juridical discourse of human rights and the literary discourse of personal narrative encourages students to become ethically engaged readers; they begin by bearing witness to the testimonial narrator's story and may be inspired to go on to become more politically active as a result. I share Elizabeth Ammons's belief that

> the tremendous value of the humanities and especially the study of literature resides in the power of texts to teach us about ourselves, individually and corporately, including the systems of injustice that we as human beings create. But the value of the humanities also resides in the power of words to inspire us, to transform us, to give us strength and courage for the difficult task of *re*-creating the world. (14)

Ammons goes on to argue in favor of an engaged pedagogical practice that is not afraid to reimagine literary study "as a progressive cultural force capable not simply of providing critique but also of offering hope and inspiration in the real-world activist struggle for social justice" (21).

In the particular context of the struggle to abolish FGM, the study of testimonial accounts by survivors has an important place in teaching us not only about the practice but also about strategies of resistance and transnational alliance in the service of human rights. While comparisons to earlier abolition movements can be useful in thinking about the potential for alliance between the privileged and the oppressed, it is important to note that the anti-FGM movement differs from the nineteenth-century antislavery movement in that FGM is not an institution like slavery that is imposed on women and girls by an oppressive outside power. Rather, it is a practice perpetuated by mothers and grandmothers, some of whose daughters and granddaughters are in fact eager to participate in what they understand to be an essential rite of passage into womanhood. As Tobe Levin observes, the question for us as readers who are cultural outsiders is "how to approach an issue viewed as urgent by only a tiny trans-national minority. For make no mistake," Levin cautions, "an enormous and powerful majority tenaciously defends the practice" (Preface xv).

If we were just to go by the published documents on FGM, whether works of fiction, personal narratives, poetry, or research-based journalistic and scholarly articles, we might have trouble believing that the majority of people concerned with the issue of FGM are in favor of it, since almost all the published work views FGM as a human rights violation to be eradicated. Defenders of FGM are more likely to make their arguments orally and through action on the ground where the cutting occurs. One published source that does an excellent job at presenting both the pro- and anti-FGM arguments is Fuambai Ahmadu's "Rites and Wrongs: An Insider/Outsider Reflects on Power and Excision." Ahmadu, raised in the United States by Sierra Leonean parents, was a college senior when she was taken back to Sierra Leone with her sister to be initiated into the Kono women's secret society, the Bundu. In Sierra Leone, according to

World Health Organization statistics, ninety percent or more of women undergo removal of the clitoris as one of many rituals required of girls seeking to join the Bundu. Ahmadu, who now holds a graduate degree in cultural anthropology, describes her FGM experience, incorporating both the anthropologist's attention to detail and the testifier's firsthand point of view:

> I was hoisted up by four or five . . . stocky women. I looked down: a large leaf had been laid on the ground directly underneath my buttocks. I looked up again. Terror finally overcame me as the women's faces, now dozens, now hundreds, moved in closer all around my near naked body suspended in mid-air. They grabbed my legs and arms apart. The women's screams, the sounds of drums and then a sharp blade cut deep into my flesh on one side and then on the other. As I cried out in unimaginable agony, I felt warm blood ooze down between my thighs. Perhaps for the first time since I was an infant, I vomited. (293)

Despite her own "agony," Ahmadu, in her culturally detailed and nuanced insider/outsider description, shows how the practice can also be, paradoxically, empowering to the women who uphold it. Kono women view their Bundu membership strategically, Ahmadu says, "women claim sole credit for everything from procreation to the creation of culture, society and its institutions" (306), and the most important rite of initiation into this sisterhood is the genital cutting that makes a girl a woman. Ahmadu ends her essay by arguing for medicalization of the procedure as a way to reduce "the immediate physical pain and risk of infection"[2] and also suggests that a "ritual without cutting model," which "positively values many cultural aspects and belief underlying female genital operations and initiation while attempting to eliminate the actual physical cutting," might be "a reasonable middle ground" (308).

Ahmadu's essay opens a window into the intracultural debates over the practice of FGM and allows students to move beyond a simple binary framework of response. Clearly it is important to guard against what Joseph A. Massad has aptly characterized as "a Western nativism armed with a Rousseauian zeal intent on forcing people into freedom, indeed one that considers assimilating the world into its own norms as ipso facto liberation and progress and a step toward universalizing a superior notion of the human" (251). One way to undermine the possible superiority of the West in regard to initiation rituals is to demystify FGM by contextualizing it as one among many initiation rituals or beautifying practices worldwide that can have harmful physical repercussions. For example, hazing practices by athletic teams, fraternities and sororities, the military, and gangs all involve putting aspirants through painful and humiliating rituals that, once survived, guarantee one's place as a bona fide member of the group. FGM's role in making girls into women can also be discussed in terms of international beauty standards for women, which can lead to harmful practices like self-starvation, skin bleaching, or plastic surgery procedures including, in the West, the ever more popular vaginoplasty. The important difference is that for the most part, participation in these self-destructive rituals is voluntary, whereas in most cases FGM is practiced on girls who have no agency to resist.

I often add films or Web-based visual narratives to our reading of human rights testimonials, especially when students are unlikely to be familiar with the sociocultural context of the testifier. One of the most effective recent films that has taken up the question of resistance is Ousmane Sembène's *Moolaadé*, in which a group of girls who decide to run away from the excisor find an ally in the form of a mother, Collé, who invokes the ancient custom of giving sanctuary ("moolaadé") to the girls to keep them intact. Collé lost her first two children because of her botched circumcision, and her third and only child, her daughter Amasatou, survived only because Collé found a midwife who "tore her apart" to deliver the baby.

Collé has refused to let Amasatou undergo FGM, and in the course of the film, she stands up to social pressure and personal violence in her determination to be a bulwark for other girls in her village as well. The film especially celebrates the courage of the men and women in the transitional generation: Collé's husband, Ciré, who finally breaks with his dominating older brother and sides with his wife, saying, "it takes more than a pair of balls to make a man"; and Collé herself, who is honored by the other women as "a warrior, more valiant than men" for standing firm against the overwhelming pressure to conform to tradition. Sembène shows us that both men and women need to be engaged in the work of change: it will take both Ciré and Collé, along with Amasatou and her fiancé, Ibrahima, to make the decisions needed to reject a harmful traditional practice.

While *Moolaadé* has been criticized for presenting the social struggle over FGM as too baldly a question of modernity, progress, and civilization as imported ideals on the one hand and backward local traditions on the other, it is a powerful and beautifully executed film that gives students a visual image of rural West Africa and opens up many productive avenues of discussion. It demonstrates that it is possible for change to come through the determination of a single strong woman like Collé, but only if she is able to rally her community—including the men and the traditional women—to her cause. The fact that this film was made by a man who is a greatly respected African elder (Sembène was born in 1923) models the necessary alliances that must occur to create the momentum for change: as long as men insist that they will only marry circumcised women, the practice will continue.

Moolaadé also clearly demonstrates that change must come from within African societies; it cannot be imposed from outside. The one outsider in Sembène's narrative, a traveling peddler from the city, meets a violent end because he is suspected of challenging local traditions. This is important for students to realize, since they often tend to imagine that quick interventions from outside—say, governments becoming signatories to human rights conventions—could put a stop to FGM once and for all. But as Nicholas Kristof and Sheryl WuDunn observe, "The impulse of Westerners to hold conferences and change laws has, on one issue after another, proved remarkably ineffective" (228). Instead, Kristof and WuDunn cite the Senegal-based nongovernmental organization Tostan as a successful model for grassroots organizing and deep, lasting change. Tostan was initially started by an American woman, Molly Melchin, who married a Senegalese man and recognized the importance of education in the struggle to eradicate the practice of FGM. Tostan trains local community activists, who speak the local dialects, to go into village communities and open up spaces for dialogue, learning, and reflection. "Hard-line efforts by abolitionists to coerce women to reject the practice and to stigmatize those who uphold their ancestral traditions as 'illiterate,' 'backward,' and against 'women's rights' and 'progress' are unacceptable," Ahmadu states unequivocally. Instead, the approach favored by Tostan, of respectfully presenting the facts to people and letting them make up their own minds, is the best way to work toward the gradual shift of the practice of FGM away from harmful cutting. "In the event that I ever have a daughter," Ahmadu says, "I would like her to be well-informed about the sociocultural and historical significance of the operation as well as its purported medical risks so that she can make up her own mind" (310).

Tostan educates communities and individuals about the dangers of FGM until they are ready and willing to outlaw the practice, offering classes that meet three times a week for two or three hours, over a period of three years. This is no quick fix but a slow, mind-altering process of community reflection that aims to proceed with what Gayatri Spivak calls "great tact," which is what "is called for if the effort is to draw forth consent rather than obedience" ("Righting Wrongs" 558). Since Tostan's founding in 1991, more than seven thousand communities from Djibouti, the Gambia, Guinea, Guinea-Bissau, Mali, Mauritania, Senegal, and Somalia have publicly declared their decision to abandon both FGM and child or forced marriages after participating in Tostan programs. Another excellent film for classroom use that shows this process of change is *Sarabah*, which documents the return of international rap star Sista Fa to her home village in Senegal, where she uses her own celebrity and talent, as well as the time-tested tools of Tostan, to successfully convince the village elders to give up the practice of FGM.

Action against FGM is taking place not just in small villages in Africa but also among African immigrant communities in some of the biggest and most cosmopolitan cities of the West. In *Bloodstains: A Child of Africa Reclaims Her Human Rights*, Koïta documents her transition from a happy, bright child growing up in a small Senegalese town, to a child bride who is married at thirteen to a cousin twenty years her senior and sent to live with him in Paris, to an empowered, trailblazing activist. Koïta's story is important because, unlike Korn, she is not the daughter of social elites, nor has she gained wealth and fame on her own, like the anti-FGM activists Waris Dirie and Ayaan Hirsi Ali. Koïta deals with the ordinary pressures of the sudden removal of her clitoris at age seven, with the attendant pain and trauma; marriage as a child to a stranger; the abrupt shift to a life as an immigrant woman in a foreign culture. Koïta's husband proves to be physically and emotionally abusive, and much of her narrative is dedicated to documenting her transition from a cowed, fearful teen mother, crowded into a small apartment with a rapidly growing family, including, eventually, a cowife, to an independent woman who educates herself, finds work, and gets herself and her children out of the reach of her abusive husband. Koïta finds support from French neighbors, other African women immigrants, and generous French social services and charitable organizations, showing once again that the struggle for empowerment may be enhanced by collaborative allies.

Koïta's story ends on a strong note, as she becomes the president of the European Network for the Eradication and Prevention of Female Genital Mutilation (Euro-Net-FGM). At the end of her testimonial, Koïta eloquently describes her journey as "an obstinate march that led me from the shadow of the mango tree to the light of international sorority, from an intimate and secret mutilation to the blaze of a public campaign trail" (212).

Testifiers like Koïta, Ahmadu, and Korn invite us to join them on their "obstinate march" toward the full enjoyment of their rights as global citizens. Through testimonial narratives, cultural outsiders can gain insight into the personal dimensions of the human rights violations that are presented at a broad, impersonal remove in the UDHR. Human rights conventions are essential as legislative policy guidelines and prescriptions, but they do not have the power to arouse compassionate empathy the way literature can. In rural locales in Africa, anti-FGM education often takes the form of creating plays to be performed for people who either cannot read or lack access to written materials. Whether in the oral, visual, or written literary tradition, the impulse is the same: to tell a new story with drama and passion, to reach the feeling place in the audience that can lead to deep social change. Even if students leave my seminar with no more than an increased awareness about the literature of human rights, this awareness is an essential first step to help them become ethical global citizens.

Notes

1. For background on the theory of testimonial literature, see Beverley, *Testimonio* and *Subalternity*.

2. The World Health Organization (WHO) takes the position that there is no medical rationale for FGM: "FGM has no health benefits, and it harms girls and women in many ways. It involves removing and damaging healthy and normal female genital tissue, and interferes with the natural functions of girls' and women's bodies. . . . WHO is particularly concerned about the increasing trend for medically trained personnel to perform FGM. WHO strongly urges health professionals not to perform such procedures" ("Female Genital Mutilation").

Neville Hoad

Sexual Orientation and Human Rights: *Walking with Shadows* in Nigeria

Jude Dibia's *Walking with Shadows* (2005), both heralded and damned as "the first gay Nigerian novel" (Uzoatu; Nwelu), can be characterized as a "coming-out narrative" set in a rapidly globalizing Nigeria (King, Burton, and Geise 376). The appellation "first gay Nigerian novel" represents a complicated claiming and may have as much to do with publishing's niche marketing as with the novel's explicit content. There is a long history of representations of homosexuality in Nigerian fiction, going back at least as far as Joe Golder in Wole Soyinka's *The Interpreters* (1965)—though, not accidentally, Golder is African American or, in the narrator's less charitable terms, "three-quarters white" (101). Such identity markers are significant in relation to human rights talk that, by definition, must claim the universal, and they render its geography and history unevenly visible at best.

In *Walking with Shadows*, a disgruntled former employee fired for embezzlement tells the family of the protagonist, Adrian (called Ebele by his family), that Adrian is gay. Not insignificantly the former employee had received this dangerous piece of information from a South African colleague of Adrian's. South Africa is the only country on the African continent that has an antidiscrimination clause on the grounds of sexual orientation in its constitution, for a range of complicated and contested reasons, and the survival of that clause is far from assured at the moment of writing (Hoad, Martin, and Reid; Reid). In something like an emergency family meeting after the unwelcome disclosure, Adrian has the following conversation with his two brothers, Chika and Chiedu:

> "Ebele, how can you say this?" Chiedu asked: "You know what the Bible says about homosexuals . . . God forbids it. The law says it's a felony for a man to practice sodomy."
>
> "I know what the Bible says," Adrian said. "And it is open to different interpretations. The law you speak about has been dictated by the society we live in . . . some societies in this country state that if an unmarried woman has sex with a man and it's discovered, the woman should be stoned to death, and that is law. Please tell me, because the law says so, does that make it right?"
>
> "Come on, Ebele," Chiedu said. "These are different things."
>
> "How so?" Adrian challenged. "Sharia law is law for the Muslims in this country and many others, who are we to say that what their law dictates is wrong? And if it is right, does that make it okay? If our society was positive about homosexuality or silent on the issue, would being gay be acceptable to you then?" (52)

This deceptively simple piece of dialogue between the brothers opens up a range of formidable and fascinating questions for the teaching of human rights in literary and cultural studies. Even just an initial parse of the passage raises the problems of the relation of law and morality, law and religion, text and interpretation, cross-cultural or religious judgment and social norms, to name a few. Revealingly, neither the terms nor the ideas of human rights appear, let alone have any critical purchase on the brothers' conversation.

Instead, we are in the complicated commonsense debates about the nature, role, and place of the law in regulating, ignoring, protecting, and prohibiting people's sexual behavior that can just as easily be found in the newish place of the undergraduate human rights classroom. The material, intellectual, ideological, and institutional determinants of such a place will vary somewhat, and vary from a literary or cultural studies classroom where human rights as a theme or unit is being taught. In the English department at the University of Texas, Austin, where I teach (mostly), my colleague Barbara Harlow has been teaching a course called Literature and Human Rights for nearly twenty years now. In 2011, the Center for Women's and Gender Studies received a grant from the Embrey Foundation to develop a curriculum on gender and human rights inter alia. I teach a course called Gender Identity, Sexual Orientation, and Human Rights under the auspices of that grant. The course is also flagged as an Undergraduate Signature course, part of a university-wide core-course initiative in response to a range of debates across often divergent pedagogical concerns from interdisciplinarity to shared college experience to service learning to the value of study-abroad programs to résumé building to the sometimes deserved cynicism of the accusation of doing good to get ahead (Kennedy). While there may be aspects of my institutional experience that may be singular, I suspect that the institutionalization of the study and practice of human rights is on the ascendant in the United States research university, whether human rights is seen as an object of research, a career, a justification for certain kinds of advocacy, an opportunity of volunteering, or an emerging moral hegemony.

How would I teach this passage in these or similar institutional circumstances, in terms of a fictional representation of a series of public debates shrunk and intensified into a family conflict? Teaching a literary text like *Walking with Shadows* in a human rights classroom, or to make human rights content and approaches relevant to such a text, requires a dialectical relation between literary close reading and supplementary contextualizing materials, with the clear proviso that neither the novel nor the background reading are reducible to each other. A familiarity with most of the arguments presented can be assumed. Almost all my students will know what Chiedu means by "You know what the Bible says about homosexuals . . . God forbids it." Like Chiedu, they might know that the reference is to the proscription in Leviticus 18.22, or, like Adrian, they might be able to open it up to interpretation by invoking other biblical passages and injunctions and by placing the Bible loosely in its moment and place of writing. Depending on the religious and political convictions of the students, this conversation can get contentious quickly, but I let them run with it, constrained by the powerful, unspoken conventions of classroom civility. The discussion can begin to assume a mimetic relation to the passage. Returning to the passage's literariness can help diffuse intense feelings on both sides; I ask, Whose position in the argument is most sympathetic in the novel? Whose consciousness does the narrative voice ask us to experience from the inside?

The next sentence in the passage—"the law says it's a felony for a man to practice sodomy"—may be vestigially familiar. The United States Supreme Court declared sodomy laws unconstitutional in *Lawrence v. Texas* in 2003, just two years before the publication of the novel. The current public debates around gay marriage in the United States ensure that students can refer to difficult arguments about religious freedom and freedom from discrimination for sexual minorities, imaginings of the separation of church and state in the United States Constitution, and secularism more generally.

On the other hand, almost no knowledge of Nigeria can be assumed—although, given the demographics of the state of Texas, the oil industry presence in Houston, and the fact that Yoruba is the only African language taught on campus, there is a good chance that there will be a Nigerian or Nigerian American student in the class, but I am careful not to place the burden of representation on any such student.

The simple question of how Nigeria acquired a sodomy law opens up complicated questions of colonial histories and legacies. Chapter 42, section 214 of Nigeria's criminal code criminalizes consensual same-sex sexual conduct between adults, allowing prison sentences of up to fourteen years: "Any person who has carnal knowledge of any person against the order of nature or permits a male person to have carnal knowledge of him or her against the order of nature is guilty of a felony and is liable to imprisonment for fourteen years" ("Sodomy Laws"). More recently, sharia penal codes, introduced in northern Nigeria in 1999, expressly criminalize what is termed "sodomy" (Ostien). Adrian's invocation of sharia law both localizes and globalizes the religious questions broached earlier. Risking a casual "Islamophobia" and relying on what he imagines to be Chiedu's anti-Islam sentiments, Adrian makes a recognizable liberal gambit. In short, if you oppose "gay rights," you are a demonized religious fanatic. In providing the necessary context for the novel for students, I would also distribute copies of the relevant Nigerian law, direct them to links to United Nations statements on sexual orientation as a human right, refer them to a few excellent blogs on the raging debate around homosexuality in Africa, and ask the students to bring in newspaper articles about the proposed antigay legislation in Uganda and Nigeria. These events are unsettling, unsettled, and unfolding and require continual monitoring, revising of positions, and ongoing research that can form an important part of classroom pedagogy.

Adrian imagines and asserts that he has no recourse, legal or otherwise, against the disgruntled fired employee: "Although under the company's staff handbook an individual could not be discriminated against due to his sexual orientation, Adrian knew that in practice if you are anything other than heterosexual, you would be discriminated against" (156). DialPlus, the United States–based multinational corporation for which Adrian works, thus clearly has policies inflected by an idea of sexual orientation as a protected human rights category. Here one can begin to ask students to think about competing notions of sovereignty at play in a globalized world. How might the company policy relate to the Nigerian national legal regime? How might these kinds of policies relate to the long debate within several African national and international public spheres on the claim that homosexuality is a decadent Western import?

I suspect that the company's name, DialPlus, could feel anachronistic and quaint for students today, if they even remember prewireless Internet technologies. How might the name contradict the phenomenon of leapfrogging technologies in developing countries (Soete)? Cell phone use in countries like Nigeria took off much faster and captured a much bigger share of the market earlier than in the United States, because fewer Nigerians ever had landlines (D. Smith). Could one use DialPlus's antidiscrimination policy to think critically and broadly about the relations between huge global forces like transnational capital and human rights and the civil society institutional sites where human rights ideas and policies have taken hold? The relatively recent arrival of sexual orientation into protected category status in university antidiscrimination language and policy may allow for some very local research assignments. At the University of Texas, Austin, there is an antidiscrimination statement on the grounds of sexual orientation in the official policy ("President's Statement"), but there are no domestic partnership benefits, since Texas has a constitutional amendment defining marriage as between one man and one woman (Texas Constitution).

In January 2006, shortly after the publication of the novel, the Nigerian minister of justice, Bayo Ojo, presented to the Federal Executive Council the Act to Make Provisions for the Prohibition of Relationship between Persons of the Same Sex, Celebration of Marriage by Them, and for Other Matters Connected Therewith, or the Same Sex Marriage (Prohibition) Bill. The proposed bill would supplement the colonial-era sodomy law by criminalizing a range of activities well beyond the sex act. If passed, the bill would provide a five-year prison sentence for any individual who "goes through the ceremony of marriage with a person of the same sex" (sec. 8.1); "performs, witnesses, aids or abets the ceremony of same sex marriage" (sec. 8.2); or "is involved in the registration of gay clubs, societies and organizations, sustenance, procession or meetings, publicity and public show of same sex amorous relationship directly or indirectly in public and in private" (sec. 7.3) ("Same Sex Marriage"). An amended version of the bill was passed by the Nigerian Senate in November 2011 and the House of Representatives in 2013 and awaits the approval of President Goodluck Jonathan before becoming law (Gambrell). (We are in a multiply ironic and belated reworking of Michel Foucault's famous dictum in *The History of Sexuality*: "The sodomite had been a temporary aberration; the homosexual was now a species" [43].) I think this piece of proposed legislation could also be used to introduce students to some of the key problems in lesbian and gay studies as it moved, and did not, into queer theory—the so-called essentialist/social constructionist debates, Eve Kosofsky Sedgwick's reframing of the problem of homosexuality into universalizing and minoritarian positions—with these discussions serving as something between necessary background and distraction.

The bill seeks to criminalize a range of social actors, potentially quite far from the scene of sodomy. The draft bill seems directed at prohibiting gay people's entry into civil society by criminalizing the registration of gay organizations and proscribing access to public recognition by banning the public display of a "same sex amorous relationship," along with the adoption of children by lesbian or gay couples or individuals. Gesturing to the uncertain global legal terrain on which the recognition or proscription of homosexuality is increasingly taking place, the draft bill would also invalidate same-sex relationships formally entered into or recognized in foreign jurisdictions.

After its first reading in the Nigerian Senate on 11 April 2006, the scope of the bill was extended to make "any individual who witnesses, celebrates with or supports couples involved in same-sex relationships" subject to a prison term ("Same Sex Marriage (Prohibition) Bill"). Imagining students' horror at some of these provisions, I would also have them read the text of the United States Defense of Marriage Act (DOMA), signed into law by President Clinton in 1996, and the 2013 United States Supreme Court decision in *Windsor v. United States*, which repealed section 3 of DOMA, alongside excerpts from Florida's recently overturned 1977 gay adoption ban (Almanzar) and Northern Ireland's recently upheld one (N. Donnelly). This comparative context is important for an understanding of how contested the idea of sexual orientation rights is, even in the putatively liberal West.

In October 2011, the British prime minster, David Cameron, threatened to suspend foreign aid to African countries with laws banning homosexuality—one type of bilateral aid known as general budget support, which would not necessarily reduce the overall amount of aid to any one country. He framed his decision in terms of human rights: "This is an issue where we are pushing for movement, we are prepared to put some money behind what we believe. But I'm afraid that you can't expect countries to change overnight. Britain is one of the premier aid givers in the world. We want to see countries that receive our aid adhering to proper human rights. We are saying that is one of the things that determines our aid policy" ("Cameron Threat"). (A bill legalizing same-sex marriage in Britain become law in July 2013.) Similar sentiments and threats were echoed by President Barack Obama after the Nigerian Senate passed the Same Sex Marriage (Prohibition) Bill (Nsehe). In a familiar scenario of unintended consequences, Cameron's actions divided the Nigerian human rights community who had formerly been solidly against the bill (Ibiwoye). These events can be used in the classroom to reinvigorate questions of the politics and historicity of human rights frames and institutions, through, for example, discussions about the accusations against human rights as the new moral imperialism from the Global North; the knot of the relation of self-determination, which can be accommodated into a human rights framework, and cultural relativism, which cannot; and the way human rights in this instance may be seen as much as a symptom of injustice in a neoliberal world as a suggested solution.

Bringing these questions back to the novel can be awkward because I find myself trapped in the paleonymy of the terms: *gay*, *sexual orientation*, *human*. What does Adrian seem to want protected, recognized, remedied? It appears in the novel as some kind of deep and necessarily incoherent psychological interiority of gayness:

> I have come to learn . . . that being gay has nothing to do with the physical action of sex nor a person's sexual preference, be it with the opposite sex or same sex. Sleeping with a man or a woman will always remain the individual's choice. I am gay because it is who I am. It is the way I see the world. It is the way I reason and live. It is waking up in the morning and going to bed at night. It is listening to music and loving it. It is watching a movie and wanting to see it over again. It is laughing when I am happy and crying when I am sad. It is appreciating the simple things that life brings and not the act of sexual intercourse. Sex on its own is a physical expression of love or lust. I could love a woman because of the qualities she possesses and still be gay. A man can be gay all his life without actually sleeping with another man. Can you understand this? (Dibia 207)

I find myself in the position of Ada, Adrian's wife, in this passage in that I don't really understand "this." But the passage does touch on many of the paradoxes in understanding the right to sexual orientation as a human right in the simultaneous effacement and assertion of gay difference. Is the right to be gay the right to be the same as everyone else, or is it the right to be different, or is it both? Adrian almost seems to agree on the terms but not on the positions of the 2006 bill that the rubric of sodomy is entirely insufficient for an understanding of gayness.

We move through a series of descriptions of ordinariness—"It is waking up in the morning and going to bed at night. It is listening to music and loving it. . . . It is laughing when I am happy and crying when I am sad." These activities are part of the lifeworld that a human rights regime seeks to protect, but none of them are named in human rights legislation or covenants. Adrian's deeply felt and incoherent attempt to explain gayness simply assumes its phenomenological reality, whereas elsewhere the novel will suggest and refuse nature/nurture arguments and typological ones on the familiar lines of effeminacy: "He was a sissy. And everyone hated a sissy. He cried easily, he was too frail and he just wasn't like any of his brothers. This on its own did not make him gay, but Chika had somehow known. There was always the suspicion" (125). The novel's overall engagement with social constructionist positions is more circumspect and broaches the problem of imagined Western taint:

> [T]he smile froze on Adrian's face. Yahaya's boldness was not something he was expecting. He didn't believe that he was so far removed from the scene that now it was perfectly tolerable for men to be so open about their homosexuality. This was not the West where it was to a degree acceptable. But then again, Yahaya looked like someone who had been exposed to the western culture and was well adjusted to it. (117)

Importantly, the strongest elements of what could be diagnosed as homophobia in the novel are also represented as alien to the novel's wobbly but frequently monolithic construction of "the African culture." The pastor who, in a disturbing scene, quite literally attempts to beat the gayness out of Adrian is initially described in the following terms:

> The most distinguishing thing Adrian could remember was the nasal American inflection in his voice when he preached. It was quite easy to believe while listening to Pastor Matthew's sermon in his church that the congregation was in faraway Harlem, New York, in one of those black Pentecostal churches with screaming, over-gesticulating pastors who preached of impending doom, hell fire and brimstone. (185)

Adrian's observation here can remind us of the role of American evangelicals in African sexual politics. So far, it appears that United States–based evangelical leaders were not as intimately involved in the making of the Same Sex Marriage (Prohibition) Bill as they were in the Ugandan proposed legislation, though the public support of a leading United States evangelical, Rick Warren, for the Nigerian archbishop, Peter Akinola, has been extensively documented (Wilson).

What is clear is that the novel's version of valorized gayness is committed to some of the very notions of respectability that are the powerful normative forces that produce Adrian's vulnerability on the question of his contested sexual identity. The novel's class politics (and, to a lesser extent, its gender politics) are uncritically bourgeois. Adrian is a rising young executive who drives a new Mercedes Benz and lives in a gated community. He would thus have easier access to legal redress than the vast majority of Nigerians. The narrator of *Walking with Shadows* claims, "The legal system in the country was not equipped to deal with anything remotely resembling 'sexual harassment' and Adrian knew that if indeed there was anything like a sexual harassment law in the country it was not meant to favor homosexuals; in fact there was a law against homosexuals in the country" (156–57). A security guard at DialPlus has accused Adrian of making sexual advances, attempting to turn a potential victim into a perpetrator. Adrian's situation in the novel can open up a discussion of many of the critiques that have been leveled at human rights institutions and practices in their attempt to create more just societies—for example, the question of who has access to legal redress, even when there is a human rights regime in place. Litigation is complicated and expensive. This is not a problem for Adrian. He is rich, educated, successful, male (and good-looking), with access to the intellectual and material resources to hire a lawyer, but the human rights regime he might be able to appeal to is a multinational corporation's antidiscrimination policy in a country with a sodomy law still on the statute books and even more restrictive legislation in the works. In addition, whom does he see as worthy of respect and dignity? "I know what you mean," Adrian says. "I got hit on tonight. As shocked as I am, when I look back on it I am sort of glad that gay men are finally coming out of hiding. I'm not talking about the divas who are so loud and effeminate but some good-looking professional type men who exude confidence" (131). The not-so-hidden norms invoked here complicate the question of who can or should be the bearers of "gay" human rights and who—socially, if not legally—should remain abject and perhaps deserving of being discriminated against.

Who is positioned to have access to human rights claims? This can also become a difficult question for people who live under a legal regime with more robust human rights protections. The South African journalist Mark Gevisser interviewed a young black South African drag queen about the new South African constitution, which included sexual orientation in its equality clause. She had this to say: "My darling, it [the constitution] means sweet motherfucking nothing at all. You can rape me, rob me, what am I going to do when you attack me? Wave the constitution in your face? I'm just a nobody black queen. But you know what? Ever since I heard about that constitution I feel free inside" (qtd. in Gevisser 136). Feeling free inside is not nothing, and it is something that the fictional Adrian seems to crave, although he seems less structurally vulnerable to violence than this "nobody black queen."

The narrative is produced in Standard English, except for a few moments of dialect and patois, which are uttered by the service-industry workers and, interestingly, Abdul, Adrian's happily coupled friend from the gay demimonde, which Adrian renounced when he married Ada. Abdul, in his language, seems to bridge the world of respectability that Adrian so fervently wishes to inhabit and the massive informal economy of a city like Lagos. Local dialect in the novel functions as local color. The novel explicitly valorizes Ada's excellent English. Ada, in thinking of cultural authenticity, is occasionally bothered by the European artifacts she sells in her interior design business but not by her impeccable English, and she offers one of the most hilarious, if irresponsible, sentences in close to three hundred years, if one goes all the way back to Edward Gibbon: "She still strongly believed that the concept of homosexuality was very much not in the African culture. It was an import like the violent rap music, sophisticated armed robbery, and nudity as a form of fashion, and all such rubbish" (149). I suspect some students will be appalled by Ada's levity, others amused. (I am both.) Both responses and the varying positions that enable them can be explored in class discussion, with a nod to what the political work of trivializing, as opposed to legislating, can do. Questions of tone and patois allow for the question of imagined readership. Who is the novel written to, for, from, and about?

In relation to the question of a human right to sexual orientation, I find myself once again returning to Gayatri Spivak's definition of deconstruction as "the critique of a structure that you cannot wish not to inhabit" ("Making" 794). That is my position. I certainly do not expect it to be my students'.

Karen Elizabeth Bishop

On Teaching the Close Reading of Torture Literature: An Approximation

> *If from the experience of torture any knowledge at all remains that goes beyond the plain nightmarish, it is that of a great amazement and a foreignness in the world that cannot be compensated by any sort of subsequent human communication.*
>
> —Jean Améry, *At the Mind's Limits*

> *Intense pain is also language-destroying: as the content of one's world disintegrates, so the content of one's language disintegrates; as the self disintegrates, so that which would express and project the self is robbed of its source and its subject.*
>
> —Elaine Scarry, *The Body in Pain*

In preparing for an oral presentation in a class on the history and literature of the legacies of torture, a student of mine stopped by our local stationer's to commission photocopies of a judicious selection of the now infamous Abu Ghraib photographs. She had intended to use the images to supplement her talk on torture and democracy, an effort foiled when the clerk refused to copy the photos and told her that she—not the photographs, not their content, not their context—was sick. The unwarranted judgment concerned me for my student's sake but also for what it revealed about how the so-called Abu Ghraib photographs have been digested since their controversial public dissemination in 2004. As far as I have been able to discern, the American reaction to the outlaw images has focused on the very fact of their existence, their digital reproducibility, the horror that it should be United States soldiers perpetrating such "abuses," or on what these images might reveal about the cultural and social values of a democratic United States of America. The reaction in the mass media, in the academy, and on the street has been an inward turn. This is part of what is laid bare in the visceral, misplaced reaction of our New England shop clerk: *you are sick*, he says. He displaces his attention to the images before him—reroutes it away from the photographs and toward my student—and in doing so betrays a kind of paradoxical and unacknowledged solipsism that allows us to look anywhere but at the suffering that is documented in the photos.

Part of the problem is certainly a human one; it is physically and psychically difficult to go through the Abu Ghraib photographs, as well as any torture report or narrative. Part of it may be that we do not know how to look at these documents, what to make of them, or how to read them. Maybe we do not know what to do with what they show us and what we learn from them; for where might we direct and to what might we apply this new and foreign knowledge? But perhaps the difficulty in examining, digesting, living with these photographs has to do with the fact that physical pain—no matter how close, how captured, how evident—always remains inaccessible. We cannot access the pain of others. So we—you, me, our young shop clerk—do not know what to do with it when it is splayed out across a page, crouched bound in a corner, or wired and hooded and balanced precariously atop a box. For empathy, as Elaine Scarry works out in her landmark *The Body in Pain*, constitutes a distance that is not more than an approach, an approximation, a move toward.

But this move toward, this moving outward away from ourselves is, as Jean-François Lyotard identifies in his short essay "The Other's Rights," premised on the possibility that "what makes human beings alike is the fact that every human being carries within him the figure of the other. The likeness that they have in common follows from the difference of each to each" (181). This constitutive otherness, proposes Lyotard by way of Hannah Arendt, provides the fundament for human rights. Being human means being more than human, indeed other than only human, so that we may live among others, speak with others, enjoy the same human rights as others. Humankind is innately othered in joining a human community; to be other is to be a "fellow man," in Arendt's words.

To recognize this "figure of the other in me," Lyotard continues, is also an Aristotelian fundament of pedagogy, a defining component of the relationship between teacher and student defined by a taciturn potentiality, an estrangement, the responsibility to say precisely what we do not know how to say, which is always a form of newness (184–85). The recognition of this selfsame other that is engendered in the teacher-student relationship—wherein the teacher, because he or she has something as yet unknown, as yet unheard to say, is "the figure of the *Other* in all its separateness"—requires a moment of stillness. The student is here silent before the unknown. "The suspension of interlocution," writes Lyotard, "imposes a silence and that silence is good. It does not undermine the right to speak. It teaches the value of that right. It is the exercise necessary for excellence in speech" (185). And this excellence, in Lyotard's estimation, is of ethical purport. For this Levinasian silence we maintain as students before the foreign—the teacher, a language we do not yet understand, "the strangeness of another logic" (185)—in pedagogical interlocution provides for the right to speak and indeed the ethical necessity of excellence in speech, of articulating something other than what has been said before that announces something to the human community. Everything turns on the enunciation of this new knowledge. So, it seems, the Abu Ghraib photographs, which command at first a withholding of speech for our speculations to be sound, also require a speaking out, a speaking anew that confirms that we recognize this congenital figure of the other, this othered figure, even if and perhaps because he suffers a pain we cannot access.

How to inhabit these movements, if necessarily uncomfortably, is a difficult thing to teach. The proposition becomes yet more complicated when the object of study is not an image but instead the written text, and we ask our students to move toward the already failed prospect of knowing another's pain by way of the already failed intermediary of language. But the hermeneutic complexities of these mounting failures is to some extent mitigated when we ask our students to take on the impossible endeavor—itself a kind of necessary fiction—of accessing another's pain by way of invention or the outright fabrication proper to works of fiction. Pathos is at play here, certainly, for we get closer to the unrealizable proximity of pain and along the way learn better what is at stake in this task, by locating the language-destroying, self-destroying, world-destroying practice of torture within the context of literary creation. Herein the act of construction, with all its constitutive failures, houses destruction and reveals its structure, so that we can get closer to it. One of the ways we can get closest to approaching another's suffering is by reading closely. What follows, then, are some ideas about how to do just that—closely read torture literature—with the aim of proffering the pedagogical possibility that close-reading practices allow us to effectively assimilate the strangeness of the ambiguity, approach, and approximation that are, at least in my teaching experience, the difficult but rich rewards that torture literature offers up.

Close Reading in the Balance

Close reading is, in literary history, credited to the school of New Critics that dominated the American institutionalization of reading practices from the 1920s to the 1950s. Its supporters would argue that it teaches students how to take apart a text from the inside out, how to identify rhythm and meter, form and structure, trope and internal coherence. Surely, learning these skills cannot be a wasted endeavor. But the detractors of New Criticism would claim that this refined reading ability comes at too high a cost: namely, the concerted disregard of the sociohistorical conditions in which a text is produced, the cultural and economic contexts in which the reading of a text is performed, and the biography and influences of the author of a work. The import of these external conditions also cannot be underestimated. Close reading—to perform or not to perform—has traditionally hung in the balance between its formalist supporters and its perhaps more postmodern, shall we say, reprovers. But it seems to me that reading a text closely—however this might differ from close reading as an institutional stronghold—is an exercise that belongs to the realm of common sense. And taking into account the cultural, political, economic, and historical circumstances that both provide for a text and for its reading consumption also makes a lot of sense, because proving the internal coherence of a text will mean something less than it might if the external coherence—or, as often is the case, rich discontinuities—remain unconsidered.

Frank Lentricchia and Andrew DuBois, editors of the 2003 reader *Close Reading*, also imagine in the preface to their work "an ideal literary critic as one who commands and seamlessly integrates both styles of reading" (ix). They explain that the division of their anthology into two major sections—"Formalism (Plus)" and "After Formalism"—is "meant to suggest that formalist critics are always interested in the vast world which lies outside literature and that the nonformalists who have dominated literary criticism and theory over the last decades of the twentieth century do their most persuasive work by attending to the artistic character of the work before them." I agree with Lentricchia and DuBois, who effectively raze the proverbial battleground between formalists and nonformalists in their astute organization of exemplar close readings. But I will add, in the context of this essay, that when approaching texts that represent the breach of that most inalienable of human rights—the right not to be tortured—the significance of this double task is redoubled.

Precisely because torture is proper to a nonformalist realm, indeed a political and extralegal limbo, particular care must be paid to how its aesthetic narrativization takes place, in what generic form, and with recourse to what literary or rhetorical devices. Understanding how torture gets told is an access point to that inaccessible region of pain that longs to be discovered, if only so that it can be assimilated into something else, its burden reduced. This is to say, there is here an ethical imperative in close reading, even if any hope of closure is always necessarily failed. And it is an imperative that students are extraordinarily capable of taking up, taking on, and taking with them into other disciplines and other pursuits, so that learning how to decipher the image or the voice of the victim on the page and assimilating the often difficult, if necessary, self-reflection that accompanies this skill becomes a new way into the world.

It was within the context of the undergraduate program in history and literature at Harvard University that I had the opportunity to teach the course The Legacies of Torture. In keeping with the interdisciplinarity of the program, I designed the course with the intention of placing the reading of torture literature within particular historical contexts while asking students to analyze historical evidence of state-sponsored torture using the close-reading techniques proper to literary scholarship. This dual approach allowed students to cultivate a broad, nuanced, and responsible understanding of the aesthetic challenges and ethical complications inherent in representing human rights abuses on the page, in art, from memory, and in history.

The syllabus opened with a study of the philosophical and linguistic structures of torture, as well as its legal history, before moving on to a closer look at both historical and literary torture texts organized geographically into units on the Trujillo dictatorship (1930–61), the Marcos dictatorship (1965–86), the Pinochet regime (1973–90), the so-called Argentine Dirty War (1976–83), the Iranian Revolution (1978–79), and the Iraq War (2003–11). As historians, we looked at United Nations conventions, legal proclamations, speeches, maps, declassified government documents from the United States and abroad, news articles, documentary journalism, transcripts of interviews, torture reports, and documentary film; as literary critics, we looked at novels, plays, poetry, literary autobiography, memoir, the graphic novel, and film. As students of aesthetics, we considered how each of these genres took up the difficult task of representing an experience that, by all accounts, lies outside the intelligible boundaries of language.

Among other assignments, the course required that each student write two close readings—one literary, one historical—and we spent a significant portion of our class cultivating these reading techniques and going through texts closely as a group. We used these readings as a way to address some of the central considerations that underpinned the course, including the following: How has torture been historically defined, especially given the recent revisions of its legal definition proffered by the Bush administration? How is torture connected, historically, to ideals of truth and, theoretically, to the structure of language? In what ways is torture documented and not documented historically and in literature? What are the aesthetic and ethical responsibilities and challenges of representing torture in literature? And, finally, how do we responsibly, in academic scholarship, comment on, evaluate, criticize, and write about what we uncover in torture literature? Ultimately, cultivating and refining close-reading techniques allowed students to better navigate the estranged voices of the survivors of torture, both real and fictional, even as students learned to reassess their difficult proximity to how the meaning of torture is made.

Close Reading, Up Close

We used close reading in this class in three ways: as an important hermeneutic exercise in its own right; as a way to enter a text during a classroom discussion; and as pieces of scholarly evidence that supported larger claims, as, for example, those put forth in the students' final papers. In teaching how to undertake a close reading, I asked students first to perform a reading as an end unto itself before discussing how to wield it as evidence integrated into a longer scholarly work. In a handout, I introduced the goals of close reading before giving step-by-step instructions for performing one and then using the analysis as proof of a larger argument. I began by explaining:

> A close reading is a three-part exercise. The first part is when you get your hands dirty and work closely with the text to determine how it functions. The second part is when you take a step back to imagine—via these observations—what a passage might mean. The third part is your attempt to connect your close reading of a passage to the larger text as a whole. Be sure not to skip step one. This is the most important step because it serves as proof for your ideas. Without it, you will be, literally, jumping to conclusions.
>
> The goal of a close reading is to show how an author creates meaning on the page via language. In order to show how meaning is constructed, you have to determine how a passage functions. Only after you have analyzed *how* meaning is made can you offer up possible conclusions about *what* that meaning might be. A good, convincing close reading will explain how a passage functions first and then, and only then, explain what it might mean.

What's crucial here is that students learn to deal with a text on its own terms before offering up possible interpretations. This is sometimes an awkward shift for students who have long viewed extracting thematic meaning from a text as the primary purpose of reading.

The first literary close-reading assignment was due in the fifth week of class, early enough that students would have plenty of time to continue building on their close-reading skills throughout the rest of the semester but late enough that we had already spent a month honing them aloud when going through texts together as a group. For this assignment, I asked my students to analyze a passage from Jessica Hagedorn's 1990 novel, *Dogeaters*. The decidedly postmodern *Dogeaters* details the lives of a wild cast of characters living in Manila that include a ten-year-old narrator, a dictator and his wife, a beauty pageant queen, the owner of several multinational corporations, a senator, a gay prostitute and DJ, leftist revolutionaries, movie stars, members of the upper class, orphans from the lower class, and the drug addicts and criminals who populate both economic spheres and everything in between. Hagedorn draws from history and popular culture; she cites canonical works of literature just as easily as she refers to a steady lineup of classic film; she mixes English with Spanish with Tagalog, integrates a variety of mixed media into the novel, and relies throughout on multiple typographical strategies. The novel, in short, is a fabulous heteroglossic, intertextual, intergeneric, popular, political, and transnational mess. Working out how the novel works, especially how it integrates a torture scene into the narrative only forty pages from the book's end, is challenging indeed.

I asked students to perform a three-page close literary analysis of any portion of the split passage that begins on page 214 with "Thirst-quencher to the stars" and ends on page 215 with "— isn't that ingenious?"). This selection is a long passage that intercalates the text of a radio melodrama called *Love Letters*, radio commercials for TruCola, and the torture of the deposed Miss Philippines, Daisy Avila, who has taken up with a leftist rebel. Daisy is repeatedly raped and tortured—in a scene that is highlighted in bolded text that occurs always between parentheses—by a general and his cronies, while the soap opera and its commercials play in the background. The torture scene comprises the questions of interrogation, the general's reflections on Bing Crosby's "White Christmas," his exhibition for Daisy of photographs of other victims who have been tortured, and, although outside the scope of what I asked the students to analyze, a gang-rape that ends with the general calling Daisy "hija" ("daughter") and promising "to make her dance," a common euphemism in torture lexicon for torture by electric cattle prod (216). There is a lot to deal with here.

While I often assign specific short passages for close reading, here I wanted students to select for themselves an excerpt from the long passage, so that their selection already functioned as a kind of criticism. Students compellingly wrote, among other things, on how the juxtaposition of the radio melodrama and the torture informed how readers might digest the torture scene; on the use of bilingualism in the lyrics of the "TruCola Calypso" playing in the background; and on the use of punctuation and typography in the interrogation scene. I would like to cite, by way of example of the fine textual readings that a close analysis can proffer, a portion of one student's close literary reading of the following passage, which depicts the general exposing Daisy to the photographs of past torture victims: "'Look—' the General shoves the last snapshot in front of her averted face. 'Look—my men rearranged him totally. A styrofoam cup where his brains should be—isn't that ingenious?'" (215). Daniela Nogueira, then a third-year government concentrator, writes:

> The first word in the passage is rife with meaning, prompting us to consider several questions. First, the separation of the word "look" from the rest of the sentence lends the word added importance; it no longer has to compete with the other words. In fact, it is so important that the General says the command even before shoving the snapshot

> at Daisy. The importance of the word "look" is only reinforced by its repetition, in which "look" remains separated from the rest of the sentence by an em dash. Why not a comma, instead of an em dash? Why not an exclamation point? The em dash is significant because it forces physical and mental distance between "look" and the following sentence. Isolated in this way, the command to "look" appears to be coming from nowhere and no one, detached from the following words or lines. This floating command suggests that not only Daisy but also everyone else in this scene must "look"—even the readers. Indeed, the imperative mood of "look" demands our attention, even though Hagedorn knows that we cannot physically see the snapshot. Our inability to see suggests that the command to "look" is directed at the entire scene, not just the snapshot. This expansion of the command to "look" is reinforced by Hagedorn's decision to make "look's" connection to the snapshot rather tenuous. The General does not directly order Daisy to look *at the snapshot.* He merely instructs her to look—without saying at what exactly—and places the snapshot before her. This tenuous link allows Hagedorn the ambiguity she needs to expand the "look" command beyond Daisy to the audience, to us. In doing so, we have become part of Hagedorn's story. We are witnesses.

This reading bodes well from the outset precisely because Nogueira has selected such a short passage; this will allow her the space to explicate in detail how she thinks Hagedorn uses language to manifest meaning on the page, the essential goal, in my estimation, of any close reading. She performs an analysis of how the imperative "look" and its attendant punctuation function both within the text and on a metanarrative level that investigates how Hagedorn renders the reader a necessary witness to Daisy's torture. Nogueira deals with the textuality of the passage first and then uses what she observes to work out how the passage functions as a larger whole and indeed as a key moment that informs how we read the novel. This marriage of textual specificity and attention to thematic and strategic import is the earmark of the finest of close readings. But, again, reflections on possible thematics or the larger significance of a text should be attempted only after a detailed analysis of how the author creates meaning on the page. Commenting on *what* a passage means before working out *how* it means often results in unfounded explanation or, worse, extrapolation. I happily accept close readings that do not even mention theme or larger significance but instead remain grounded in close textual reading. Students quickly, and gratifyingly, learn just how much space on the page this exercise can take up. Nogueira's reading, however, proffers the best of both, an integrated application of meaning to text.

The Figure of the Other

The above close reading proves how Hagedorn wields language to construct a deftly placed and generically complicated torture scene. But it also works out the strategies that the author employs to implicate the reader as a necessary, if always contingent, witness to the torture scene. In this way, insomuch as this reader identifies herself in the work, the reading also serves as evidence of how close reading can bring students closer to a text and thus closer to understanding the challenges of representing torture, to comprehending what it means that torture remains essentially unrepresentable, and to grasping the significance of working one's hermeneutic way toward something that lies always beyond complete understanding. The close and careful reading and analysis of torture literature allows students to inhabit the unknowable and still find knowledge in that foreign realm. For if our students can work out how meaning works, instead of moving directly to what means what, then they can find the genesis of knowledge anywhere.

Working through the mechanics of closely reading torture texts also provides students something identifiable, material, and concrete to hang onto during a learning process whose end result is never more than a necessary and fertile ambiguity. As they take on the task of interpreting and trying to make sense of what survivors' voices, real or fictional, reveal to us about the experience of torture, tropes and typography and textual machinations prove both stable points of departure and of reference. They allow students to return to the very structure of language as proof and possibility while working out the structure of torture and its psychological, political, and cultural aftermaths.

Close reading, then, allows students to approach, to start to envision, to begin to sound out the prolonged suffering that torture engenders. That sounding out requires a careful and quiet move toward the page; a silence before the unfamiliar interlocutors that speak, that teach through literatures of torture; and a taking up of, if uncomfortably, that Lyotardian "labour of estrangement" to learn to make sense of the unknown language the stranger—he who makes us most human—speaks ("Other's Rights" 185). When students then go on to speak for themselves, to announce to another something other than what has already been said, to in turn point to the experiences and voices of a foreign suffering in their own intellectual work, they can be sure they have witnessed something sound from within the void. And if they can work out what is sound in a text—its rhythm and beat, its syllables and synecdoches, the metaphor and metonym that hold it together and explode it apart—they might espy, if from a distance, that close figure of the other.

Note

I am indebted to the students of my Harvard spring 2010 course The Legacies of Torture: Eva Harvey, Katherine Lugo, Natalie McBride, Melanie Naranjo, Daniela Nogueira, Catherine Ntube, Beau Tremitiere, and Nicolas Zuvia; this essay would not have been possible without the benefit of their insightfulness and intellectual openness. A particular thanks to Kathy Lugo and to Daniela Nogueira for permission to use her close reading as exemplum. I would also like to thank the students of my spring and summer 2010 graduate proseminars, Human Rights and Latin American Literature, at the Harvard University Extension School, whose collaborative insight into the close reading of torture texts proved invaluable.

The writing of this essay was generously assisted by an ACLS New Faculty Fellows Award, with the support of the Andrew W. Mellon Foundation.

Brenda Carr Vellino

Cultivating the Translocal Citizen Witness: Contemporary Human Rights Poetry as "Remembrance/Pedagogy"

> Some would ask us what does poetry have to do with the life of a city, the life of the world; some would go further and say . . . what does poetry have to do with citizenship. . . . The language of citizenship is a capacious language, it is a language where we engage and elaborate ideas of equality, social justice, social responsibility, and social well-being. I propose, that it is in this language that . . . poetry may live. (Brand, "Poet Laureate Speech")

If the "capacious language" of citizenship is the matrix for the public life of poetry as the Trinidadian Canadian poet Dionne Brand suggests, I propose that the reverse is also true: the capacious language of poetry might cultivate modes of socially responsible citizenship among its readers. Human rights witness poems, especially, call into being ethical responsiveness as a practice of critical citizenship. The United States poet Carolyn Forché emphasizes how witness poetry, marked by its passage through extremity, "calls upon the reader, who is the *other* of this work, to be in turn marked by what such language makes present before her, what it holds open and begets in the reader, for witness begets witness" ("Reading" 137). Notwithstanding the significant intervention of Forché's 1993 anthology, *Against Forgetting: Twentieth-Century Poetry of Witness*, most literary human rights studies focus almost exclusively on testimonial, legal, fictional, and cinematic narrative (Dawes, *That the World*; Goldberg, *Beyond Terror*; Slaughter, *Human Rights*; Schaffer and Smith; Hesford). More so than narrative often does, primary and secondary witness poems summon the reader to the position of cowitness in the testimonial transaction. As mediated secondary and tertiary witnesses, readers are invited by such poems into classroom conversations about engaged citizenship as a standpoint of relational "response-ability" toward speakers, subject positions, and historical contexts activated by human rights witness poems.

Human rights poets frequently use the second-person pronoun *you*, constructed witness figures and subjectivity, and embodied tropes of witnessing such as eyes, ears, tongues, lips, and voice to conjure the reader as a kind of cowitness, without whom the testimonial transaction is incomplete, as Shoshana Felman and Dori Laub demonstrate in *Testimony* (71, 85). Consider Forché's testament to the death squad years in El Salvador in "The Colonel." This poem closes with the arresting image of a bag of human ears being swept off an opulent dinner table. These ears "pressed to the ground" capture a "scrap" of the ruthless colonel's voice; they call on readers to catch the echo of his voice to amplify the chain of witnessing. Through its rhetoric of speaker, voice, and address, poetry enables intimate, intense encounters with witness subjectivity. As a secondary witness to the witnesses, a reader may have his or her sense of entitlement, privilege, and beneficiary status unsettled by questions of positional distance, spectatorship, complicity, and commodification.

My engagement with contemporary human rights poetry starts with the premise that all societies are postconflict; that is, they are marked by the legacy of brutal application of state, military, economic, institutional, or social power, which continues to affect local indigenous communities as well as other diasporic and social minorities. Transitional justice processes and studies on postconflict societies have focused mainly on legal and quasi-legal trials and commissions, although collections like Kieran McEvoy and Lorna McGregor's *Transitional Justice from Below* have given more priority to the work of local activist networks often catalyzed by survivors or families of victims. It is within this context of poststate reckoning "from below" that I situate the work of many poets writing in the aftermath of atrocity. I am interested in the ways human rights poetry sometimes works as an adjunct to the mandate of official transitional justice initiatives by contributing to the alternative memory archive; sometimes enacts complex reckoning with aftermath legacies for victims, survivors, perpetrators, beneficiaries, and bystanders; and sometimes envisions what coexistence projects and conflict transformation between former or current antagonists might look like. Speakers and protagonists in human rights poems take up the labor of mourning like unappeased Antigone figures who relentlessly keep those vulnerable bodies and subjectivities positioned outside the law in the public eye. Part of the work of public mourning for human rights poets involves representing traumatic and unresolved aftereffects that exceed state mechanisms of social redress. In what follows, I establish the conjunction of witness poetry, translocal citizenship, and "remembrance/pedagogy" before turning to the work of the Armenian American poet Peter Balakian as a case study for creating a genocide poetry unit.

Translocal Citizen Witness

> . . . let's never discount it—within every official, statistical, designated nation, there breathes another nation: of unappointed, unappeased, unacknowledged clusters of people who daily, with fierce imagination and tenacity, confront cruelty, exclusions, and indignities, signaling through those barriers—which are often literal cages—in poetry, music, street theatre, murals, videos, websites—and through many forms of direct activism. (Rich, "Poetry" 133)

Adrienne Rich reworks Percy Bysshe Shelley's notion of the poet as unacknowledged legislator to consider the artist as "unappeased" citizen, witnessing what George Oppen calls the "unacknowledged world" as the geography of poetry (267). Elsewhere, Rich suggests that a poet's work consists of engaging not only what is "there" but also "what is missing, desaparecido, rendered unspeakable, thus unthinkable. It is through these invisible holes in reality that poetry makes its way" ("Arts" 150). She thus positions poetry's work as a form of (counter)memory that is contestatory, interrogative, and dissident (as James Young defines it [7]). In a manner complementary to Liz Sevcenko's conception of the transnational network of museum "sites of conscience" such as the Gulag Museum in Russia or the District Six Museum in South Africa, human rights witness poems in the classroom may function as portable alternative memory sites.

The stance of witness in postconflict locations is entangled with questions of critical citizenship. Reader witnesses are compelled to work through the ongoing claims historical and current human rights violations make on them—from genocides, dictatorships, eco-catastrophes, and border security regimes to the legacies of settler colonialism still manifesting in the lives of indigenous peoples around the globe. The model of citizenship that human rights poems invoke is less defined by national locations than by translocal affiliation as theorized by Paul Gilroy in *Postcolonial Melancholia*. He envisions translocal citizenship—simultaneously contingent and planetary—as the basis for emergent cosmopolitan social movements, responding to the ongoing violations of economic, ecological, and racialized neo-imperialism (72). While many theorists have worked on alternative forms of affiliation such as diasporic or cosmopolitan citizenship, the translocal suggests a productive ethical standpoint of oscillation between accountability to local contexts and ethical connection across borders, communities, and continents. Gilroy's concept of translocal citizenship not only finds "civic and ethical value in the process of exposure to otherness" but insists it must also be grounded in "principled and methodological *cultivation* of a degree of *estrangement* from one's own culture and history" (xv, 68; my emphasis). This suggests that accountability to one's situated, contingent locations is manifested through cultivated estrangement from them. Such self-critical exile from one's embedding in national, ethnic, racialized, economic, and gendered locations of power is essential to translocal critical citizenship. Cultivation suggests time-intensive human-scale labor, seeding, weeding, watering, and harvesting. Human rights witness poetry is a significant site of literary engagement for such cultivation.

Primary and Secondary Witnesses

For instructors who want to create a unit or a course on post-nineteenth-century human rights poetry, Forché's *Against Forgetting* is an obvious starting place. This anthology, which could easily have been two volumes instead of one, benefits from supplementation with further poems that contemporize and expand the repertoire, including poems responding to the repression of the peoples of Tibet (Woeser; Tsundue); the genocides in Rwanda (Kimani; Kimenyi), the former Yugoslavia (Mehmedinovic), and Darfur (Kusserow); the enduring colonization of indigenous peoples of the Americas (Armstrong and Grauer; Harjo); the Israeli occupation of Palestine (Nitzan and Back); and the war on terror (Brand, *Inventory*; Mikhail; Falkoff), among others.[1]

In her introduction to the anthology, Forché offers key insights into several modes of witness poetry. She suggests that poets who adopt a documentary aesthetic may offer a kind of affect-laden "evidence," as do the poems testifying to the exigencies of a forced march found in the pockets of the Hungarian Jewish poet Miklós Radnóti when his widow claimed his remains from a mass grave (29–33). Alternatively, poems that adopt a modernist fragmentary or surrealist aesthetic bear the trace of trauma as markers of aftermath consequences in consciousness, language, and psyche (40–43): "[p]oem as trace, the poem as evidence" (31). Because of her focus on the trace of trauma, Forché reads the witness poem as an ethical event rather than "political confessionalism" or "mimetic narrative" ("Reading" 138, 145). While the ethical for Forché (as for Levinas) precedes the political, I do not entirely agree with her assessment that the witness poem is "not a means to an extra-literary end" (145). A witness poem registers on many levels and can never be *solely* a means to an extraliterary end. Yet, the very notion of witness poetry as evidentiary begs the question, What kind of evidence and before what court? The poem as "ethical tribunal" (Forché, Introd. 37) becomes a space of literary reckoning where readers as secondary witnesses confronted by the evidentiary event of the poem may be asked to consider their own agency and accountability (Vellino, "Human Rights Poetry" 218, 220). As Forché asks, when we read poems as evidentiary rather than representational, "what new 'ethical forensics' is demanded by such a reading?" ("Reading" 140). Witness poetry persistently advances its claims for extraliterary efficacy in the realm of readers' lives and, by extension, our classrooms.

In addition to the victim-survivor witnesses whom Forché prioritizes, I expand her framework in conjunction with Susan Gubar's insights in *Poetry after Auschwitz* to consider the ethically complicated work of the secondary or proxy witness. Indeed, as the Holocaust survivor Primo Levi suggests, all witnesses to atrocity are in some sense belated and substitutionary for the voices of those who did not survive: "We stand in their stead, by proxy" (qtd. in Gubar 23). Poets of secondary witness like Ingrid De Kok, from South Africa, take up problems of representational ethics, namely the (potential) betrayal of traumatic experience by its cultural mediations across linguistic, temporal, spatial, and subjective distances. De Kok's "The Sound Engineer" makes explicit the cultural violence done by severing survivor testimony from context and body even in the service of truth production:

> For truth's sound bite,
> tape the teeth, mouth, jaw,
> put hesitation in, take it out

. . . .

Keep your ear to the ground,
to pain's surfacing
its gulps for air, its low ragged flight
over history's topography. (110)

Yet if the reader is in some sense like the sound engineer, our hearing and thus our witnessing capacity changes in response to what we receive through the ear phone "static": "The sound engineer hears / his own tympanic membrane tear" (111). Secondary witness poems, with varying degrees of success and failure, elicit reader responses beyond mere voyeurism or spectatorship, often through critical questions posed by the poets themselves.

Political Antielegy as "Remembrance/Pedagogy"

> We all know that atrocities have taken place [and continue] on an unprecedented scale. It becomes easier to forget than to remember, and this forgetfulness becomes our defense against remembering . . . These poems will not permit us diseased complacency. They come to us with claims that have yet to be filled . . . (Forché, Introd. 32)

Forché's anthology situates poetic witness as an act of memory against forces that mandate forgetting in the aftermath of more than a century of state-inflicted disappearances, genocides, and mass graves. Witness poems may work in complementary ways to dissident remembrance tactics such as the photographs of the disappeared displayed by Latin American family members. As Thomas Laqueur in "Mourning, Pity, and the Work of Narrative" and Judith Butler in *Precarious Life* demonstrate, the unrecovered body, the unmarked grave, and the unmourned dead are all indexical for those beyond the regard of law and community; the converse is also true: public remembrance of the dead restores their ethical and rights claims to humanity (38; xiv–xv). Witness poems thus work to restore those regarded as "relative humanity" to their place in the communal memories of the living (Barghouti 1537; Laqueur, "Dead Body" 90). Human rights poetry often orchestrates a dialogue with the missing, the dead, and the ungrieved in the form of political "anti-elegy" (Frazier 109; Vellino, "History's Pulse" 254–56). Further, political antielegies refuse the traditional form's turn to consolation, redemption, and resolution, taking up prolonged mourning as a political tactic of confronting unredressed trauma

(Ramazani 30–31). They thus seek to intervene in ongoing atrocity denial, such as Turkey's refusal of responsibility for the Armenian genocide. They also continue to press for more comprehensive justice in societies like South Africa that have unresolved transitional issues long past the tabling of Truth and Reconciliation Commission reports. In so doing, human rights witness poems enact a pedagogy of remembrance that compels readers (from unevenly privileged locations) to critically engage issues arising from post- and mid-conflict societies.

The concept of "remembrance/pedagogy" presented in Roger Simon, Sharon Rosenberg, and Claudia Eppert's *Between Hope and Despair* provides an essential theoretical framework for bridging human rights poetics and critical citizenship pedagogies. Informed by Michel Foucault, "remembrance/pedagogy" seeks to interrogate particular memory or power formations by inviting each testimonial addressee to become ethically attentive to what it means to listen to, be taught by, and respond to the narratives and subjectivities of those victimized by or surviving social, structural, or state violence (Simon, Rosenberg, and Eppert 2–6). If official versions of history are often sanitized, nation-confirming narratives defined by myths of social progress and reform, "remembrance/pedagogy" calls readers to engage in a "difficult return" to traumatic and occluded histories, a process that may serve to unsettle privileged subjectivity and locations (Simon, Rosenberg, and Eppert 4–5; Simon 135). For readers positioned as secondary witnesses, such self-aware critical reflection would involve consideration "of to what and to whom I must be accountable," as well as "what attention, learning and actions such accountability requires" (Simon 4–5). When paired with Forché's sense of the transactive agency of witness poetry—"these poems come to us with claims that have yet to be filled, as attempts to mark us as they have themselves been marked" (Introd. 31)—it is worth considering what kinds of claims witness poems make on their readers. Poetry makes its claims, in part, by compelling slow reading and contemplative encounters that, in turn, facilitate a quality of ethical attention that unsettles one's relation to historical suffering (135).

To stimulate active critical engagement with conflict-aftermath legacies in my upper-year classrooms, I start a term with several introductory classes focused on theoretical readings paired with poems on the following: witness poetry (Forché, Introd. and "Reading"; Gubar; Vogler); human rights problematics of Western universalism and sentimental reading (Spivak, "Righting Wrongs"; Scarry, "Difficulty"; Atwood, "Notes"); bystanders, complicity, and apathy (Cohen; Cohen and Seu; Atwood,

"Footnote"); readers and cowitnessing in the testimonial transaction (Felman and Laub; Siamanto); alternative memory within transitional justice frameworks (Amstutz; Minnow; Jelin; J. Young; De Kok's post-TRC poems in *Seasonal Fires*); and atrocity appropriation (Kleinman and Kleinman; Dorfman's poem "First Prologue, Simultaneous Translation"). Ariel Dorfman's poem explores the similarities between the secondary witness poet and human rights tribunal translators:

> interpreters
> in their glass booths
> at endless international conferences
> translating what the peasant from Talca
> tells about torture. (*In Case of Fire* 3)

Ultimately, our responses to witness poetry requires a critical translation poetics, accounting for both what does get through and what can never be fully accounted for and accommodated in the testimonial transaction.

One of my assignments takes up the reading position of becoming a witness to the witnesses. I invite students to write biweekly "shadow texts," or "secondary narratives a reader or listener writes . . . in response to the unresolved questions a primary narrative elicits" (Simon 58–59, 62). While the assignment has a literary analysis component, it also asks students to offer their responses to "the unresolved questions" through narrative, poetry, visual arts, or other creative mediums. This has led to the creation of several class anthologies and a course blog.

Another of my pedagogical priorities is to mentor ways of reading in class that enable us to see how each poem works in a field of alternative remembrance and human rights discourses and practices. This requires apprenticeship to the contexts that produce human rights violations underlying—if not explicit in—the poetry, as well as to local and transnational human rights instruments, networks, and tactics that emerge as aftermath responses in the postconflict setting. This further involves comparative study between human rights poems and alternative memory tactics in other mediums (film, documentaries, Web sites, museums, and historical sites). Below I offer a case study that builds on Peter Balakian's testimonial poetry of the Armenian genocide to suggest a genocide poetry unit as a practice of "remembrance/pedagogy." Because of the ongoing Turkish denial of the Armenian genocide, the literary witness of Balakian—a third-generation descendent of a survivor—is a particularly significant case study. Most students are familiar with the Shoah (which I also teach) but are surprised to realize they know little about the Armenian genocide or its significance as the first high-profile transnational human rights campaign of the twentieth century (Balakian, *Burning Tigris* xix).

Balakian, a one-man Armenian cultural industry, has produced a prolific array of literary interventions: a volume of poems, *June Tree*; an award-winning memoir, *Black Dog of Fate*; a historical narrative, *The Burning Tigris*; translation work on his grandfather's poet friend Siamanto's *Bloody News from My Friend*; and literary essays ("Falling" and "Poetry"). When taken together with his poetry, these texts form a matrix of life writing that performs a powerful antidote to the century-long campaign of Turkish genocide denial. Students may productively consider how the postmemory work undertaken by the third generation after genocide remains urgent in the wake of ongoing genocide denial. Balakian's poem "The History of Armenia" represents elements of the traumatic past disrupting the present of an ordinary moment in contemporary East Orange, New Jersey: "in the grocery store / a man is standing / to his ankles in blood" (*June Tree* 125). "The Claim" interpolates fragments of a recovered document filed by Balakian's grandmother with the United States State Department after she survived a forced death march into the Syrian desert (after most of her family perished in Turkey) and arrived on United States shores as a refugee in 1919. Here she refutes the genocidal logic by declaring, "I am / I am human herewith affidavit" (139). In Balakian's most well-known poem, "The Oriental Rug," the carpet may be read as an archive of cultural, historical, and genocidal memory, a transgenerational genealogy transmitted to a boy who first sleeps on the rug, then sinks into a dream space of simultaneously sensual and dangerous memory, until as a young man, he shoulders the burden of history: "I walk with a rug on my back. / Become to myself a barren land" (51).

Adam Jones's comprehensive study *Genocide* has important contextual chapters on the Armenian genocide and others. Walter Kalaidjian's chapter "History's 'Black Page'" provides a substantial critical reading of Balakian's poetry (15–48). Taner Akcam's *A Shameful Act* provides an important historical counterbalance to Turkish denial. To compare poetry with other kinds of documentary archives, I show images from Alex Alexanian's online project *Armenian Genocide—The Forgotten*, which features clandestine photographs taken by the German soldier and bystander witness Armin T. Wagner, who was posted to Turkey in 1915. To invite connections between genocides, I encourage students to visit the United States Holocaust Museum's interactive online project *Confront Genocide* and to learn about Genocide Watch's student campus campaigns. Further weeks in this unit may include a focus on the Stalin terror years, which enacted "politicide" as witnessed by poet dissidents, including Osip Mandelstam, Boris Pasternak, and Anna Akhmatova; on the Shoah, as witnessed by survivor poets such as Nelly Sachs, Paul Celan, and Primo Levi; and on the late-twentieth-century genocides in Rwanda, Bosnia, and Darfur.

A final research project for the course asks students to take their citizen witness work a step further by developing a comparative analysis of a poetic alternative remembrance project and an activist alternative remembrance project that respond to the same context. Students working on Balakian, for example, may choose to compare his work with Fergal Keane's BBC film *Armenia: The Betrayed*, Andrew Goldberg's PBS film *The Armenian Genocide*, or the material available on the Web site of the Armenian Genocide Museum-Institute. The students' task is to consider literary points of convergence with, divergence from, and contribution to the intersecting fields of transitional justice and alternative remembrance interventions. Another option is Michael Rothberg's (counter)memorial assignment, which offers students an active way to engage the "founding crimes" of the Americas—slavery and the genocide of the indigenous peoples (469). Such an assignment could be turned toward direct activism or service learning depending on the parameters of the institution or course.

Seamus Heaney's poetic caution—"No poem or play or song / can fully right a wrong / inflicted and endured"—moderates the temptation to overidealize the cultural work of poetry (77). Yet I am convinced by my classroom experience that poetry as a catalyst for empathy, ethics, and critical citizenship is underengaged in the narrative dominant interdiscipline of the human rights humanities. Because of its compact form—brief, intense, intimate—poetry invites close textural and ethical attention to its witness questions and insights within classroom reading communities. These small texts, sometimes framed on a single page, offer contemplative spaces, formalized by page borders and stanza breaks, within which the work of difficult remembrance may be undertaken. As an embodied form—rhythmic, aural, and sensory—witness poetry read aloud makes visceral links between witness bodies, reader bodies, and the bodily rhetoric of human rights advocacy campaigns (Vellino, "Human Rights Poetry" 221–23). Because of their figural, imaginative, and semiotic richness, poems resist easy access and thus commodification, affirming the gifts of the small and the slow. I am sometimes in awe of the ways a single slender poem can cultivate ethical attentiveness through sustained conversations among readers. In this way, the poetry classroom may become a site of countermemory that contributes to what the Chilean human rights lawyer Naomi Roht-Arriaza calls the "justice cascade," in which poetic questions and readerly engagement reinforce and interrogate the ongoing interventions of community and transnational projects (210).

Notes

I dedicate this essay to Adrienne Rich (1929–2012) and Roger I. Simon (d. 2012).

1. Additional anthologies from which to build human rights poetry curriculum include Flattley and Wallace-Crabbe; Cronyn, McKane, and Watts; Hull; McClatchy; P. Forbes; and Chang, Handal, and Shankar.

Susan Spearey

Reconstituting Community, Identity, and Belonging: Classroom Encounters with Postconflict Texts

When literary, cinematic, and other artistic texts bear witness to mass violations of human rights from a postconflict vantage point, they almost inevitably engage in two related and necessarily open-ended processes. On the one hand, they grapple with the tensions between the impossibility and the urgency of articulating histories that are often unspeakable, incomprehensible, or largely irretrievable and with the attendant problematics of representation. On the other hand, they examine various and ongoing efforts (discursive, legal, political, therapeutic) to renegotiate and recalibrate the very conditions out of which the conflict has issued. These conditions include the prevailing social relations, operations of power, strategies of representation, epistemological assumptions, conceptions of justice, and modes of access to cultural and material resources that are understood to have framed the conflict and that have positioned its actors, casualties, beneficiaries, and witnesses in particular ways. When examining both processes in a classroom setting, it is crucial, I argue, to keep clearly in view the differences between bearing witness—an undertaking that is performative and intersubjective and that requires of us what Kelly Oliver has termed "infinite response-ability" (87)—and adopting a stance of objective distance in relation to the events and processes that the texts address. Any artistic mediation of histories of brutality and disenfranchisement runs a number of risks for artists, and these risks extend also to their audiences. The potential to turn the suffering of others into a spectacle or to retraumatize survivors with repeated demands for—or insufficiently sensitive receptions of—their eyewitness accounts may be the most obvious cases in point. The problems of objectification may be further exacerbated in a classroom context if instructors and students understand their—indeed, our—academic training to require us to treat such artistic texts and the histories on which they focus principally as objects of analysis. As the title of Oliver's *Witnessing: Beyond Recognition* suggests, the ethical imperative to bear witness demands much more of us than simply recognizing that injustice has been done and that profound suffering has ensued or recognizing as legitimate certain claims of belonging or agency that have heretofore been disavowed. It requires our meticulous attention to the complex intersubjective relations inherent in any scenario of witnessing. And it requires that we continually ask, in the words of James Orbinski, former president of Médecins Sans Frontières / Doctors without Borders, "How am I to be, how are we to be in relation to the suffering of others?" (4).

Oliver's account of witnessing beyond recognition provides a generative point of departure from which to begin to answer this question. Oliver pairs the terms "responsibility" and "response-ability," positing them jointly as the "founding possibility of subjectivity and its most fundamental obligation" and therefore as the constitutive conditions of bearing witness (91). In so doing, she emphasizes the necessity for each artist or reader who approaches histories of extreme violence and dehumanization to assume responsibility for addressing the legacies of these events while also continuing to open spaces for testimonies and for responses to our actions and utterances. Oliver writes:

> Subjectivity requires the possibility of a witness, and the witnessing at the heart of subjectivity brings with it responsibility, response-ability, and ethical responsibility. Subjectivity is responsibility: it is the ability to respond and to be responded to. Responsibility, then, has the double sense of opening up the ability to respond—response-ability—and ethically obligating subjects to respond by virtue of their very subjectivity itself. (91)

The emphasis that Oliver places on the interdependence of subjects serves as a reminder that the experience of subjectivity, which is always relational, entails much more than mobilizing the capacity to exert agency in a given context; it also carries with it the obligation not to incapacitate others, or, stated more positively, the obligation to safeguard or enhance the capacities of others to exercise agency. Such an obligation does not, of course, presume, anticipate, or dictate any specific response; it requires only that the possibility of further response be kept in play. Working in dialogue with Oliver's conception of witnessing, I explore here how best to cultivate conditions in which responsibility and "response-ability" might be fostered pedagogically, so that histories of atrocity are not simply events that students come to "know" by assimilating the contents of the materials they read but that such histories instead serve to engender the enactment of witnessing, along with an increasingly nuanced awareness and practice of ethical relationships. As I introduce students to postconflict literature, drama, and film in contexts ranging from large-enrollment, first-year undergraduate courses to graduate seminar courses, my consistent objective is to engender a sustained engagement with the summons to "infinite response-ability" and to examine how the very difficult questions raised by the primary texts might be negotiated on both the global scale that frames the histories addressed by the texts and the intimate scales of each student's particular interrelations with others, in the classroom and beyond. I am interested, in other words, in how students engage with provisional reconstitutions of community, identity, belonging, and agency, both through their encounters with course texts and through their encounters with their own and others' understandings and experiences of each of these concepts.

Striving toward such an objective is, admittedly, ambitious, especially given the limited contact time instructors generally share with students, as well as the institutional constraints that regulate modes of course delivery and evaluation. Yet the work of witnessing is incremental and ongoing, and much of what is yielded by this pedagogical approach unfolds beyond the times and spaces in which formal meetings with students are held. In attempting to foster responsibility and "response-ability," I encourage students to cultivate attentiveness to both the sociopolitical dimensions of the humanitarian crises we study and those dimensions of histories of conflict that lie beyond our capacity to conceptualize. In an impassioned call to make pedagogy a key site of political engagement, Henry A. Giroux suggests why the classroom is ideally suited to the task. He urges educators to "engag[e] students in robust dialogue," to "challeng[e] them to think critically about received knowledge," to "energiz[e] them to recognize their own power as individual and social agents," to model forms of democratic participation, and to instill a recognition of the ways that such engagement might contribute to the alleviation of human suffering. Such practices, Giroux suggests, also enable learners to keep clearly in view the differences between "the promise of an unrealized democracy" and "its really existing and grievously incomplete forms" ("Cultural Studies"). Giroux envisions classroom encounters as collaborative negotiations of received and emergent understandings in which learners may begin to realize how various sociopolitical experiences have been shaped and also how they might be transformed. The likelihood of students' engaging directly in democratization is increased by their gathering in seminar groups—or wherever readers gather together, in book clubs, for example—to reflect on and respond to texts that focus explicitly on the painstaking work of rebuilding shattered communities in the aftermath of conflict and of working toward a more equitable sharing of power, land, resources, and stories of self-definition.

And yet, when I invite students to discuss texts that are produced in or about societies striving to redress past injustices, eradicate their living legacies, and fulfill the promise of unrealized democracy, clearly even more is at issue than a sharpening of our critical faculties and a recognition of our respective potential for agency. Entering into a sustained dialogue with these texts also enables us, individually and collaboratively, to explore the very process of bearing witness, as we become witnesses to the histories explored in the course texts and also to our evolving learning processes. It affords us the opportunity to consider what is at stake in this intersubjective endeavor; to examine precisely how each of us is bound up in relations of "infinite response-ability"; to grapple with the obstacles and the resistances to bearing witness that we may encounter in the face of feelings such as horror, perplexity, guilt, despair, or shame; and to examine the implications of our responses to these obstacles. Almost inevitably, both students and instructors will feel challenged to mobilize capacities that exceed the limits of the conceptual. As Oliver puts it:

> To recognize others requires acknowledging that their experiences are real even though they may be incomprehensible to us; this means that we must recognize that not everything that is real is recognizable to us. Acknowledging the realness of another's life is not judging its worth, or conferring respect, or understanding or recognizing it, but

> responding in a way that affirms response-ability. We are obligated to respond to what is beyond our comprehension, beyond recognition, because ethics is possible only beyond recognition. (106)

This move toward ethical engagement, then, requires witnesses to acquire skills beyond those we are accustomed to honing in the classroom. For seasoned instructors and students alike, our academic enculturation may impel us, when responding to accounts of the dissolution and attempted reconstitution of a given set of social relations, to give priority to the refinement of our powers of cognition: to analyze, to judge, to "problem-solve," to attempt to make conclusive sense of the experiences to which we are exposed, and perhaps to apportion blame. Our less scholarly inclinations may also lead us to confer respect, to empathize, to attempt to identify with—or, alternatively, as in the case of eyewitness accounts of perpetrators or beneficiaries of violence, to scapegoat and distance ourselves from—those who share their stories and testimonies. Oliver reminds us, though, that each of these impulses, however well intentioned, may provide insufficient scope for "affirm[ing] response-ability." She suggests that the most profoundly transformative work in which witnesses can engage unfolds beyond the limits of any of these conceptual operations or empathic urges, that it requires us to acknowledge the excess of meaning and potentiality that testimony always entails, and that it challenges us to find other ways of relating (to) the experiences with which we are confronted in the course of bearing witness.

Most, if not all, of the postconflict texts I teach dramatize the problems encountered by the artists and their interlocutors, narrators, or fictional characters, as each attempts to bear witness to histories of profound suffering. These stagings of moments of crisis provide a very important focus of discussion, but as readers we must not forget that we are also addressees of the testimonies contained within and performed by the primary texts and that as their imagined audiences we are caught up in the circuits of testimony's transmission. Oliver points out that our awareness of this relationship makes a significant qualitative difference in the work that testimony can perform. Looking to the example of survivors of dehumanizing histories who bear witness to their experiences, she writes:

> [I]n the case of bearing witness to your own oppression, the performative is in special tension with the constative element of speech. The performative is one of a human subject in a dialogic relation with another human subject while the constative element—what is said—

> tells the tale of dehumanization and objectification. The content of testimonies of oppression reinscribes the survivor as victim and object even while the act of testifying restores subjectivity to the experience of objectification. (98)

The circumstance that Oliver describes here illustrates the dangerous implications of focusing exclusively on what is said and failing to attend to our obligations as addressees to the speaking or writing subjects whose testimonies we are offered. Moreover, when the monumental and often perilous task of reconstituting broken communities is approached by proxy witnesses from a cultural, geographic, or historical distance and when our access to the lived experiences of others is mediated by a written text, a film, or a play—when those who testify are not immediately, physically, present to us—we must seek all the more strenuously to find ways of affirming "response-ability" for those whose realities may not be readily available to us. We must attempt to open up possibilities for response not only for those with whom we discuss the texts but also for those to whose experiences the texts expose us, in addition to the multiple, dispersed, and ever-proliferating audiences with whom we share the position of addressees. Even if we engage in highly sophisticated, thoughtful, and open-ended dialogue with each and every person present in the classroom, we may inadvertently situate other witnesses outside the purview of our intellectual and ethical work and thereby foreclose the possibility of "infinite response-ability." We must be especially vigilant in our attempts not to preempt potential responses and be careful to speak to those who are not physically present as well as those in our immediate surroundings, so that we are more likely to affirm their subjectivity, to begin to address their claims on us, and to keep in play the summons to ethical encounter.

Thus far the case for the importance of affirming possibilities for "response-ability" when learners gather to reflect on postconflict texts has been couched largely in theoretical terms. There are, however, a number of concrete, practical steps that can be taken to ensure that fostering "response-ability" remains a priority and a touchstone as classroom discussions unfold. Teachers can begin by stressing the importance of open-ended dialogue and collaborative learning and by providing guidance, incentives, and a pedagogical rationale for students to index their contributions toward generating the responses of others within and beyond the classroom. Students can be assigned, individually or in pairs or groups, the task of facilitating (rather than leading) class discussions; if they are required to come to class with discussion questions prepared, instructors can work with them to ensure that such questions are both focused and open-ended; assignments can be crafted that help students formulate probing essay questions; and all learners—but especially those who participate frequently or those who are seen to dominate discussions—can be encouraged to push toward complex analyses by framing or reformulating their contributions as queries that invite the responses and the participation of their peers. Lectures and course outlines can open with questions that invite students to examine their existing assumptions about some of the key concepts that they will be addressing in a given course, and instructors can encourage them to revisit these questions. Doing so invites the participation of students from the outset while also reminding all of us as we proceed that the problems under investigation do not have easy or definitive answers. It enables each participant to see and to begin to explore the implications of the differences between our responses and those of other class members and to recognize each other as valuable resources and coinvestigators, each of whom approaches the course with a particular set of knowledge, interests, and life experiences.

Instructors can also encourage students to be careful and precise about the use of pronouns, especially where any collective is invoked, and to indicate exactly who is understood to be included or excluded by each referent. This attention to pronouns is particularly urgent when dealing with texts that situate their audiences as proxy witnesses; using pronouns such as *we* keeps clearly in view our role as addressees who are being entreated to respond and reminds us that we are not distant or objective commentators who are analyzing discrete and self-contained cultural artifacts. We can also be self-reflexive about the cognitive operations we enlist and examine when and where our judgments, analyses, attempts at synthesis, or articulation of seemingly definitive statements come into play; why we might mobilize these strategies or capacities at any given moment; and what they might accomplish as well as occlude. Together, we can foreground and attend carefully to the performative dimensions of the testimonies we examine, especially when their speakers lay claim to the right to participate fully in the reconstitution of community and when they engage in the difficult work of negotiating with others the very terms and conditions of that participation. In other words, every participant in discussion can raise questions about what these testimonies say as well as examine the ongoing cultural work they perform and how our role as addressees might contribute to this work. As witnesses, we can be mindful of the extent to which these efforts are carried out in the absence of any guarantee of their eventual outcomes, that they are serious and committed gestures of hope. Just as crucially for those of us located in the Global North, we can measure the attempts to effect processes of democratization in postconflict settings against our experiences of democracy's "grievously incomplete forms" (Giroux, "Cultural Studies"), and we can take up the work that these texts set in motion in our local, national, and global contexts by examining precisely where we might be implicated in practices that disempower others or ourselves.

If discussions are conducted as though every author, director, playwright, fictional character, narrator, or nonfictional interlocutor were present in the classroom, we can potentially heighten our sense of responsibility toward each of these subjects as well as our sense of accountability for the positions we adopt, we will open space for "response-ability," and we will have to confront the often fraught and complex politics of address. We may, for instance, be forced to consider how we would speak about inconceivably brutal experiences if someone who had survived them were in our midst or how we would engage with those whose use of violent tactics in the course of a liberation struggle horrifies us, despite our sympathies with the cause. To speak to the latter point, in one cohort of a second-year undergraduate course on South African literatures of transition, I realized that many of the students were having difficulty coming to terms with the use of violence against civilians by various antiapartheid organizations and operatives and with the apparent endorsement—if not outright celebration—of these actions by the primary texts. When, in the course of a lecture, a heartfelt question was raised by a student who wondered in what circumstances the use of violence should be condoned, I put my lecture notes down and asked students to choose the individual, whether real or fictional, whose story had troubled them the most and to begin to write a letter to this person with a view to expressing what was disturbing them or to seeking answers to their most pressing questions. Most students chose Mxolisi, the semifictionalized murderer of the American Fulbright scholar Amy Biehl in Sindiwe Magona's novel *Mother to Mother*, or Mongezi Manqina, the actual Truth and Reconciliation Commission amnesty applicant on whom Mxolisi is based. While I allocated only ten minutes of lecture time for students to write their letters, several opted to complete them afterward or reflected insightfully and candidly on the experience in subsequent seminar and online discussions, as well as in their exam papers. In their reflections, they explored the limits they had reached when passing judgments or invoking moral absolutes, and they began to rethink some of their convictions about the concept of justice, the constituency it serves, and the means of its execution. No conclusive "resolutions" were reached, but the impromptu exercise pushed the students who pursued the writing and those with whom they discussed it toward more subtle engagements with the key problems raised by the course and toward greater receptivity to experiences very unlike their own. It also helped students understand the extent to which their reactions to histories of struggle and resistance reflect or contest hegemonic constructions of concepts such as social order and terrorism. It is important also to note that this anecdote is but one of many that I might have cited and that I have consistently been impressed by the range of thoughtful and creative pedagogical strategies and exercises introduced by students in their seminar facilitations.

Examining societies in the process of reconstituting community structures and of renegotiating the terms according to which identity and participation can be experienced also affords learners the opportunity to explore how power, authority, belonging, agency, and legitimacy are constituted in our more immediate circumstances, including in our classroom dynamics, and how these, too, might be beneficially renegotiated. Obviously, the stakes are highest in contexts of heightened conflict; at issue are the physical safety, well-being, and health of human beings and ultimately the very possibility of self-determination and survival for individuals, their children and descendants, their communities, and their cultures. The reconstitution of community in these circumstances is indexed toward living beyond the limits of what Giorgio Agamben has termed "bare life" (*zoe*) and acceding to the realm of "the good life" (*bios*) promised by a given polity. By way of contrast, what is at stake for students in classrooms such as mine is a rethinking of the principles that structure their understandings of "the good life" and inform the strategies enlisted to procure its achievement and, following Agamben's lead, an examination of the connections between *zoe* and *bios*. One colleague of mine, a sociologist whose research focuses on the operation of alternative economies, uses a pedagogical exercise that helps make transparent the operation of power dynamics that are often invisible to students and possibly even instructors in the day-to-day running of classes and helps students begin to explore how certain mechanisms of exclusion and silencing function. During a given seminar, she will distribute some kind of currency (knowing this colleague, it is unlikely to be Monopoly money) to students each time they make a contribution to seminar discussion. A few minutes before the class ends, she will ask students to take stock of who has currency and who does not, who has the most and who has the least, and how these distributions speak to broad considerations of voice, agency, and the circulation of power and knowledge. While I have never enlisted this technique in the classroom, I have on several occasions related it as an anecdote, and even the narrative account of the exercise has given rise to subtle and probing discussions of how, in a situation in which equal participation is strongly encouraged, often invisible inequities are reproduced and how these unintentional exclusions might begin to be redressed.

Because it is crucial to consider the context specificity of the conditions that precipitate such exclusions and silencings, I have found the work of Sherene H. Razack invaluable in teaching postconflict literature in the specific sociopolitical context in which I work. Razack's *Dark Threats and White Knights: The Somalia Affair, Peacekeeping and the New Imperialism*, for example, traces connections between the unspoken principles that, under the auspices of the advancement of civility and humanitarianism, shape social relations in Canada's domestic sphere and those that determine the terms of its participation on the international stage. In both cases, Razack argues, the maintenance of peace and order is secured by perpetuating pervasive and long-standing practices of disenfranchisement, dehumanization, and exclusion, all of which work to legitimize the white Western subject as the rightful arbiter of just and fair governance. In her introductory chapter, "Savage Wars of Peace," Razack takes a critical look at the role of peacekeeping operations in Canada's self-imagining and makes visible the violence that is often elided in accounts of these military missions and of Canada's role in the maintenance of global order. The chapter takes as one of its epigraphs an excerpt from the fiftieth-anniversary edition of W. E. B. Du Bois's *The Souls of Black Folk*, in which Du Bois asserts that the logic of the "color line" continues to be "a great problem of this century," an argument that Razack extends to her own twenty-first-century Canadian context (qtd. in Razack 3). Du Bois's argument that an elite minority enjoys comfort and security at the expense of the vast majority and protects this privilege through militarism is readily recognizable to any of my students familiar with the politics and economics of globalization and tends to encounter little resistance. Razack's invocation of "the color line" and race, however, strikes many of my students as counterintuitive, if not misplaced, in a study of Canada's contemporary domestic and international relations. The prevailing national mythologies in Canada celebrate notions of inclusivity and fair-mindedness, which are seen to be exemplified in our cherished system of universal health care, in our asylum policies, in our embrace of the principle of multiculturalism, in our advocacy of tolerance for diverse cultural practices, and, to cite Razack's specific focus of investigation, in our role as a "middle power" in international peacekeeping and humanitarianism (10).

In Canada as elsewhere, the assurances so emphatically asserted by the dominant national mythologies produce certain dynamics in the public sphere that regulate what can and cannot be said and how far critiques may extend. These dynamics are often replicated in my classrooms, making it difficult for those who have not experienced the celebrated ethos of inclusiveness or ease of participation to be heard or taken seriously. Razack, however, invites her readers to respond to Du Bois's observation through a process of self-reflection. She writes, "Du Bois's insight that we are somehow able to live with the pernicious effects of the colour line suggests that it is imperative to understand how our daily participation in a colour-lined world is secured" (9). One salient example of how such participation may operate that students have found especially compelling is Razack's discussion of the reception and circulation in Canada of the story of General Roméo Dallaire, head of the United Nations Assistance Mission for Rwanda during the 1994 genocide. Razack contends that the very accounts that celebrate Dallaire as a national hero, a champion of human rights, and an exemplar of Canadian peacekeeping are actually premised on racist assumptions barely distinguishable from those that animated and justified the most egregious exploits of European colonialism. In these accounts, Dallaire is depicted as a valiant "white knight" crusading to bring peace and civilized conduct to the dark regions of the world, whose brush with the "evil" of Africa (as suggested by the title of his memoir, *Shake Hands with the Devil*) almost destroyed him. Razack argues that the widespread circulation of these accounts, in which the genocide becomes a story about Dallaire's trauma rather than that of its nearly one million casualties and their survivors, serves to reinforce the dominant myths about Canada as a benevolent, civilized, unaggressive, and legitimate actor in the advancement of justice and reestablishes white settler society as the rightful and established locus of this identity within Canada and the world at large. She elaborates:

> This [Canadian] national mythology has always depended on race. It is informed by the notion that "we" know about democracy and

> "they" do not; "we" have values of integrity, honesty, and compassion that "they" do not; that "we" are a law-abiding, orderly, and modest people while "they" are not. As an immigrant to Canada from the Third World, I have long understood that the 'we' is a white category and that it refers to people who imagine themselves to be the original citizens (Aboriginal peoples are considered dead or dying and people of colour are considered recently arrived). . . . The instruction of the natives that is so central to peacekeeping is also central to the everyday experiences of immigrants of colour in the North. It is a civilizing process that is deeply familiar and utterly dehumanizing. My impulse to name the colour line in peacekeeping springs from this everyday experience of eviction from the national, an eviction that swiftly occurs whenever racism is named. (13)

Here, Razack makes transparent several troubling assumptions that inform the dynamics of Canada's domestic and international social relations and complicates notions that Canadian domestic and international policy exemplifies the principles of human rights. She simultaneously traces the continuities between current and historical, local and global manifestations of a politics of exclusion by locating her own experience of "eviction from the national" as symptomatic of larger processes that exclude, demean, and disavow.

Razack's work challenges students to rethink some of their most deeply held convictions. For some, it can be profoundly unsettling, whereas for others, especially those who have felt inhibited in their attempts to articulate their experiences of "eviction" from various communities and to elicit responses to these experiences, it is immediately embraced as affirming and empowering. It is important for all class members to be attentive to each of these reactions as discussions of the text unfold and not, for example, to belittle the responses of those who are perhaps encountering aspects of their privilege in unanticipated and disconcerting ways. A vital part of my role as a teacher, regardless of the subject matter at hand, involves encouraging in students a confidence that the sometimes deeply disquieting experience of seeking complexity is worth the effort, that it is potentially enabling and transformative. The value of Razack's work, to my mind, is not ultimately that it offers hard-hitting and unflinching critiques of race relations in Canada but that it is indexed toward the unmaking of forms of social cohesion and belonging that are premised on unacknowledged mechanisms of exclusion. Razack explicitly expresses the hope that her examination of "how a racially specific national and international subject is performed, produced, and sustained and how such performances keep the global order in place" might "reveal that subject's fictive and destructive core and . . . suggest another, more ethical way of imagining our selves and of living in the world" (9). It is precisely this process of reimagining community and engaging in ethical encounter that shapes my pedagogical aspirations.

Bearing witness as a classroom practice, then, is performative and intersubjective not only to the extent that it enables instructors and students to cultivate a fuller awareness of, and "response-ability" and responsibility for, our positions and obligations as addressees of the texts with which we engage but also to the degree that we take up this work at affective and embodied—as well as cognitive, sociopolitical, and ideological—levels in our daily lived practices of community and collectivity. To do so is to commit ourselves to addressing and to renegotiating the constraints on and potentialities for our capacities as individual and social agents, as witnesses, and as ethical beings.

Part IV

Classroom Contexts

Introduction to Part 4

Human rights content poses particular challenges for teachers of literature and cultural studies: the need to create space for affective responses to powerful material as well as to teach analytical approaches to the texts at hand; to attend to the productive work that human rights may accomplish as well as its limitations; to build historical or geopolitical context for understanding the violations at hand without subsuming the literature to that context. The eight essays in this section take up these challenges. They present specific classroom practices, assignments, and teaching materials, as well as provide conceptual framings that are broadly applicable to many different kinds of classes.

The first two chapters present pedagogical approaches to linking textual analysis with ethical practice. Kimberly A. Nance notes that students frequently embrace either a poetics of celebration (that human rights stories are being told) or a poetics of mourning (of the immense and unrelenting violations they encounter as readers)—two positions Greg Mullins also delineates in the first essay in this volume. Both, she argues, delimit students' ability to analyze the persuasive dimensions of the text as well as their willingness to answer, for themselves and on their own terms, the call of the text. In place of celebratory or wholly critical or sorrowful readings,

Nance advocates instead a prosaic approach that counteracts defensive reading strategies to pursue measured reading of the text's persuasive powers (and failures). Crucial to her argument is that students consider not just how a text cultivates compassion (stemming from identification) but whether or how it moves the reader back to exotopy (Bakhtin), to a considered evaluation of one's position and thus capacity to act. Alexander Hartwiger focuses similarly on student expectations for course work in human rights and on the project of cultivating students' capacity for ethical reading practices. Although students enroll in particular courses for myriad reasons, they tend to share expectations of a trajectory of rights stories that moves from violation to redemption. To acknowledge these expectations and to complicate them, Hartwiger makes the case for an unhomely cosmopolitan pedagogy that encourages students to recognize their assumptions and privileges as integral to their reading practice and to build on that recognition through exercises that gradually defamiliarize students from their initial positions. The process of disorientation, he asserts, can steer students away from default readings—those that never move beyond either sympathy for victims or denial—and create the intellectual and emotional space for new interpretations.

The two essays that follow delve into the pedagogical imperative of human rights as well as the need to develop students' capacities as critical and dialogic interpreters of rights. Both essays suggest teaching materials and assignments that position students not solely as readers but also as performers or creators of human rights narratives. The authors argue that active participation asks students to reflect critically on the stakes of different narrative forms through which rights are articulated. Belinda Walzer provides an overview of several different pedagogical initiatives on human rights sponsored by the United Nations and other organizations before focusing on Kerry Cuomo Kennedy's multimodal project *Speak Truth to Power*. Walzer presents a rhetorical approach to *Speak Truth to Power* that can give students the tools to unpack the difficult questions of what it means—in the context of egregious human rights violations—to speak effectively, to define truth, and to address power, even as the project performs its consciousness-raising objectives. Also describing a rhetorical approach, Ryan Omizo and Wendy Hesford theorize and describe an assignment that asks students to create and critique their human rights visual narratives. Reflecting critically on their own work, students become savvy manipulators of its emotional pull as well as deeply cognizant of the stakes of representation.

The next two essays present examples of cross-disciplinary approaches to human rights literature. Erik Juergensmeyer and Bridget Irish describe the development of a common reading experience that, although located in the composition program and tied to its learning goals, also engages students and faculty in various other disciplines as well as strengthens links between the college and the community. Lisa Eck and Ben Alberti take a different approach to the interdisciplinary potential of human rights through their coordinated or clustered classes in expository writing and anthropology. In both essays, the authors underscore how specific textual choices, student assignments, and interdisciplinary conversations can help students develop deeper understandings of the structural dimensions of human rights and their cultural contexts. In addition to contributing to the student learning outcomes in developing reading and writing skills, these approaches seek to foster students' sense of global citizenship beyond awareness or consciousness-raising.

Marike Janzen's exploration of service learning in the next essay does not take as a given the pursuit of real-world action after classroom readings of human rights stories; instead, implicitly following Thomas Keenan in his essay "Mobilizing Shame," Janzen questions what Keenan calls the "lockstep logic of if-then, in which knowledge generates action (reaction)" on the grounds of its connection to an Enlightenment ontology that suggests that knowledge can be known, unconditionally, and that it will then produce a rational response from a presumptively rational subject (Keenan 437). Janzen argues that service learning, instead of making the classroom materials relevant in the real world, as much of the research suggests, deepens lessons in the literature classroom about the interrelation of narrative forms of human rights and our understandings of what it means to be human. Service learning in human rights and literature, in other words, can enhance student understanding of the literary dimensions of human rights narratives, as opposed to solely their applicability.

This section concludes with an essay by Megan Sweeney in which she presents the relation of two dimensions of her teaching—in a university and at a women's prison—as an example of how to teach students to acknowledge other readers' perspectives and to begin to build for themselves a "rickety bridge" to the world beyond the classroom.

Collectively, the essays in this section theorize and demonstrate approaches to interpretative, emotional, and ethical dimensions of human rights and literary and cultural studies in traditional and experimental class contexts.

Kimberly A. Nance

Empirical Ethics, Theoretical Mechanics: Toward a Prosaics of Teaching Human Rights Literature

Human rights literature points back to an experience of violation and at the same time forward toward a project to bend the arc of justice. As a defining feature of the genre, this double connection between the page and the world presents formidable challenges to literary critics. Faced with a project that is social as well as literary and whose expected time frame often exceeds the human lifespan, critics have tended to make the task manageable by shrinking its scope. In the case of Latin American testimonial texts, a euphoric first wave of criticism reduced the project to the page, declaring victory as soon as a previously marginalized voice gained publication. A suspicious second wave did acknowledge human rights literature's goal of working on the world but went on to truncate its time line. Seeing little immediate effect, those critics declared the project impossible; all that was left, they insisted, was the work of mourning. Procrustean as well as premature, readings of human rights literature through either celebration or mourning effectively served to insulate readers from any sense of personal obligation to work for human rights. If the project was already done or could never be accomplished anyway, the reader's role was reduced to either applause or tears.

In *Can Literature Promote Justice?* I argue that because the goals of human rights literature extend beyond the page, any poetics is fundamentally inadequate to the task of an engaged critique. Accounting for literature's social objectives requires instead a *prosaics*, a term employed by the Bakhtin critics Gary Saul Morson and Caryl Emerson to describe a solidarity founded not on ecstatic fusion or abjection but instead on considered, contingent, and concrete actions in everyday life (15). Rejecting both euphoria and despair regarding the social potential of literature, the premises of a prosaics are at once more ambitious and more modest. Prosaics insists that literature can change the world but at the same time acknowledges that the task is powerfully difficult, since texts can only operate by persuading their readers to act. "Literary texts are tools," observes Michael Holquist, "they serve as a prosthesis of the mind. As such, they have a tutoring capacity that materially effects change by getting from one stage of development to another" (83). Owing to readers' defenses against calls to action, the requirements for socially effective human rights literature are exigent. Evidence based and outcomes focused, a prosaics of human rights literature is profoundly improvisational and interdisciplinary. In addition to drawing on work from psychology, rhetoric, philosophy, communications, media studies, and any other area that might shed light on a practical project of persuasion, it is informed by the empirical expertise of community organizers and other human rights workers. In its approach to human rights literature as a concrete social project, a prosaics facilitates dialogue between literature and law, sociology, and other kindred disciplines, as well as with service learning.[1] This essay considers how the concept of prosaics might inform teachers' goals and practice in teaching human rights literature.[2]

The title, a nod to Valerie Nollan's *Bakhtin: Ethics and Mechanics*, reflects prosaics' emphasis on practice. In courses on human rights literature the objective of a prosaic approach is to teach students how human rights literature works in the world and how to evaluate the likely effectiveness of individual texts as instruments in what is ultimately a project of persuasion. Students learn to recognize what action a particular text seeks from its readers, to understand the processes of persuasion and how it succeeds or fails, to identify the techniques of persuasion deployed in a text, and, finally, to make an educated estimate of whether and why those techniques might or might not work. A prosaics does not seek to indoctrinate students to a particular political perspective or to persuade them to support the projects of any particular text. Questions of whether students (or teachers) agree with the goals of a given text, whether they plan to respond to the appeals of that text, and, if so, how they might go about responding are explicitly excluded from both class discussion and written assignments.

I realize that taking questions of individual conscience and action off the table in the classroom might appear counterintuitive, particularly to teachers accustomed to pedagogies of advocacy that frame classes in human rights literature as promotions of selected projects, but that exclusion is not an attempt to avoid conflict or controversy. Instead it reflects a conviction that the negative consequences of classroom advocacy—albeit unintended—outweigh the hoped-for rewards. Given the dynamics of power in the classroom it is likely that at least some students will feel coerced to endorse political projects with which they do not agree—hardly a formula for changing hearts and minds. And further, even if we stipulate in our classes that all the texts as well as the teacher's advice will be impeccable guides to ethical behavior, encouraging students to rely passively on others to set their moral compass for them is not a productive social strategy for the long run. As I caution in *Teaching Literature in the Languages*,

> [T]hroughout their lives students will be subject to all manner of textual propositions—some worthy, some not, some appalling. Rather than conceiving their educational project as convincing students to act on behalf of their own carefully selected set of textual propositions, teachers need to think about how they hope students will respond in the future when the text is not one they would have selected for the class, and when the action it suggests is not moral at all. (145–46)

I begin class by writing on the board some of the questions raised by human rights literature that we will be considering for each text: What project is being proposed here? What actions are proposed or implied for readers? What arguments or other strategies of persuasion does the text employ? How likely is it that those strategies will work? I pause and draw a double line before adding two more questions: Should I support this project, or not? If I choose to support this project, what should I do? I explain to students that their answers to those last two questions will not be subject to written assignments or to class discussion, and I tell them the reasons. Lest my rationale that they need to work out their own ethical answers be taken as pro forma, I note that the reading list for class includes human rights texts that reflect a variety of political viewpoints, so that in this class all students are bound to encounter some texts with whose agenda they will disagree as well as some they are likely to endorse—just as they do in the world, and just as they will for the rest of their lives. I offer students the advice of the Nicaraguan human rights worker Elvia Alvarado: "I've learned that if you want to know what's going on in the world, you should study as much as you can. You should read or listen to the news as much as you can. You should take it all in, but digest it in your own way, and judge for yourself what you think the truth is" (64).

A prosaics of teaching human rights literature depends first on recognition of the genre's double connection to the lifeworld, acknowledgment that its social goals can be attained only by persuading its readers to act, and conviction that such persuasion is indeed possible. While for a course on literature of human rights those premises might appear to go without saying, students entering any class will have encountered words to the contrary. Students who have so far been persuaded by a poetics of celebration may believe that human rights literature succeeds simply by documenting injustice or by giving voice to hitherto marginalized people. Students whose experience of human rights literature has been shaped by the poetics of mourning may see the genre's project of persuading readers to act as well intentioned but unfortunately quixotic.

Taking note of those poetic lessons to be unlearned, teachers may be tempted to begin by surveying students' assumptions regarding human rights literature, but compelling students to unpack their critical baggage for inspection at entry may well prove counterproductive. Even if meant in the kindest possible way, opening class by directing students to rehearse publicly beliefs that will soon be explicitly contested is unlikely to encourage future participation. Students who feel stung by such an exercise may feel compelled to protect their sense of competence by rejecting those new premises. A more effective means of establishing the foundations for prosaics is to present evidence and ask students to discuss what they see. Confirmation of the practical objectives of human rights literature might take the form of excerpts from some of the texts to be read in class or clips from audio or video interviews in which writers or subjects discuss their objectives. For instance, an introduction to a class on Latin American *testimonio* might include a passage from *Don't Be Afraid, Gringo*, in which Alvarado addresses readers regarding her goals for her text.

> If you sit around thinking what to do and end up not doing anything, why bother even thinking about it? You're better off going out on the town and having a good time. No, we have to think and act. That's what we're doing here, and that's what you have to do.

> I hate to offend you, but we won't get anywhere by just writing and reading books. I know that books are important, and I hope this book will be important for the people who read it. But we can't just read it and say "Those poor campesinos. What a miserable life they have." Or others might say "What a nice book. That woman Elvia sounds like a nice woman." I imagine there'll be others who say "That Elvia is a foul-mouthed, uppity campesina." But the important thing is not what you think of me, the important thing is for you to do something. (146)

In the same vein, for students who have already learned the lesson that human rights literature cannot change anything, merely declaring that for purposes of this class we will assume that it can is unlikely to be persuasive. Here the counterevidence takes the form of articles and audio or video segments of research on the power of justice as a motive in human life and on literature's capacity to evoke that motive. Social psychologists and just-world theorists such as Melvin Lerner, Adrian Furnham, Michael Ross, and Dale Miller present compelling observational and experimental evidence that "people want to and have to believe in a just world so that they can go about their lives with a sense of trust, hope, and confidence in their future" and that people will make great sacrifices to restore justice—up to and including their own lives (Lerner 14; see also Furnham; Ross and Miller). As the developmental psychologist Paul Bloom reports, evidence is mounting that even very young infants have the ability to recognize injustice and that even they are inclined to reward just actors and punish unjust ones ("New Science"). Neuroscientists such as Nancy Eisenberg offer accounts of subjects' physiological responses to witnessing the suffering of others, physical evidence that, as Dascher Keltner puts it, "compassion can be cultivated" (248). Work by Lerner, Markus Appel, Tobias Richter, Melanie Green, Timothy Brock, Jeffrey Strange, Cynthia Leung, and Leslie Paul Thiele, among many others, confirms that both factual and fictional narratives of injustice can change the attitudes of readers about injustice, their sense of urgency, and the likelihood that they will act (see Lerner; Appel; Appel and Richter; Green and Brock, "In the Mind's Eye" and "Role"; Green, Strange, and Brock; Strange; Strange and Leung; Thiele).

But while literature can change the world, not every text is an effective tool for that purpose. Prosaics draws clear distinctions between the goals of human rights literature, on the one hand, and its real-world outcomes, on the other. Conceptualizing human rights literature's project of persuasion as a difficult practical task as opposed to a foregone conclusion helps counter the constraints of both prevailing poetics. Acknowledgment that persuasion is difficult and often unsuccessful helps forestall the possibility of premature celebration and also makes it clear that one or even many failures do not define a given project as impossible. One useful model of the task of persuasion, as well as an index of its difficulty, comes in the form of Bakhtin's description of the fraught double passage required for ethical witness, a process described in *Art and Answerability* as empathy and exotopy. "Let us say that there is before us a human being who is suffering," he begins. The witness's first obligation is empathy, insofar as it is possible to "come to see and know what [the other] experiences," but empathy is by no means an ethical end in itself. Instead, Bakhtin insists, ethical witnesses must continue on to exotopy, "return to [their] own place," where they can recognize the unique ways in which their situation enables them to assist and take action accordingly (25–26). Jean-François Lyotard reaches a similar conclusion in *The Differend* with his description of the "testimonial pact." When faced with "something that resembles a call," he argues, it is not sufficient for addressees to acknowledge the occurrence of injustice. For witnesses to hear that "something" as a call addressed to them, they must first believe that they are able to help: to hear "you ought to" they must first hear "you are able to" (121). Both accounts of the process of persuasion underscore the formidable task of human rights literature. It is one thing to convince readers that human rights violations have occurred and that someone ought to do something about them and quite another to persuade readers to see themselves, now, as the appropriate agents.

A key task for a prosaic pedagogy of human rights literature is consideration of the human factors that enable or inhibit the project of persuasion, including the capacities and constraints of those who shape the texts. Examination of persuasion in practical terms reveals that the failure of a given text to promote action does not necessarily stem from lack of dedication or belief. Even people who believe sincerely in human rights and who work diligently for justice may not be very good at persuading others to do so. Indeed, the very fervency of one's beliefs may become an obstacle to effective persuasion, especially when a value is so closely held that it is impossible to imagine that anyone could fail to share it, a phenomenon that Bloom terms "the curse of desire" (*Descartes' Baby* 22).

Prosaics likewise takes note of the capacities and constraints that characterize readers of human rights literature, including the fact that the appeal of any given text comes in the midst of a daily barrage of other appeals. Teachers might ask their students to consider all the pleas for time and money that they see and hear each day. While a few of those requests might be dismissed out of hand as frivolous or unworthy, most are probably for needs and causes that the students see as legitimate. But could anyone ever act on every plea? The same just-world theory that explains the force of the justice motive in human life also explains why people who learn about human rights violations—even decent people who feel a strong impulse to work for justice—only rarely act on that impulse. Given the demonstrated strength of the justice motive, which under certain circumstances can overcome not only self-interest but even the instinct for self-preservation, people who lacked any brake on that motive would instantly place themselves in harm's way. "One's resources are limited and finite," reminds Lerner, so that "no matter how one may feel, there is only so much that can be accomplished with these resources without doing harm to one's self and family" (19). Lerner and other just-world theorists posit that human beings' very survival requires a means to selectively inhibit action on the impulse to do justice. To avoid becoming overwhelmed by demands for help, they find, most people will engage in action to restore justice only when specific criteria are met. If the appeal of a particular text does not meet those requirements, readers of human rights literature will seek to restore justice not by changing the world but instead by changing their minds. Lerner takes pains to note that even decent and caring readers are likely to engage in a vast range of cognitive defenses, up to and including derogation of victims, to avoid feeling called on to act when the cost seems too high or the cause too uncertain (122). In fact, he suggests, people who place a higher value on justice may even be more prone to those cognitive defenses, only because they feel more keenly the impulse to act. Just-world theorists contend that the enormous array of cognitive defenses against feeling called to action in fact testifies to the strength of the human impulse to act for justice. If it were easy for humans to ignore injustice, they argue, those inhibitory defenses would never have evolved (172–76).

One common example of a cognitive defense against answerability, a means by which one can read all about human rights violations without feeling obligated to do anything, occurs when readers fail to continue to exotopy, instead stopping short at empathy. Bakhtin warns sternly against lingering in such an imaginative identification with sufferers, on grounds that the result will be "an infection with the other's suffering, and nothing more" (26). In *Pathologies of Power*, a critical analysis of responses to crises in world health, the physician-activist Paul Farmer calls out such sentimental occupation of the place of the other as an unsatisfactory substitute for a "pragmatic solidarity" that "move[s] beyond sentiments to action" (230). As Farmer observes, it is all too easy for witnesses of injustice to recast themselves as fellow victims, evading the sense of responsibility that might come with recognition of their relative privilege. "Not all forms of suffering are equivalent," Farmer insists, and "the risk of stretching the concept of rights to cover every possible case is that obscene inequalities of risk will be drowned in a rising tide of petty complaint" (231). For this reason teachers of human rights literature who hope that their students might take action for the rights of others should be wary of encouraging them to spend too much class time sharing their own experiences of injustice.

Another example of a defensive reading that short-circuits the process of persuasion is a misprizing of reading itself as the desired outcome, so that readers can enjoy the satisfaction of having responded to a situation merely by having read a book about it. The possibilities for defensive readings are endless: readers may evade responsibility by redefining the situation, suffering, sufferer, expectations for response, chances of success, or even themselves. Given the magnitude of the "asks" for work for human rights—not only the demands of any individual text but also the cumulative effect of all the evidence of injustice that readers encounter every day—it is no wonder that defensive readings of human rights literature that permit readers to witness without feeling called to act would far outnumber productive ones.

The real wonder is that, as a social project, human rights literature ever works at all. For teachers, prosaics poses an ongoing challenge to maintain students' sense of the genre's possibilities. While it is relatively easy to persuade students to abandon a poetics of celebration, as they learn about all the ways that the process of persuasion can fail it can be difficult for them to avoid falling back into a poetics of mourning. As students come to understand the precariousness of the project of human rights literature, teachers do well to remind them of that literature's real-life successes. It is in this way, by making and keeping students keenly aware of both the contingency and the possibility of human rights literature as persuasion—rather than by advocating any particular project—that courses informed by prosaics come to serve as metaprojects of social justice. As an approach to reading human rights texts, prosaics serves to counter two major sources of defensive readings—the illusion that the work of justice does not require reader participation and the illusion that such work cannot be done at all. Moreover, just-world theorists have observed that the power of cognitive defenses may diminish when they are brought to conscious attention (Lerner 80). As a result of a prosaics of teaching human rights literature, students who have learned about the many means by which readers resist answerability and the ways in which that resistance can be countered may be more likely to recognize in that literature "something that resembles a call," more apt to see themselves as answerable, and better equipped to persuade others to help.

Notes

1. My *Can Literature Promote Justice?* constructs a provisional rhetoric for texts in service of human rights and analyzes the capacities and constraints of speakers, writers, editors, critics, and readers in the production and reception of such texts. See Nance, "'Something,'" for a brief survey of recent developments in the theory and practice of one genre of human rights literature, including its relation to efforts such as Vincent Farenga's Literature and Justice Project. For information on Farenga's project, see his "Authoring Justice" and "Report."

2. For further analysis of the capacities and constraints of teachers and students of human rights literature, as well as practical details of a prosaics of teaching and suggestions for its relation to service learning, see Nance, "*Mountains*," "Only Connect?," *Teaching*, and "Reading."

Alexander Hartwiger

Locating Difference: Addressing Student Expectations in the Human Rights and Literature Classroom

In 2006, then MLA president Domna Stanton issued a challenge for scholars in the humanities "to deconstruct fixed and unexamined ideas, language, and representations in human rights to expose the ways in which they compromise the struggle for freedom, equality, justice, and tolerance, however complex and vexed those ideals may be" ("Foreword" 1523). Stanton prodded scholars in the humanities to explore the complexity of human rights issues, moving research and teaching beyond consciousness-raising to critical, imaginative, and ethical involvement. Heeding Stanton's call, I explore one particular aspect of the classroom environment—student expectation—as it pertains to the challenge of ethical engagement with human rights literature. Addressing this often overlooked aspect of the classroom is foundational to implementing any theoretical and practical approach to teaching human rights because it accounts for the perspectives of students as they initially engage with the material and as they continue to develop their relationship with it. I offer a pedagogical approach mediated through cosmopolitanism, the philosophical belief in a shared ethical orientation across differences, that works to build in students a dynamic and responsible connection to human rights literature.

As the number of courses on human rights, social justice, and cultural encounters grows, it is important to pause for a moment and consider the experience students have with these topics before they enter a class. Why do students sign up for courses that engage with human rights issues? What expectations do students bring to those courses? Having taught at a midsize state institution in the United States and at an international university that offers an American-style education, I have encountered a variety of responses to these questions, yet in both locations I hear surprisingly similar responses: "I needed it to fulfill a requirement," "It fits my schedule," "I am committed to activism," "I wanted to learn more about the subject." These comments reflect two ends of the spectrum, students who are there through interest or those there through convenience, but both groups, in my experience, share similar expectations of what a human rights narrative should look like: a victim experiences a gross human rights violation and overcomes a major obstacle to find a redemptive ending in which the victim has been vindicated or saved in some way. But where does this narrative expectation originate? How does this "horizon of expectation," to use a term from the reception theorist Hans Robert Jauss, develop? How are students preconditioned to see human rights through this model even when they profess to have no expectations or experience in the subject? Answering these questions is the necessary first step for teachers who hope to help students engage critically with human rights literature.

In the codicil of *Human Rights, Inc.*, Joseph Slaughter quotes a speech President George Bush delivered about Afghanistan on 1 March 2006. President Bush describes what an honor it is to be involved in helping Afghanistan build its future. He goes on to say, "we like stories of young girls going to school for the first time so they can realize their potential." Only a few lines later, President Bush reiterates his point, explaining, "we like stories, and expect stories, of young girls going to school in Afghanistan" (317). These lines are revealing not only because they "lift the veil," exposing Western spectators' cultural expectations of human rights, but also because they offer a less than subtle reminder to those who have endured human rights violations of the kinds of stories their self-proclaimed benefactors wish to hear. This perspective creates a supply and demand in terms of expectations of human rights literature in which trauma and suffering are commodified. Makau Mutua, in *Human Rights: A Political and Cultural Critique*, invoking the savage-victim-savior metaphor, suggests that without "the victim there is no savage or savior, and the entire human rights enterprise collapses" (27). Gayatri Spivak presents a similar argument in "Righting Wrongs," in which she identifies a structure of rights that reinforces the West as the righter of wrongs and the non-West as the victims. In this framework, victims of human rights abuse are denied agency in changing their situation and must rely instead on protection and justice from intervening forces.

This narrative construction is not only articulated in political rhetoric, but it is also prominently featured in literary, cinematic, and popular culture depictions of human rights issues. For several years, the *New York Times* best-seller list has been populated by works like *Reading* Lolita *in Tehran*, *The Kite Runner*, and *A Long Way Gone*, narratives that offer arcs that reinforce the basic premise of President Bush's comments. Popular movies such as *Blood Diamond*, *The Constant Gardner*, and *Tears of the Sun* also reinforce this trajectory of victimization to vindication with the aid of Western influence. The Kony 2012 video is perhaps the most striking recent example. This viral video, with 35 million views in the first week alone, directly targeted high school and college students through social media in an attempt to raise awareness for the plight of Ugandan children and to apply pressure on the United States government for the capture of the Lord's Resistance Army's leader, Joseph Kony. Such narratives position readers from the West as, on the one hand, consumers of human rights trauma and emotional testimonies and, on the other hand, somehow outside global political, social, and economic structures that are often implicated in the violations. Exemplifying the problems that Mutua and Spivak have identified, this familiar story situates victims of human rights abuse as the producers (or, at the least, the subjects) of stories about loss and suffering. This expectation of fixed positions within the structure of rights results in a dual reaction for many Western readers: feeling bad about others' circumstances and feeling relieved about one's own. In both cases, a troubling gap exists between the reader and the material.

In "Reading Human Rights Literature in Undergraduate Literature Classes," Kimberly Nance identifies many of the defensive reading strategies that prevent students from taking social action. Some of the examples Nance provides include seeing suffering as "natural" and "inevitable," taking a passive appreciation of one's own "luck of the cosmic draw," engaging in "hagiographic" readings that turn victims into saints, and experiencing "imaginative fusion" between the reader and the sufferer (164–65). I would argue that such defensive reading practices, like students' expectations of human rights literature, are established well before students enter a literature class. Whereas Nance focuses on the outcome—lack of demonstrable action—I contend that these defensive reading strategies need to be addressed from the outset of the course. How can we challenge students to recognize their positions within large geopolitical and economic structures that frame many of the violations? How can we encourage students to reconsider their approach to human rights literature before or as they read?

Cosmopolitanism provides a philosophical foundation that promotes an alternative framework in which individuals see themselves as responsible to and for others irrespective of race, gender, class, nationality, and other identificatory markers. Cosmopolitanism is not a magic remedy for students, and it has too often appeared as a utopian one in global contexts, but in the past several years theories have transformed cosmopolitanism from an elite project of a privileged minority to one grounded in the lived realities of individuals forced to enter an unwelcoming global public sphere. This shift provides the grounds for my argument that cosmopolitanism informs a useful pedagogy for human rights.

Historically, cosmopolitanism has been closely linked with human rights projects, from its inception in Greek Stoic and Cynic thought to its development in Enlightenment philosophy to its manifestation in twentieth-century human rights discourse. This intellectual trajectory of cosmopolitanism has been well documented by David Harvey, Robert Fine, and others. The recent critiques of cosmopolitanism as complicit in universalizing a normative Western culture and an elitism that privileges those with the economic and cultural capital to be able to comfortably inhabit a globalized world generate a space for useful reimaginings of cosmopolitanism as a potential counterhegemonic project. It is this impulse toward a cosmopolitanism from below that provides the impetus for understanding its potential productivity in the classroom. Projects such as Walter Mignolo's "de-colonial cosmopolitanism" and Costas Douzinas's cosmopolitanism to come provide examples of this work. Reframing cosmopolitanism allows a shift from the perspective of being at home in the world to being "unhomed" in the world. When introduced in the classroom, this process of disorientation and disidentification can help students establish different frameworks for how they engage with texts. What I term an "unhomely cosmopolitanism" does not seek to make others as weighty and significant as the self but rather challenges readers to destabilize their position to create, albeit temporarily, an unmoored space for encounter with the text. Elaine Scarry, in "The Difficulty of Imagining Other Persons," frames this process as becoming "weightless" instead of "trying to make one's knowledge of others *as weighty as* one's knowledge of oneself" (51). This formulation of cosmopolitanism is predicated not on integration but rather on disintegration, and as such it gives rise to an ethical framework that preserves the difference of others. For students, the struggle in the process is in letting go of assumptions and expectations that allow them to feel grounded in a comfortable and comforting worldview. This pedagogical model productively pushes students to reexamine and perhaps revise those familiar perspectives and maybe also to construct new experiences with knowledge and knowledge production.

The imaginative engagement between reader and text provides a space for an ethical encounter that mirrors a cosmopolitan engagement with difference. If we understand ethics in Levinasian terms as grounded in the preservation of the difference of an other, then we can introduce a cosmopolitanism in the literature classroom that locates and preserves that difference between reader and text. Within the reader/text paradigm, an example of an unethical encounter with difference is when the reader subsumes difference: in the bid to identify with the text, the student eradicates the difference of the other. In these readings, students force similarities between circumstances that are incompatible or reap the emotional returns from identification with a character at the expense of recognizing the enormous gaps that might trouble that identification. Another form of elision is when students deny the existence of difference by not acknowledging the presence or authority of the other. In the classroom, this takes the shape of rejecting the accuracy and authenticity of both fictional and nonfictional texts. To engage ethically, then, would be to read with the irreducibility of another to one's self, a state that calls for responsibility to and for another. This approach challenges a reading process in which identification and expectation usually play a major role. Again, I turn toward disorientation, in this case in how students approach reading, as a way of accessing a space in which new relationships might emerge. How a reader negotiates difference is too often addressed at the point of contact with difference, and I suggest it is equally important to examine and attend to the conditions preceding that encounter. Before that connection to a text can be cultivated, students must first build a level of self-awareness that allows them to see their place in the world. This "conscientization," Paulo Freire's term for the critical consciousness that helps individuals recognize their place in structures of power and work toward changing the world, is built through practical pedagogy.

In developing a critical consciousness, students can continue to negotiate these emerging positions, providing new perspectives to see themselves and others. Yet the "unhomely cosmopolitan" pedagogy that I advocate does not require a radical reshaping of the classroom. Many classrooms already incorporate the types of assignments that I describe below. These strategies usually work metacognitively by helping students understand how they learn. The goal, though, is not simply for students to think about how this piece of literature makes them feel but rather to challenge them to see how they are implicated in the structures of power that shape those feelings, their catalysts, and potential responses. If students remain fixated solely on their feelings in regard to a text, they risk reinforcing the established power dynamic between human rights protector and human rights beneficiary or losing sight of the differences between self and other. Destabilizing, or disorienting, as I like to think of it, those positions requires work from the outset.

During the first class, I incorporate two activities that work to make more transparent the perspectives and expectations students bring to the course. First, I ask students to participate in a short cartography exercise in which they draw a map of the world, labeling it in as much detail as possible. Clearly this is a difficult task. In fact, most students struggle mightily with it, but surprisingly they still engage enthusiastically because there is a sense of camaraderie as they attempt to tackle such a daunting assignment. I have conducted this exercise in the United States, Hong Kong, and Lebanon and observed strikingly similar tendencies. Most students place the Atlantic in the center, revealing a heavy reliance on Western representations of the world, and draw their locations in greater scale and detail than the other parts of the world. After students complete their maps we hang them up in the room and take a few minutes for a gallery walk. In that time I ask students to take notes regarding the maps' similarities and differences. Once they have had a chance to look and giggle with some of their neighbors at the impossibility of the task, I provide a set of questions to help them engage more critically with what they saw: What is at the center of the maps? What did you notice about the scale of the maps? What is biggest? What is smallest? How does how we see the world shape our understanding of it? How does representation become a source of power? During this time, I also project two maps, one that is Atlantic centered and one that is Pacific centered. By showing students these two different perspectives, I encourage them to see how something as familiar as a map of the world can become unfamiliar when viewed from a different vantage point. From a cosmopolitan perspective, this activity challenges students to see the world from several standpoints and to acknowledge that their positionality is mutable. This exercise initiates a momentary disorientation of location that helps destabilize fixed expectations.

The second assignment is a short journal activity in which I ask students to detail their expectations for the course. Writing—and journaling in particular—can provide a valuable space for students to synthesize and arrange ideas, construct knowledge, make visible their thoughts, and engage in critical self-reflection. (I think it is important to point out that journaling risks becoming unproductive when it is used as a forum for students only to describe their feelings.) This journal entry and the subsequent class discussion call attention to conscious and subconscious expectations students bring to the course and the potential issues that may arise because of those expectations. Typically after this journal activity, as a class we work to construct a set of learning outcomes and goals that reflect this new self-awareness of what we, as a group, hope to achieve.

Addressing student expectation is an ongoing process. Once the readings for the semester begin, I continue to incorporate journal prompts that help students recognize the presence of the other in the text by bringing attention to the name of the other. I ask students to write about how they negotiate names of people or places that may be culturally or linguistically dissimilar. Typical responses range from abbreviating long names to anglicizing names to eliding them completely. When my students read Tsitsi Dangarembga's *Nervous Conditions*, for example, they often struggle with the name Babamukuru. In some cases, they end up abbreviating it to "Baba" or even simply to "B," but most students see the word as a symbol for the character without even attempting to pronounce it; they end up seeing the word but not reading it. At other times, these moments allow students with more knowledge or background in the culture represented to bring their experience to the forefront of discussion, underscoring again the partiality of each person's approach to the text. The follow-up discussion tends to be a moment of classroom solidarity when students realize that others struggle with these encounters, if from potentially vastly different points of entry. But instead of calling attention to this approach to unfamiliar names, and subsequently risking approving it, I confront students with the consequences of this practice. Are there implications of renaming, misnaming, or ignoring the name of characters? How might students be rerepresenting or misrepresenting that character? How does this give power to the student in relation to the text? How do the unfamiliar names potentially give power to the text? It is in these moments that the cosmopolitan principles grounded in a Levinasian ethics that underscore this pedagogical approach emerge, asking students to be responsible at least for the name of the other. For human rights literature this recognition of the name of the other is particularly important because it prevents the appropriation of another's difference as well as the silencing of specific voices in the text, which can lead to the types of homogenizing and universalizing reading practices that are at the heart of Mutua's and Spivak's critiques.

Toward the end of the semester, I offer a more complex approach to engaging with student expectation by pairing materials that seemingly promote a normative culture of rights often grounded in the savage-victim-savior metaphor with texts that upset that narrative. I might pair Khaled Hosseini's *The Kite Runner*, a novel that closely follows Mutua's human rights metaphor, with Michael Winterbottom's film *In This World*, a documentary-style depiction of the plight of two Afghan refugees. The temptation might be to use the film to critique the novel, but this maneuver would diminish the process of identifying how readers are complicit in completing the metaphorical frame Mutua describes. In other words, when students recognize their susceptibility to a specific horizon of expectation, whether it is through the bildungsroman structure that *The Kite Runner* employs or the identification of a normative culture of rights that anticipates an savage-victim-savior metaphor (Assef, Sohrab, and Amir, respectively, in *The Kite Runner*), they will be more likely to recognize those patterns in the future. The second text then works as an alternative to that normative model, and I ask the same questions about students' frames of reference to both texts. As students become adept at understanding the effects of their reading predilections, they can more easily reorient themselves in relation to the second text.

Another short writing assignment, a take on Ann Berthoff's double-entry notebook, offers a way to move journal activities beyond initial emotional responses. The double-entry notebook helps students reflect on their thoughts while they are engaged in the reading process. As Berthoff explains, the double-entry journal "raise[s] consciousness of texts as [an] intermediary form . . . develop[ing] a method of critical reading" (46). The goal of the journal is to help students understand why they respond the way they do to the text. On one side of the page, students record their reactions to the narrative. On the other side, they identify what in the text prompted those first responses. As the journals progress and reading skills develop, I ask students to offer more analytical readings of the text to help them recognize its complexity. I find this type of journal to be particularly effective in the study of works that include traumatic and upsetting passages because it requires students to acknowledge and engage with issues that often remain outside public view but that elicit deep emotional responses. The double-entry notebook provides a space for students to confront expectations; acknowledge their initial, often emotional reaction; and respond to both that reaction and the text through critical self-reflection and textual analysis.

A pedagogical approach mediated through cosmopolitanism provides the grounds for a rigorous examination of how and why we imagine others the way we do. Our pedagogical strategies influence how students will interact with human rights issues and questions of difference in the classroom, but ultimately these strategies factor into how they will face the material realities from which these imaginings emerge. It is imperative then that we identify and address how and where students develop their understanding of and responses to human rights issues. Confronting student expectation is the first step in pushing past consciousness-raising that elides the structural inequities at the roots of so many rights violations, to help students craft an ethical approach to these issues. A pedagogical process that fosters disorientation, disintegration, and disidentification at the outset of a course can provide the groundwork toward productive reframings of the ways in which students orient themselves toward and integrate and identify themselves with others.

Belinda Walzer

Rhetorical Approaches to Teaching Human Rights: The Pedagogy of *Speak Truth to Power*

> The pedagogic effort that may bring about lasting epistemic change in the oppressed is never accurate, and must be forever renewed. (Spivak, "Righting Wrongs")

> Every individual and every organ of society, keeping this Declaration constantly in mind, shall strive by teaching and education to promote respect for these rights and freedoms and by progressive measures, national and international, to secure their universal and effective recognition and observance. (preamble to the Universal Declaration of Human Rights [res. 217.A.III])

The Universal Declaration of Human Rights (UDHR) and other United Nations rights instruments were constructed to serve a pedagogical function. In other words, education underwrites the project of human rights. The preamble to the UDHR, quoted above, declares from the outset how important this pedagogical function is to the promotion, foundations, and principles of human rights. In addition to the call for education about rights in the preamble, article 26 of the UDHR declares, "Education shall be directed to the full development of the human personality and to the strengthening of respect for human rights and fundamental freedoms," embedding education as a fundamental right, indivisible from the rest. Furthermore, article 13 of the 1976 International Covenant on Economic, Social and Cultural Rights (ICESCR) reiterates that it is through education that rights can be guaranteed.

Out of the UDHR has grown an entire industry and culture of educational bodies devoted to teaching about human rights, some developed and promoted by the UN, some developed within academia, and many developed externally by nongovernmental organizations (NGOs) and individuals. In this essay I discuss the pedagogical and rhetorical foundations of the UDHR and provide a brief overview of several UN-sponsored, academic, and external pedagogical projects before interrogating one particular human rights teaching project, *Speak Truth to Power*. I chose *Speak Truth to Power* because, as a popular and well-known external project, it exemplifies the kind of pedagogy to which the UDHR gives rise and because it has the potential either to reinforce or to question the paradoxical and structural issues problematic in the human rights regime. Ultimately, I argue that a rhetorical pedagogical approach to projects like *Speak Truth to Power* can encourage students to examine their relation to those structures of power rather than to fortify them unwittingly.

To make the pedagogical impulse of the UDHR and surrounding documents a reality, the United Nations developed UNESCO (United Nations Educational, Scientific and Cultural Organization), which was charged with promoting education as a human right and education in human rights: "from the very beginning the promotion of human rights in the framework of the United Nations system was intimately associated with their dissemination and their teaching" (Senarclens 7). In 1982 UNESCO hosted a conference of international experts in pedagogy to discuss the progress of the UDHR's educational agenda and teaching of human rights throughout the world. Most important for this essay, the conference determined that it should be the responsibility of academia to realize the pedagogical imperative founding the UDHR and surrounding documents of human rights (Senarclens 13). The 2003 World Conference on Higher Education echoed this sentiment: "At no time in human history was the welfare of nations so closely linked to the quality and outreach of their higher education systems and institutions" (*Final Report*). Thus, UNESCO created a branch devoted solely to human rights education, which was ratified as part of its strategy on human rights (*Human Rights Education* 12). Through this branch and the OHCHR (Office of the High Commission for Human Rights) the UN has developed several pedagogy manuals and curricula for teaching about human rights violations and the UDHR, adding to material published by the many academic research organizations and NGOs devoted to raising awareness and inspiring action for specific and general human rights issues.

Human Rights Education in the School Systems of Europe, Central Asia and North America: A Compendium of Good Practice, released in celebration of the results of the so-called decade of human rights (1995–2004), compiles strategies from governments, NGOs, professional bodies, and individual educators from throughout North America, Central Asia, and Europe and lists programs, manuals, and best practices for educating about human rights so as to help inform policy makers, administrators, individual educators, and the general public. Most pedagogical strategies articulated by the UN promote an often problematic narrative of fostering individual identification and thus compassion, whether instructors use international issues as a lens through which to view local human rights issues or use a local approach to enable recognition of the global. For example, one best practice for learning about rights for refugees and asylum seekers asks students to imagine that they are part of a family group who can only bring three things with them when they flee a conflict to a refugee camp and later to a relocation country (Advocates). This approach encourages further consciousness-raising and humanitarian intervention as the appropriate outcome of rights pedagogy. The manual *ABC: Teaching Human Rights*, listed in the compendium, defines two pedagogical strategies for teaching human rights courses in the United States. The first approach seeks to foster individual compassion and empathy for others locally that can then be transferred to an international context. This is similar to the traditional notion of stoic cosmopolitanism that Martha Nussbaum articulates in which local affiliations are linked through reason first to the family, then to the local community, and finally to humanity as a whole in a series of expanding concentric circles ("Kant"). The second pedagogical model also has an individual focus but asks students to consider their local situation through an examination of international or global human rights abuses. This strategy is similar to what Elaine Scarry calls "generous imaginings" ("Difficulty" 41). This kind of imagining, in which literature plays an especially powerful role, can, according to Scarry, supplement a policy approach to rights with a bottom-up daily imagining of others (which requires a radical unimagining of the depth of ourselves). In both approaches, students are encouraged to act in response to the identifications they make.

Given the deliberate link between academia and human rights education, it is not surprising that in the second half of the twentieth century human rights education became a major focus on college campuses and in pedagogy throughout the world. Today one can browse university Web sites in the United States and find student groups dedicated to raising consciousness about international human rights issues such as the genocide in Darfur (STAND), displaced children in Uganda (Invisible Children), ending slavery throughout the world (Free the Slaves) and local rights issues such as holding United States presidents accountable for crimes against humanity (The World Can't Wait). Many colleges and universities have also developed human rights projects and networks (e.g., the Human Rights Project, at Bard College; the Lowenstein Project in the Orville H. Schell, Jr. Center for International Human Rights, at Yale; UCLA's Sanela Diana Jenkins Human Rights Project; the program in human rights and humanitarianism at Macalester College; and the University of Connecticut's Human Rights Institute). There are also national initiatives spearheaded by NGOs such as Amnesty International and the Human Rights Education Associates (HREA), an organization that provides support, training, and assistance to human rights educational initiatives. This industry of postsecondary educational bodies and groups devoted to teaching human rights, for humanitarian ends, often reflects the UN's normative model of human rights pedagogy, which advances consciousness-raising that leads to action. To further examine the UN's conventional narrative of promoting human rights, I am particularly interested in unaffiliated projects that have a specific focus on human rights educational curricula, such as the high-profile *Speak Truth to Power.*

Speak Truth to Power is a multidisciplinary and multimedia pedagogical project that uses testimony by human rights defenders from all over the world translated into performance, photography, and an educational curriculum to raise students' awareness of international human rights violations and to inspire activism. I examine *Speak Truth to Power* in particular because its diverse approach reflects the ways rights discourse gets performed across different media. The project began in 2000 when Kerry Kennedy Cuomo published a book, *Speak Truth to Power: Human Rights Defenders Who Are Changing Our World*, featuring the testimony of over fifty human rights activists, many of whom are also victims of human rights abuses, accompanied by photographic portraits of the defenders taken by the Pulitzer Prize–winning photojournalist Eddie Adams. The photographs also travel throughout the world as an autonomous exhibit. The book features contributions from renowned human rights figures such as Desmond Tutu, the Dalai Lama, and Elie Wiesel, but it also includes others, including Kailash Satyarthi, "India's lodestar for the abolition of child labor" (213), and Fauziya Kassindja, a woman from Togo who escaped female genital mutilation. One of the most powerful images and testimonies comes from a Sudanese rights activist working for women's rights in the Sudan who cannot be named. His or her striking portrait depicts the activist covered entirely in black and with a noose around his or her neck. The image serves as the cover for the book and represents all the others who cannot speak for fear of reprisal. The book embraces the founding principles of the UDHR and is dedicated to "all the unsung who show us not how to be saints, but how to be fully human." The human rights issues represented range from "freedom of expression to the rule of law, from environmental defense to eradicating bonded labor, from access to capital to the right to due process, from women's rights to religious liberty" (6). The defenders are defined nationally and hailed as the "Martin Luther Kings of their countries" (6). While the book aims less to herald the UDHR and more to feature extraordinary courage in the face of adversity, it promotes a similar narrative of rights advocacy.

The project also includes *Speak Truth to Power: An Educational and Advocacy Package*, developed in conjunction with Amnesty International (Cuomo and Richardson). This supplemental publication contains Ariel Dorfman's play *Speak Truth to Power: Voices from beyond the Dark*, which rearranges the defenders' testimony from the book into monologues, and encourages students to produce and perform the play and to participate in local and international activism related to the issues profiled. The educational component has expanded its curriculum to a Web site in conjunction with the New York Teacher's Union. The Web site offers free, downloadable lesson plans, complete with pedagogical techniques, goals, readings, activities, assignments, and essay contests. Finally, the project includes a documentary film that presents the premiere of Dorfman's play acted by Hollywood actors and intersected with interviews and footage of human rights violations and the activists' work (*Speak Truth*). The project hopes to raise awareness and to inspire: "these voices are, most of all, a call to action. . . . The more voices are raised in protest, the greater the likelihood of change" (Cuomo and Richardson 3). It is this sense of responsibility, this sense of personal accountability to action pervasive throughout the entire project of *Speak Truth to Power*, that echoes Edward Said's conception of the phrase from which the title is drawn (*Representations*).

It is clear that student-run groups and educational projects such as *Speak Truth to Power* are an extremely important addition to college campuses and curricula. They can generate a faculty and student body conscious of human rights violations and provide tools to contribute to the alleviation of suffering, through consciousness-raising, fund-raising, volunteering, and influencing policy. My concern, however, is that the pedagogical strategies surrounding these projects often lack the depth to prepare students to engage in the issues critically and to interrogate their responsibility toward action. Simply learning that such violations occur throughout the world and at home and encouraging students to participate in humanitarian action, while necessary and important work, does not often prompt students to understand their implications in the geopolitical power structures that might contribute to the perpetuation of rights abuse. If, according to Domna Stanton, part of the role of the humanities is to interrogate the discourse of human rights without foreclosing on or giving up on its very concepts ("Foreword" 1523), then projects such as *Speak Truth to Power* are a productive site through which to explore the tension between, on the one hand, the humanities mission to interrogate and, on the other, a normative culture of rights pedagogy that privileges action and often oversimplifies the structural relationship between the would-be bestower and the recipient of humanitarian aid as the (only) response to rights violations.

One of the many paradoxes of rights is a linguistic one, in which there can be no rights without wrongs and the claiming of rights accompanies the responsibility to right wrongs (Spivak, "Righting Wrongs" 523–24). This structural responsibility contributes at once to the alleviation of the suffering of others and, in doing so, the substitution of assistance for the recipients' acknowledged claims to rights. Makau Mutua locates this dynamic of mutual dependency in both the human rights regime as well as in the familiar metaphor of savage-victim-savior, which runs through many humanitarian narratives (*Human Rights*). This dynamic in turn leads to human rights' functioning as an alibi for further political, economic, and military intervention (Spivak, "Righting Wrongs" 524). In other words, rights require a response, but how we respond, as well as who that "we" should be, is key. To address those questions, education must move beyond pedagogy that seeks only to raise consciousness (potentially reifying the structure of rights) and instead must move toward a self-conscious, critical approach that destabilizes the positions of those who believe it is their responsibility to give rights without questioning why they can claim rights and others cannot (530). That is, a critical approach to the pedagogy and pedagogical impulse of human rights work is necessary to cultivate an engagement that is dialectic. To do so, teacher-scholars must bring an overtly rhetorical lens to the pedagogy of human rights discourse so as to further examine the ways in which pedagogy enables or disables the work of human rights.

I initially taught *Speak Truth to Power* in a first-year seminar course at a midsize public institution with a diverse student body. I screened the documentary film and asked my students to write a reflective journal on it as a foundation for discussion. My students' responses to the film varied from surprise that these human rights violations were occurring to a desire to know more. Often the general reaction was, "I didn't know that was going on over there; it's too bad that they can't just be more like us." In fact, many of my students believed that the issues profiled had been resolved. In my own reflective work, I faced difficult pedagogical questions: Where was the self-reflexivity on the part of my students? Where was the decentering of privilege that leads to a critical awareness of the paradoxes and structures of rights? What my students were showing me in their analysis of the project was its potential to allow for a position of spectatorship and consumption of these issues rather than a position of witness. What seems to be missing at the heart of the project, or at least my initial approach to it, are the rhetorical questions that *Speak Truth to Power* implicitly produces: What is the truth that this pedagogical mission is attempting to speak, who is speaking, and to what power? More important, how are we teaching our students to engage in this process of speaking truth to power in ethical ways?

By only screening the film, my students came away knowing more about the issues profiled through the singular voices of their spokespeople; however, I did not create an environment that fostered self-reflexivity or examined the structural imbalances behind many of the issues profiled and behind the project as a whole. By not attending directly and deeply to rhetorical concerns, my students simply learned about the other instead of learning from the other. I discovered later that my students' reactions were classic examples of defensive reading strategies in which the reader keeps the sufferer at a distance in order to preserve his or her ability for inaction in the face of seemingly insurmountable odds (Nance, "Reading"). And so I returned to the pedagogical drawing board and focused on rhetoric.

I locate human rights pedagogy in rhetorical studies, including composition classes, for four reasons. First, pedagogy that employs a rhetorical approach teaches writing and argument through perspectives of how language shapes and is shaped by power and epistemology, the very skills that are necessary in considering the implications of speaking truth to power. Second, considering Min-Zhan Lu's reminder that composition and rhetorical studies do not always have to be the "ungrateful receiver" of other disciplines' theoretical histories (11), rhetorical studies and writing has long been engaged in issues of ethics and social justice, from service learning to critical pedagogy to the ethical impulses that underscore the rhetorical project of argumentation exemplified by none other than Aristotle. Rhetoric and composition as a field is thus poised to bring this history to bear on the pedagogical project of human rights discourse (see, e.g., Olson and Lyon). And vice versa: human rights discourse can bring its history and vocabulary to bear on the pedagogy and subject matter taught in composition and rhetoric classrooms. Stated another way, the discourse surrounding human rights is implicitly rhetorical and pedagogical, and, consequently, locating it in a writing or rhetoric class enables participants to pay greater attention to the ethical ramifications of speaking truth to power.

In its overall approach, *Speak Truth to Power* relies on powerful images and performance to draw attention to individual and structural human rights abuses. It encourages students to act as witnesses to these abuses and, ideally, to feel the same sense of responsibility to act as do the human rights defenders profiled. Dorfman describes the human rights advocates: "They understood that if they witnessed this suffering inflicted on themselves or on others, and did nothing, they were, in some twisted way, being turned into accomplices" (Introduction). A rhetorical perspective of a project that exemplifies and encourages witnessing with an aim toward action, then, demands consideration of the implications of speaking truth to power.

The third reason I locate human rights pedagogy in rhetorical studies is in response to Kimberly Nance's "Reading Human Rights Literature in Undergraduate Literature Classes." Nance argues that literature can elicit defensive readings in which readers become overwhelmed and shut down when faced with the gravity of a situation (as happened with my students in the freshman seminar). Empathy and overidentification, she argues, erase critical distance, thereby preventing action. However, since a rhetorical perspective encourages students to interrogate the how of a text more explicitly in terms of the ways in which they engage with language and its effects, rhetorical studies has the potential to push students' engagement beyond the affective space of the issue at hand to a critical engagement that leads them to consider the responsibility of the reader.

Finally, the fourth reason a rhetoric and composition classroom is a productive place to use a project like *Speak Truth to Power* is that the writing and revising process is intrinsically self-reflexive, and students who can pay close attention to their positions as speakers and audience learn to be sensitive to the delicate rhetorical negotiations important in any exchange but crucial in human rights discourse. In teaching *Speak Truth to Power* through writing and acting, students must be witness, listener, and actor. These multiple points of engagement not only teach them the skills necessary for participating with awareness in discourse communities but also enable students to gain the rhetorical tools necessary to speak truth to power, whatever that might look like.

Keeping these four reasons in mind, when I use *Speak Truth to Power* now, it is not so much to teach it as it is to enable students to participate in facets of the project and then reflect on that engagement through written exercises, both high and low stakes (graded and ungraded). In addition to screening the documentary, I now also encourage students to analyze the photographs and the play, or better yet, to perform or produce the play either as a school-wide production or as an in-class exercise, depending on the additional goals of the course. With these several points of engagement, *Speak Truth to Power* has the ability to provide students with the necessary imaginative space through which to engage critically with the structure of rights because the project does not invite identification with the human rights defenders as static subjects. Instead, its goals of representing the violations, contexts, and subjects of violations through different media and discourses draw attention to the distance between the original enunciation, the subsequent layers of representation, and the additional layers of audience (the activists speaking about it in the documentary, the celebrities performing the play, the students themselves watching and performing the play).

Dorfman's play, for example, has nine speaking parts. There are eight parts for students to play human rights defenders (Dorfman suggests that several people can play each defender) and one part for a student to play The Man, a character who represents oppression (Dorfman suggests that two students can play The Man). The stage notes call for the names or images of the defenders to be displayed behind the actors onstage. Dorfman also suggests in his stage notes that the voices of the activists should "flow through the bodies of the actors and actresses in a natural manner. . . . Each actor and actress is not pretending to be that person, but is the channel through which that person is reaching the audience" (*Speak Truth* 60). I find that asking my students the foundational questions of who is speaking, why, and to what power can draw attention to this gap between the speech that is permissible (the script) and the speech that is impermissible (the activists' voices within their own contexts, speaking out against their particular forms of oppression). The speaking through, or rerepresentation of the activists' words by student actors, disrupts the students' understandings of the production of knowledge as individual, static, cognitive, and rational and suggests instead that it can be polyvocal, fluid, affective, and corporeal.

I have also found it is important to draw specific attention to the ethos of the character of The Man by asking the students to do a rhetorical analysis of the character, in either a class discussion or a writing assignment. The Man is the one character who does not speak the words of a human rights activist. Instead, he speaks back to the activists' testimony, representing the "evangelist of multiple evils, who reminds us by his words and presence what the defenders are up against" (60). The Man is meant to be the embodiment of state and social oppression (jail, torture, exile) as well as discursive oppression (apathy and unethical action). For example, The Man says:

> All those names. Names we won't forget, not me. Others will forget those names. They're already fading from memory, those names. . . . The lights on them now and the applause about to start and surround and caress them, the lights that begin to dim, go out one by one, as the audience goes home and a faraway face, perhaps one of these very faces, flares up in pain and then dies down, and it's time for dinner and it's time again for sleep, and tomorrow it will be back where it has always been. (58)

I ask students to pay close attention to The Man's ethos and his attempts to embody oppression that is "more perverse and pervasive and closer to home both to those who stage this and those who watch it" (60). As Dorfman says, The Man represents the person who does nothing in the face of injustice, "the forces of indifference and apathy that are the world's enemies of the struggle for a better world" (60). Asking students to analyze The Man's rhetorical appeals draws attention to the fact that his homogenized power assumes that witnessing and thus ethical action will not work. This rhetorical exercise is a crucial moment in the class because students can either walk away thinking that The Man wins, so to speak, or that, as the final line of the play states, "[t]he work has just begun" (59).

To stack the deck in favor of the second option and since drama educates through reflection (Zatzman), performing the play must be supplemented with exercises that ask students to be self-conscious about their rhetorical stances. Reflective writing assignments such as Ann Berthoff's double-entry notebook are particularly useful, although any assignment that encourages students to witness their witnessing—in other words, to observe their own reactions and then comment on how and why they had those reactions—is productive. I usually ask students to address their initial reactions by paying attention to the ways in which human rights texts often appeal to pathos and then ask them to move beyond those initial emotional reactions to consider the appeals to ethos and thus the structural interventions that the text might be making. Conceptually, a rhetorical lens turns the gaze onto readers or audience members and asks them to consider their role as meaning makers in their interaction with the text.

In considering the telos of human rights pedagogy after my first, failed lesson in human rights pedagogy, I realized my need for critical pedagogy that has as its end result not only humanitarian action but also self-reflexivity and the critical interrogation of discourse as action. Let me be clear: this pedagogy by no means precludes or forecloses the kind of humanitarian work that remains still so necessary. Nor do I mean to promote consciousness-raising as the end result of human rights pedagogy. Rather, this renegotiation of what action looks like within a pedagogical setting enables teachers, particularly at the university level, to engage in the structural and rhetorical interrogation of human rights discourse and ultimately provide students with the tools to determine their own engagement with human rights within and beyond the classroom.

Ryan Omizo and Wendy S. Hesford

Cultivating the Dialogic Subject of Human Rights Pedagogy

In *Cultivating Humanity*, Martha Nussbaum calls for a cosmopolitan approach to civic education based on the view that we are all citizens of the world and members of a common humanity. For Nussbaum, world citizenship involves our "imaginative capacity to enter into the lives of people of other nations" (51). To become a "good interpreter of cultural difference," Nussbaum claims, drawing on Marcus Aurelius, we need to "[a]ccustom [ourselves] not to be inattentive to what another person says, and as far as possible enter into that person's mind" (qtd. on 63). Cosmopolitan education requires that students and educators transcend the inclination "to define themselves primarily in terms of local group loyalties and identities. . . . The world citizen must develop sympathetic understanding of distant cultures and of ethnic, racial, and religious minorities within her own" (67–69). Failing to make a broad world perspective a central part of education, Nussbaum warns, undercuts the case for multicultural respect in a nation.

In Nussbaum's framework, human rights education emerges as a form of cosmopolitan multiculturalism, wherein literature and the cultural arts play "a vital role [in] cultivating powers of imagination that are essential to citizenship" (85). According to Nussbaum and others, such as Lynn

Hunt in *Inventing Human Rights*, imaginative identifications across cultural and national boundaries were crucial to the historical development of the concept of universal human rights. Both Nussbaum and Hunt make an important argument about how cultural practices and human rights law are constituted in and through each other. Yet both fall short of detecting the force of sentimentality in their valorization of imaginative capacities, which are caught up in hidden subjectivities, unaccounted privileges, and social and political inequities. Imaginative identifications may function as no more than pedagogical scenes of self-recognition, a process through which privileged readers and writers distance themselves from hegemony and reinforce their status before the law as rights-bearing subjects distributing rights to those unable to claim them.

Nussbaum acknowledges that the primary function of cosmopolitan education is not to confirm "the foreign or minority student's personal sense of dignity" (*Cultivating Humanity* 69). Imagining, she suggests, should promote the view of the other as an agent and not simply as a "passive recipient of benefits and satisfactions" (97). Yet she nevertheless embraces the confirmation of the other as a byproduct of rhetorical, namely narrative, imagination (69). Thus *Cultivating Humanity*, aligned as it is with a cosmopolitan model of human personality development, which suggests that the route to human rights is through the acquisition of a humanitarian sensibility toward the other, repeats at the pedagogical level the warring struggles for recognition that sustained colonial relations and have long constrained the radical potential of human rights. For instance, non-Western sociocultural practices have been the prime targets of human rights education; the "messianic ethos" of human rights is pitched to "help those who cannot help themselves" (Mutua, "Savages" 231). The inability of the United States to recognize its own violations of human rights—American rhetoric assumes the violations are elsewhere—is a classic example of this messianic ethos.

We share Nussbaum's rhetorical orientation and interest in understanding how cultural practices function as pedagogical surrogates for the legal development and enforcement of human rights. But what neither Nussbaum nor Hunt sufficiently addresses, which is crucial to our argument, is how human rights law and culture work together to sustain normative frameworks of inclusion and exclusion and how cultural predilections and entrenched conceptions of identity and difference shape an individual's imaginative capacity to identify with others. In other words, we also recognize the need to acknowledge the potential risks of cosmopolitan identifications in reproducing sociopolitical hierarchies, especially when individual subjectivity and agency are predicated on the Hegelian self-other dialectic, which itself is symptomatic of the "pathology of oppression" (Oliver 3). As Kelly Oliver points out, "Oppression creates the need and demand for recognition" (9). In contrast to theories of subjectivity that replicate the subject-other or subject-object hierarchy and therefore are caught up in the trap of recognition and "logic of oppression that made [struggles for recognition] necessary in the first place" (26–27), Oliver calls for a dialogic understanding of subjectivity as "response-ability" and "address-ability" (6). Oliver's dialogic view of subjectivity as address-ability provides a useful way to conceptualize how students and teachers negotiate the subject positions, self- and social recognitions, and affective responses that human rights representations compel.

Contemporary human rights pedagogy, tethered as it is to a cosmopolitan imaginary, carries the legacy of the colonial enterprise and its hierarchy of self- and social recognition. Our aim here, however, is not merely to point to the duplicity of sentimental education, in which the goal is to form "between reader and text . . . a friendship and/or community" predicated on compassionate identification in neocolonial, colonial, and imperialist projects (Nussbaum, *Cultivating Humanity* 101). Rather, we are interested in how legally and culturally based human rights discourses, exploited and inflected by hegemonic powers, may provide a pedagogical locus for the cultivation of critical, rhetorical agency and a dialogic human rights subjectivity attuned to the limitations of a moral cosmopolitan framework for addressing social injustices. Heeding Oliver's point, we seek to trace how such discursive matrices position subjects to address and respond to human rights representations and how these positions confirm, disrupt, and revise normative assumptions about such concepts as victimhood and bearing rights. We therefore propose an intercontextual rhetorical approach to human rights pedagogy, which takes as its point of departure the ethical and pedagogical ramifications of framing students as moral cosmopolitan subjects of human rights internationalism. We use the term *moral cosmopolitan subjects* in this context to refer to human rights representations that position privileged peoples and nations as the distributors of rights and recognitions to those unable to claim them. We are particularly interested in drawing attention to the pedagogical work that human rights images perform and the mediation of suffering by sociopolitical relations, discourses, aesthetics, and technologies. Attention to the mediation of suffering prompts us to engage the dialogism of human rights rhetoric and to trouble the binary configurations of the moral vernacular of official and resistant human rights discourses, in order to account for how victims appropriate the "official" human rights language used by governments and nongovernmental organizations to create narratives of experience (see Hauser).

Intercontextual Productions

During the spring 2012 quarter, Wendy Hesford taught Human Rights Law, Literature, and Film, a special-topic course in the Department of English at Ohio State University. The course focused on international human rights law and contemporary human rights literature and film, with an emphasis on the tensions that arise when representations of crimes against humanity and humanitarian interventions are written and marketed for Western audiences. Topics under consideration included representations of genocide in Darfur, apartheid and reconciliation in South Africa, child soldiers in Sierra Leone, and the United States war on terror. The curriculum included essays on the history of human rights and key debates in the field, human rights documents, and several memoirs, among them Brian Steidle's *The Devil Came on Horseback: Bearing Witness to the Genocide in Darfur*, Loung Ung's *First They Killed My Father: A Daughter of Cambodia Remembers*, Ishmael Beah's *A Long Way Gone: Memoirs of a Boy Soldier*, and films, including Emmanuel Jal's *War Child* and Rory Kennedy's *Ghosts of Abu Ghraib*. Hesford's curriculum and pedagogical approach derived from an earlier version of the course and collaboration with Ryan Omizo. Although we emphasized truth-telling texts and contexts (memoirs, testimonials, documentary films, and so on), our pedagogy did not focus on issues of resemblance or misrepresentation. Our goal was not to direct students to make judgments about whether a certain representation captured the truth, nor were we interested in elevating truth-telling genres over other cultural forms. Rather we hoped to engage our students in an analysis of the intercontextuality of truth-telling texts to better understand the forces that shaped their interpretations and affective responses.

Intercontextuality is a key element of a rhetorically oriented pedagogical vision that seeks to understand how arguments and images travel across cultural and national borders; how symbols and symbolic practices are appropriated, translated, and historicized; and how human rights subjectivities are discursively constituted. As Hesford explains in *Spectacular Rhetorics*, to read intercontextually is to identify the referents to other texts or rhetorical acts in a composition or performance and to reflect on the social codes and habits of interpretation that shape its meaning and that it enacts. Our approach to human rights pedagogy attends to the material circumstances and ideological formations that shape the movement and contextual and yet provisional meanings of rhetorical acts. In discussing student texts, therefore, we move beyond consideration of authorial intention to track how students' engagement with human rights texts and images represents their rhetorical negotiation with or appropriation of cosmopolitan narratives, culturally sanctioned modes of identification and affect, and technologies of interaction. Such a view necessitates an understanding of rhetoric as action—rhetoric activates social, historical, and political relationships; consolidates identities; and configures material relations of power and difference (Riedner and Mahoney 7). As Carole Blair rightly notes, "[R]hetoric has material force beyond the goals, intentions, and motivation of its producers. . . . Rhetoric enables some actions and prohibits or at least discourages others; it promotes particular modes of identity and not others" (22–23).

Cosmopolitan and human rights rhetoric hover between closeness and distance in configuring the "global as the human" (Cheah 3). In *Inhuman Conditions*, Pheng Cheah observes, "Both phenomena are generally viewed as placing actual and normative limits on the efficacy of national culture and the sovereignty of the nation-state, which is seen as particularistic, oppressive, and even totalitarian" (3). Similarly, the shared pedagogical dimension of cosmopolitanism and human rights resides in the "normative concept of culture as the human power of transcendence" (5). But, rejecting the notion that reflexivity is akin to the transcendence of discursive confirmations, we involve our students in the critical analysis of the normative dimensions of human rights representations, including how human rights images of atrocity or advocacy imagine audiences as part of a transnational or national witnessing public—a public that more often than not calls forth the sentiment of cosmopolitanism that seeks to close moral distance between spectators and those suffering.

Correspondingly, we approach our students' responses to and production of human rights texts and images as intercontextual productions. Just as any given text or image is intercontextual, the spectator is intercorporeal; he or she cannot be conceived outside a web of interrelations and discourses of which he or she is a living part (Holquist). We therefore embrace a Foucauldian view of human agency as implicated in, though not necessarily entrapped by, cultural discourses, ideologies, and technologies of interaction. In other words, we argue for an understanding of the intersubjectivity of human rights subjects. Consequently, we emphasize that agency is not a quality possessed by any one individual to be voluntarily activated, as modernist notions have maintained. We locate agency in the orientations to and enactments of rhetorical opportunities historically conditioned by intercontextual fields. In mapping our students' entries into the rhetorical fields of mass media, human rights, and academic discourse we are thus investigating how human rights representations are authored and authorized under prevailing notions of cosmopolitanism, moral universalism, and human agency.

Through the lens of intercontextuality, we inspect the mobility of our students' texts—their capacity to travel and converse with other discourses—and complicate notions of authorial intent by identifying recurrent rhetorical strategies and situating these strategies within domains of mass media such as journalism or documentary film. These domains provide students not simply with models of emulation or targets for critique but also with the conditions that constrain or allow the articulation of certain statements and social relations.

In the following section, we have identified two such rhetorical strategies typified by student image-texts and arrayed on a continuum that spans the iconic to the iconoclastic. The iconic encompasses a text that attempts to represent an entire complex of issues through a reduction of messages, often synecdochic. On the opposite end, the iconoclastic mode thoroughly disrupts the iconic and calls attention to the gaps and ideological contingencies in meaning making. While we have derived these categories in part from the formal qualities of students' image-texts and their expressed motivations, we do not intend them as purely generic definitions. The iconic and iconoclastic also register the levels of intercontextuality and reflexivity manifest in the visualizations and, by extension, track paths of rhetorical agency.

Pedagogical Reflections and Challenges

We present here two student examples of a visualization assignment. In this assignment, students assembled three images in a linear sequence and then overlaid a quotation from one of the class readings over the three images in *Microsoft Word* or *Adobe Photoshop* (we offered a *Photoshop* workshop in preparation for the assignment). Students were asked to explore the relation of the images and the text and to deliberate on the meanings of each combination and those conveyed across the series. Instead of collecting images that simply illustrated the selected quotation, students were asked to complicate the signification of image and text and then create a visual argument about the representation of human rights. Students submitted their visualization drafts for peer review, and reviewers responded to the visualizations' pairing of text and image (Does the quotation mirror, revise, restrict, or expand the meaning of the images?), the narrative potential of the series (What effect does the initial image have on the understanding of the second and third?), and its rhetorical persuasiveness (How do the image-text combinations appeal to an audience? What audience does the image-text imagine?). Lastly, students reflected on their artistic and rhetorical decisions and evaluated the shortcomings and successes of their compositions in an artist's statement that accompanied the final visualization. The artist statements allowed students to clarify the goals of their creations, but they also served as snapshots of students' positioned, intercontextual engagements within a matrix of discourses. Consequently, we pay specific attention to how students' reflections reproduce or complicate dominant rhetorical strategies employed in the legitimation of human rights cases and the pursuit of public support. Doing so, we believe that we move beyond authorial intent, examining instead how students authorize their arguments.

The Iconic: Student 1

The iconic point on our continuum includes visualization projects that attempt to represent large-scale issues in human rights through shorthand imagery. This procedure is related to the rhetorical trope of synecdoche, which evokes a whole through its parts. According to his artist statement, Student 1 focused his visualization project on the atrocities occurring in Syria to "start off showing violence plain and simple." He begins the visual sequence with an exterior shot of a doorway stained with blood. The quotation superimposed on the photograph is culled from the byline of a *New York Times* op-ed piece by Andrew Stobo Sniderman and Mark Hanis, founders of the Genocide Intervention Network, which advocates the use of drone planes to document violence in Syria. It reads, "The world could get clear, instant evidence of atrocities in Syria." The second image captures an older man carrying a wounded boy away from the throes of a skirmish that erupted during a demonstration against Syrian President Bashar Assad. The quotation for Stobo Sniderman and Hanis is situated in the lower right corner beside the Samaritan and the wounded boy. The final image presents an infographic map of the death and casualty toll in Syria originally created by the *Guardian* ("Syria Crisis"). Death counts are clustered in lurid red, and a line graph depicts the casualties reported each day, showing a large spike on 4 February 2012. The quotation, in blue, overlays the center of the map and blends with the muted greens and reds of the infographic so that it almost appears to be a native caption.

Student 1's professed intent to depict the Syrian government's repression of its citizenry in a "plain and simple" visual argument indicates two key engagements with the iconic pole of our spectrum. First, the image of spilled blood in the initial photograph serves as a sign of generalized violence. The act of bloodshed recorded in the photograph could have occurred anywhere, at any time, affecting anyone. Thus Student 1 leverages the image's symbolic and synecdochic capacities over the documentary to portray the direness of the Syrian situation. He then extends this iconic argumentation in the second image of the sequence. Although the photograph does serve as a more definitive record of the Syria's civil strife, Student 1's artist statement draws attention to a universalized notion of fatherhood and the status of children: "This is the culmination of my ethos rhetorical appeal, which not only appeals to fathers, but also anyone who has, or is considering having children, as well as those who believe children have no place in war and conflict." However, as Student 1 acknowledges in his artist statement, this picture "looks to be" a father carrying his son away from a violent encounter with Syrian authorities. Whether this father-son relationship actually describes the connection between the elder man and the boy is undefined in Student 1's artist statement and in the online source of the image. What is discernible from the image is that the altruistic action of the elder man resembles that of a caring parent. As such, Student 1 employs this image as an icon that both activates universalist concepts of the family in audiences and corroborates the imaginary projections of these concepts. This strategy of iconization consequently serves as a figurative bridge connecting the national struggles of Syria with audiences across the globe, despite cultural and geographic distance. By demonstrating how a withdrawal from particularity can make the other more familiar, Student 1's visualization emphasizes the need for a fine-grained analytic with which to understand how the exercise of the imaginative capacities Nussbaum advocates can produce discourses that increase necessary emotional investment in human rights cases within audiences and collapse the historical specificity of the afflicted into a series of tragic archetypes—what might be considered, paraphrasing Nussbaum's formulations, familiarization gone too far ("Compassion" 10).

The third image in Student 1's visualization enacts his second key engagement with the iconic. Here, the image illustrates clusters of casualties in red across a regional map of Syria, further divided into sectarian zones. The iconicity of this image departs from the previous images in the sequence. Rather than a photograph whose content lends itself to the invocation of generalized themes of suffering, war, and the family, the map relies on abstract shapes—icons—to visualize the statistics of Syrian unrest. As Student 1 writes, "I chose what seems to be a fairly accurate representation of the deaths and casualties that have occurred according to region." The red circles metonymically replace images of carnage and the hard numbers, which also appear on the map.

Reviewing Student 1's artist statement, we can discern a rhetorical strategy that attempts to move the audience from the general to the concrete. A doorway splashed with blood signals a crime or social breakdown. The image of the Syrian man rescuing a battered child puts a human face on the state of emergency, while the lack of provenance allows the audience to synecdochically conflate these subjects with wider themes of family, fatherhood, and the innocence of childhood confronted with war. The final image then locates the previous two images within a specific time in a specific location, supported by numerical facts. We can also trace in Student 1's composition a tendency that distinguishes the iconic pole of our spectrum: the use of reduced but allusive imagery as evidence in the substantiation of claims. Student 1's quotation, "The world could get clear, instant evidence of atrocities in Syria," calls attention to this strategy and further obliges viewers to consider the status of this type of evidence. What do "clear" and "instant" mean when associated with the use of icons? Discussing the final image in his sequence, Student 1 refers to an "obvious ease" with which readers can "access" the casualty figures, connecting the use of icons with an enhanced mental digestibility. When assessing his use of the second image, Student 1 refers to the photograph as the "emotional bombshell of the piece," further inflecting this attribute of accessibility with a sense of impact. Here the evidentiary value of the iconic is its readability and its ability to maximize audience impact on an emotional level. Thus the iconic shortens the gap in reception, announcing the extremity of the Syrian political climate with a minimum of easily registered signs: blood in a doorway, the injured fleeing from conflict, a rash of red circles representing death.

The task of an intercontextual rhetorical analytic is to interrogate such uses of evidence, especially considering how important the subject is for the prosecution of human rights violations, donor involvement, and the legal recognition of individuals or groups as bearers of certain rights. That said, such interrogations are incomplete if they merely unmask the rhetorical strategies motivating a student text. Locating Student 1's visualization on the iconic pole of our spectrum, we must also attend to the discursive formations that authorize this iconization, or what Foucault would term a domain's "principle themes" or "governing statements" that regulate the possibilities for action (147). For Student 1, we can start this process by examining the source of his chosen quotation. The *New York Times* op-ed by Stobo Sniderman and Hanis, "Drones for Human Rights," argues for employing military drone planes to record video of the human rights abuses occurring in Syria. These records could then be used as legal evidence in International Criminal Court proceedings and as tools to mobilize global support against Syria's oppressive acts. The quotation's linkage to a journalistic artifact is significant to the iconic mode of representation, given that mass media news reporting routinely incorporate images synecdochically. Indeed, this is most apparent in human-rights-related stories, in which an interview subject is often asked to comment on the struggles of his or her community, offering less of an individual account and more of a testimonial that represents a general state of affairs. In the process, the interview subject serves as an exemplum (or icon) of humanitarian need. Thus Student 1's employment of the iconic mode participates in a well-established, recognizable image economy—mass media journalism—whose ethos of truth telling grants legitimating authority to the iconic mode and, further, sets the grounds for Student 1's visual argumentation.

Stobo Sniderman and Hanis's proposal to deploy military drones in the service of human rights causes also reflects a thoroughgoing priority of the Western human rights project: documenting incidents for the legitimation of human rights appeals. Undergirding this preoccupation is the assumption that photographs or video footage can prove the truth of human rights appeals by capturing an objective moment of reality, by showing what really happened. This weight placed on visual evidence in human rights discourse consequently contributes to an iconic understanding of the human rights image because such images are conceived as imminently meaningful. Whether or not the man cradling the bloodied boy in Student 1's visualization is the boy's father can be elided by the tacit acceptance that this photograph does show the horrors of political oppression. The boy's injuries did occur. The elder man did rescue him. The photograph does refer to a real event whose capture can satisfy the ethical imperative of human rights projects—to protect people from the abrogation of their natural rights as human beings—even if it cannot substantiate a legalistic claim. When considered in this particular intercontextual weaving, Student 1's visualization prompts critical questions about how human rights rhetoric mobilizes the visual as a means toward legitimating human rights appeals and rallying public support. For example, what is the evidentiary status of the iconic image in human rights advocacy?

In addition, Student 1's rhetorical negotiations bring to light a critical misprision in cosmopolitan pedagogical orientations: that the imaginative identification with the difference of the other grounds itself in universalist construals of human subjectivity. The imaginative capacities that Nussbaum cites as the animus for a cosmopolitan world citizenry are attributed to all subjects equally, disregarding cultural, economic, and political differences that operate between subjects as subjects are advised to understand and embrace them. To what degree, then, is cosmopolitan multiculturalism a byproduct of iconic modes of representation commodified by mass media? What does it mean to imagine oneself in the position of the other when the other is so readily commuted into an object, an icon?

Iconoclastic: Student 2

We employ a literal definition of the iconoclastic: a rhetorical strategy that disrupts the material image. The most apparent difference between Student 2's visualization and Student 1's is the amount of digital manipulation. The first image in Student 2's sequence features a compilation of various signs protesting gay marriage, which nearly completely obscures the Human Rights Campaign logo, a yellow equal sign against a purple field, in the background. Slogans in the collage include "Defend Marriage," with icons of a man and woman; "A True Marriage. Male and Female and God" on a church sign; and "Marriage: One Man & One Woman," held aloft by a white male in military fatigues. The image of the United States flag inserted in the right third of the collage locates this controversy within the United States. Moreover, the compositing of a saluting protester in the military fatigues evokes notions of United States patriotism and citizenship. Student 2's quotation, "They are entitled to equal rights as to marriage," culled from article 16, section 1, of the Universal Declaration of Human Rights (UDHR), mingles with the anti-gay-marriage typography, the key phrase, "equal rights as to," suppressed in the collage through the use of a minuscule font size. The second image features a competing sign that reads, "It's Wrong to Vote on Rights," nested within the Human Rights Campaign logo. Two key revisions are operant. First, the quotation from the UDHR is more prominent, if still interrupted. Second, the Human Rights Campaign logo is more opaque, although it is still ghostly in comparison with the other elements of the composition. In the final image of the sequence, Student 2 presents an extracted image of President Barack Obama sourced from the speech in which he publicly proclaimed his belief in marriage equality, composited over a fully realized Human Rights Campaign logo. The segments of the UDHR quotation are now united so that it reads as one complete sentence.

In one sense, Student 2's visualization enacts a narrative of progress. The sequence begins with rightist arguments that dissent from the ostensible ideals of the UDHR article and seek to crowd out marriage equality supporters by asserting normative conceptions of marriage as an institution exclusively involving a man and a woman. The second image responds to these charges by foregrounding a sign that adheres to the principles of the UDHR and is LGBTQ inclusive. The third image represents the resolution of these two positions. Combined, the image of President Obama, a powerful political advocate for marriage equality, and the Human Rights Campaign logo repair the heretofore fractured proposition of the UDHR, thus connecting marriage equality for LGBTQ groups with inalienable human rights.

We can also trace a pervasive use of iconic imagery. The messages on the protest signs in the first and second images operate as metonyms for both anti-gay-marriage and marriage-equality platforms. The photoshopped image of President Obama casts him as the decisive political authority on the marriage-equality debate, referencing both his affirmative statements on gay marriage and the mystique surrounding the office of the president of the United States. Finally, Student 2 employs the Human Rights Campaign logo as a condensed symbol for LGBTQ struggle for civil recognition and as a mark of success for the fair application of human rights to all groups, regardless of sexuality. What distinguishes Student 2's project as iconoclastic is the internal dialogue that it enacts among its pictorial elements and the process of its composition, which prominently foregrounds its manipulation of the iconic. Student 2's mosaic of anti-gay-marriage signage functions as a gestalt figure of conservative ideologies; however, what is critical about this mosaic is how Student 2 pieced it together from a variety of referential images to create an iconic picture, a fact she draws attention to in her artist statement. This assembly work relies on and reveals to the reader how icons work rhetorically as a series of cultural associations between texts and concepts. Thus, in contrast to Student 1's definitional use of images (e.g., the photographic realism of the elder man and wounded boy or the infographic of casualty rates), Student 2 emphasizes the relational animation of images in the making of an icon.

The other significant contrast between Student 1's more iconic visualization and Student 2's iconoclastic argument is in the way that the pictorial elements operate in tension with one another. We can trace this technique in her project through her use of the Human Rights Campaign logo and the quotation from the UDHR. Student 2 offers both in their iconic modes—the Human Rights Campaign logo as a synecdoche for LGBTQ justice and the UDHR quotation as a reference to a foundational and authoritative human rights document. By introducing the Human Rights Campaign into the same frame as the anti-gay-marriage mosaic, she embroils each into a contest that mimics the oppositional lines drawn by the real defense-of-marriage and marriage-equality proponents. At the same time, the imposition of the UDHR quotation serves as an adjudicating mechanism within the composite, placing both marriage camps under a juridical lens, admittedly not on level terms. Much of this strategy conforms to the genre of a progress narrative. Regarded as a duel of iconic imagery, Student 2's visualization is also an attempt at a dialectical negotiation of statement and counterstatement. Her innovation is her visual adulteration of the chosen icons in the first image, in which the Human Rights Campaign's logo is nearly translucent and the quotation from the UDHR features a novel typography. Both techniques make conspicuous the material status of the icons as graphics, not simply abstract principles or legal stipulations. Student 2's visualization obliges the reader to see the use and reception of icons as a result of material and technological practices that can create a truth as much as it can render a preexisting convention more accessible. Furthermore, by showing the iconic as a precession of signs and rhetorical techniques, Student 2's visualization holds out the possibility for people to intervene in the construction of iconic imagery through the use of programs such as *Photoshop* or even through the cutting and pasting of printed imagery. We would contend that Student 2's visualization functions as what W. J. T. Mitchell calls a "meta-picture"—a picture about pictures and about picturing (35–45).

Given the technical skill demonstrated by Student 2 and the extent of her digital alterations, it would be easy to privilege the iconoclastic over the iconic pole of our continuum. But instead of leveraging one form over another, an intercontextual analytic should investigate how and why student texts come to inhabit the positions that they do and how texts slide back and forth along this continuum. As we have argued, the iconoclastic visualization project contains tendencies of the iconic—just as the elements of the iconic text can lead to the iconoclastic.

Although these two visualization projects cover a spectrum of intercontextuality and reflexivity, one tendency cuts across this continuum: the prevalence of emotional appeals (pathos) in engaging with human rights discourse. Specifically, we see among the sampled visualizations a vacillation between outrage and empathy. Student 1's visualization proceeds along these very lines. The image of the blood-drenched doorway suggests that some violence has penetrated the stable normality of a civilized space. The second image then inserts an instance of humanity in the scene of the crime, eliciting an empathetic response on two counts. First, by showing a child in jeopardy, the photograph attempts to arouse viewer compassion for the injured child. Second, by depicting an act of care between the elder man and the child, the photograph fosters empathetic identification between the viewer and the capacity for humanitarian sacrifice that the image renders iconic. In Student 2's visualization, the outrage over the marriage equality debate is staged in the collection of protest signs, themselves synecdochic reminders of passionate rallies from both sides of the issue, and in the typographic defacement of the excerpt from the UDHR. Like Student 1, Student 2 also presents to the viewer an empathetic action with which one should identify: the acknowledgment by President Obama that the LBGTQ community deserves the right to marry.

This is not to say that representations of empathy and outrage are not appropriate rhetorical appeals in human rights discourse. Empathy for the human rights victim and outrage against the victimizer delineate commonsense reactions to obvious wrongs—which obliges the question, Commonsense for whom? Thus drawing on the work of Sara Ahmed, we locate the vicissitudes of emotional appeals in a wider intercontextual sociality. According to Ahmed, emotions do not emanate from within the individual; rather, they emerge from the impressions left by a collectivity of others, which then configure a subject's relationship with others in society (31–35). Consequently, emotions, even responses to sheer brutality, arise through social interaction, itself conditioned by discourse, and must therefore be read as another text in the dialogic matrix of human rights.

The cause of human rights may presuppose a cosmopolitan audience with the social and economic capital to effect far-flung change and the freedom to publicly deliberate on moral, political, and legal matters. Likewise, the student examples imagine the audience as part of a larger human-rights-witnessing public. Student 1 creates varying proximities between the distant viewer and violence: from the blood-stained stairs to the intimacy of familial embrace to the wide-angle statistical viewpoint. He prompts the audience to oscillate between objective observation and emotional identification. The scene of emotion—the second image in the series—is preceded and followed by images that gesture toward a rational predisposition, which suggests that the emotional appeal must in the end be objectified and quantified (that is, removed from the realm of the personal) to enable a commitment to a moral cause. The idea of agency as possession, particularly as individual possession, is unsettled in this project precisely because it is not the final appeal. The final appeal is one that re-secures the distance between viewers and sufferers by commuting Syria's national situation into fungible visual currency, which can circulate in the broadest media economies. And so the notion that this "hard data" can clinch the case of Syrian human rights violations presupposes a rational liberal subject with the ability to deliberate in an established democratic public, which implicitly separates the danger zones from those countries, agencies, or collectives secure enough to help. Student 1 moves beyond sentimental cosmopolitan representations that position the human rights victim as the other awaiting recognition by emphasizing the significance of human suffering. At the same time, the appeal through tabulation throws the principles of moral universalism back on itself by also framing Syrian human rights abuses as a crisis of scale. The casualty counts are sizable enough to deform the lines of the map with red circles, suggesting that the numbers are too high to tolerate. Given a moral universalist orientation, should the scale of human rights abuses matter? Should the infringement of the rights of many outweigh the few, or would that lead to a dangerous precedent? Student 1's visualization thus alerts us to the need to unpack common construals of cosmopolitan donor audiences, especially when the significance of human rights cases is couched in utilitarian appeals.

The pedagogical value of the visual project is that it provides a mechanism through which we can work with students to trouble the commonplace narratives of human rights education, which presume the existence of a transnational public sphere wherein all participants are equally able to speak and to be heard. Likewise, our focus on the dialogism of human rights discourse aims to trouble the idea that cultural productions transcend difference through rhetorical identification. In other words, our goal is to enable our students to recognize how both spectatorship and witnessing are implicated in the production of socially recognizable subjects and subjectivities and to attend to how both culturally and legally based human rights discourses substantiate normative frameworks of inclusion and exclusion and thereby legitimatize certain identities, subjectivities, and social relationships over others. Attuned to the potential ideological capture by the image, as Student 2 demonstrates, we need not remain caught in a critical paralysis over the spectacle of victimization or objectification of suffering.

Acting as witnesses in the sense argued by Oliver, we can move our students beyond the pathology of recognition in responses to atrocity by placing under inspection the dialogic conditions of viewing practices, specifically the ways in which such scenes of suffering address the audience and assume normative responses. For example, even though human rights politics and its visual and affective economies are tainted with power difference, a savvy rhetor (activist, artist, teacher, and scholar alike) can strategically mobilize normative legal frameworks in ways that point to new sociopolitical relationships and new forms of legal recognition that imagine cultural productions as sites of possibility and contestation. We can trace such a move in Student 2's interpretation of article 16 of the UDHR. Student 2 treats the UDHR's terminology of *men* and *women* as strictly gender categories, thus removing sexuality as a contingency for marriage. Although the original framers of the UDHR likely did not share Student 2's conceptualization of *men*, *women*, or *marriage*, the language of article 16 does permit this reconfiguration. Given the UDHR's status as the definitive modern statement of human rights and its roles in shaping subsequent policies and laws, Student 2's resignification of marriage beyond conventional gender roles demonstrates how alternative applications of normative frameworks can open new possibilities for the distribution of social equity.

Erik Juergensmeyer and Bridget Irish

Teaching Human Rights in the Composition Classroom: Engaging Students through Common Curricula

> *The moral imagination suggests that education and training are incomplete . . . if they do not build early and continually the space to explore the meaning of things, the horizons toward which to journey, and the nature of the journey itself.*
>
> —John Paul Lederach, *The Moral Imagination* (176)

The purpose of the composition course has always been contested. Different stakeholders in higher education look to composition courses to provide a service for higher-level disciplinary studies, build skills necessary for students' future job placement, cultivate communication norms as well as individual voice, and teach students to become powerful public rhetors. In the Gary Tate–Erika Lindemann exchange of the early 1990s in *College English*, for example, scholars debated how literature contributed to or detracted from disparate goals in composition classes. For Lindemann, there is no place for ("imaginative") literature in the composition classroom; instructors would do better spending their time on "audience, purpose, and form that rhetorical training has always prepared students to address" ("Freshman Composition" 313; see also Lindemann, "Three Views"). For Tate, however, such texts can help students look beyond their immediate studies and become better citizens, people "whose most important conversations will take place outside the academy, as they struggle to figure out how to live their lives—that is, how to vote and love and survive, how to respond to change and diversity and death and oppression and freedom" ("Place" 320; see also Tate, "Notes"). This conversation still exists today (for a more historical overview of the debate, see Crowley) and poses particular challenges to composition faculty members who would pursue a human-rights-oriented pedagogy to teach the necessary skills expected from varying stakeholders and to engage students in larger social issues.

Complicating these pedagogical decisions are eras of accountability and resource scarcity (brought on through the Department of Education, state priorities, accreditation organizations, and financial crises) that bring with them an even broader set of outcomes, budgetary restrictions, resource challenges, and general institutional trepidation. Such challenges can be especially prevalent at small institutions that seek to create environments for students to engage in ideas deemed worthy of the entire student population: global citizenship, human rights, service learning, sustainability, and so on. Here we discuss the theory behind and implementation of an action-oriented pedagogy of human rights that articulates "the universal elements of human rights as a basis for promoting social progress, better living conditions and greater freedom" at our small public college (Lenhart and Savolainen 146). We pay particular attention to the competing demands in lower-division composition courses that focus on human rights education (HRE) for assessing student competencies as well as for fostering interdisciplinary work that deepens students' sense of their places and responsibilities in the world.

Educators can draw on helpful scholarship that addresses why lower-division courses are appropriate for non-skills-based instruction. Sabine Hornberg, for example, believes general education is the most effective place to locate HRE work because it is "a topic which has the potential to help students transcend national, social, cultural and economic and other boundaries" (190). On the administrative level, Hornberg, constructing an argument on the German educational model, reasons that because HRE work encourages interdisciplinary thinking, general education is a good fit. And, on the instructional level, Hornberg sees the alignment of the contextual and critical aspects of general education outcomes with the critical-thinking and critical-awareness goals of many general-education writing courses.

Recent movements in composition theory have helped foster an environment where students learn more than just basic skills (Cushman, "Rhetorician"; Flower; Herzberg). As Paula Mathieu explains in *Tactics of Hope: The Public Turn in English Composition*, the composition classroom is experiencing a "public turn" as instructors are using topics beyond the traditional academic scope. Aided by scholarship on action research, community literacy, and service learning, instructors at myriad institutions have embraced this "turn" and enacted critical pedagogies and curricula that seek to empower students as agents of change as well as effective communicators. Whereas Mathieu appropriately cautions instructors to remain thoughtful in their public critiques and activism, the ubiquity of such pedagogies in programs across the country suggests composition instructors are finding appropriate spaces for the critical examination of issues beyond prescribed academic skills.

Moreover, movements and developments of critical pedagogies are also helpful for locating human rights in the composition classroom. This relevant branch of composition instruction establishes a foundation for a "democratic public discourse" (George 97). As explained by the composition scholar Ann George, critical pedagogy "envisions a society not simply pledged to but successfully enacting the principles of equality, of liberty and justice for all" (92). With roots in work by Paulo Freire, Henry Giroux, Jürgen Habermas, and Ira Shor, critical pedagogies can directly contribute to our attempts to transcend boundaries because they seek both to imagine a world that is different from the present and to empower students to create that change. Giroux sees critical pedagogy as a "part of a broader ethical and political project wedded to furthering social and economic justice and making multicultural democracy operational" ("Pedagogy" 3). Although teaching human rights in the composition classroom may not radically develop students' critical consciousness—what Freire calls *conscientização*—it hopes to increase their capacities for creating change. We find the composition classroom a perfect fit for such empowerment because our classes focus on the rich dialogue of human interaction, the "daily verbal and literate interactions [that] mark the very places where composition teachers can begin to look for the impact of our critical pedagogy and activism, both in the classroom and when we approach the community" (Cushman, "Rhetorician" 14).

This essay considers these challenges and offers educators—especially those involved in general education and composition instruction—a heuristic for creating opportunities to teach human rights while providing skills-based disciplinary instruction; it explains how to successfully bring HRE issues into classes. Drawing on our experiences as both writing instructors and administrators in a stand-alone writing program, we suggest a structure for implementing a common theme across campus that allows composition students, instructors, administrators, and the community to participate in a shared learning experience that brings human rights issues to the forefront and empowers all participants. Reflecting on a variety of data, including instructor feedback, student comments, and administrative records, we share our experiences from five years of planning and experimenting with HRE curricula. We detail the ways in which writing teachers can pursue their passions for engaging students in topics that involve HRE without bypassing the significant skills that accompany writing instruction and general education.

By instituting a form of common reading experience (CRE), a common text shared across the disciplines, teachers can create a conceptual framework that can unite students, faculty members, administrators, and the community. As we have instituted different themes and texts across the college in a CRE at our institution—Fort Lewis College, in Durango, Colorado—we have identified several simple criteria that have been key to making our experiences more successful: points of inquiry, campus and community involvement, and pedagogy and teacher preparation.

Student feedback reveals effective learning of disciplinary content. The following sampling of data illuminates experiences from two years of composition courses using CREs and suggests the HRE curricula contributed to students' disciplinary learning:

85% of students either agreed or strongly agreed that the course helped them "read and write academic texts."

82% of students either agreed or strongly agreed that the course helped them "[u]se content and style appropriate to academic audiences."

81% of students either agreed or strongly agreed that the course helped with "[c]ompetency in mechanical and stylistic features."

77% of students either agreed or strongly agreed that the course helped them "[u]se specialized vocabulary, format, and documentation."

We find this information comforting as we often struggle with the potential side effects of consciousness-raising pedagogy and the pressure to demonstrate skills-based outcomes.

The Right to a Nuclear-Free Society: CRE 1

Our first attempt at formally teaching HRE used *Folding Paper Cranes: An Atomic Memoir.* Written by Leonard Bird, an emeritus professor in our college's English department, the book deals with issues of nuclear weapons and human rights, focusing on the nuclear disaster in Hiroshima (and thus international humanitarian law) and the long conversation it has produced about possibilities for peace in a nuclear age. As an autobiography, poem, and history lesson, it appeals to a variety of student and faculty interests.

Because of the text's clear themes, identifying analytical frames was easy. We emphasized general themes such as poetry, narrative, nuclear weapons, World War II, controversial physicists and their ethical dilemmas, the Doomsday Clock, the "red scare," and how world peace fits in existing frameworks of human rights. Local themes involved community participation and regional responsibility, since a uranium mine in our community contributed to the nuclear weaponry of World War II, and Los Alamos National Lab is located in nearby northern New Mexico. These local themes were also helpful in generating campus and community involvement.

Consistent with the text's imagery, our campus was vibrant with colorful origami cranes constructed by faculty members, staff members, and students during collaborative workshops. Art students built a large iron crane to house the paper cranes and erected it in a small park on campus that then became officially named Hesperus Peace Park. The music department created a peace bell from an oil drum, and everyone rang it as they displayed their cranes at the dedication ceremony. Community members participated in the ceremony and celebrated our new park. Bird and the college president, Brad Bartel, elaborated on the importance of such activities, setting the stage for future academic investigations into the topic. The theater department presented a version of the book as a play and delivered it first in the new park and then as a full-blown evening production in the theater. Finally, at another public event, a panel of four historians discussed the decision to drop the atomic bomb.

Our first attempt at teaching HRE was comparatively uncomplicated since *Folding Paper Cranes* was already a popular text on campus, and faculty familiarity with the work facilitated curricular design. Instead of reaching out to the broader campus community, we worked closely with the writing program and the English department. Some instructors focused on biographies of nuclear scientists and their ethical dilemmas, some encouraged visual representations of the Doomsday Clock, and some focused on one of the text's main characters, Sadako, the young Japanese woman who associates paper cranes with good luck.

The variety of campus and community involvement indicates a great deal of support. During the project, students folded one thousand paper cranes and donated them to local nursing homes, and to this day the community has continued the tradition of folding origami cranes and donating them (one of us even received a crane years later during a hospital stay). Moreover, keeping our curricula within two programs that specialize in writing allayed our fears that the content matter would distract from sharpening students' awareness of the effects of rhetoric and writing skills.

Using *Folding Paper Cranes* in these composition classes enabled us to demonstrate how activism manifests in dialogue. This awareness not only takes place in the assigned texts but also in the accompanying readings and activities. The curriculum created opportunities for faculty members and students to attend events together that deepened the students' understandings of the human rights issue at hand. By attending a public screening of the atomic bomb documentary *The Day after Trinity* and a facilitated discussion by philosophy and chemistry professors, students gained a more critical understanding of the topic from varied disciplinary perspectives. In this case, the classroom revolved around discussion of the ethical dilemma of physicists who were creating a weapon of mass destruction, a topic that deeply challenges the right to a nuclear-free society.

Medicine and the Right to Health Care: CRE 2

Our second text, Tracy Kidder's *Mountains beyond Mountains: The Quest of Dr. Paul Farmer, a Man Who Would Cure the World*, required a different approach. Based on the life of Paul Farmer and his mission to improve public health care, *Mountains* ranges from the slums of Haiti to the prisons of Russia. The book traces Farmer's whirlwind life as his organization, Partners in Health, eventually seeks to influence World Health Organization policy on multidrug-resistant tuberculosis as well as the global AIDS campaign.

Teachers designed curricula around global issues of human rights, philosophical issues of health care as a right or privilege, world geography, American foreign policy, current health issues in American politics, public policy, social justice, and critical thinking. In addition, some chose to examine the personal challenges to individuals' taking on such ambitious work.

Generating campus and community involvement and collaboration comparable to the *Folding Paper Cranes* project required a variety of media. As our college's composition outcomes seek to expose students to an array of genres, such multimodality easily aligned with our curricular goals. A series of radio shows with the author, Partners in Health staff members, local not-for-profit organizations, and students broadened the types of texts and research opportunities available to our students, as did film screenings on health-care-related issues, panel discussions with Center for Disease Control experts, and community and faculty workshops and discussions. Interestingly, the theater department paralleled our themes by staging Ariel Dorfman's play *Speak Truth to Power: Voices beyond the Dark*, one component of a multimedia project on global human rights (see Belinda Walzer's essay in this volume for a pedagogical approach to *Speak Truth to Power*). Finally, discounted books at area book stores and on campus, a student writing competition, as well as an honors residence hall on campus that focused its extra- and cocurricular activities on health care exposed students to community connections they might not have made through a more traditional curriculum.

Accompanying such varied modes is a need for increased teacher preparation and resources. The potential for teachers to become overwhelmed by such broad themes can be alleviated through program administrators' providing clearly articulated outcomes for teaching the text and suggested assignments. Before the semester begins, composition instructors can invite all interested faculty members, from any discipline, to attend discussion workshops about how to incorporate the book and its themes in their classes. Interested faculty members can also create instructional materials, general outlines, and discussion questions, creating an open environment for faculty adoption of the theme.

This particular topic and text also offered important inter- and transdisciplinary connections. Interdisciplinary themes involving philosophical approaches to social justice that asked students to familiarize themselves with John Rawls's examinations of equality and with ethnographic studies of the people affected by the lack of access to medical care proved especially effective (*Theory*). Consistent with hands-on learning pedagogies espoused by some writing programs, the topic offered students on our campus the opportunities to hold clothing drives and purchase clothes for Haitian citizens affected by the lack of just medical treatment.

Perhaps the biggest issue from both the administrative and instructional standpoint for such an undertaking can be logistics and timing: preparing instructors ahead of time requires choosing a theme and text early enough to contact authors and arrange the accompanying events. Experimental pedagogies and pilot projects also need to have clear means of assessing student learning, something that can be relatively easily accomplished through creating a CRE assessment institute at the end of the academic year to examine student learning and identify which pedagogical strategies worked best.

For our efforts, student reactions were generally positive. When asked to "name one way that reading *Mountains beyond Mountains* influenced [their] skills," students claimed to have increased their knowledge of "social awareness," "social justice," and "health care social justice" and to have "bec[o]me much more interested in social justice." One student appreciated the hands-on experiences because "[r]eal life events helped to give insight," and another claimed to be inspired "to think more deeply about fairness and public health." At the same time, students were asked to identify improvements in their academic and nonacademic literacies and writing skills. Balancing their increased awareness in HRE, they identified increased skills in general rhetorical principles such as seeing "exigence in texts," becoming "more analytical in terms of rhetorical content," and gaining "ideas of new perspectives in writing."

The activities accompanying *Mountains* also increased students' critical awareness through dialogue. A community forum entitled Creating a Safer, More Compassionate World, for example, brought hundreds of students, faculty members, and community members, ranging from individual health practitioners to staff members at local not-for-profit organizations to representatives of national efforts, together for a weekend to share ways of being activists in the world of public health. After the participants shared their experiences, the forum then ventured into the question of whether access to health care is a right or a privilege.

Planning Future Human Rights Education

Based on these experiences, we have learned that to focus on the future, we must outline not only relevant paths of action and curriculum but also means of making human rights issues relevant for our students. We must create ways for our students to become involved with issues beyond their immediate worlds, to engender thinking that reaches across disciplines and courses. Such increased participation, according to the public health scholars Richard Wilkinson and Kate Pickett, is key to creating change within contemporary societies. For Wilkinson and Pickett, increased ownership fosters "social emancipation" and ultimately creates a society less influenced by the hierarchical divisions that lead to human rights violations (253). To achieve such change, they suggest increased political participation that stems from increased interest:

> Political will is dependent on the development of a vision of a better society . . . : a more equal society in which people are less divided by status and hierarchy; a society in which we regain a sense of community, . . . in which we own and control our work democratically as part of a community of colleagues. . . . The task now is to develop a politics based on a recognition of the kind of society we need to create and committed to making use of the institutional and technological opportunities to realize it. (264)

Integrating common themes in composition classes creates an opportunity for such awareness. When first-year writing students are confronted with problems of injustices and inequities, they are often quickly and emotionally involved with the subject. This attachment can be alluring to teachers as they feel the classroom move and shake—something that doesn't happen enough with composition instruction. At the same time, one must be vigilant to the possibility that such emotional responses intensify students' humanitarian urges at the expense of a deeper understanding of the structural conditions that too often separate the bestower and receiver of aid, if not rights, along all-too-familiar geopolitical lines. We sought to counter that tendency through a multimodal approach to each topic that disrupted fixed understandings of the issue at hand. Assigning a human rights issue for students new to college to read and write about can be successful, but it also can be problematic if instructors overemphasize the content, issue, or ideas. We have found, however, that a focus on contextualization, scholarly interrogation, theme-related cocurricular activities, engaged reading and writing assignments, and a campus-wide discussion of themes associated with each text helps lessen these complications.

At Fort Lewis College, we have learned a great deal from our CREs, and as they have built on each other, they have created a significant place for HRE at our institution. This action-oriented pedagogy directly aligns with the mission of our institution, a public liberal arts college, to encourage students "to take responsible, informed action toward a less violent and more just world" (Reardon 283). Directly connected to our college's mission is the desire to increase our students' capacities to be more engaged global citizens. Our recently developed peace initiative and minor in peace and conflict studies are expanding HRE on campus, building on the success of our common reading program and creating more opportunities for students to make the type of society that we need to challenge the inequities that lead to the abuse of human rights. Such efforts offer hope for the future.

Lisa Eck and Ben Alberti

Reading Culture and Writing Rights

The aim of this essay is to reveal the resources, or teachable moments, literary studies and anthropology each offer to the discussion of human rights, including the useful dialogic tensions they produce in combination. At our small, public university, we developed an ambitious human rights unit in the form of two "clustered" classes: Expository Writing and Introduction to Cultural Anthropology, linked by schedule, content, and a shared roster of students. Our collaborative pedagogy sought to move beyond the most commonly cited reason for reading literature in the service of human rights: to tap the power of identification between reader and character (or reader and first-person narrator) that promises to generate empathy in a reader, who might someday turn spokesperson or activist. In contrast, an anthropological discussion of human rights moves the focus from the individual to groups; individual rights are suddenly rendered illegible without the context of cultural rights. Our pedagogical goal was to introduce this oversimplified opposition between defending individuals and defending culture, to critique the notions of a bounded individual and bounded culture. We sought to create a third space in which students would be urged to think about the structural causes of human rights violations and their complex, situated solutions.

As new historicist methodologies remind us, no firewall exists between the discursive practices of literary and nonliterary texts—between, for example, a science-fiction drama and an ethnography, or a contemporary film and the Universal Declaration of Human Rights. By foregrounding the related challenges of reading culture and writing rights, our hope was that our students would come to see human rights subjects—victims, perpetrators, and all difficult subject positions in between—as never isolated from an engagement with interconnected cultural contexts and with the politics of representation. Thus we extend Mark Goodale's claim for an anthropological approach to rights to the realm of literary studies as well: that "the comparative practice of everyday life must be understood," or, in the case of literature, represented, in "the conjunctive and the disjunctive," as "both an expression of certain vague universal patterns and a reflection of what is absolutely irreducible about *this* practice in *this* place at *this* particular moment" ("Introduction" 1).

What follows is an analysis of a grouping of texts that, when taught in combination, urged our students to question their prior conceptions about what is right, and necessary, about the project of articulating rights. Chief among these correctives was first learning to question the tendency to demonize cultural otherness as the de facto cause of human rights violations and then learning to think in structural terms—economically and politically—about genuine threats to human agency, citizenship, and free will.

Module 1: Approaching Human Rights through Anthropology: The UDHR and AAA Statements as Teaching Tools

The intellectual changes we expected our students to undergo mirrored debates between the drafters and heirs of the Universal Declaration of Human Rights (UDHR) and members of the American Anthropological Association (AAA). Melville Herskovitz (a former student of Franz Boas) wrote the AAA's 1947 statement on human rights in response to an invitation by the United Nations to provide input into the process of formulating the UDHR ("Statement"). His critique, not of core tenets of tolerance, freedom, and free will, but of their definition and imposition by forces outside specific cultural context to which they might be applied, reflected one aspect of the debate at the time. Other anthropologists distanced themselves from the AAA's statement based on the argument that they were not, in fact, in a position to comment on the UDHR, as their role was to critique rather than prescribe.[1] Indeed, many anthropologists lamented the explicitly political tone of the AAA statement in its concern over the possibly imperializing reach of human rights, for what was supposed to be "a value-free science" (Merry 56).

The AAA statement defends the one value, it seems, anthropologists could agree on: their strong belief in culture as an indispensable resource for the individual. The AAA's 1947 statement stresses the point that individuals "can develop only in terms of the culture of [their] society" ("Statement" 540). In other words, from an anthropological point of view, the sovereign individual of modernity, so central to human rights discourse, does not rightly exist outside his or her culture.

When mischaracterizations occur in human rights discourse about the role of culture in perpetuating human rights abuses, they often result from an easy polarization: anthropologists are labeled as relativists—strident supporters of cultural sovereignty over human rights—and human rights activists are labeled as universalists—vocal supporters of individuals, over and above the cultures they live in.[2] The traditional view of the concept of culture derives both from the sociologist Talcott Parsons, who makes the problematic assumption that culture equates with values, and from the equally problematic Boasian notion of bounded cultures (pure versus porous) that exist within specific historical trajectories (Merry 64, 65). The definition of culture as a sum of values (e.g., rather than concrete practices) makes cultural relativism appear resistant to ethical critique (64), whereas the view of culture as bounded implies incommensurability across cultures and immunity from historical processes (65). The human rights anthropologist Sally Engle Merry argues that these popular misreadings of culture often enable human rights scholars and activists to villainize traditional practices that contravene universal rights. According to Merry, one of the serious consequences of the rush to demonize culture has been the tendency to "culturalize" issues that more accurately stem from economic or political causes.

As a corrective counterpoint, the AAA's 1947 statement draws explicit attention to the political context in which the UDHR was developed. On first inspection, the UDHR reads as a courageous defense of the human qua human (denuded and deracialized) against the xenophobic logic of genocide. But the UDHR also reads as a document written in the wake of European expansionism and inflected by the specific ideology of the "white man's burden." In the classroom, we wanted our students to recognize the historical context of the UDHR and to become critical of the potential imposition of their own (Euro-American) tradition on others.

Ultimately, our students came to see that cynical definitions of culture and cultural relativism are often inscribed in human rights documents, with potentially negative consequences. Merry provides examples from documents from the Convention on the Elimination of All Forms of Discrimination against Women (CEDAW) hearings and recommendations that "see culture as an obstacle to the human rights of women" (60). If "culture . . . [subordinates] women" in many of these documents, Merry continues, then it is "modernity that frees them" (62). Merry argues that adopting this outmoded view of culture provides students, activists, anthropologists, and scholars with a dangerous "sense of moral certainty," one that can be "disrupt[ed]" through an understanding of culture as constellations of flexible and contingent processes and of ostensible universality as a product of its own particular circumstances (72).

Module 2: Global Citizenship: Addressing the Implications of Organ Trafficking through Film and Ethnography

After analyzing these debates over universality and particularity from the standpoints of both culture and the law, we moved to a case study. We chose organ trafficking because it encouraged our students to consider their connectivity with global markets, conceived in terms of both supply and demand. Indeed, we picked the problem of organ trafficking because it disturbs the "us versus them," "here versus over there" geography that characterized our initial class discussions on human rights topics. Early brainstorming questions for our classes ranged from "Do you know where the shirt you're wearing was made, and under what conditions?" to "Given the current costs of health care, how many black-market kidneys do you suppose arrive in Boston each month?" The latter question, students soon discovered, was no easy hypothetical, meant simply to provoke, but instead referred to a specific trade route, documented by the medical anthropologist Nancy Scheper-Hughes, between a Nigerian doctor-broker who arranged foreign transplants in Boston with "a ready supply of poor Nigerian kidney sellers" ("Keeping" 1646). Conceptualizing the reach of global markets—for goods, for organs, for labor, for health—was an important foundational issue in the unit, because it asked students to theorize their possible complicity as participants, alongside their unanimous moral outrage at the sometimes fatal risks taken by impoverished organ donors.

Teaching Scheper-Hughes's anthropological essays in conjunction with Manjula Padmanabhan's play *Harvest* allowed us to follow the intellectual development we had established in module 1.[3] We continued the process of questioning an easy identification with the abstract positions of Western legal theory, which focus on the individual, to a systemic critique of market conditions that limit or deny rights, reflecting the current anthropological understanding of culture as "unbounded, contested, and connected to relations of power" (Merry 67). The aim, ultimately, was to find that desired third space in which sympathy could not be used in any easy way to sort right from wrong and where anthropology and literature's shared advantage promised to be their emphasis on careful reading of context or situated practices.

Scheper-Hughes opens her article "Keeping an Eye on the Global Traffic in Human Organs," published in the *Lancet*, by quoting a rhetorical question: "If a living donor can do without an organ, why shouldn't the donor profit and medical science benefit?" (1645).[4] Just as we had asked students to question the American-style individualism embedded in the UDHR, Scheper-Hughes's article pounces quickly on the position inferred in the question: that organ trafficking can represent a "win-win" proposition for all parties. Instead, Scheper-Hughes exposes the impossibility of the classical liberal position in the sociopolitical context of globalization. Put plainly, she argues that the free choice of the donor is a chimera in this context. Indeed, the list of problems faced by organ donors, from a lack of postoperative care to outright lies to induce them to give up an organ, serve to complicate our understanding of what it means to choose.

In addition, the article offers students a useful testing ground for holism, or what it means to theorize using transnational or global contexts. As a case in point, Scheper-Hughes stresses the relation of rights, bodies, and culture when she argues that "deeply held beliefs in human dignity and bodily integrity are not solely the legacy of Western Enlightenment" (1648). Comments from donors reinforce that message: "We are treated worse than prostitutes," declares one donor from Turkey, "[and, in a sense,] we are worse than prostitutes—we have sold something we can never get back; we are a disgrace to our families and country" (1647). In this example, the donor's culture supplies both a cost and a corrective for would-be organ donors: a cost, in the form of social stigma, and a corrective represented in the numerous disincentives embedded in various discourses (both religious and secular) that warn against the cultural consequences of the harvesting of one's organs.

The plot thickened, however, for our class, when they read Scheper-Hughes's "Postcard from Brazil," a series of three short articles written on Gaddy Tauber, a convicted organ trafficker, for *Anthropology News*. Scheper-Hughes's portrayal of Tauber disrupts the tidy moral positions our students adopted after reading her other article. Tauber, we learn, languishes in a Brazilian prison after being convicted of "kidney hunting" and organizing the transportation of fifty donors from Recife to Durban in 2002–03 ([Mar.] 19). He is a Holocaust survivor who was abandoned as a child, and he justifies his actions (providing organ donors from the poor of Brazil for ailing Israelis) on the grounds that he is saving two lives: the Israeli's and the impoverished donor's. Scheper-Hughes had heard similar justifications before, citing one surgeon in Jerusalem who had said, half in jest, that "the world owes Israel 8 million hearts and 16 million kidneys" ([Apr.] 24). In fact, Tauber had no problem recruiting donors, some of whom paid to be on the waiting list, since the $10,000 cash payments for an organ (which quickly fell to $3,000) was a huge sum to Recife's impoverished inhabitants ([Mar.] 19).

By analyzing Scheper-Hughes's use of what, in literary terms, might be called characterization and plot, four related issues surfaced: Tauber is not a simple, evil purveyor in organs; organ donors do not unilaterally damn the trafficker (readers are presented with a photograph of a broadly smiling organ donor, Geremias, who acted as a defense witness at Tauber's trial, his arm around an equally beaming Tauber); wrongdoers can also be victims (e.g., Tauber was taunted with anti-Semitic slurs by his prison guards); and, finally, Scheper-Hughes cannot be understood simply as the objective social scientist, or conversely, as the well-intentioned activist on the right side of the issue. Instead, she, like the rest of us, was forced to complicate the literary tropes of victim and villain we all bring, consciously or unconsciously, to our interpretations of human rights issues.

Building on this new self-consciousness about form, specifically the literary qualities of nonliterary texts, we posed to the class one of the unit's overarching questions: "Are there right and wrong ways to write about human rights?" Padmanabhan's 1997 play, *Harvest*, proved ideal for this line of questioning. By staging an Orwellian vision of the future in which organ trafficking is entirely legal and carried out by completely mechanized, faceless, multinational corporations and their nameless goons, *Harvest* uses artifice, fantasy, and allegory to stage a "real-world" political debate, in what is now the recent past: 2010. In the 2003 edition of the play, Padmanabhan explains that her inspiration for the play was "the flourishing illegal trade in human organs in India," in which poor villagers "donate" organs to both Indian and non-Indian buyers, for as little as $400 (4). Besides functioning as a piece of activist literature aimed at a particular national problem, *Harvest*, Padmanabhan insists, ought to be read as a portable, "situated" script, whose activism could be made site specific. "Ideally," she argues in her dramaturgical notes for the play, "the Donors and Receivers should take on the racial identities, names, costumes and accents most suited to the location of the production" (6).[5]

Responding to the play as a piece of political satire, several student essays focused on the dehumanizing aspects of Western responses to Third World poverty—the dramatic ways in which the "West feeds off the rest" and then finds the resulting poverty "shocking," "disgusting," and unacceptable (Padmanabhan 26). In contrast, a handful of essays stopped at a kind of "blame the victim" stance, since, after all, Om, Padmanabhan's protagonist, chooses to become an organ donor. But even these papers ended up critiquing the ways in which the economic opportunities produced by this legal example of global trade were disruptive to the family structure, to cultural and religious traditions, and to the integrity of the local body politic. These conclusions highlight the same kinds of cultural fallout experienced by the organ donors whom Scheper-Hughes interviewed in the course of her research.

Juxtaposed with the political body (the presumed subject of human rights discourse), the anthropological body also becomes legible in the play, as Jaya, Om's wife, grieves the ways in which the donor's body no longer makes sense as an object of ritual or site of belief: "Were you dead, I could shave my head and break my bangles—but this? To be a widow by slow degrees? To mourn you piece by piece? Should I shave half my head? Break half my bangles one at a time?" As Padmanabhan's imagery suggests, the slow death of the donor's body represents a kind of splitting of the self into competing pieces.

Using two specific plot devices, Padmanabhan's play dramatizes how globalized organ trafficking violates the rights of both individuals and groups, producing, in each case, a loss or fracturing of identity. In act 1, the audience learns that to meet the company policy that donors need to be single males, Om willingly misleads his employer by claiming his wife is not his wife but instead his sister-in-law. This single misrepresentation reconfigures the economies of intimacy in this extended family of four, which includes Om; Jaya; his younger, "good for nothing" brother, Jeetu; and his sixty-year-old mother, Ma. In addition, viewers are compelled to compare Jeetu's profession as a male prostitute with Om's decision to sell his body to Western strangers. "At least when I sell my body," Jeeta editorializes to Jaya, "I decide which part of my body goes into where and whom" (33). This scene reminded our students of the regret voiced by the Turkish donors cited in Scheper-Hughes's article who argued that perhaps donors "are worse than prostitutes" for allowing themselves to be not sold but harvested.

In *Human Rights as Politics and Idolatry*, Michael Ignatieff makes the argument that the whole purpose of human rights is to protect human agency. If this weren't the case, Amy Gutmann argues in her introduction to Ignatieff, human rights might be misunderstood as simply aiming to protect a "negative freedom, the freedom from abuse, oppression and cruelty" (ix). Gutmann argues, however, that for Ignatieff, human rights are meant to defend both positive and negative freedoms. The examples she gives reflect the economic power relations in Padmanabhan's play. "The right to subsistence is as necessary for human agency," Gutmann insists, "as the right against torture" (ix). Om's human right to agency, our students determined, was undercut by the economic conditions that denied him and his family the right to safe sources of subsistence.

Of the various subgenres Padmanabhan combines in her play, we were surprised to find that science fiction, arguably the most artifice-laden of forms, proved to be the best suited for inspiring our students to interrogate current structures of inequality. Several student essays interpreted the futuristic, mechanistic imagery in the play as a critique of modernization in general and Westernization in particular. When Jeetu is taken by the guards instead of Om and his eyes are harvested rather than the expected kidney, Jeetu literally sees the world through Western eyes, since the company has conveniently provided him with a pair of sci-fi goggles, or artificial eyes, equipped with free Wi-Fi that continually streams images of the virtual West. In the final plot twist of the play, Virgil, the male Organ Receiver who had earlier been posing in cyberspace as the "angelic" female avatar Ginnie, has now targeted Jaya for her fertile ovaries and uterus. Jaya's final act of resistance is to insist that the ironically named Virgil make the epic journey to see her "in person," or she'll kill herself—that is, she'll take these goods off the market (91). Ultimately, our students argued in their essays on the play that, here, global "contact" between donors and receivers proves no substitute for the pleasures of family, culture, vocation, and citizenship.

Module 3: An Invitation to Write Rights

When Joseph Slaughter argues in his chapter "The Legibility of Human Rights" that human rights offer a kind of "enabling fiction," "fiction" is not intended as a pejorative term, precisely because the working fiction of human rights supports the existence of what he calls "an egalitarian imaginary" (*Human Rights* 5). For our part, we were pleased to see that the liberal idealism of the UDHR was not entirely sabotaged for our cohort of students, but instead they were able to project their own "egalitarian imaginary" in two final writing assignments: an independent research paper and a cowritten statement of rights. *Reading* dialectically as anthropologists (between polarities such as liberalism and social constructivism), our students shifted from simply *declaring* the rights of the sovereign individual to *imagining* the rights of the situated individual, whose culture they no longer understood to be a de facto threat to human rights. Reading in equal measure as literary critics, our students learned how to spot tropes in literary, ethnographic, and legal discourses that reproduce, among other effects, a reductive imaginary of victims and villains, while appreciating, in the end, the power of literary genres, such as science fiction, or literary modes, such as satire, to contribute to a structural understanding of human rights violations and their working solutions.

Writing about rights in a similarly dialectical fashion proved harder. The shocking nature of what our students were reading about in their independent research for their capstone papers—the Rwandan genocide, child labor, female genital cutting—was sometimes privileged over the more self-conscious issue of how they might choose to interpret and write about it. Rhetorical strategies aimed at raising awareness (e.g., the opening hook of a research paper) had the undesired effect of reinscribing a clear "us versus them" gap between the Western reader and human rights victims in Africa, Southeast Asia, the Middle East, and elsewhere. Here, our students had stumbled on a key difficulty: namely, What is the genre of the human rights research paper? The way in which our students often assumed their readers had no knowledge of a topic, or little incentive to identify or engage with said topic, seemed to deny both module 1's study of fifty years of human rights theory and the research process itself, which revealed a history of scholarship and activism, both local and global.

Ultimately, however, our desire to see our students write about rights in a way that was both situated and self-reflexive was partially satisfied.

On the last day of class, we surprised our students with one final writing task: divided into groups, they were asked to reflect on the process of writing their research papers and coming to the position they did on human rights, in the light of their specific topic. These final rights statements followed Goodale's prescription: they were both conjunctive and disjunctive; they presumed shared definitions of the human when it would be ethnocentric or xenophobic not to do so, but they also made provisions for cultural difference in a move that avoided demonizing culture. All the papers directly quoted from the UDHR or the AAA statements, and all made an attempt to merge the two documents in reflecting on their new positions. One group chose to stress the AAA's 1999 statement that "Human rights is not a static concept" and further that "anthropology's cumulative knowledge of human cultures . . . attests to the universality of the human capacity for culture" (*Declaration*). Another group advocated that the first fifteen articles of the UDHR are applicable to all people: "though culture may shape a person's beliefs," they argued, "it does not necessarily bind them."

All told, writing about rights proved to be the most telling assessment. Our students demonstrated that they could, on paper, occupy that difficult third space. Whether it was a student presentation on the efforts of Kazakhstani women to fight domestic violence with culturally specific strategies or one group's efforts to rearticulate article 26 of the UDHR, the right to an education, from the combined perspectives of indigenous peoples and their own interests as working-class American youth at a state institution, the students made legible at the very least the question of a right way to write about rights.

Notes

1. For two contemporaneous examples of dissent, see Julian H. Steward's and H. G. Barnett's responses (Amer. Anthropological Assn., Steward, and Barnett 27–31).

2. See Kymlicka for an influential argument on the need to translate claims for individual rights into claims for collective rights.

3. Module 2 also included a film: Stephen Frears's 2002 *Dirty Pretty Things*. Set in London among a diverse community of illegal immigrants, the film tracks the work and legal pressures that lead a Nigerian doctor, Okwe, to operate illegally and a young, attractive Turkish woman, Senay, to want to sell an organ in insalubrious circumstances.

4. Scheper-Hughes, because of her thorough grounding in this human rights issue and her position in the discourse of academic anthropology, is a good model

for how an anthropologist can both support cultural difference and work for human rights. In addition to establishing Organs Watch with Lawrence Cohen, she has presented before United States congressional hearings, medical boards, and ministries of health (Scheper-Hughes, "Keeping" 1645).

5. Editors' note: Rolan Schimmelpfennig's play *The Golden Dragon* offers an alternative approach to the representation of global trafficking circuits (of labor and sex trafficking, rather than organs). Schimmelpfennig breaks convention and narrative rules by having single actors play characters of different ages, genders, and nationalities. Actors give their lines as well as their pauses and stage directions. As opposed to emphasizing the situatedness of given subject positions in a local context, as Padmanabhan suggests, *The Golden Dragon* underscores the interconnections in the global economy that challenge the fixity of identification.

Marike Janzen

Experiencing Form: Service Learning in the Literature of Human Rights Classroom

In a literature of human rights course, facilitating a link between service learning and reflection on literary form can make pertinent a fundamental paradox of human rights narratives. Such texts serve a critical role in calling attention to human rights violations and are therefore seen as contributing to larger efforts in redressing human rights abuses. Since the narratives employ formal strategies that either occlude or privilege certain perspectives, however, they cannot be seen as transparent records of wrongs done. Incorporating service learning into a literature of human rights course concretizes the ways in which form affects our understanding of human rights concerns. As just one approach to service learning, students can volunteer at not-for-profit agencies in the community and then document their experiences in a creative piece of writing in a genre of their choosing. One desired outcome of such an assignment is that students recognize that human rights issues occur where they live and not only in geographically distant contexts—a rationale shared by other instructors for engaging service learning in a human-rights-related course (Krain and Nurse 190). By taking on the role of authors of human rights narratives and crafting a textual representation of local human rights concerns, students encounter firsthand the fact that formal decisions necessarily result in a contingent version of the events they witness. Consequently, they must contend with a central problem of both literature and human rights: the difficulty of locating a fixed referent for either a narrative point of view or the subject of human rights.

In what follows, I describe how service learning can contribute to an overall course goal to promote critical reflection on the relation of narrative and experience in human rights literature. This practice leads to questioning the assumed usefulness—and benefit—of such works for describing human rights and its abuses. In this way, my view on service learning diverges somewhat from research premised on the notion that the purpose of service learning in a literature course is to demonstrate and clarify the utility of literary study. As I argue, however, using service learning as a tool to foster critique of the way authors represent the human resonates with a central thesis of scholarship on human rights literature—namely, that form and our understanding of human-ness are mutually constitutive.

Service Learning and the Literature of Human Rights

Literary scholars who argue for the relevance of community engagement in the context of a literature course are often writing in response to what Ann Marie Fallon describes as literature professors' prevailing view that literature exists as a critical "counterpoint" to the world of practice and "realpolitik" and should not be accorded a use value (xvii).[1] Yet according to Ellen Cushman, it is imperative that literary scholars—both professors and students—consider their work in terms of its public utility ("Service Learning" 213). Following Cushman, coupling literary study with service learning is a prime mode for the production and implementation of "utilitarian knowledge" (213). In her view, as students and professors "test the merit of what they learn in the university classroom against their experiences as volunteers at local sites," they create ways of knowing about and addressing local issues relevant to those in "under-served neighborhoods" ("Public Intellectual" 329). This form of knowledge is not a top-down application of, for example, literary-theoretical insight but derives from a combination of expertise developed within and outside the academy ("Service Learning" 213).

This view, that service learning can highlight the usefulness of literary study for social analysis and activism, serves as a rationale for scholars who advocate engaging service learning in the literature classroom. Scholars do recognize the risk that an emphasis on the social relevance of literary study can result in students' understanding of literature as a self-evident "sociological document," an instrument for "[illustrating] the reality beyond a text" (Grobman, "Is There" 130). Nevertheless, a key argument in scholarship on service learning and literary study is that literary analytical insight helps students make sense of the complexities of real-world concerns.[2]

In my experience, students who enroll in my course Literature of Human Rights—predominantly majors or graduate students in "practical" or professional fields such as international relations, law, business, or social welfare—are drawn to the class because they expect that the assigned texts will be necessarily useful works. That is, they conceive of a literature of human rights as comprising documents that reveal human rights violations. As a result, I do not primarily engage service learning to lead students to recognize texts' utility. On the contrary, I treat service learning as a tool for troubling assumptions about works' instrumentality as platforms for voicing human rights violations. In this way, my view of service learning aligns with Dan Butin's notion that service learning ought to be seen as an "anti-foundational" practice that forecloses any "easily achieved end goal" (13). This is not to be obstructionist. To understand how a text can make an intervention—how it can be useful—it is imperative to gain a sophisticated understanding of narrative modes and their implications.

When students struggle to shape their experiences at local not-for-profit organizations into a creative piece, they encounter the theoretical crux of human rights literature as a tangible experience—namely, that literary genres not only reflect but also inform our understanding of the human. This relation of form and the human is the focus of major recent scholarship on the literature of human rights. On one hand, Lynn Hunt and Joseph Slaughter explore the relation of literature and rights discourse. Specifically, they show how Enlightenment-era genres shaped conceptions of human subjectivity. While the epistolary novel posited a subject with a rich inner life—one with which others could identify despite differences in gender or social status (Hunt 39), the bildungsroman implied a natural developmental course through which subjects freely become productive participants in civil society (Slaughter, *Human Rights* 26). These genres in turn align with foundational and normative discourses on human rights such as the Declaration of the Rights of Man (1789), which assumes equality between men, and the Universal Declaration of Human Rights (1948), which posits the ideal conditions in which development of free subjects can take place (Hunt 21, 29; Slaughter, *Human Rights* 46).

On the other hand, Kay Schaffer, Sidonie Smith, Elizabeth Swanson Goldberg, and James Dawes examine both the development and constraints of specific formal parameters within a global human rights regime. Schaffer and Smith chart the development and reception of "life narratives" in various global contexts of the post–World War II world where "storytelling and rights claims [intersect]" (36, 12). Goldberg identifies how contemporary representations and interpretations of political trauma—particularly those emanating from the West—can reinforce notions of the primacy of a Western perspective or other ideologies (*Beyond Terror* 32). In his examination of the modes by which human rights activists speak with and for others, Dawes traces the way human rights infrastructures shape stories told by and about victims and pushes us to consider how interviews of the violated by human rights workers might echo the formal conditions of those being interrogated in a prison (*That the World* 77). Collectively, these investigations into writing and rights show, in Dawes's words, the centrality of "storytelling" to our understanding of the "self," and thus the need for "[sensitivity] to the structure of narrative and the role of storytelling" when "considering basic issues about the 'self' that are fundamental to the work of human rights and humanitarianism" ("Human Rights" 395).

Students' work to tell stories about service-learning experiences offers a way to foster this kind of sensitivity to narrative. Specifically, my aim is that this process will clarify the fact that narrative not only represents reality but refracts the reality that is its object and of which it is part.

Recognizing and Discussing Form

In a course on the literature of human rights, readings and discussion of texts that relate historical and contemporary instances of human rights crises provide the foundation for the practice of translating service-learning experiences into narrative. To this end, generic diversity is a key criterion for text selection. In my course, I regularly assign students to read several texts that represent the same historical event in diverse ways so that they might gain insight into the way form shapes content. We read Rigoberta Menchú's testimonial of her political "conscientization" during the Guatemalan civil war along with Horacio Castellanos Moya's *Senselessness*, the narrative of an unnamed protagonist (in an unnamed Central American country) charged with editing a collection of oral testimonies by indigenous people about atrocities committed against them. This pairing presents students with distinct formations of the subject related to the protagonist's status as either victim of or witness to the Central American civil wars of the 1970s and 1980s. In Menchú's work, students grapple with the tension between the narrator's depiction of a communally based subjectivity—through which Menchú claims others' experience of abuse by the Guatemalan armed forces as her own—and Menchú's critics, who claim Menchú lied because she did not see specific events she purports to have witnessed (Fernández García 68). When reading Castellanos Moya's text, we examine the implications of the fact that the protagonist's increasing inability to maintain any separation between his role as an objective reader of the document and his identification with the abused—a development possibly understandable as empathy—is registered by his peers and the reader as growing paranoia and even insanity. By reading these two works, students not only gain awareness of specific contours of Central American conflict in the last century but also explore how form shapes our conception of the parameters of subjectivity.

Students can practice reflecting on how such articulations of the human and human rights relate to each other by creating analytic outlines or précis on the way that textual strategies affect a text's message. This assignment, developed by Janet Swaffar and Katherine Arens to cultivate awareness of the relation of the conventions of discursive practices and cultural contexts in the foreign language, literature, and cultural studies classrooms, works well as a tool for identifying the consequences of narrative. The précis, which asks students to make connections among context, message, and form, pushes them to recognize the social embeddedness of genre. It requires them to identify specific, component parts of a text as well as to articulate the potential implications of the way in which the work presents information. First, students produce a statement that describes the work's focus, or its content or topic (Swaffar and Arens 110). Second, students name the logic, or strategy, the author uses to present information related to that topic and explain the author's goal in employing particular rhetorical strategies (110). Then students use a chart to draw on specific examples to illustrate the strategies at play in the text, such as what elements the author is emphasizing, defining, contrasting, or correlating (110). In a final section on implications, students examine what is at stake if material related to a particular topic is presented in the way identified. According to Swaffar and Arens, this section of the précis articulates what is potentially new, traditional, or challenging in presenting the material in this way (110, 181–82).

In my course, I ask students to consider how the text's makeup shapes readers' understanding of the human or of a particular human rights violation. By leading students to an understanding of the analytical distinction between form and content, and then pushing them to consider the relation of form to a larger social or political context, they arrive at a textually informed perspective of how a work means—both at the textual and cultural levels. Furthermore, by prompting students to reflect on the assigned literary works as "specifically placed cultural artifact[s]" that reinforce or challenge culturally and historically defined "communication conventions" (141, 147), they ideally move to an understanding that these texts do not depend on universally understood notions of the human that exist a priori to representation. Instead, they grasp the interrelation of textual strategies, or genre, and definitions of the human.

Students' précis of specific texts, which they complete before class, provide a good basis for in-class discussion. While the text's parameters provide limiting boundaries for analysis, students will identify various textual strategies at work in the assigned narrative. In other words, while each reading must accurately reflect the work's structure, there is no single possible correct reading. Furthermore, since each analysis identifies distinctive elements of a text, students' findings of the implications of these elements will vary. In this way, students' collective expertise on a work's makeup, as well as their reflections on the implications of the author's formal strategies for representing the human and human rights violations, inform class discussion of the readings.

Creating Form out of the Service-Learning Experience

The précis on individual readings offer a critical foundation for students' written pieces based on their volunteer work. Through this writing assignment, students engage in what Swaffar and Arens describe as an advanced task in a curriculum designed to promote awareness of the relation of genre and cultural context. By producing a creative piece, or "[performing] a genre's features as personal expression," students enact and demonstrate a meta-level understanding of condensing and representing experience into form (153).

Transforming hours spent working with a local not-for-profit agency into a coherent narrative, informed both by a sophisticated understanding of a range of formal options for representing human rights issues as well as—ideally—an awareness of the ramifications of representational choices, requires several steps. First students select and commit to a work site. Next, they document their volunteer experience to create the raw material for their creative piece. Finally, they engage the writing process, which requires the conceptual work of making formal decisions as well as reflecting on the kinds of formal choices they made.

To facilitate students' contact with appropriate local organizations, faculty members may take advantage of the resources available at their institution's center for service learning or engaged learning. Faculty members without these campus centers can draw on material available through the national service-learning organization Campus Compact, which also maintains a network of state affiliates who can advise faculty members on service-learning-related questions. Faculty members may want to develop a relationship with one local agency that represents a particularly pressing regional human rights concern—it may be that certain organizations would particularly welcome the kind of documentation that students working on this assignment can provide. But students do not necessarily need to be paired with a self-described human rights organization to be able to reflect on the establishment and maintenance of key human rights in the community. The local homeless shelter, for example, could be viewed as working to ensure the possibility of article 25 of the Universal Declaration of Human Rights (UDHR), "the right to a standard of living adequate for the health and well-being of [the individual] and of his family, including food, clothing, housing and medical care" ("Universal Declaration").

Once students choose the organization where they will work, they should make contact with the agency and arrange a schedule that guarantees that they work there a minimum of twenty hours over the course of the semester. This time frame is recommended by the Center for Civic and Social Responsibility (CCSR) at the University of Kansas, which warns that fewer contact hours with the agency may reinforce stereotypes of others in the community who are in need of help. This is a potential problematic consequence of service learning recognized by scholars who are concerned about the way that community service at times "devolve[s] into a cultural safari into the jungle of 'otherness'" (Forbes et al. 158). The CCSR also offers methodological guidelines for students recording their experiences at the service-learning site in a journal, a process that can help students make sense of their subjective and objective observations of a work site. Specifically, the CCSR recommends that students write about each visit to the organization in two columns. In one column, they are to describe as objectively as possible what they did and saw during each visit to the agency. In the other column, students are to record their subjective responses to what they have done and seen. This system of journal writing allows space for students' emotional reactions to their work while also ensuring a detailed record of the particular tasks they completed and experiences they witnessed. In my course, I ask students to turn in their journals for evaluation twice during the semester, since the journal provides the exclusive source material for students' final projects (no secondary research is required). Students receive a grade for each "journal check" based on the level of detail provided as well as on the evidence of substantive reflection on the service experience.

The writing stage of the assignment requires preliminary conceptual work. Here, the précis again serves an important function. Instead of analyzing someone else's work, students can produce a draft outline of the final assignment in which they describe its focus, rhetorical strategies, as well as the potential implications of their formal decisions. This third and final stage of the service-learning process is a key step in students' transformation of their experiences working with and witnessing human rights issues at the local level into the ordered framework of a narrative. At this point, students ideally come to confront the primary pedagogical goal of the course—namely, to apprehend the process and ramifications of shaping a "messy" context into a bounded story.

Along with their final project, students can be asked to write an essay in which they explain or justify the formal choices they made by referencing works read during the semester. This essay serves as a way for students to describe the process of crafting their narrative and to articulate their understanding of the ethical dimensions of generic choices. Furthermore, by having to situate their work within a larger literary historical context of writing about human rights issues that they encountered in the course readings, students engage in a synthetic, critical evaluation of course material.

In my course Literature of Human Rights, students' final projects have both responded to the particular service-learning contexts and drawn on the course material in productive and compelling ways. One student, Blaise Cannon, wrote about his experiences at Douglas County Court Watch, a program that places volunteer witnesses in the courtroom to document proceedings with the aim of providing a transparent record of court activities by neutral parties. Cannon's creative piece, entitled "Guilty, Your Honor," is a fictional first-person account of the way that a court bailiff comes to question his own sexist and racist preconceptions after realizing the structural impediments to due process for all. By tracking the transformation of a prejudiced bailiff, a seemingly neutral figure in a supposedly transparent judicial system, Cannon implicitly questions whether the local courts comply with article 7 of the UDHR, which claims that "all are equal before the law and are entitled without any discrimination to equal protection of the law" ("Universal Declaration"). Cannon justified his formal choices by citing specific works read during the semester. For example, Moya's *Senselessness* modeled the "[depiction] of moral development through exposure to the suffering of others" and *I, Rigoberta Menchú* showed him that "one of the most effective ways of awakening an audience's consciousness to . . . human rights issues is by depicting an individual becoming conscious of those same . . . issues."

Another student, Michael Schepers, documented his work at Women's Transitional Care Services (WTCS) in Lawrence, Kansas—primarily caring for children so that their mothers could attend meetings at the center—in the form of a graphic novel. Unlike Cannon's fictional bailiff who serves as the focal point for his narration of a human rights issue, Schepers's protagonist, Mike, is a self-described "weird punk kid with a bad smoking habit" who dreads working with children. Mike, however, comes to the realization that his seemingly small contributions to WTCS make a difference in women's and children's lives. Though he does not explore this explicitly in the graphic novel, his work, as well as the work of the WTCS, can be viewed in connection with recent global efforts to put an end to systemic violence against women, such as the United Nation's 2007 Convention on the Elimination of All Forms of Discrimination against Women (CEDAW). Yet just as Cannon argues that a first-person fictional narrator functions as a fitting mode for representing the many instances of unequal access to due process he witnessed, Schepers's emphasis on his transformation is an appropriate strategy for depicting the world of WTCS: the women and children cannot be the subject of realist representation in Schepers's story because their identities must remain anonymous. Schepers's treatment of this reality—a fully fleshed-out Mike who stands in contrast to the stick-figure children he supervises—implicitly references Art Spiegelman's use of different animal species to reflect varying social groups in *Maus*, which we read in class.

Quite opposite of some expectations, the use of service learning for a literature of human rights course, then, is as a tool for leading students to question the role of literature as instrument. They do this by reflecting, in a very concrete way, on the relation of form and content. By crafting a coherent narrative from their collection of experiences doing human rights work—work that often includes tedious tasks essential for institutions seeking to promote human rights at a local level, such as listening to long court cases and giving children rides—students confront the power of form to give meaning to lived experience and the limitations thereof. In other words, they must wrestle with the fact that representational strategies constitute our view of reality while reflecting it in a contingent manner. Ultimately, students' process of telling about the local human rights concerns they witnessed at their service-learning sites becomes a personally and intellectually relevant act. Not only do they produce texts based on the "street smarts" they gain—to use Gerald Graff's term for expertise not necessarily valued within the bounds of academia (213)—but they also acquire a framework for recognizing the strategies, and thus the stakes, of cultural texts.

Notes

1. While research on the theory and practice of service learning has boomed since the mid-1990s (Speck and Hoppe vii), the corpus of publications investigating the place of service learning in literature courses is slim and has not included discussions of integrating service learning into a course on literature and human rights. For reflections on the minimal engagement with service learning in literature classrooms thus far, see Zlotkowski; Grobman, "Is There" and "Service Learning"; E. Cushman, "Service Learning" and "Public Intellectual." Grobman and Rosenberg's recent volume on service learning and literary studies offers an important contribution to the field.

2. This position is characteristic of the scholarship on service learning in the literature classroom. See, e.g., Comstock; Grobman, "Is There"; and Mollis.

Megan Sweeney

The Rickety Bridge: Prisoners and Human Rights in the Literature Classroom

> *When the prison gates slam behind an inmate, he does not lose his human quality; his mind does not become closed to ideas; his intellect does not cease to feed on a free and open interchange of opinions.*
>
> —Thurgood Marshall, *Procunier v. Martinez*

While teaching in divergent contexts—including bilingual elementary schools, universities, and men's and women's prisons—I have found that literature serves as an effective means to facilitate dialogue across lines of difference. As my students encounter unfamiliar characters, histories, cultures, and ideas, they begin to step outside their comfort zones, question some of their assumptions, and increase their awareness of the particular positions they occupy in the world. Discussing encounters across lines of difference, Peggy Phelan writes, "It is in the attempt to walk (and live) on the rickety bridge between self and other—and not the attempt to arrive at one or the other—that we discover real hope" (174). As Anne Anlin Cheng suggests, putting oneself on that rickety bridge entails both a responsibility to enter "the space of the other" and a deep awareness of "the limits of that ingress" (191). As a teacher, I seek to foster students' ability to take some steps toward others—and to understand the stakes of doing so—on bridges of their own making.

The metaphor of the rickety bridge has proven especially helpful for framing my efforts to bring prisoners and human rights into my literature classes at the University of Michigan. I have been involved with women prisoners for more than twenty years, as a social worker, volunteer tutor, book club facilitator, and researcher. For my recent book, *Reading Is My Window: Books and the Art of Reading in Women's Prisons*, I conducted extensive interviews and group discussions with ninety-four women prisoners. Although I am keenly aware of the limits of my ingress into these women's lives, our interactions continue to inform my thoughts about literature, pedagogy, and human rights. I now view my university classroom as a site for engaging in the broader human rights project of challenging the presumed divisions between incarcerated and nonincarcerated people. During our discussions of literary texts, I draw attention to the thoughts and experiences of women involved in my research, emphasizing how they use reading as a means to make meaning from their experiences, situate those experiences within broader contexts, experiment with new ways of being, and cultivate relationships with people on both sides of the prison fence. By positioning prisoners as integral members of our community and as thinkers whose ideas merit careful engagement, I invite my university students to consider how social justice, rather than imprisonment, might serve as the foundation of our communal well-being.

Some central insights that I gained from teaching in prisons seem useful for teaching in a variety of university settings. The first insight is that access to books and opportunities for reading is a human rights issue. Second, readers productively engage with the subject of human rights through a variety of reading practices, some of which are devalued in academic contexts. Third, a wide variety of literary genres can serve as resources for addressing human rights issues. Fourth and finally, collective discussions of literary texts can foster participants' recognition of their human dignity and shared humanity. By reflecting on these insights here, I hope to inspire new possibilities for a range of educators—including those who will never teach in prisons—to address human rights issues in literature classrooms.

Reading as a Human Rights Issue

In prisons, where women have limited access to books, education, and spaces conducive to reflection, it quickly becomes apparent that reading is a human rights issue.[1] Since the birth of the penitentiary in the early 1800s, dehumanizing conceptions of prisoners have led to restrictions on prisoners' right to read. Such restrictions increased with the shift toward a retributive justice framework in the 1970s, as penal authorities reduced prison library budgets, converted library space into prison cells, and installed televisions as a pacification tool. In 1994, Congress eliminated merit-based Pell Grants for prisoners who were seeking higher education, contributing to a decline in all levels of educational programs in prisons. And in 2006, the United States Supreme Court ruled in *Beard v. Banks* that denying access to reading materials serves as an "incentiv[e] for inmate growth"—even for prisoners who have no contact with others and no access to television, radio, or telephone—because it encourages prisoners' compliance with prison rules (Breyer 8).

As I talk with university students about the dehumanizing consequences of such restrictions, many begin to recognize that they have had greater access to books and education than many of their fellow citizens. At the same time, we discuss how material and institutional forces such as rising costs also delimit university students' engagements with books. Such contextualization of the act of reading helps students understand the unexpected roles that books and reading can play in environments that impede human flourishing. For instance, curling up in bed with a book can offer incarcerated readers a sense of refuge from the unrelenting noise of the prison. Books can also provide soothing touch and aesthetic pleasure in environments where gentle human contact and sensory delight are lacking; as one prisoner noted, she never reads hardback books because she finds it much more comforting to touch and hold paperbacks. Moreover, women counter the myriad institutional forces that thwart interpersonal connection by reading to each other as a form of nurturance and by sharing and discussing books with family members and friends. Even when women can barely read, borrowing books from the prison library can serve as a means—in the words of one reader—"to feel a part of society as a whole." My university students learn to situate reading in a human rights framework by discussing these institutional, material, and embodied dimensions of reading.

Identificatory Reading Practices

A second pedagogical insight that I gained from working with prisoners is that readers bring a wide range of needs and motivations to their engagements with literary texts, and it is crucial to focus on understanding, rather than judging, reading practices that differ from one's own. As Michael Warner argues, educators tend to dismiss as "uncritical" "any style of actual reading that we can observe in the world," including identification, sentimentality, enthusiasm, and aversion (15). By jettisoning the critical/uncritical distinction, Warner suggests, we can better understand the roles that a variety of reading practices play in readers' projects of self-creation.

In both penal and university settings, identification is a central component of many readers' engagements with texts. I gained a deeper understanding of the importance and complexity of identificatory reading practices during the earliest phase of my research, when some prisoners and I were discussing Pearl Cleage's *What Looks like Crazy on an Ordinary Day*. Cleage tells a tale of redemption that features an HIV-positive woman, a former cocaine addict who served time in prison for murder, and a crack-addicted baby whose mother abandoned her. These three characters embody the novel's credo that "people have a right to change, to grow, *to get better*" (131). Cleage's tale of redemption is predicated, however, on an intertwined story about an unredeemable class of "crack-heads" and "superpredators" who must be expelled from the community—through incarceration or death—to ensure the well-being of the main characters.

While discussing Cleage's novel with incarcerated women, I quickly learned that our approaches to the book sharply differed. I presumed that women in the group—many of whom have struggled with crack addiction—would share my desire to challenge the novel's dehumanizing depiction of "crack-heads" and its suggestion that incarcerating drug users ensures communal safety. However, all the readers embraced the novel's depiction of the drug-addicted characters, sharply distanced themselves from such characters, and emphasized their identification with characters who are overcoming "obstacles" and "accept[ing] responsibility" for their circumstances. A woman named Arlene summarized the group's response in these terms: "That book gives a lot of ladies in here as well as myself a lot of support, because a lot of us are trying to change."[2]

These readers' responses to Cleage's novel helped me recognize the complex work that readers can perform in identifying and refusing to identify with various characters. On the one hand, prisoners' embrace of discourse that demonizes drug addicts illuminates our ongoing need for cultural and jurisprudential narratives that better account for the social and structural factors that fuel our communal problems of addiction and crime. On the other hand, when I criticized Cleage's depiction of drug addicts as unredeemable and utterly expendable, a prisoner named Patty responded, "That's the way society looks at inmates. We're expendable. It's just like we stay in a human warehouse. *We* know that." As Patty's comment clarified, women in the group had firsthand knowledge of the detrimental effects of demonizing discourse, but in reading Cleage's novel, they found it more useful to identify with characters that enabled them to sort out the parameters of individual agency and served as models for reclaiming their own life stories. Such strategic identification with characters can seem especially helpful for women who have faced numerous social and structural obstacles such as poverty, racism, and gendered violence and for women who live with daily reminders of their captivity and dependence.

Learning to recognize how incarcerated women—like all of us—read for different purposes at different times has heightened my awareness of the wide range of needs and desires that college students bring to the study of literature. Acknowledging students' own entry points and motivating questions is crucial, I now see, for constructing knowledge together in the literature classroom. When teaching texts that address human rights issues, I have also learned to help students analyze their affective responses—including outrage, grief, guilt, frustration, contempt, pity, relief, and sometimes joy—and recognize what is at stake in identifying or refusing to identify with particular characters. For instance, I encourage students to avoid both distancing themselves from imprisoned people and conflating their own experiences with those of prisoners by asking themselves, "Where am I in this story? How do my own experiences intersect with, and diverge from, the experiences of these people?"

To foster such encounters, I frequently ask students to read essays that feature women prisoners' readings of some books on our syllabus. These reading-based encounters do not enable actual dialogue between incarcerated and nonincarcerated readers, but they encourage students to consider the intellectual and emotional lives of prisoners and to regard prisoners as thinkers whose ideas merit discussion in a college course. My essay "Prison Narratives, Narrative Prisons: Incarcerated Women Reading Gayl Jones's *Eva's Man*" can encourage students to situate their experiences in relation to those of women prisoners. Jones's novel offers the first-person fictional account of Eva Medina Canada, an African American woman who is incarcerated in a prison psychiatric hospital for killing a man with whom she spent four days in a hotel. Although her written narrative conveys her continual exposure to sexual harassment, Eva remains silent when others insist that she explain her violent acts. In their responses to *Eva's Man*, women prisoners generate important insights about the potential connection between sustaining and perpetrating violence and about the ways in which ideologies of race, class, and sexuality shape cultural and legal responses to women's victimization. As my students struggle to reconcile prisoners' responses with their own responses to Jones's novel, I encourage them to consider social, structural, and interpersonal factors that may delimit one's sense of agency and lead one to commit a criminal act. We also discuss what is at stake in efforts to protect the human rights of someone who has violated another person's human rights. Furthermore, we explore possibilities for protecting women from violence without relying on the penal system, which participates in, and contributes to, cycles of violence. Although our conversations often generate more questions than answers, they foster students' intellectual humility, capacity for ethical inquiry, and willingness to learn about—and learn from—imprisoned women.

Whereas identification is central to many undergraduates' engagements with literary texts, graduate students have often learned to be suspicious—if not dismissive—of identificatory reading practices. As we engage with prisoners' responses to texts, I therefore encourage my graduate students to question presumed hierarchies of reading practices, including the belief that a deconstructive reading practice is more valuable or productive of knowledge than an identification-based reading practice. Students learn to consider the cognitive dimensions of identification and affect: the ways in which readers, including themselves, produce crucial forms of knowledge through their complex identifications with texts, characters, and authors. In my view, preparing graduate students for their roles as teachers entails encouraging them to expand the spectrum of reading practices they consider legitimate and potentially productive of knowledge.

Expanding the Scope of Human Rights Literature: Popular Genres

Teaching in penal contexts has also helped me recognize how texts that neither promote a human rights ethos nor typically count as literature can serve as valuable resources for engaging with human rights issues.

Although some of my discussions with women prisoners focused on texts that foreground such issues—including Dorothy Allison's *Bastard Out of Carolina* and Ernest J. Gaines's *A Lesson before Dying*—our discussions of human rights issues often revolved around popular genres that academics tend to dismiss. A prime example is urban fiction, an immensely popular genre that features African Americans who are involved in drug dealing, hustling, prostitution, and murder. Penal officials have banned this genre in the prisons where I conducted research, but many works of urban fiction make it onto prison grounds and become part of "the Underground Book Railroad." While some prisoners argue that urban fiction glorifies crime, fans of the genre often map their own psychological interiority onto urban fiction's thinly drawn characters, transforming the books into templates for reflecting on their experiences as drug users and drug sellers, victims and perpetrators, neglected children and neglectful parents. For many women, reading urban fiction involves grappling with pressing questions, including whether crime is a necessary stepping-stone to financial success, and whether sustaining abuse is a necessary price to pay for maintaining men's financial support.

Using popular genres to address human rights issues also presents unique pedagogical challenges. In penal contexts, I found myself searching for respectful and pedagogically productive ways to encourage prisoners to grapple with urban fiction's ideological assumptions and contradictions. At one point, I felt so discouraged by a group's unquestioning embrace of the genre that I asked them to read an urban fiction novel in conjunction with Harper Lee's *To Kill a Mockingbird*. My attempt to shape our discussion was misguided and ineffective—only one participant actually read Lee's novel—but it pushed me to develop other strategies for introducing alternative perspectives during our discussions of urban fiction. I learned, for instance, to ask readers to consider other paths that the protagonists might have followed, to reflect on the effects of protagonists' actions or modes of thinking, to unpack particular contradictions, and to imagine alternative endings.

I have since found that urban fiction is a valuable resource for addressing human rights issues in my university courses. I often ask students to read a cluster of texts such as the following: Nikki Turner's novel *A Project Chick*; Nick Chiles's *New York Times* op-ed about urban fiction; Percival Everett's *Erasure*, a novel that satirizes the genre; and "Fear of Books: Reading Urban Fiction," a chapter from *Reading Is My Window* in which I discuss women prisoners' engagements with the genre. Juxtaposing these materials invariably generates the liveliest discussions of the semester. In addition to sparking debate about definitions of *literature*, expectations paced on black authors, and the value of analyzing popular texts, this unit prompts important dialogue about the ways in which cultural representations can perpetuate or challenge patterns of injustice and human rights violations.

For instance, *A Project Chick* focuses on a young black woman who struggles to support herself and her sons while her boyfriend is incarcerated for drug dealing. Turner draws a sharp distinction between the protagonist and the long-term residents of the projects, whom she characterizes as lazy, criminal, neglectful of their children, and deserving of punishment. As my students and I work to untangle the novel's ideological threads, some students argue that Turner offers an accurate depiction of irresponsible "project chicks." Students tend to yoke class ascendancy to individual effort for a variety of reasons: the ideology of self-determination remains powerful across racial lines, some students who grew up in the projects are seeking to educate themselves into middle-class status, and we lack readily available solutions for systemic problems such as racialized poverty. In an effort to help students analyze—and ultimately revise—some of their assumptions about demonized others, we discuss the origins and histories of such assumptions, the purposes they serve, and the kinds of questions they obscure or prevent us from addressing.

Discussing my chapter about prisoners' engagements with urban fiction further enables students to rethink their assumptions about poor women and women in prison. We explore how incarcerated women use urban fiction to grapple with racism, intraracial class tensions, educational and employment inequities, gendered violence, and the personal costs of sustaining and perpetrating violence. During these conversations, students often learn about, and from, one another's varied experiences. In fact, a subtle shift in power dynamics frequently ensues. Students who have grown up reading urban fiction gain confidence as we discuss the genre, as if their knowledge, interests, and perspectives have moved from margin to center. By contrast, students who have little familiarity with the genre struggle to find their bearings; their frameworks for engaging with literature seem inadequate in this context. As they learn to recognize how readers' racial, class, gender, and educational backgrounds affect their responses to texts, students often deepen their understanding of perspective. Moreover, they realize that what is at stake in restricting prisoners' right to read is their status as complex human beings who are trying to make meaning from their experiences in a dehumanizing, infantilizing, and resource-poor environment.

Reading and Recognition

My conversations with women in prison have also helped me understand how discussing literary texts can open up crucial possibilities for recognition: readers often learn to recognize experiences that differ from their own, to recognize the complexity and humanity of other readers, and to recognize long-forgotten, disavowed, or emerging aspects of their own subjectivity. In penal contexts, discussing books enables women to witness not only to their experiences of victimization but also to the ways in which they have harmed others. Publicly articulating how they have violated others' human rights can feel urgently important to some women, not because they desire the absolution that confession affords, but because they seek recognition of their own humanity, an affirmation that who they are and who they might become is not encompassed by the self who performed reprehensible deeds.

A young Latina woman named Nena often seemed to be seeking such recognition during our group conversations. As we were discussing T. D. Jakes's novel *Woman, Thou Art Loosed!*, other readers were denigrating a character named Cassey for denying her daughter's sexual abuse, particularly since she sustained such abuse herself. Comparing herself with Cassey, Nena acknowledged, "I think about what I did with my son. I let him be abused even though my sister abused me." When another woman said of Cassey, "It's I hurt, so you hurt. Isn't that crazy?" Nena responded, "That's like me. . . . I have to get help for future generations." A bit later in the conversation, Nena identified herself as both victimizer and victim when she shared, "My sisters locked me in the trunk, put me in the dryer, did all kind of things to me. . . . But then I chose a man over my own daughter and I lost my parental rights. I felt really messed up reading this because my daughter was molested due to my drug use." Drawing parallels between herself and the protagonist of Jakes's novel, Nena then emphasized the difficult decisions that she has been making in trying to change her life, concluding: "It took a drastic change for me to look at me and not blame others for me being a victim. . . . I used to be a clown. I was a complete jerk. My life from birth to twenty-nine years old was a play. Now it's time to put the masks away, pull down the curtain, and pack up fantasy island. . . . I got to do some work." As Nena offered these reflections, other women in the group responded with expressions of understanding and encouragement. Eva Illouz argues that publicly narrating one's injuries allows for "symbolic reparation" in the form of recognition while compelling one to assume responsibility for improving one's condition (185). In a related vein, bell hooks argues that "story-telling becomes a process of historicization" that "enables us to see ourselves as part of history" (qtd. in Alcoff and Gray-Rosendale 216). As she weaves between her own and others' stories, situating herself within a broader history and a personal history that is still unfolding, Nena seems to be seeking recognition of her ability to rescript her life story—in its past and future forms—in more bearable and hopeful terms.

Like Nena, all of us bring complex selves to discussions of literature, and all of us seek recognition as members of the human community. In my university classes, I seek to help students recognize the myriad ways in which prisoners—some of whom are responsible for egregious violations of others' human rights—struggle to come to terms with their experiences, repair their relationships, and find new ways of being in the world. At the same time, I strive to create an atmosphere that allows students to grapple with their personal experiences, wrestle with their contradictions, and try out new forms of engagement with others. As in penal contexts, university discussions of literary texts offer students much-needed opportunities for coming into existence through dialogue: for experimenting, within a community of interlocutors, with whom they might become, and for being recognized as contributing members of the human community.

"[W]e cannot pretend," Sophia McClennen and Joseph Slaughter caution, "that literature or literary studies . . . rises like an answer to the problem of human rights violations" (7). Replenishing prison libraries will not prevent further violations of prisoners' human rights or diminish the economic and political centrality of prisons. Likewise, offering more literature courses that foreground the ideas and experiences of incarcerated people will not guarantee enlightened responses to the profound social problems that fuel crime. Nonetheless, teaching at the juncture of prisoners, literature, and human rights can open up opportunities for countering dehumanizing policies that restrict prisoners' intellectual lives and challenge their status as human beings capable of deep thought, growth, and change. Moreover, facilitating literature-based encounters with prisoners can foster university students' awareness that each of us plays a role in perpetuating the world's largest penal system and that each of us can play a role in changing the structures, policies, and institutions that keep so many members of our community in prison. As a teacher, I cannot guarantee that my students will step onto a rickety bridge that links them to others, and I cannot guarantee that their bridges will be structurally sound. I can, however, create an atmosphere and provide intellectual tools that may increase students' awareness of all the bridges that remain to be built. I can then encourage them to step onto, or move a little farther along, a rickety bridge of their own design.

Notes

1. See Stevens; Sweeney, "*Beard*" and "Legal Brutality"; Buntman; James; and K. Warner.

2. All prisoners' names in this essay are pseudonyms.

Part V

Resources

Alexandra Schultheis Moore and Belinda Walzer

Resources

Chronology of the Core International Human Rights Instruments

1948	Universal Declaration of Human Rights (UDHR)
	Convention on the Prevention and Punishment of the Crime of Genocide
1949	Geneva Convention relative to the Treatment of Prisoners of War
	Geneva Convention relative to the Protection of Civilian Persons in Time of War
1961	Convention on the Reduction of Statelessness (CRS)
1965	International Convention on the Elimination of All Forms of Racial Discrimination (ICERD)
1966	International Covenant on Civil and Political Rights (ICCPR)
	International Covenant on Economic, Social and Cultural Rights (ICESCR)
1979	Convention on the Elimination of All Forms of Discrimination against Women (CEDAW)

1984	Convention against Torture and Other Cruel, Inhuman or Degrading Treatment or Punishment (CAT)
1986	Declaration on the Right to Development
1989	Convention on the Rights of the Child (CRC)
1990	International Convention on the Protection of the Rights of All Migrant Workers and Members of Their Families (ICRMW)
2000	Optional Protocol to the Convention on the Rights of the Child on the Involvement of Children in Armed Conflict (OP-CRC-AC)
2002	Optional Protocol to the Convention against Torture and Other Cruel, Inhuman or Degrading Treatment or Punishment (OP-CAT)
2006	International Convention for the Protection of All Persons from Enforced Disappearance (CPED)
	Convention on the Rights of Persons with Disabilities (CRPD)
2007	Declaration on the Rights of Indigenous Peoples

Histories of Human Rights and Humanitarianism

Barnett, Michael. *Empire of Humanity: A History of Humanitarianism.* Ithaca: Cornell UP, 2011. Print.

A history of humanitarianism(s) based on archival work. Examines the ethics of humanitarianism from the early nineteenth century to today.

Baxi, Upendra. *The Future of Human Rights.* 2nd ed. Oxford: Oxford UP, 2006. Print.

Problematizes the origins, ideologies, and enunciations of human rights. Distinguishes between modern and contemporary human rights and suggests an alternative paradigm for its future through a link with global capital.

Donnelly, Jack. *Universal Human Rights in Theory and Practice.* 2nd ed. Ithaca: Cornell UP, 2002. Print.

Donnelly, a long-standing contributor to human rights discourse, updates his hopeful and approachable exploration of the potential for the universality of human rights in a second edition.

Evans, Tony. *Human Rights Fifty Years On: A Reappraisal.* Manchester: Manchester UP, 1998. Print.

A collection of essays that provides a critical historical overview of human rights in the twentieth century, marking the occasion of the fiftieth anniversary of the UDHR.

Glendon, Mary Ann. *A World Made New: Eleanor Roosevelt and the Universal Declaration of Human Rights.* New York: Random, 2001. Print.

More than just a clear and insightful account of Eleanor Roosevelt's role in leading the Human Rights Commission, because of Glendon's exclusive access to personal correspondence and diaries, this work is also a uniquely well-informed history of the drafting of the UDHR.

Hunt, Lynn. *Inventing Human Rights:. A History.* New York: Norton, 2007. Print.

Provides a historical connection between individuality and rights discourse and argues a correlation between the rise of the novel, as a means of fostering empathy for distant others, with the rise of rights discourse.

Iriye, Akira, Petra Goedde, and William I. Hitchcock, eds. *The Human Rights Revolution: An International History.* Oxford: Oxford UP, 2011. Print.

Part of the National History Center's Reinterpreting History series, this collection of fifteen essays provides a diverse survey of the history of rights from World War II to the UDHR's sixtieth anniversary.

Ishay, Micheline R. *The History of Human Rights: From Ancient Times to the Present.* Rev. pref. Berkeley: U of California P, 2008. Print.

A history of human rights that takes into account perspectives ranging from early ethics and the Enlightenment to globalization and the twenty-first century. Also includes a chronology of events and writings on and about human rights.

Lauren, Paul. *The Evolution of Human Rights: Visions Seen.* 2nd ed. Philadelphia: U of Pennsylvania P, 2003. Print.

A history of human rights that uses the operative metaphor of visions, past, present, and future, to organize and frame its argument about universality.

Moyn, Samuel. *The Last Utopia: Human Rights in History.* Cambridge: Harvard UP, 2010. Print.

In this controversial reframing of history of rights discourse, Moyn locates the rise of contemporary international human rights, what he calls the last utopian idea, in the 1970s rather than immediately after World War II.

Neier, Aryeh. *The International Human Rights Movement: A History.* Princeton: Princeton UP, 2012. Print.

Traces the historical rise of the movement from the seventeenth century to the Arab uprisings in 2011 with primary focus on the 1970s and the Cold War.

Normand, Roger, and Sarah Zaidi. *Human Rights at the UN: The Political History of Universal Justice.* Bloomington: Indiana UP, 2008. Print.

A recent history of the role of the United Nations in promoting human rights; spans the first half of the twentieth century to post–Cold War development of rights.

Whelan, Daniel. *Indivisible Human Rights: A History.* Philadelphia: U of Pennsylvania P, 2010. Print.

A historical approach to the concept, rhetoric, and debate over the indivisibility of the covenants of civil and political rights and social, cultural, and economic rights.

Williams, Randall. *The Divided World: Human Rights and Its Violence.* Minneapolis: U of Minnesota P, 2010. Print.

Provides a critique and examination of the rise of a liberal model of humanism that was parallel with the United States' rise to global power during the postwar years.

Anthologies of Human Rights Literature and Poetry

Agosín, Marjorie. *A Map of Hope: Women's Writing on Human Rights: An International Literary Anthology.* New Brunswick: Rutgers UP, 1999. Print.

A comprehensive collection of over seventy poems, narratives, and essays written by women from all over the world on human rights issues and discourse. The sections range from war and remembrance to childhood to resistance and refusal.

Agosín, Marjorie. *Writing Toward Hope: The Literature of Human Rights in Latin America.* New Haven: Yale UP, 2006. Print.

Organized thematically around topics like witness, memory, fear, history, exile, and women's rights, this anthology brings together voices from twentieth-century Latin America to explore human rights issues.

Amnesty International. *Freedom: Stories Celebrating the Universal Declaration of Human Rights.* Edinburgh: Mainstream, 2009. Print.

Amnesty International brings together contemporary, influential fiction writers from around the world to provide thought-provoking short fiction organized according to the articles of the UDHR. Each author identifies the specific article of the UDHR that motivated the story, and the stories dramatize and personalize the stakes of those rights. Authors include Chimamanda Ngozi Adichie, Paulo Coelho, Nadine Gordimer, Joyce Carol Oates, and Walter Mosley, among others.

Flattley, Kerry, and Chris Wallace-Crabbe, eds. *From the Republic of Conscience: An International Anthology of Poetry.* Fredonia: White Pine; Amnesty Intl., 1993. Print.

Gathers over one hundred thirty poems about human rights injustices in seven topical groupings; includes biographical information on contributors.

Forché, Carolyn. *Against Forgetting: Twentieth-Century Poetry of Witness.* New York: Norton, 1993. Print.

This landmark anthology compiles work from over one hundred forty poets as a means to bear witness to some of the twentieth century's most heinous human rights violations and atrocities. Forché's introductory essay offers a compelling definition and discussion of poetry of witness.

Godrej, Dinyar, ed. *Fire in the Soul: One Hundred Poems for Human Rights.* Oxford: New Internationalist, 2009. Print.

A collection of poems written by poets from all over the world including Chris Abani, Margaret Atwood, Mahmud Darwish, and Ken Saro-Wiwa. Sales proceeds support Amnesty International.

Scheffler, Judith A., ed. *Wall Tappings: An International Anthology of Women's Prison Writings, 200 to the Present.* 2nd ed. New York: Feminist, 2002. Print.

An exhaustive compilation of women's prison writing.

Anthologies of Critical Approaches to Rights Discourses and Documents

Belgrade Circle, ed. *The Politics of Human Rights.* New York: Verso, 1999. Print.

An excellent collection edited by the Yugoslavian dissident intellectual group the Belgrade Circle, containing essays by key theorists such as Jean Baudrillard, Charlotte Bunch, Noam Chomsky, and Richard Rorty. Highlights Eastern European perspectives on the promise and pitfalls of rights discourse in the so-called new world order.

Cushman, Thomas, ed. *Handbook of Human Rights.* New York: Routledge, 2012. Print.

This comprehensive, highly recommended resource brings together over sixty authors from a variety of fields who explore the complexities of human rights in the twenty-first century from traditional and nontraditional perspectives. Individual essays frame central concerns and debates in geographic contexts as well as specific kinds of human rights.

Goodale, Mark. *Human Rights: An Anthropological Reader.* Oxford: Blackwell, 2009. Print.

Provides an excellent overview of the relation of anthropology and human rights, moving from anthropology's limited role in postwar rights discussions to its presence in human rights conversations today. In defining and demonstrating what Goodale calls a "critical anthropology of human rights," the essays look closely at epistemological, institutional, and moral dimensions of human rights in a variety of cultural contexts.

Hernández-Truyol, Berta Esperanza, ed. *Moral Imperialism: A Critical Anthology.* New York: New York UP, 2002. Print.

Organized by three generations of rights (civil and political; social, cultural, and economic; solidarity or collective), this text gathers twenty essays from scholars to examine the United States' claims of moral supremacy on issues of human rights.

Ishay, Micheline, ed. *The Human Rights Reader.* 2nd ed. New York: Routledge, 2007. Print.

This reader organizes human rights around five historical periods (the origins, the Enlightenment, the industrial age, the imperial age, and globalization) through the incorporation of political, legal, philosophical, and religious texts. Also arranged thematically, it facilitates comparative readings of different approaches to issues ranging from justice in war to environmental rights. Another strength is the attention to the political contexts that frame the historical development of human rights.

Lockwood, Bert, ed. *Women's Rights: A Human Rights Quarterly Reader.* Baltimore: Johns Hopkins UP, 2006. Print.

Collects nineteen influential articles in five sections (history, religion, violence, economic rights, and reproductive rights) to explore the relation of women's rights and human rights.

Peters, Julie, and Andrea Wolper, eds. *Women's Rights, Human Rights: International Feminist Perspectives.* New York: Routledge, 1995. Print.

Although some of the legal frameworks have changed since this volume was released, it still contains essays that provide an excellent overview of central problems in theorizing women's rights as human rights from an international or transnational perspective. Divided into sections on background and key concepts, regional case studies, and specific kinds of violations, including issues of health and economics.

Sriram, Chandra Lekha, Olga Martin-Ortega, and Johanna Herman, eds. *War, Conflict, and Human Rights: Theory and Practice*. New York: Routledge, 2010. Print.

Explores the important debates regarding conflict and human rights, moving from foundational theoretical issues to specific case studies and ending with peace and reconciliation projects.

Wilson, Richard Ashby, and Richard D. Brown, eds. *Humanitarianism and Suffering: The Mobilization of Suffering*. Cambridge: Cambridge UP, 2009. Print.

Composed of thirteen essays on humanitarianism that arose out of the Humanitarian Narratives of Inflicted Suffering conference at the University of Connecticut in 2006, this collection looks at the ethos of humanitarianism in contemporary civil society.

Cross-Cultural Approaches to Human Rights

An-Na'im, Abdullahi Ahmed, ed. *Cultural Transformation and Human Rights in Africa*. London: Zed, 2002. Print.

This collection explores the tension between local and universal conceptions of rights in an African context. Essays include Makau Mutua's analysis of the Banjul Charter and several discussions of economic and development rights and women's rights.

An-Na'im, Abdullahi Ahmed, ed. *Human Rights in Cross-Cultural Perspectives: A Quest for Consensus*. Pittsburgh: U of Pennsylvania P, 1992. Print.

An exploratory collection of essays that examines cross-cultural interpretations of human rights, both productive and problematic, from various disciplinary perspectives in an effort to negotiate between cultural specificity and the ideals of universality.

Bergoffen, Debra, Paula Ruth Gilbert, Tamara Harvey, and Connie L. McNeely, eds. *Confronting Global Gender Justice: Women's Lives, Human Rights*. New York: Routledge, 2011. Print.

A collection of eighteen essays drawing from multiple disciplines in the humanities that examines human rights and gender internationally. Organized into four parts, each with an operative verb: "Complicating Discourses of Victimhood," "Interrogating Practices of Representation," "Mobilizing Strategies of Engagement," and "Crossing Legal Landscapes."

Ibhawoh, Bonny. *Imperialism and Human Rights: Colonial Discourses of Rights and Liberties in African History*. Albany: State U of New York P, 2007. Print.

The first in the SUNY series in Human Rights, this text offers a critical look at the uses of rights discourse in colonial Nigeria by British colonizers and missionaries to further legitimate the colonial agenda and by the colonized to speak back to imperial powers.

Jolly, Rosemary. *Cultured Violence: Narrative, Social Suffering, and Engendering Human Rights in Contemporary South Africa*. Liverpool: Liverpool UP, 2010. Print.

Brings together fictional narratives and factual testimonies from South Africa to explore the cultural formations of violence.

Keown, Damien V., Charles S. Prebish, and Wayne R. Husted, eds. *Buddhism and Human Rights.* Richmond: Curzon, 1998. Print.

A foundational collection of essays that explores, among other issues, whether the concept of rights is compatible with Buddhist philosophy and the relation of rights and compassion.

Marrero-Fente, Raúl. *Bodies, Texts, and Ghosts: Writing on Literature and Law in Colonial Latin America.* Lanham: UP of Amer., 2010. Print.

Specifically dealing with the cross-cultural exchange between Spain and Spanish America, this book argues for a transatlantic approach to human rights law and literature.

Martin-Cabrera, Luis. *Radical Justice: Spain and the Southern Cone beyond Market and State.* Lewisburg: Bucknell UP, 2011. Print.

Focusing on Spain, Argentina, and Chile, this monograph considers the traumatic past of dictatorial regimes through an exploration of popular culture, specifically political documentaries and detective fiction.

Musa, Bala A., Jerry Domatob, and Cees J. Hamelink, eds. *Communication, Culture, and Human Rights in Africa.* Lanham: UP of Amer., 2011. Print.

A collection of essays on the relation of communication, culture, and human rights in Africa, including theoretical perspectives on media, gender, and health.

Mutua, Makau. *Human Rights: A Political and Cultural Critique.* 2nd ed. Philadelphia: U of Pennsylvania P, 2008. Print.

A critique of the Eurocentric civilizing mission of human rights, this monograph outlines the now foundational metaphor of human rights of savage-victim-savior that often defines the relation of human rights and humanitarianism among nations of the Global North and the Global South.

Niezen, Ronald. *The Origins of Indigenism: Human Rights and the Politics of Identity.* Berkeley: U of California P, 2003. Print.

Provides a thorough overview of the philosophical and practical questions surrounding the growing movement of indigenism (especially in contradistinction to ethnonationalism) as legal category, self-identification, and political strategy for collective action, including both its local contests as well as its efforts in United Nations frameworks and alliances.

Nnaemmeka, Obioma, and Joy Ngozi Exeilo, eds. *Engendering Human Rights: Cultural and Socioeconomic Realities in Africa.* New York: Palgrave Macmillan, 2005. Print.

Fourteen essays, from postmodern literary perspectives to case studies, that provide a comprehensive look at gendered human rights issues and abuses in Africa.

Theories of Human Rights in Literary and Cultural Studies

Agosín, Marjorie. *Inhabiting Memory: Essays on Memory and Human Rights in the Americas.* San Antonio: Wings, 2011. Print.

A powerful collection of essays on the relation of memory, witness, and trauma in Latin America.

Agosín, Marjorie, ed. *Women, Gender, and Human Rights: A Global Perspective.* New Brunswick: Rutgers UP, 2002. Print.

Sixteen essays grouped into four sections: "Theoretical Visions," "Women and Health," "Women, Activism, and Social Change," and "Women and the Cultures of Displacement." Worth noting is this last section, which includes essays by Barbara Harlow and by Joseph Slaughter and Jennifer Wenzel.

Anderson-Gold, Sharon. *Cosmopolitanism and Human Rights.* Cardiff: U of Wales P, 2001. Print.

Provides a historical overview of the development of human rights normativity and explores the complicated relation of human rights and Kantian cosmopolitanism, arguing for the potential of a global community bound by an international legal structure.

Anker, Elizabeth S. *Fictions of Dignity: Embodying Human Rights in World Literature.* Ithaca: Cornell UP, 2012. Print.

From Arundhati Roy's *The God of Small Things* to Salman Rushdie's *Midnight's Children*, Anker's monograph develops a phenomenological approach to reading human rights in fiction as a way to reconsider the currently disembodied and abstract subject of rights.

Anthonissen, Christine, and Jan Blommaert, eds. *Discourse and Human Rights Violations.* Philadelphia: Benjamins, 2007. Print.

Originally a special issue of *Journal of Language and Politics*, this collection of essays in discourse analysis and linguistics investigates primarily the discourses of the South African Truth and Reconciliation Commission to consider the role of language in fostering and mediating reconciliation.

Azoulay, Ariella. *The Civil Contract of Photography.* New York: Zone, 2008. Print.

Develops a bold theory of the "civil contract of photography" that binds the subject, photographer, and viewer in an ethical and political relationship vis-à-vis images of atrocity depicting the status of Palestinians and violence against women.

Boltanski, Luc. *Distant Suffering: Morality, Media, and Politics.* New York: Cambridge UP, 1999. Print.

Looks at the relation of spectatorship, media, and action and considers the role of speech in human rights work.

Bradley, Mark Philip, and Patrice Pietro, eds. *Truth Claims: Representation and Human Rights.* New Brunswick: Rutgers UP, 2002. Print.

Thirteen interdisciplinary and transnational essays on the making of human rights claims in the shift from a nationalist framework to the individual in an era of globalization.

Butler, Judith. *Frames of War: When Is Life Grievable?* New York: Verso, 2010. Print.

The follow-up to *Precarious Life*, in which Butler first asked the question, What makes a life grievable?, this set of essays continues her critique of military intervention and war, this time through an analysis of the media's dehumanizing role.

Butler, Judith. *Precarious Life: The Powers of Mourning and Violence.* New York: Verso, 2004. Print.

A theoretical perspective on violation and mourning as a way to rethink the United States' response to the violence of 9/11 with further violence. The chapter "Violence, Mourning, Politics" in particular articulates the transformative power of mourning in relation to human rights and the need for a recognition of shared human vulnerability.

Cheah, Pheng. *Inhuman Conditions: On Cosmopolitanism and Human Rights.* Cambridge: Harvard UP, 2006. Print.

A dense and complex critique of the ways in which human rights and an emerging new cosmopolitanism are situated in and defined by a global capitalist framework.

Cubilié, Anne. *Women Witnessing Terror: Testimony and the Cultural Politics of Human Rights.* New York: Fordham UP, 2005. Print.

A monograph that uses first-person survivor testimony by women to speak to theoretical accounts of witnessing. An important book for those interested in the relation of theoretical and practical roles of ethical witnessing.

Dawes, James. *That the World May Know: Bearing Witness to Atrocity.* Cambridge: Harvard UP, 2007. Print.

An important contribution to scholarship on human rights and humanitarianism, Dawes draws on personal narratives, media accounts, and other genres to consider the role of narrative in witnessing.

Douzinas, Costas. *Human Rights and Empire: The Political Philosophy of Cosmopolitanism.* New York: Routledge, 2007. Print.

Divided into two sections, on the paradoxes of human rights and on human rights normativity, Douzinas provides a critical evaluation of the co-opting of contemporary human rights for military and political purposes.

Doxtader, Erik. *Faith in the Work of Words: The Beginnings of Reconciliation in South Africa.* East Lansing: Michigan UP, 2009. Print.

A close look at the discursive process of reconciliation from a rhetorical perspective through an analysis of lesser-known texts in South Africa that precede the Truth and Reconciliation Commission. Doxtader is also a senior research fellow for the Institute for Justice and Reconciliation in South Africa.

Felman, Shoshana, and Dori Laub. *Testimony: Crises of Witnessing in Literature, Psychoanalysis, and History.* New York: Routledge, 1992. Print.

A collection of essays by a literary critic (Felman) and psychoanalyst (Laub) that consider witnessing from their perspectives of bearing witness to other people's firsthand accounts of atrocity. Presents a theory of testimony that considers the role of narration in postviolation witness, memory, and response.

Goldberg, Elizabeth Swanson. *Beyond Terror: Gender, Narrative, Human Rights.* New Brunswick: Rutgers UP, 2007. Print.

A literary interrogation of postviolation witness, testimony, and representation that takes a gendered perspective to examine the work of fictional narrative in human rights redress.

Goldberg, Elizabeth Swanson, and Alexandra Schultheis Moore, eds. *Theoretical Perspectives on Human Rights and Literature.* New York: Routledge, 2012. Print.

A foundational collection of fourteen essays from leading scholars in human rights and the humanities that examines what literature and theory in the humanities can offer the exhausted language of rights. The introduction provides an overview of the theoretical perspectives, challenges, and paradoxes of human rights discourse as they intersect with literature.

Harlow, Barbara. *Resistance Literature.* New York: Routledge, 1987. Print.

From the perspective of postcolonial literature, this text provides the groundwork for much of the work on human rights and literature by considering the performative nature of noncanonical resistance literature, including texts and authors from Palestine, South Africa, and South America, and how literature can confront the political work of writing history.

Hauser, Gerard A. *Prisoners of Conscience: Moral Vernaculars of Political Agency.* Columbia: U of South Carolina P, 2013. Print

A prizewinning look at vernacular human rights discourse.

Hesford, Wendy S. *Spectacular Rhetorics: Human Rights Visions, Recognitions, Feminisms.* Durham: Duke UP, 2011. Print.

Hesford takes a necessary and sophisticated rhetorical approach to her analysis of the relation of the textual, the visual, and the audience or reader in human rights discourse—what she calls "spectacular rhetoric"—ultimately asking, "Who are we becoming in this spectacular discourse?" (203).

Hesford, Wendy S., and Wendy Kozol, eds. *Just Advocacy? Women's Human Rights, Transnational Feminisms, and the Politics of Representation.* New Brunswick: Rutgers UP, 2005. Print.

A collection of eleven important essays that critique and interrogate the ways in which gender is deployed in transnational rights discourse in often problematic ways. The introduction also provides a good overview of the scholarship on the relation of gender to rights discourse.

Jensen, Meg, and Margaretta Jolly, eds. *We Shall Bear Witness: Life Narratives and Human Rights.* Madison: U of Wisconsin P, 2014. Print.

A strong collection of essays on witnessing and life writing from an international group of scholars, activists, and survivors. Includes a final section on pedagogy.

Kaplan, E. Ann. *Trauma Culture: The Politics of Terror and Loss in Media and Literature.* New Brunswick: Rutgers UP, 2005. Print.

This monograph, coming out of trauma studies, speaks to human rights and literature in its exploration of the ethics of witnessing and issues of memory and trauma.

Kennedy, David. *The Rights of Spring: A Memoir of Innocence Abroad.* Princeton: Princeton UP, 2009. Print.

One long essay, this quick read presents the problematic elements of the structure of rights and international humanitarianism told from the perspective of Kennedy's personal account of his humanitarian work one spring over twenty years ago in Uruguay.

Marsden, Peter, and Geoffrey Davis, eds. *Towards a Transcultural Future: Literature and Human Rights in a "Post"-Colonial World.* New York: Rodopi, 2004. Print.

Emerging from the twenty-third Annual Conference of the Association for the Study of New Literatures in English, this collection spans a broad range of geographic locations and subject matter to investigate postcolonial studies' engagement with human rights.

Milosz, Czeslaw. *The Witness of Poetry.* Cambridge: Harvard UP, 1984. Print.

A thoughtful expression on how the poetry of the twentieth century contains the traces of testimony and at times may hold a more accurate reflection of the world than journalism does.

Nance, Kimberly. *Can Literature Promote Justice? Trauma Narrative and Social Action in Latin American* Testimonio. Nashville: Vanderbilt UP, 2006. Print.

Nance explores the genre of the *testimonio* and the role it plays in furthering human rights concerns, connecting with the larger issue of the role literature plays in initiating action.

Owen, Nicholas, ed. *Human Rights, Human Wrongs: The Oxford Amnesty Lectures.* Oxford: Oxford UP, 2003. Print.

A collection that emerged from the Oxford Amnesty Lectures and contains influential essays on a broad range of topics from intervention to the representation of violence by Tzvetan Todorov, Michael Ignatieff, Gayatri Chakravorty Spivak, Susan Sontag, and others.

Robbins, Bruce. *Feeling Global: Internationalism in Distress.* New York: New York UP, 1999. Print.

Robbins examines the role of the public intellectual in international rights discourse and suggests that cosmopolitanism is a potential way to revitalize the universality of the discourse.

Sanders, Mark. *Ambiguities of Witnessing: Law and Literature in the Time of a Truth Commission.* Stanford: Stanford UP, 2007. Print.

Using the South African Truth and Reconciliation Commission and literature surrounding it as a case study, Sanders argues that literary reading is vital to the legal undertakings of testimony and witness.

Scarry, Elaine. *The Body in Pain: The Making and Unmaking of the World.* New York: Oxford UP, 1985. Print.

A foundational text that articulates the relation of pain and language, namely that pain destroys language. Divided into two parts, "Unmaking" and "Making," Scarry details the structures of power of torture that "unmake" worlds before examining the kinds of creative acts of language that produce worlds.

Schaffer, Kay, and Sidonie Smith. *Human Rights and Narrated Lives: The Ethics of Recognition.* New York: Palgrave Macmillan, 2004. Print.

Important for anyone thinking about the relation of life writing, including testimony, and human rights. Chapters range from South Africa to Australia to China and examine the ways in which life narrative is produced, circulated, and received in local and global settings.

Slaughter, Joseph R. *Human Rights, Inc.: The World Novel, Narrative Form, and International Law.* New York: Fordham UP, 2007. Print.

A significant text for human rights and literature that reads the legal documents through the literary, articulating "mutually enabling fictions" of the narrative form of the bildungsroman and the UDHR.

Sontag, Susan. *Regarding the Pain of Others*. New York: Picador, 2003. Print.
Sontag's last publication before she died, this book revisits and furthers many of the issues in *On Photography* on the role of art in human rights, specifically war photography.

Special Issue Journal Publications

And Justice for All? The Claims of Human Rights. Ed. Ian Balfour and Eduardo Cadava. Spec. issue of *South Atlantic Quarterly* 103.2–3 (2004).

The Humanities in Human Rights: Critique, Language, Politics. Spec. issue of *PMLA* 121.5 (2006).

Human Rights and Cultural Forms. Ed. Elizabeth Swanson Goldberg, Alexandra Schultheis Moore, and Greg Mullins. Spec. issue of *College Literature* 41.3 (2013).

Human Rights and Literary Forms. Ed. Sophia A. McClennen and Joseph R. Slaughter. Spec. issue of *Comparative Literature Studies* 46.1 (2009).

Human Rights Rhetoric: Traditions of Testifying and Witnessing. Ed. Arabella Lyon and Lester C. Olson. Spec. issue of *RSQ* 1.3 (2011).

Select Web Resources

Amnesty International Educators Resources (amnestyusa.org/resources/educators?id=1102117).
Detailed resources for educating about human rights including film, curriculum and teaching guides, and lesson plans.

Duke Human Rights Center (humanrights.fhi.duke.edu/study-human-rights/resources-for-teachers).
An interdisciplinary center, supported by Duke University's Franklin Humanities Institute, with links to syllabi, reading lists, and human rights films.

Facing History and Ourselves (facinghistory.org).
An organization with relationships to schools and offices all over the world intending to foster democracy and principles of human rights. The site includes curricula and information on workshops, seminars, benefits, and conferences.

H-Human-Rights (h-net.org/~hrights/).
A subscription-based international and interdisciplinary discussion network devoted to the history, theory, and practice of human rights. Hosts discussion forums and distributes calls for papers, conferences, and other global events and information relating to human rights.

Human Rights Center (http://www.law.umn.edu/humanrightscenter/index.html).
A useful and comprehensive library and resource center for electronic and

print media related to human rights education, sponsored by the University of Minnesota.

The Human Rights Curriculum Development Project (https://humanrights.uchicago.edu/page/syllabus-bank).

Linked to the University of Chicago's Pozen Family Center for Human Rights, a database that compiles human rights syllabi from scholars and teachers throughout the United States.

Human Rights Education Associates (hrea.org).

A Web-based forum, database, and repository of educational and training materials for both formal and informal human rights education.

Human Rights in the Humanities (hrhdatabase.com/).

A forum for academics, students, and activists, the site offers syllabi, teaching sections, and links to resources on other sites, all organized according to themes in human rights and literature. Particularly useful is the database of human rights literature and film.

Human Rights Research Tools (depts.washington.edu/hrights/resources.htm).

This network includes links to human rights research tools and legal resources and has bibliographies for human rights literature and film in Central and South America and the Caribbean.

Human Rights Syllabi for the College Classroom (learning.berkeley.edu//aiusa-syl/toc.html).

Hosted by Undergraduate and Interdisciplinary Studies at University of California, Berkeley, a comprehensive list with links to human rights syllabi for higher education in the humanities from well-known scholars and teachers across the United States.

International Coalition for the Responsibility to Protect (responsibilitytoprotect.org).

A coalition founded in 2009 that works to protect people at risk through shared responsibility. Published the report of the International Commission on Intervention and State Sovereignty on the so-called right of military and humanitarian intervention articulating the responsibility to protect.

The Office of the High Commissioner for Human Rights (ohchr.org/EN/ProfessionalInterest/Pages/UniversalHumanRightsInstruments.aspx).

A comprehensive database with links to the full text of all core international human rights instruments and many others; includes further information about ratification.

PEN International (pen-international.org).

An international organization that promotes freedom of expression and campaigns on behalf of persecuted writers.

Speak Truth to Power (rfkcenter.org/speak-truth-to-power; blogs.nysut.org/sttp/).

An interdisciplinary and multimedia pedagogical project profiling over fifty human rights defenders. Now joined with the New York State Union of Teachers, it is also a pedagogical database with lesson plans, exercises, and resources.

United Nations Educational, Scientific and Cultural Organization (unesco.org/new/en/education/).

UNESCO is the United Nations body tasked with promoting global education of human rights at all levels.

Witness (www.witness.org).

This international nongovernmental organization promotes video advocacy of human rights abuses. The site includes training for video advocacy.

James Dawes

Afterword: Human Rights Formalism

Literature and human rights has, as a subfield, come into its own. It is the topic of books like this one and its theoretical predecessor by the editors, *Theoretical Perspectives on Human Rights and Literature*. Literature and human rights panels regularly assemble at the annual conventions of the American Comparative Literature Association and the MLA; graduate students write dissertations on and self-describe as working in literature and human rights; independent conferences are convened on literature and human rights from Chicago to Beirut to London; and a search of the *MLA International Bibliography* for the subject "literature and human rights" yields hundreds of results. Here's an especially striking detail. In 2012 the visionary National Humanities Center held the first of three interdisciplinary conferences on human rights. Literature professors were in the majority. As somebody who had been, often, alone as a literature professor at interdisciplinary conferences on human rights ten years earlier—and then, typically, invited only as a resource for recommending stories to spice up the syllabi of proper human rights historians, philosophers, and political scientists—this was a gratifying moment.

This shift has been a long time coming. For those looking for origin stories, as Elizabeth Swanson Goldberg and Alexandra Schultheis Moore emphasize ("Human Rights"), one could do worse than to start with the 1985 publication of Elaine Scarry's *The Body in Pain*. Shortly after that book came out, I (then a young graduate student) took a human rights and literature course with Scarry—although neither of us would've recognized that description at the time. The course, organized around the concept of consent, did not fit easily into any existing categories. For many unfamiliar with Scarry's work, it wasn't even clear that she was still professing literary studies. What she was doing seemed closer to theory—but again, nothing like theory as we understood the term in the early 1990s. It was something more like political science theory or (non-Continental) philosophy. But not really. One thing was clear: what it wasn't was formalism. People looking at her courses from the outside couldn't make sense of the palpable esteem and respect between Scarry and her colleague Helen Vendler, the Anglo-American world's leading formalist. Wasn't the whole point that scholars like Scarry instrumentalized literary experience? That they used texts to learn about human rights discourse rather than to learn about the text? What possible intellectual kinship could they have shared? For those who never read Scarry's corpus, there was a worry that for her the literary text as such was not significant, except as a springboard for considering larger philosophical or cultural issues. But Scarry was, as a target of such criticisms, far from unique. The text/context tension people read (wrongly) into the work of Scarry—and into the work of those like her who were committed to philosophical and ideological contextualization—cut through all the disciplinary movements that, as Goldberg and Moore persuasively argue elsewhere ("Human Rights"), collectively intersected to make possible the interdiscipline of literature and human rights: law and literature, trauma theory, queer theory, Holocaust studies, postcolonial studies, and the ethical turn in 1990s literary studies.

Terry Eagleton, writing with defensive panache in his after-theory phase, characterizes this charge of aesthetic impoverishment as a cliché—that is, a claim whose breadth is only matched by its emptiness: "The idea that literary theorists killed poetry dead because with their shriveled hearts and swollen brains they are incapable of spotting a metaphor, let alone a tender feeling, is one of the more obtuse critical platitudes of our time" (1–2). But decades later, echoes of such worries linger. You've probably encountered them in one way or another yourself, if you've taught human rights and literature. Sophia McClennen and Joseph Slaughter tried to address the problem in *Human Rights and Literary Forms*, a special issue of *Comparative Literature Studies.* This sense of a formalism gap has made teaching human rights seem more difficult than it need be. Because whatever our theoretical or ideological commitments, we literary professors are—in the undergraduate classroom—almost always, at one time or another, formalists and aestheticists. Close reading, as the practice of formalism, is the meat and potatoes of the one-hour seminar. If your method seems incompatible with close reading—as appeared to be the case with literature and human rights for many years—you'd need to be a rather exceptional teacher to thrive in the classroom.

One of the great delights of this collection is the way its focus on pedagogy reveals so effortlessly—without strenuous theoretical positioning or argument—the seamless fit between deeply contextualized global or regional human rights study and careful attention to aesthetic form. Close reading is modeled in many different ways in this volume, from textual examples to specific pedagogies to analysis of frames within which we structure our close readings. McClennen, in her reading of *The Official Story*, *I, Rigoberta Menchú*, and *Death and the Maiden*, insists that "ethics and aesthetics are necessarily intertwined." As Eve Wiederhold does in her close reading of rhetoric in *The Visitor*, McClennen demonstrates her claim through careful attention to both micro and macro aesthetic choices: How long is the take? How close is the close-up? How do these decisions affect popular appeal and the nature of the audience one reaches? Neville Hoad's analysis of sexual orientation and human rights in *Walking with Shadows*, like Brenda Carr Vellino's reading of human rights poetry, is untroubled by the history of binary thinking around aesthetics. Theirs is the logic of *both/and* rather than *either/or*. Hoad writes, "Teaching a literary text . . . in a human rights classroom, or to make human rights content and approaches relevant to such a text, requires a dialectical relation between literary close reading and supplementary contextualizing materials, with the clear proviso that neither the novel nor the background reading are reducible to each other." Marike Janzen even goes so far as to show how service learning—what some see as, quite literally, a matter of walking away from the text—can be treated as a deliberate step in teaching students to understand the formal parameters of textual production and reception. Finally, in what is perhaps the most direct characterization of the relation of close reading and sociopolitical contextualization in this volume, Karen Bishop explains that their compatibility is simply "common sense."

So, in this brief afterword, I would like to take advantage of the permission given by these scholars to luxuriate in text, to give one last example of how human rights and literature work together—not only in the service of illuminating larger political and discursive movements but in the service of illuminating the aesthetic artifact. I would like to show how the human rights approach to literature can be a matter of aesthetic wonder, first and last, rather than a matter of discerning larger cultural logics or unmasking systems of power. I invite you to try this one, from Dave Eggers's *What Is the What*, in your own classrooms. It often takes me two full class sessions to go through the first two paragraphs of the novel, reading it this way. And that, for me, is the best way to start a course on literature and human rights. The political science majors who come to your course for the "human rights part" will think you've performed magic. "One paragraph per class session?!" they will ask, scratching their heads. And the English majors will know right away that the skills they've developed as literary critics remain relevant and valuable, even in the face of a topic as stratospheric as human flourishing.

The only thing you need to know about this book to discuss the first two paragraphs is that it is about somebody who fled to the United States as a war refugee. Here are the first two paragraphs:

> I have no reason not to answer the door so I answer the door. I have no tiny round window to inspect visitors so I open the door and before me is a tall, sturdily built African-American woman, a few years older than me, wearing a red nylon sweatsuit. She speaks to me loudly, "You have a phone, sir?"
>
> She looks familiar. I am almost certain that I saw her in the parking lot an hour ago, when I returned from the convenience store. I saw her standing by the stairs, and I smiled at her. I tell her that I do have a phone. (9)

On the first day, I ask my students to spend about ten minutes reading it closely. To help out those new to literary studies, I tell them to look for anything that seems unusual: unexpected word choices, repetitions, anything that draws attention to the fact that the author is making a deliberate decision. Over the next couple of hours, they draw attention to individual words and patches of language, and they offer theories that we will discuss.

One of the first things they notice is the repetition of "I have no." This is important, I tell them. The first words of a novel are carefully chosen and carry great weight. When the author chooses, then, to *repeat* those words, it is the literary equivalent of grabbing somebody by the collar. Here, in short summary, is the plot of the entire book to come. *I have no.* This is a book about a life of subtractions. What happens when you take away a boy's family? his village? his country? his language? (The book opens by emphasizing that he doesn't know the word *peephole.*) What is left of a person after all of those things have been removed? We discuss these questions for a while until, inevitably, one bright student notices the dramatic inversion at the end: "I *do* have." This is an exciting moment, I say, waving my hands in the air. The author now has repeated three times! Clearly what follows is going to be one of the most important words in the text.

The word is "phone." This puzzles them, especially with the over-excited hand waving. I let them puzzle. Either they finally figure out, or I eventually say, why the phone is one of the most important symbols in this book. What do you have left when everything has been taken away from you? Where do you go when every hoped-for safe place, every place to which you have fled (Ethiopia, refugee camp, United States), turns out to be unsafe once again? What safe space is there? For these war refugees resettled in pockets across the country, the imagined community of the phone is the only unburnable village. It is the one place those who have survived may gather and not become targets. I leave it to the students to discuss whether this should be considered a moment of hope or existential despair. Sometimes, in this conversation, a student asks why war refugees are separated during resettlement, why they aren't allowed to move in groups so as to preserve their sustaining relationships. That question becomes their first group research assignment. The result always astonishes them and generates our first policy-oriented discussion of human rights.

Students also notice the repetition of the word "door" in the first sentence. "Eggers is grabbing us by the collar again," they say. Discussion leads us to recognize that in this moment we are, once again, being emotionally prepared for everything that is to follow. The "door" is harder for them to suss out than the "have no"s, generally, so I help them along by asking why it is "the" door rather than "my" door. Soon, students are explaining it isn't "his" door because he has no home anymore, even if he lives there. Nothing can be "my." I push them further by asking them to explain the door as a concept. They explain, eventually, that we are being asked to think about doors because doors are about entries and exits, about transitions, and Eggers is showing us what it means to be continually in transitional space, always running, like the image of the young man on the spine of the first hardcover edition. The door is, then, an entryway, but it is also another kind of subtraction: homelessness. The perpetual motion of escape is homelessness.

Students soon notice, sometimes at my prompting, that the architecture of these first paragraphs offer up *only* transitional spaces, spaces designed so that you will pass through them as quickly as possible, without leaving a mark. What do we get to see? A door, a parking lot, a convenience store, stairs. These are, so to speak, the architectural equivalents of running. In a life defined by these kinds of spaces, what does it mean for somebody to be, as the narrator describes the woman he meets, "familiar"? If I were to say somebody looks familiar, I say to my students, it would suggest depth in time. A woman is familiar because I knew her from long enough ago and far enough away that her identity has begun to blur. Or else she is somebody I have seen frequently—because I have a stable enough life to be brought together often with the same clusters of people—but I have never taken the time or had the opportunity to cement her identity in my head. She is familiar rather than remembered or known. That is what it would mean to me and to you, I tell my students, if we said somebody looked familiar.

So what does "familiar" mean to the protagonist in this paragraph? Somebody he saw once in the parking lot of a convenience store, somebody he smiled to because he didn't know any better, because he didn't know that in this, once again new, environment, smiling would make him a target. That is familiarity only for a person who has spent his life running.

Talking about the woman lets me ask this question: What are the first spoken words? The first of anything is important, so what are the first spoken words? Are they unusual? When somebody finally identifies the odd grammatical structure of the woman's question—"You have a phone, sir?"—I clarify. The protagonist is being asked a question, but it is delivered in a grammatical form that echoes the structure of command. From here it is a short leap to Althusser's theory of subject interpellation, which depicts the individual as constituted through the ideology and language of a culture in much the same way that a pedestrian is hailed and accosted on the street by a police officer. Only a few paragraphs later the narrator will be named by his visitors—they will call him "Africa." He is, in short, called into being through a form of address that attempts to categorize and dismiss him. What follows is always an interesting theoretical discussion. Is it true that the language that constitutes you—that seems, like the structure of question itself, to acknowledge you as an independent source with autonomy and integrity of identity—is in fact a command in disguise?

Endings are returns to the beginning, but with a difference. I often pair these opening paragraphs with the third-to-last paragraph of the book. In a deliberate echo, it begins: "Today I have options." Recently one student pointed out that this mirror paragraph is an almost hysterical catalog of contradictory motions: "drive," "drive on," "swim," "drive the other way," "drive all day and night," "walk," "walk," "walk barefoot" (474). The narrator is now an American, and Americans "have options." But even in these final pages of the book, after a lifetime of running, the narrator has no place where he can be still. The "options" of freedom in the United States are only one more form of dissatisfied motion. The final word, which echoes a series of "ma" words throughout the paragraph, is "madness."

There is much more to say about these paragraphs, and all those paragraphs in between. But for the purposes of this afterword, that should be enough. Teaching literature and human rights can, and should, involve using novels like *What Is the What* to get students interested in researching settlement policies for war refugees and to help them see the immediate relevance of difficult and sometimes distant-seeming high theory. But it is also, like everything else we do, poetry.

Notes on Contributors

Marjorie Agosín is Luella LaMer Slaner Professor in Latin American Studies and professor of Spanish at Wellesley College. Her work includes *A Map of Hope: Women's Writings on Human Rights: An International Literary Anthology*, *Women, Gender, and Human Rights: A Global Perspective*, *Secrets in the Sand: The Young Women of Ciudad Juárez*, and *The Light of Desire / La Luz del Deseo*. She has been honored with human rights awards from the Chilean government, the Jeannette Rankin Foundation, and the United Nations.

Ben Alberti is associate professor of anthropology at Framingham State University. He is the editor of three volumes and the author of journal articles and book chapters on masculinity, queer theory, and gender in Bronze Age Crete, pre-Hispanic South America, and contemporary Tunisia.

Elizabeth S. Anker teaches in the English department at Cornell University. Her first book is titled *Fictions of Dignity: Embodying Human Rights in World Literature*, and she is currently working on a project that places comparative constitutionalism in dialogue with literature, architecture, and film.

Karen Elizabeth Bishop is assistant professor of Spanish and comparative literature at Rutgers University, New Brunswick. She writes on twentieth-century literary representations of torture and disappearance, exile, cartography, architecture, and the poetics of form.

Jennifer Browdy de Hernandez teaches comparative literature and media studies at Bard College at Simon's Rock, with a focus on narratives of social and ecological justice. She is the founding director of the annual Berkshire Festival of Women Writers and the editor of two anthologies on African, Latin American, and Caribbean women writers. She blogs on politics, education, and the environment at *Transition Times* (http://bethechange2012.wordpress.com).

James Dawes is chair and professor of English at Macalester College and founder and director of the program in human rights and humanitarianism. He is author of *Evil Men*, *That the World May Know: Bearing Witness to Atrocity*, and *The Language of War*.

Ira Dworkin is assistant professor of English at Texas A&M University and previously taught at the American University in Cairo. He is the editor of *Daughter of the Revolution: The Major Nonfiction Works of Pauline E.*

Hopkins and the author of the forthcoming book “Congo Love Song: African Americans and the Congo, 1884–1965.”

Lisa Eck is professor of contemporary world literature at Framingham State University. She has published essays in journals and collected volumes on the work of authors from Zimbabwe, Denmark, Iran, England, Sri Lanka, and India that represent a unified body of work on the “nervous conditions” of cross-cultural literacy.

Elizabeth Swanson Goldberg is professor of English at Babson College. The author of *Beyond Terror: Gender, Narrative, Human Rights*, she edited *Theoretical Perspectives on Human Rights and Literature* with Alexandra Schultheis Moore and a special issue of *Peace Review* on the film and literature of human rights. Her many articles on human rights, gender studies, and literature can be found in edited volumes and in journals such as *Callaloo*, *Humanity*, and *South Atlantic Review*.

Alexander Hartwiger is assistant professor of world literature at Framingham State University. He has also taught at the American University of Beirut and was an international fellow at the Center for Online International Learning. His research interests include contemporary world literature, postcolonial studies, cosmopolitanism, and globally networked learning.

Wendy S. Hesford is professor of English at Ohio State University. She is the author of two monographs, *Framing Identities: Autobiography and the Politics of Pedagogy* and *Spectacular Rhetorics: Human Rights Visions, Recognitions, Feminisms*. She edited two collections with Wendy Kozol, *Haunting Violations: Feminist Criticism and the Crisis of the “Real”* and *Just Advocacy? Women’s Human Rights, Transnational Feminisms, and the Politics of Representation*, and a textbook with Brenda Brueggemann, *Rhetorical Visions*.

Heather Hewett has published work in a range of publications, including *WSQ*, *English in Africa*, *MELUS*, *Journal of the Association for Research on Mothering*, and *Women’s Review of Books*. She is associate professor of English and women’s, gender, and sexuality studies at the State University of New York, New Paltz.

Neville Hoad is associate professor of English and women’s and gender studies at the University of Texas, Austin. He is the author of *African Intimacies: Race, Homosexuality, and Globalization* and the editor (with Karen Martin and Graeme Reid) of *Sex and Politics in South Africa*. He is working on a book about the literary and cultural representations of the HIV/AIDS pandemic in sub-Saharan Africa.

Bridget Irish is retired assistant dean of the School of Arts, Humanities, and Social Sciences at Fort Lewis College. She coordinated the First Year

Experience, including the Common Reading Experience and the Learning Communities. She also taught in the college's writing program.

Marike Janzen is assistant professor of humanities at the University of Kansas. Her research focuses on world literature, human rights, solidarity, and authorship. She has published in *German Quarterly*, *Comparative Literature*, and *Seminar* and is at work on a book titled "Writing to Change the World: Anna Seghers, Authorship, and International Solidarity in the Twentieth Century."

Erik Juergensmeyer is associate professor of composition and rhetoric at Fort Lewis College, where he is also writing program director and coordinator of the new minor in peace and conflict studies. His research examines how rhetorical theories and research can transform social conflict. His work has appeared in *Community Literacy Journal*, *Composition Studies*, *Peace Studies Journal*, *Rhetoric Review*, and *Writing Program Administration.*

Nicholas Matlin is lecturer and postdoctoral teaching fellow in the College Core Curriculum at New York University. He is working on a book project derived from his dissertation, "Crime as Punishment: South African Literature and the Experience of Violence," which investigates how literature from the apartheid era shapes contemporary discussions of violent crime in South Africa.

Sophia A. McClennen is professor of international affairs and comparative literature at Penn State University, University Park, where she directs the Center for Global Studies. Her recent books include *Ariel Dorfman: An Aesthetics of Hope*, *Representing Humanity in an Age of Terror* (edited with Henry James Morello), and *America according to Colbert: Satire as Public Pedagogy.*

Alexandra Schultheis Moore is associate professor of English at the University of North Carolina, Greensboro. She is the author of *Regenerative Fictions: Postcolonialism, Psychoanalysis, and the Nation as Family* and editor, with Elizabeth Swanson Goldberg, of *Theoretical Perspectives on Human Rights and Literature* and of, with Goldberg and Greg Mullins, a special issue of *College Literature* on human rights and cultural forms.

Greg A. Mullins is academic dean at the Evergreen State College. He is the author of *Colonial Affairs*, a study of colonialism and sexuality, and of a series of essays that explore literary engagements with the cultural politics of human rights.

Kimberly A. Nance, professor of languages, literatures, and cultures at Illinois State University, has chaired the MLA Division on the Teaching of Literature and is secretary of the Division on Teaching as a Profession. Her books include *Can Literature Promote Justice?* and *Teaching Literature in the Languages.*

Ryan Omizo is visiting assistant professor in Michigan State University's Department of Writing, Rhetoric, and American Cultures. He is also a postdoctoral researcher at MSU's Matrix: Center for Digital Humanities and Social Sciences, studying computational rhetorics.

Crystal Parikh is associate professor in the Department of English and the Department of Social and Cultural Analysis at New York University. She is the author of *An Ethics of Betrayal: The Politics of Otherness in Emergent U.S. Literatures and Culture* and is completing a second book, "Writing Human Rights."

Manav Ratti is assistant professor of English at Salisbury University in Maryland. He has been a Fulbright Scholar at New York University and is Fellow Designate at the Institute of Advanced Study at Jawaharlal Nehru University. He is the author of *The Postsecular Imagination: Postcolonialism, Religion, and Literature.*

Susan Spearey is associate professor in the English department, the interdisciplinary MA program in social justice and equity studies, and the interdisciplinary humanities PhD program at Brock University, where she has also held the Chancellor's Chair for Teaching Excellence. Her research focuses on the ethics of witnessing contemporary postconflict histories and transitional justice initiatives as they are mediated through artistic texts.

Megan Sweeney is Arthur F. Thurnau Professor and associate professor of English and Afro-American and African studies at the University of Michigan, Ann Arbor. Her publications include an award-winning monograph, *Reading Is My Window: Books and the Art of Reading in Women's Prisons*, and an interview collection, *The Story within Us: Women Prisoners Reflect on Reading.*

Brenda Carr Vellino is associate professor of English at Carleton University with a focus on transnational human rights poetry and conflict transformation theater. She has published on Dionne Brand (*University of Toronto Quarterly*) and on redress theater (*College Literature, Canadian Literature*) and has a chapter on transnational human rights poetry forthcoming in the *Routledge Companion to Literature and Human Rights.*

Belinda Walzer is a lecturer in English at Northeastern University. She researches the intersections between rhetoric, human rights, and transnational gender studies. Her current project examines the pedagogical imperative underwriting human rights instruments and the normative culture it produces. She teaches rhetoric and composition, literature, and gender studies.

Eve Wiederhold, assistant professor of English at George Mason University, focuses her research and teaching on feminist rhetoric, sentiment, and judgment in critical theory and contemporary media. She is the author of the forthcoming book "Expel the Pretender: Rhetoric Renounced and the Politics of Style" and has published essays in *JAC*, *Rhetoric Review*, *Symplokē*, and *Transformations*, as well as in two edited collections.

Sarah Winter is professor of English and comparative literary and cultural studies at the University of Connecticut, Storrs. Her current book project investigates the conceptualization of human rights in the long nineteenth century in habeas corpus jurisprudence, abolitionist writings and activism, and the novel.

Works Cited

ABC: Teaching Human Rights: Practical Activities for Primary and Secondary Schools. HR/PUB/2004/2. *Office of the United Nations High Commissioner for Human Rights.* OHCHR, 2003. Web. 21 July 2014.

Advocates for Human Rights. "Energy of a Nation: Immigrants in America—Resources for Learning about Immigration." *Human Rights Education in the School Systems of Europe, Central Asia and North America: A Compendium of Good Practice.* HR/PUB/09/3. *Organization for Security and Co-operation in Europe.* OSCE/ODIHR, Council of Europe, UNESCO, and OHCHR, 2009. Web. 21 July 2014.

Aegerter, Lindsay Pentolfe. "A Dialectic of Autonomy and Community: Tsitsi Dangarembga's *Nervous Conditions.*" *Tulsa Studies in Women's Literature* 15.2 (1996): 231–40. *JSTOR.* Web. 14 Jan. 2009.

Agamben, Giorgio. *Homo Sacer: Sovereign Power and Bare Life.* Trans. Daniel Heller-Roazen. Stanford: Stanford UP, 1995. Print.

Agid, Shana, Michael Bennett, and Kate Drabinski, eds. *Radical Teaching against the Prison Industrial Complex.* Spec. issue of *Radical Teacher* 88 (2010): 1–80. Web. 1 Sept. 2010.

Ahmadu, Fuambai. "Rites and Wrongs: An Insider/Outsider Reflects on Power and Excision." *Female "Circumcision" in Africa: Culture, Controversy, and Change.* Ed. Bettina Shell-Duncan and Yiva Hernlund. Boulder: Rienner, 2000. 283–312. Print.

Ahmed, Leila. *A Border Passage: From Cairo to America—A Woman's Journey.* New York: Penguin, 1999. Print.

Ahmed, Sara. "Collective Feelings; or, The Impressions Left by Others." *Theory, Culture, and Society* 21.2 (2004): 25–42. Print.

Akcam, Taner. *A Shameful Act: The Armenian Genocide and the Question of Turkish Responsibility.* New York: Henry Holt, 2006. Print.

Alcoff, Linda Martin, and Laura Gray-Rosendale. "Survivor Discourse: Transgression or Recuperation?" *Getting a Life: Everyday Uses of Autobiography.* Ed. Sidonie Smith and Julia Watson. Minneapolis: U of Minnesota P, 1996. 198–225. Print.

Alexanian, Alex. *The Armenian Genocide.* Armenian Natl. Committee of Amer., 2012. Web. 26 Sept. 2014. <theforgotten.org>.

Almanzar, Yolanne. "Florida Gay Adoption Ban Is Ruled Unconstitutional." *The New York Times.* New York Times, 25 Nov. 2008. Web. 6 June 2012.

Alvarado, Elvia. *Don't Be Afraid, Gringo: A Honduran Woman Speaks from the Heart.* Ed. and trans. Medea Benjamin. San Francisco: Inst. for Food Development Policy, 1987. Print.

American Anthropological Association, Julian H. Steward, and H. G. Barnett. "Statement on Human Rights (1947) and Commentaries." Goodale, *Human Rights* 23–31.

Améry, Jean. *At the Mind's Limits: Contemplations by a Survivor on Auschwitz and Its Realities.* Trans. Sidney Rosenfeld and Stella P. Rosenfeld. Bloomington: Indiana UP, 1980. Print.

Ammons, Elizabeth. *Brave New Words: How Literature Will Save the Planet.* Iowa City: U of Iowa P, 2010. Print.

Amstutz, Mark R. "Confronting Human Rights Abuses: Approaches to Transitional Justice." *The Healing of Nations: The Promise and Limits of Political Forgiveness.* Ed. Amstutz. Lanham: Rowman, 2005. 17–40. Print.

Anderson, Carol. *Eyes Off the Prize: The United Nations and the African American Struggle for Human Rights, 1944–1955.* Cambridge: Cambridge UP, 2003. Print.

Anker, Elizabeth S. *Fictions of Dignity: Embodying Human Rights in World Literature.* Ithaca: Cornell UP, 2012. Print.

An-Naʿim, Abdullahi Ahmed. *Human Rights in Cross-Cultural Perspectives: A Quest for Consensus.* Philadelphia: U of Pennsylvania P, 1992. Print.

———. *Muslims and Global Justice.* Philadelphia: U of Pennsylvania P, 2011. Print.

Appel, Markus. "Fictional Narratives Cultivate Just World Beliefs." *Journal of Communication* 58.1 (2008): 62–83. Web. 12 June 2012.

Appel, Markus, and Tobias Richter. "Persuasive Effects of Fictional Narratives Increase over Time." *Media Psychology* 10 (2007): 113–14. Web. 12 June 2012.

Arendt, Hannah. "The Decline of the Nation-State and the End of the Rights of Man." *The Origins of Totalitarianism.* New York: Schocken, 1951. 341–84. Print.

Arias, Arturo, ed. *The Rigoberta Menchú Controversy.* Minneapolis: U of Minnesota P, 2001. Print.

Aristotle. *Politics.* Trans. T. A. Sinclair and T. J. Saunders. *A New Aristotle Reader.* Ed. J. L. Ackrill. Princeton: Princeton UP, 1987. 507–39. Print.

Armenia: The Betrayed. Dir. Fergal Keane. BBC, 2003. Film.

The Armenian Genocide. Dir. Andrew Goldberg. PBS, 2006. Film.

The Armenian Genocide Museum-Institute. Armenian Genocide Museum-Inst., 2007–14. Web. 26 Sept. 2014. <genocide-museum.am>.

Armstrong, Jeanette, and Lally Grauer. *Native Poetry in Canada: A Contemporary Anthology.* Peterborough: Broadview, 2001. Print.

Atwood, Margaret. "Footnote to the Amnesty Report on Torture." *Two-Headed Poems.* Toronto: Oxford, 1978. 45–46. Print.

———. "Notes toward a Poem that Can Never Be Written." *Selected Poems II: Poems Selected and New, 1976–1986.* Boston: Houghton, 1987. 71–74. Print.

Avelar, Idelber. *The Letter of Violence.* New York: Palgrave, 2004. Print.

Bahri, Deepika. "Disembodying the Corpus: Postcolonial Pathology in Tsitsi Dangarembga's *Nervous Conditions.*" *Postmodern Culture* 5.1 (1994): n. pag. *Project Muse.* Web. 15 Sept. 2008.

Bakhtin, Mikhail. "Author and Hero in Aesthetic Activity." *Art and Answerability: Early Philosophical Essays.* By Bakhtin. Ed. Michael Holquist and Vadim Liapunov. Trans. Liapunov. Austin: U of Texas P, 1990. 4–256. Print.

Balakian, Peter. *Black Dog of Fate.* New York: Broadway, 1997. Print.

———. *The Burning Tigris: The Armenian Genocide and America's Response.* New York: Harper, 2003. Print.

———. "Falling into a Rug: Notes on Imagination and the Artifact." *Introspections: American Poets on One of Their Own Poems.* Ed. Robert Pack and Jay Parini. Hanover: UP of New England, 1997. 35–39. Print.

———. *June Tree: New and Selected Poems: 1974–2000.* New York: Harper, 2001. Print.

———. "Poetry, Ancestors, History." *Centennial Review* 35.3 (1991): 519–28. Print.

bandele, asha. *The Prisoner's Wife.* New York: Scribner, 1999. Print.

Barghouti, Omar. "Relative Humanity: Identity, Rights, and Ethics—Israel as Case Study." *PMLA* 121.5 (2006): 1536–43. Print.

Barnett, Michael. *Empire of Humanity: A History of Humanitarianism.* Ithaca: Cornell UP, 2011. Print.

Baucom, Ian. *Specters of the Atlantic: Finance Capital, Slavery, and the Philosophy of History.* Durham: Duke UP, 2005. Print.

Bauman, Zygmunt. *Community: Seeking Safety in an Insecure World.* Cambridge: Polity, 2001. Print.

Bayoumi, Moustafa. "The Race Is On: Muslims and Arabs in the American Imagination." *Middle East Report Online.* The Middle East Research and Information Project, Mar. 2010. Web. 24 Aug. 2010.

Berlin, James A. *Rhetorics, Poetics, and Cultures: Refiguring College English Studies.* Urbana: NCTE, 1996. Print.

Bernasconi, Robert, and Anika Maaza Mann. "The Contradictions of Racism: Locke, Slavery, and the Two Treatises." Valls 89–107.

Berthoff, Ann. *The Making of Meaning.* Upper Montclair: Boyton, 1981. Print.

Beverley, John. "The Margin at the Center: On Testimonio." Gugelberger 23–41.

———. *Subalternity and Representation: Arguments in Cultural Theory.* Durham: Duke UP, 1999. Print.

———. *Testimonio: On the Politics of Truth.* Minneapolis: U of Minnesota P, 2004. Print.

———. "What Happens When the Subaltern Speaks: Rigoberta Menchú, Multiculturalism, and the Presumption of Equal Worth." Arias 219–36.

Bhana, Hershini. "The Political Economy of Food: Hunger in Tsitsi Dangarembga's *Nervous Conditions.*" *Proteus* 17.1 (2000): 18–24. Print.

Bielefeldt, Heiner. "Muslim Voices in the Human Rights Debate." *Human Rights Quarterly* 17.4 (1995): 587–617. Print.

Bird, Leonard. *Folding Paper Cranes: An Atomic Memoir.* Salt Lake City: U of Utah P, 2005. Print.

Blackburn, Robin. *American Crucible: Slavery, Emancipation and Human Rights.* London: Verso, 2011. Print.

———. "Reclaiming Human Rights." Rev. of *The Last Utopia: Human Rights in History,* by Samuel Moyn. *New Left Review* 69 (2011): 126–38. Web. 6 June 2011.

Blair, Carole. "Contemporary U.S. Memorial Sites as Exemplars of Rhetoric's Materiality." *Rhetorical Bodies.* Ed. Jack Seltzer and Sharon Crowley. Madison: U of Wisconsin P, 1999. 16–57. Print.

Bloom, Irene, J. Paul Martin, and Wayne L. Proudfoot, eds. *Religious Diversity and Human Rights.* New York: Columbia UP, 1996. Print.

Bloom, Paul. *Descartes' Baby: How the Science of Child Development Explains What Makes Us Human.* New York: Basic, 2004. Print.

———. "The New Science of Morality." Edge Seminar. 20–22 July 2010. *Edge.* Web. 12 June 2012.

Born into Brothels: Calcutta's Red Light Kids. Dir. Ross Kauffman and Zana Briski. Red Light Films, 2005. Film.

Born into Brothels *Curriculum Companion. Kids with Cameras.* Amnesty Intl., n.d. Web. 20 Aug. 2014.

Brand, Dionne. *Inventory.* Toronto: McClelland, 2006. Print.

———. "Poet Laureate Speech on the Occasion of the Toronto Book Awards." *Toronto.* City of Toronto, n.d. Web. 15 Oct. 2009.

Breyer, Stephen. Majority opinion. Beard, Secretary, Pennsylvania Dept. of Corrections v. Banks. 04-1739. Supreme Court of the US. 28 June 2006. *Lexis/Nexis.* Web. 2 Dec. 2014.

Browdy de Hernandez, Jennifer. "Of Tortillas and Texts: Postcolonial Dialogues in the Latin American Testimonial." *Interventions: Feminist Dialogues on Third World Women's Literature and Film.* Ed. Bishnupriya Ghosh and Brinda Bose. New York: Garland, 1997. 163–84. Print.

Brown, Christopher Leslie. *Moral Capital: Foundations of British Abolitionism.* Chapel Hill: U of North Carolina P, 2006. Print.

Brown, Wendy. "'The Most We Can Hope For . . .': Human Rights and the Politics of Fatalism." *South Atlantic Quarterly* 103.2–3 (2004): 451–63. Print.

Brysk, Alison. "Introduction: Transnational Threats and Opportunities." *Globalization and Human Rights.* Ed. Brysk. Berkeley: U of California P, 2002. 1–16. Print.

Buck-Morss, Susan. *Hegel, Haiti, and Universal History.* Pittsburgh: U of Pennsylvania P, 2009. Print.

Bunch, Charlotte. "Women's Human Rights: The Challenges of Global Feminism and Diversity." *Feminist Locations: Global and Local, Theory and Practice.* Ed. Marianne DeKoven. New Brunswick: Rutgers UP, 2001. 129–48. Print.

———. "Women's Rights as Human Rights: Toward a Re-vision of Human Rights." *Human Rights Quarterly* 12.4 (1990): 486–98. Print.

Buntman, Fran Lisa. *Robben Island and Prisoner Resistance to Apartheid.* Cambridge: Cambridge UP, 2003. Print.

Burke, Edmund. *Reflections on the Revolution in France.* Ed. Conor Cruise O'Brien. London: Penguin, 1968. Print.

Burke, Roland. *Decolonization and the Evolution of International Human Rights.* Philadelphia: U of Pennsylvania P, 2012. Print.

Butin, Dan W. *Service-Learning in Theory and Practice: The Future of Community Engagement in Higher Education.* New York: Palgrave, 2010. Print.

Butler, Judith. *Precarious Life: The Powers of Mourning and Violence.* London: Verso, 2004. Print.

Butler, Judith, and Gayatri Chakravorty Spivak. *Who Sings the Nation-State? Language, Politics, Belonging.* London: Seagull, 2007. Print.

Cadava, Eduardo. "The Monstrosity of Human Rights." *PMLA* 121.5 (2006): 1558–65. Print.

"Cameron Threat to Dock Some UK Aid to Anti-Gay Nations." *BBC News*. BBC, 30 Oct. 2011. Web. 29 Dec. 2014.

Carey-Webb, Allen. "Transformative Voices." *Teaching and Testimony: Rigoberta Menchú and the North American Classroom*. Ed. Carey-Webb and Stephen Benz. Albany: State U of New York P, 1996. 3–18. Print.

Castellanos Moya, Horacio. *Senselessness*. Trans. Katherine Silver. New York: New Directions, 2008. Print.

Chang, Tina, Nathalie Handal, and Ravi Shankar, eds. *Language for a New Century: Contemporary Poetry from the Middle East, Asia, and Beyond*. New York: Norton, 2008. Print.

Cheah, Pheng. *Inhuman Conditions: On Cosmopolitanism and Human Rights*. Cambridge: Harvard UP, 2006. Print.

Cheng, Anne Anlin. *The Melancholy of Race: Psychoanalysis, Assimilation, and Hidden Grief*. New York: Oxford UP, 2001. Print.

Chiles, Nick. "Their Eyes Were Reading Smut." *The New York Times*. New York Times, 4 Jan. 2006. Web. 25 Jan. 2008.

Chow, Rey. *The Protestant Ethnic and the Spirit of Capitalism*. New York: Columbia UP, 2002. Print.

Clarkson, Thomas. *The History of the Rise, Progress, and Accomplishment of the Abolition of the African Slave Trade by the British Parliament: A New Edition with Prefatory Remarks on the Subsequent Abolition of Slavery*. London: John W. Parker, 1839. *Google Books*. Web. 21 Sept. 2012.

Cleage, Pearl. *What Looks like Crazy on an Ordinary Day*. New York: Avon, 1997. Print.

Clifford, James. "Traveling Cultures." *Cultural Studies*. Ed. Lawrence Goldberg, Cary Nelson, and Paula A. Treichler. New York: Routledge, 1992. 96–116. Print.

Cohen, Stanley. *States of Denial: Knowing about Atrocity and Suffering*. Malden: Polity; Blackwell, 2001. Print.

Cohen, Stanley, and Bruna Seu. "Knowing Enough Not to Feel Too Much." *Truth Claims: Representations and Human Rights*. Ed. Mark Bradley and Patrice Petro. New Brunswick: Rutgers UP, 2002. 187–201. Print.

Cole, Teju. "The White-Savior Industrial Complex." *The Atlantic Monthly*. Atlantic Monthly, 21 Mar. 2012. Web. 11 Nov. 2013. <http://www.theatlantic.com/international/archive/2012/03/the-white-savior-industrial-complex/254843/>.

Comaroff, Jean, and John Comaroff. "Alien-Nation: Zombies, Immigrants, and Millennial Capitalism." *South Atlantic Quarterly* 101.4 (2002): 781–805. Print.

Comstock, Cathy. "Literature and Service Learning: Not Strange Bedfellows." *Building Community: Service Learning in the Academic Disciplines*. Ed. Richard J. Kraft and Marc Swadener. Denver: Colorado Campus Compact, 1994. 83–89. Print.

Con Davis, Robert, and David S. Gross. "Gayatri Chakravorty Spivak and the

Ethos of the Subaltern." *Ethos: New Essays in Rhetorical and Critical Theory.* Ed. James S. Baumlin and Tita French Baumlin. Dallas: Southern Methodist UP, 1994. 65–90. Print.

Confront Genocide. United States Holocaust Memorial Museum. US Holocaust Memorial Museum, n.d. Web. 21 July 2014.

Conlin, Jennifer. "For American Students, Life Lessons in the Mideast." *The New York Times.* New York Times, 6 Aug. 2010. Web. 6 Sept. 2010.

Connelly, Karen. *The Lizard Cage.* New York: Talese; Doubleday, 2005. Print.

"Convention against Torture." *United Nations.* United Nations, 10 Dec. 1984. Web. 20 July 2010. <http://www.ohchr.org/EN/ProfessionalInterest/Pages/CAT.aspx>.

"Convention on the Elimination of All Forms of Discrimination against Women." *United Nations.* United Nations, n.d. Web. 9 Aug. 2010. <http://www.un.org/womenwatch/daw/cedaw/text/econvention.htm>.

"Convention on the Rights of the Child." *United Nations.* United Nations, 2 Sept. 1990. Web. 10 June 2015. <http://www.ohchr.org/en/professionalinterest/pages/crc.aspx>.

Creamer, Heidi. "An Apple for the Teacher? Femininity, Coloniality, and Food in *Nervous Conditions.*" *Kunapipi* 16.1 (1994): 349–60. Print.

Cronyn, Hume, Richard McKane, and Stephen Watts, eds. *Voices of Conscience: Poetry from Oppression.* Northumberland: Iron, 1995. Print.

Crowley, Sharon. *Composition in the University: Historical and Polemical Essays.* Pittsburgh: U of Pittsburgh P, 1998. Print.

Cuomo, Kerry Kennedy. *Speak Truth to Power: Human Rights Defenders Who Are Changing Our World.* Ed. Nan Richardson. Photographs by Eddie Adams. New York: Crown, 2000. Print.

Cuomo, Kerry Kennedy, and Nan Richardson. *Speak Truth to Power: An Educational and Advocacy Package in Collaboration with Amnesty International and Umbrage Editions.* New York: Umbrage, 2000. Print.

Cushman, Ellen. "The Public Intellectual, Service Learning, and Activist Research." *College English* 61.3 (1999): 328–36. *ProQuest.* Web. 30 Aug. 2010.

———. "Rhetorician as an Agent of Social Change." *College Composition and Communication* 47.1 (1996): 7–28. Print.

———. "Service Learning as the New English Studies." *Beyond English, Inc.: Curricular Reform in a Global Economy.* Ed. David B. Downing, Claude Mark Hurlbert, and Paula Mathieu. Portsmouth: Boynton; Cook, 2002. 204–18. Print.

Cushman, Thomas, ed. *Handbook of Human Rights.* New York: Routledge, 2012. Print.

Dangarembga, Tsitsi. *Nervous Conditions.* New York: Seal; Oxfordshire: Ayebia Clarke, 2004. Print.

Danielson, Susan, and Ann Marie Fallon, eds. *Community-Based Learning and the Work of Literature.* Bolton: Anker, 2007. Print.

Davis, Angela Y. Introduction. *Narrative of the Life of Frederick Douglass, an American Slave.* By Frederick Douglass. Ed. Davis. San Francisco: City Lights, 2009. 21–37. Print.

Davis, David Brion. *The Problem of Slavery in the Age of Revolution, 1770–1823.* New York: Oxford UP, 1999. Print.

Dawes, James. "Human Rights in Literary Studies." *Human Rights Quarterly* 31.2 (2009): 394–409. *Project Muse.* Web. 20 May 2010.

———. *That the World May Know: Bearing Witness to Atrocity.* Cambridge: Harvard UP, 2007. Print.

The Day after Trinity. Dir. Jon Else. Perf. Hans Bethe, Holm Bursom, and Haakon Chevalier. KTEH, 1981. Film.

Dayan, Colin. "Words behind Bars: Do Prisoners Have a Right to Read What They Want?" *Boston Review.* Boston Review, 1 Nov. 2007. Web. 5 Feb. 2010.

De Bolla, Peter. *The Architecture of Concepts: The Historical Formation of Human Rights.* New York: Fordham UP, 2013. Print.

Declaration on Anthropology and Human Rights. American Anthropological Association. Amer. Anthropological Assn., 1999. Web. 1 Sept. 2010.

Defense of Marriage Act. Pub. L. 104-99. 110 Stat. 2419–20. 21 Sept. 1996. *U.S. Government Printing Office.* Web. 7 June 2012.

De Kok, Ingrid. *Seasonal Fires: New and Selected Poems.* New York: Seven Stories, 2006. Print.

Desai, Manisha. "Transnational Solidarity: Women's Agency, Structural Adjustment, and Globalization." *Women's Activism and Globalization: Linking Local Struggles and Transnational Politics.* Ed. Nancy A. Naples and Desai. New York: Routledge, 2002. 15–33. Print.

Devi, Mahasweta. *Imaginary Maps: Three Stories.* Trans. Gayatri Chakravorty Spivak. London: Routledge, 1995. Print.

Dibia, Jude. *Walking with Shadows.* Lagos: BlackSands, 2005. Print.

Dirty Pretty Things. Dir. Stephen Frears. BBC Films, 2002. Film.

Donnelly, Jack. *Universal Human Rights in Theory and Practice.* Ithaca: Cornell UP, 1989. Print.

———. *Universal Human Rights in Theory and Practice.* 2nd ed. Ithaca: Cornell UP, 2003. Print.

Donnelly, Nick. "Northern Ireland Ban on Gay Adoption Upheld by Attorney General as in Best Interest of Children." *Protect the Pope.* Protect the Pope, 24 Mar. 2012. Web. 7 June 2012.

Dorfman, Ariel. *Death and the Maiden. The Resistance Trilogy.* London: Hern, 1998. 87–148. Print.

———. *In Case of Fire in a Foreign Land: New and Collected Poems from Two Languages.* Durham: Duke, 2002. Print.

———. Introduction. Cuomo and Richardson 4.

———. *La muerte y la doncella (Teatro 1).* Buenos Aires: Flor, 1992. Print.

———. *Speak Truth to Power: Voices beyond the Dark.* Cuomo and Richardson 47–60.

Douglass, Frederick. *Narrative of the Life of Frederick Douglass, an American Slave.* 1845. New York: Penguin, 2014. Print.

———. *Narrative of the Life of Frederick Douglass, an American Slave, Written by Himself.* Ed. William L. Andrews and William S. McFeely. New York: Norton, 1997. Print.

Douzinas, Costas. *Human Rights and Empire: The Political Philosophy of Cosmopolitanism.* New York: Routledge, 2007. Print.

Drescher, Seymour. *Abolition: A History of Slavery and Antislavery.* Cambridge: Cambridge UP, 2009. Print.

Drowning by Bullets. Dir. Philip Brooks and Alan Hayling. First Run; Icarus Films, 1992. Film.

DuBois, Page. *Slaves and Other Objects.* Chicago: U of Chicago P, 2003. Print.

Eagleton, Terry. *How to Read a Poem.* Malden: Blackwell, 2007. Print.

Eck, Lisa. "Thinking Globally, Teaching Locally: The 'Nervous Conditions' of Cross-Cultural Literacy." *College English* 70.6 (2008): 578–98. *EBSCOhost.* Web. 12 Jan. 2009.

Edwards, Brian T. "Cairo 2010: After Kefaya." *A Public Space* 9 (2009): 128–33. Print.

"Effective Functioning of Human Rights Mechanisms." *Report of the United Nations Commissioner for Human Rights.* E/CN.4/2003/NGO/225. *Office of the United Nations High Commissioner of Human Rights.* OHCHR, n.d. Web. 17 Mar. 2003.

Eggers, Dave. *What Is the What.* San Francisco: McSweeney's, 2006. Print.

Eisenberg, Nancy. "Empathy-Related Emotional Responses, Altruism, and Their Socialization." *Visions of Compassion: Western Scientists and Tibetan Buddhists Examine Human Nature.* Ed. Richard J. Davidson and Anne Harrington. New York: Oxford UP, 2002. 131–64. Print.

Elmusa, Sharif S. "Poetry of the Revolution." *Al-Masry Al-Youm.* Egypt Independent, 20 Feb. 2011. Web. 23 Feb. 2011.

Equiano, Olaudah. *The Interesting Narrative of the Life of Olaudah Equiano, or Gustavus Vassa, the African, Written by Himself.* Ed. Angelo Costanzo. Toronto: Broadview, 2001. Print.

Euripides. *Hecuba. Fabulae.* Vol. 1. Ed. James Diggle. Oxford: Oxford UP, 1984. 331–98. Print.

———. *Hecuba.* Trans. Robin Mitchell-Boyask. Newburyport: Focus, 2006. Print.

Everett, Percival. *Erasure.* New York: Hyperion, 2001. Print.

Falicov, Tamara L. "Film Production in Argentina under Democracy, 1983–1989: *The Official Story* (*La historia oficial*) as an International Film." *Southern Quarterly* 39.4 (2001): 123–34. Print.

Falkoff, Marc. *Poems from Guantanamo: The Detainees Speak.* Iowa City: U of Iowa P, 2007. Print.

Fallon, Ann Marie. Preface. Danielson and Fallon xv–xxii.

Farah, Nuruddin. *Gifts.* New York: Penguin, 2000. Print.

Farenga, Vincent. "Authoring Justice: A Dialogue between Contemporary Theories of Justice and the Literature of Injustice." *UCLA.* Dept. of Political Science, U of California, Los Angeles, 2 Oct. 2012. Web. 21 July 2014.

———. "Report: The Literature and Justice Project, 2007–2008." *University of Southern California.* Dept. of Compar. Lit., U of Southern California, 2008. Web. 11 June 2012.

Farmer, Paul. *Pathologies of Power: Health, Human Rights, and the New War on the Poor.* Berkeley: U of California P, 2003. Print.

Feldman, Keith. "Towards an Afro-Arab Diasporic Culture: The Translational Practices of David Graham Du Bois." *Alif: Journal of Comparative Poetics* 31 (2011): 152–72. Print.

Felman, Shoshana, and Dori Laub. *Testimony: Crises of Witnessing in Literature, Psychoanalysis, and History.* New York: Routledge, 1992. Print.

"Female Genital Mutilation: Fact Sheet No. 241." *World Health Organization.* WHO, Feb. 2014. Web. 17 Sept. 2014. <http://www.who.int/mediacentre/factsheets/fs241/en/>.

Fernández García, Dina. Interview with David Stoll. Arias 66–69.

"Fighting War Crimes, without Leaving the Couch?" *The New York Times.* New York Times, 9 Mar. 2012. Web. 11 Nov. 2013. <http://www.nytimes.com/roomfordebate/2012/03/09/kony-2012-and-the-potential-of-social-media-activism>.

Final Report of the Meeting of Higher Education Partners (World Conference on Higher Education + 5). UNESCO. UNESCO, 2004. Web. 22 July 2014.

Fine, Robert. "Cosmopolitanism and Human Rights: Radicalism in a Global Age." *Metaphilosophy* 40.1 (2009): 8–23. Print.

Flattley, Kerry, and Chris Wallace-Crabbe, eds. *From the Republic of Conscience: An International Anthology.* Fredonia: White Pine; Amnesty Intl., 1993. Print.

Flower, Linda. "Partners in Inquiry." *Writing the Community: Concepts and Models for Service-Learning in Composition.* Ed. Linda Adler-Kassner, Robert Crooks, and Ann Watters. Urbana: NCTE, 1997. 95–117. Print.

Forbes, Kathryn, et al. "Punishing Pedagogy: The Failings of Forced Volunteerism." *Women's Studies Quarterly* 27.3–4 (1999): 158–68. *Wilson OmniFile: Full Text Select.* Web. 30 Aug. 2010.

Forbes, Peter, ed. *Scanning the Century: The Penguin Book of the Twentieth-Century in Poetry.* New York: Penguin, 2000. Print.

Forché, Carolyn, ed. *Against Forgetting: Twentieth-Century Poetry of Witness.* New York: Norton, 1993. Print.

———. "The Colonel." *Poetry Foundation.* Poetry Foundation, n.d. Web. 21 July 2014.

———. Introduction. Forché, *Against Forgetting* 29–48.

———. "Reading the Living Archives: The Witness of Literary Art." Goldberg and Moore, *Theoretical Perspectives* 135–48.

Foreman, Amanda. *A World on Fire: Britain's Crucial Role in the American Civil War.* New York: Random, 2010. Print.

Foucault, Michel. *The History of Sexuality.* Vol. 1. Trans. R. Hurley. New York: Pantheon, 1990. Print.

Frazier, Leslie Jo. "'Subverted Memories': Countermourning as Political Action in Chile." *Acts of Memory: Cultural Recall in the Present.* Ed. Mieke Bal et al. Hanover: UP of New England, 1999. 105–19. Print.

Freire, Paulo. *Pedagogy of the Oppressed.* New York: Herder, 1970. Print.

Furnham, Adrian. "Belief in a Just World: Research Progress over the Past Decade." *Personality and Individual Differences* 34.5 (2003): 795–817. Web. 12 June 2012.

Gallagher, Susan VanZanten. "Contingencies and Intersections: The Formation of Pedagogical Canons." *Pedagogy: Critical Approaches to Teaching Literature, Language, Composition, and Culture* 1.1 (2001): 53–67. *EBSCOhost.* Web. 14 Jan. 2009.

Gambrell, Jon. "Nigerian Senate Approves Anti-Gay Marriage Bill." *Associated Press.* Assoc. P, 29 Nov. 2011. Web. 4 June 2012.

George, Ann. "Critical Pedagogy: Dreaming of Democracy." *A Guide to Composition Pedagogies.* Ed. Gary Tate, Amy Rupiper, and Kurt Schick. New York: Oxford UP, 2001. 92–112. Print.

Gevisser, Mark. "Mandela's Stepchildren: Homosexual Identity in Post-apartheid South Africa." *Different Rainbows.* Ed. Peter Drucker. London: Gay Men's, 2000. 111–36. Print.

Ghachem, Malick W. *The Old Regime and the Haitian Revolution.* Cambridge: Cambridge UP, 2012. Print.

Gilroy, Paul. *Postcolonial Melancholia.* New York: Columbia UP, 2005. Print.

Giroux, Henry A. "Cultural Studies in Dark Times: Public Pedagogy and the Challenge of Neoliberalism." *Fast Capitalism* 1.2 (2005): n. pag. Web. 6 July 2005.

———. "Pedagogy of the Depressed: Beyond the New Politics of Cynicism." *College Literature* 28.3 (2001): 1–32. Print.

Glausser, Wayne. "Three Approaches to Locke and the Slave Trade." *Journal of the History of Ideas* 51.2 (1990): 199–216. Print.

Gluck, Carol, and Anna Lowenhaupt Tsing, eds. *Words in Motion: Toward a Global Lexicon.* Durham: Duke UP, 2009. Print.

Goldberg, Elizabeth Swanson. *Beyond Terror: Gender, Narrative, Human Rights.* New Brunswick: Rutgers UP, 2007. Print.

———. "Intimations of What Was to Come: Edwidge Danticat's *The Farming of Bones* and the Indivisibility of Human Rights." Goldberg and Moore, *Theoretical Perspectives* 103–19.

Goldberg, Elizabeth Swanson, and Alexandra Schultheis Moore. "Human Rights and Literature: The Development of an Interdiscipline." Goldberg and Moore, *Theoretical Perspectives* 1–16.

———. eds. *Theoretical Perspectives on Human Rights and Literature.* New York: Routledge, 2012. Print.

Goodale, Mark. *Human Rights: An Anthropological Reader.* Oxford: Blackwell, 2009. Print.

———. "Introduction: Human Rights and Anthropology." Goodale, *Human Rights* 1–18.

Graff, Gerald. *Clueless in Academe: How Schooling Obscures the Life of the Mind.* New Haven: Yale UP, 2003. Print.

Gravers, Mikael. "Monks, Morality and Military: The Struggle for Moral Power in Burma—and Buddhism's Uneasy Relation with Lay Power." *Contemporary Buddhism: An Interdisciplinary Journal* 13.1 (2012): 1–33. Print.

Green, Melanie C., and Timothy C. Brock. "In the Mind's Eye: Transportation-Imagery Model of Narrative Persuasion." Green, Strange, and Brock 325–41.

———. "The Role of Transportation in the Persuasiveness of Public Narratives." *Journal of Personality and Social Psychology* 79.5 (2000): 701–21. Web. 12 June 2012.

Green, Melanie C., Jeffrey J. Strange, and Timothy C. Brock, eds. *Narrative Impact: Social and Cognitive Foundations.* Mahwah: Erlbaum, 2002. Print.

Greiner, Rae. "1909: The Introduction of the Word 'Empathy' into English." *BRANCH: Britain, Representation and Nineteenth-Century History.* Dino Franco Felluga, gen. ed. BRANCH, n.d. Web. 22 Nov. 2013.

Grobman, Laurie. "Is There a Place for Service Learning in Literary Studies?" *Profession* (2005): 129–40. Print.

———. "Service Learning in the Literature Classroom: Initiating Conversations." *Journal on Excellence in College Teaching* 18.1 (2007): 79–95. Print.

Grobman, Laurie, and Roberta Rosenberg, eds. *Service Learning and Literary Studies in English.* New York: MLA, 2015. Print.

Gubar, Susan. *Poetry after Auschwitz: Remembering What One Never Knew.* Bloomington: Indiana UP, 2003. Print.

Gugelberger, Georg M. *The Real Thing.* Durham: Duke UP, 1996. Print.

Gutmann, Amy. Introduction. Ignatieff vii–xxviii.

Gyatso, Tenzin. "Human Rights and Universal Responsibility." Keown, Prebish, and Husted xvii–xxi.

Hagedorn, Jessica. *Dogeaters.* New York: Penguin, 1990. Print.

Harjo, Joy. *How We Became Human: New and Selected Poems, 1975–2001.* New York: Norton, 2001. Print.

Harpham, Geoffrey. "Human Rights in the Humanities." *The Chronicle of Higher Education.* Chronicle of Higher Educ., 23 July 2012. Web. 16 Sept. 2012.

Harvey, David. *Cosmopolitanism and the Geographies of Freedom.* New York: Columbia UP, 2009. Print.

Hauser, Gerald A. *Introduction to Rhetorical Theory.* 2nd ed. Prospect Heights: Waveland, 2002. Print.

Hayden, Patrick, ed. *The Philosophy of Human Rights.* St. Paul: Paragon, 2001. Print. Paragon Issues in Philosophy.

Heaney, Seamus. *The Cure at Troy: A Version of Sophocles'* Philoctetes. New York: Farrar, 1991. Print.

Herzberg, Bruce. "Community Service and Critical Teaching." *College Composition and Communication* 45.3 (1994): 307–19. Print.

Herzberger-Fofana, Pierrette. "Excision and African Literature: An Activist Annotated Bibliographical Excursion." Levin and Asaah 142–55.

Hesford, Wendy S. *Spectacular Rhetorics: Human Rights Visions, Recognitions, Feminisms.* Durham: Duke UP, 2011. Print.

Hill, Janice E. "Purging a Plate Full of Colonial History: The *Nervous Conditions* of Silent Girls." *College Literature* 22 (1995): 78–90. *Wilson Select Plus.* Web. 26 Oct. 2008.

La historia oficial. Dir. Luis Puenzo. Almi Pictures, 1985. Film.

Hoad, Neville, Karen Martin, and Graeme Reid, eds. *Sex and Politics in South Africa.* Cape Town: Double Storey, 2005. Print.

Holquist, Michael. *Dialogism: Bakhtin and His World.* London: Routledge, 1990. Print.

Hornberg, Sabine. "Human Rights Education as an Integral Part of General Education." *International Review of Education* 48.3–4 (2002): 187–98. Print.

Hosseini, Khaled. *The Kite Runner.* New York: Riverhead, 2003. Print.

House, Jim, and Neil MacMaster. *Paris 1961: Algerians, State Terror, and Memory.* New York: Oxford UP, 2006. Print.

Hull, Robert. *Breaking Free: An Anthology of Human Rights Poetry.* New York: Thomas Learning, 1995. Print.

Human Rights Education in the School Systems of Europe, Central Asia and North America: A Compendium of Good Practice. HR/PUB/09/3. *Organization for Security and Co-operation in Europe.* Council of Europe, OSCE/ODIHR, UNESCO, and OHCHR, 2009. Web. 21 July 2014.

Hunt, Lynn. *Inventing Human Rights: A History.* New York: Norton, 2007. Print.

Ibiwoye, Dotun. "Gay Right Controversy: A Gathering Storm over Cameron's Comments." *Vanguard.* Vanguard Media, 23 Nov. 2011. Web. 7 June 2012.

Ignatieff, Michael. *Human Rights as Politics and Idolatry.* Ed. Amy Gutmann. Princeton: Princeton UP, 2001. Print.

Ihara, Craig K. "Why There Are No Rights in Buddhism: A Reply to Damien Keown." Keown, Prebish, and Husted 43–52.

Illouz, Eva. *Saving the Modern Soul: Therapy, Emotions, and the Culture of Self-Help.* Berkeley: U of California P, 2008. Print.

In This World. Dir. Michael Winterbottom. IFC, 2002. DVD.

Ishay, Micheline R., ed. "Human Rights: Historical and Contemporary Controversies." Introduction. Ishay, *Human Rights Reader* xxi–xxviii.

———. *The Human Rights Reader: Major Political Essays, Speeches, and Documents from Ancient Times to the Present.* 2nd ed. New York: Routledge, 2007. Print.

Ishiguro, Kazuo. *Never Let Me Go.* New York: Vintage Intl., 2005. Print.

Jaggi, Maya. "Speaking for the Dead." *The Guardian.* Guardian News and Media, 13 June 2003. Web. 10 June 2005. <http://books.guardian.co.uk/review/story/0,12084,975904,00.html>.

James, Joy, ed. *The New Abolitionists: (Neo)Slave Narratives and Contemporary Prison Writings.* Albany: State U of New York P, 2005. Print.

Jarratt, Susan C., and Nedra Reynolds. "The Splitting Image: Contemporary Feminisms and the Ethics of Ethos." *Ethos: New Essays in Rhetorical and Critical Theory.* Ed. James S. Baumlin and Tita French Baumlin. Dallas: Southern Methodist UP, 1994. 37–64. Print.

Jauss, Hans Robert. "Literary History as a Challenge to Literary Theory." Trans. Elizabeth Benzinger. *New Literary History* 2.1 (1970): 7–37. Print.

Jelin, Elizabeth. "Political Struggles for Memory." *State Repression and the Labours of Memory.* Minneapolis: U of Minnesota P, 2003. 26–41. Print.

Jones, Adam. *Genocide: A Comprehensive Introduction.* London: Routledge, 2006. Print.

Kalaidjian, Walter. *The Edge of Modernism: American Poetry and the Traumatic Past.* Baltimore: Johns Hopkins UP, 2006. Print.

Kaplan, Amy. "Violent Belongings and the Question of Empire Today: Presidential Address to the American Studies Association, October 17, 2003." *American Quarterly* 56.1 (2004): 1–18. Web. 7 June 2009.

Keating, AnaLouise. *Teaching Transformation: Transcultural Classroom Dialogues.* New York: Palgrave, 2007. Print.

Keen, Suzanne. "'Altruism' Makes a Space for Empathy, 1852." *BRANCH: Britain, Representation and Nineteenth-Century History.* Dino Franco Felluga, gen. ed. BRANCH, n.d. Web. 22 Nov. 2013.

Keenan, Thomas. "Mobilizing Shame." *South Atlantic Quarterly* 103.2–3 (2004): 435–49. Print.

Keltner, Dascher. *Born to Be Good.* New York: Norton, 2009. Print.

Kendall, Frances E. *Understanding White Privilege: Creating Pathways to Authentic Relationships across Race.* New York: Routledge, 2006. Print.

Kennedy, David. *The Dark Sides of Virtue: Reassessing International Humanitarianism.* Princeton: Princeton UP, 2004. Print.

Keown, Damien V. "Are There Human Rights in Buddhism?" Keown, Prebish, and Husted 15–42.

Keown, Damien V., Charles S. Prebish, and Wayne R. Husted, eds. *Buddhism and Human Rights.* Richmond: Curzon, 1998. Print.

Kidder, Tracy. *Mountains beyond Mountains: The Quest of Dr. Paul Farmer, a Man Who Would Cure the World.* New York: Random, 2004. Print.

Kids with Cameras. Kids with Cameras, n.d. Web. 21 Aug. 2014. <http://www.kids-with-cameras.org/>.

Kimani, Mary W. *He Didn't Die Easy: The Search for Hope Amid Poverty, War, and Genocide.* New York: iUniverse, 2006. Print.

Kimenyi, Alexandre. "Poetry on Tutsi Genocide." *Alexandre Kimenyi.* N.p., n.d. Web. 25 Sept. 2014. <kimenyi.com>.

King, Laura A., Chad M. Burton, and Aaron C. Geise. "The Good (Gay) Life: The Search for Signs of Maturity in the Narratives of Gay Adults." *The Story of Sexual Identity: Narrative Perspectives on the Gay and Lesbian Life.* Ed. Phillip L. Hammack and Bertram J. Cohler. New York: Oxford UP, 2009. 375–96. Print.

Kleinman, Arthur, and Joan Kleinman. "The Appeal of Experience; the Dismay of Images: Cultural Appropriation of Suffering in Our Times." *Social Suffering.* Ed. A. Kleinman, Veena Das, and Margaret Lock. Berkeley: U of California P, 1997. 1–23. Print.

Koïta, Khady, with Marie-Thérèse Cuny. *Bloodstains: A Child of Africa Reclaims Her Human Rights.* Trans. Tobe Levin. Frankfurt am Main: UnCUT/VOICES, 2010. Print.

"Kony 2012." *YouTube.* Invisible Children; YouTube, 5 Mar. 2012. Web. 20 Feb. 2013. <http://www.youtube.com/watch?v=Y4MnpzG5Sqc>.

Korn, Fadumo. *Born in the Big Rains: A Memoir of Somalia and Survival.* Trans. Tobe Levin. New York: Feminist, 2004. Print.

Krain, Matthew, and Anne M. Nurse. "Teaching Human Rights through Service Learning." *Human Rights Quarterly* 26 (2004): 189–207. *Project Muse.* Web. 16 May 2010.

Kriger, Clara. "*La Historia Oficial*: The Official Story." *The Cinema of Latin America.* Ed. Alberto Elena and Marina Díaz López. London: Wallflower, 2003. 177–83. Print.

Kristof, Nicholas D., and Sheryl WuDunn. *Half the Sky: Turning Oppression into Opportunity for Women Worldwide.* New York: Knopf, 2009. Print.

Kusserow, Adrie. "War Metaphysics for a Sudanese Girl." *Winning Writers: Best Resources for Poets and Writers.* Winning Writers, n.d. Web. 21 July 2014.

Kymlicka, Will. "The Good, the Bad, and the Intolerable: Minority Group Rights." Goodale, *Human Rights* 58–67.

Laqueur, Thomas. "The Dead Body and Human Rights." *The Body.* Ed. Sean T. Sweeney and Ian Hoder. Cambridge: Cambridge UP, 2002. 75–93. Print.

———. "Mourning, Pity, and the Work of Narrative in the Making of 'Humanity.'" *Humanitarianism and Suffering: The Mobilization of Empathy*. Ed. Richard Ashby Wilson and Richard D. Brown. Cambridge: Cambridge UP, 2009. 31–57. Print.

Lauren, Paul Gordon. *The Evolution of International Human Rights: Visions Seen*. 2nd ed. Philadelphia: U of Pennsylvania P, 2003. Print.

Lawrence v. Texas. 539 US 558; S. Ct. 2472. Supreme Court of the US. 2003. Print.

Lederach, John Paul. *The Moral Imagination*. New York: Oxford UP, 2005. Print.

Lenhart, Volker, and Kaisa Savolainen. "Human Rights Education as a Field of Practice and of Theoretical Reflection." *International Review of Education* 48.3–4 (2002): 145–58. Print.

Lentricchia, Frank, and Andrew DuBois, eds. *Close Reading: The Reader*. Durham: Duke UP, 2003. Print.

Lerner, Melvin. *The Belief in a Just World*. New York: Plenum, 1980. Print.

Levin, Tobe. "Assaults on Female Genitalia: Activists, Authors, and the Arts." Levin and Asaah 1–14.

———. Preface. Levin and Asaah xiv–xvii.

Levin, Tobe, and Augustine H. Asaah, eds. *Empathy and Rage: Female Genital Mutilation in African Literature*. Banbury: Ayebia Clark, 2009. Print.

Lewis, Reina, and Sara Mills, eds. *Feminist Postcolonial Theory: A Reader*. New York: Routledge, 2003. Print.

———. Introduction. Lewis and Mills, *Feminist Postcolonial Theory* 1–21.

Lindemann, Erika. "Freshman Composition: No Place for Literature." *College English* 55.3 (1993): 311–16. Print.

———. "Three Views of English 101." *College English* 57.3 (1995): 287–302. Print.

Liu, Lydia H. "Injury: Incriminating Words and Imperial Power." Gluck and Tsing 199–218.

Locke, John. *An Essay concerning Human Understanding*. Ed. Peter H. Nidditch. Oxford: Clarendon, 1975. Print.

———. *Two Treatises of Government*. Ed. Peter Laslett. Cambridge: Cambridge UP, 1960. Print.

Loury, Glenn C. *Race, Incarceration, and American Values*. Cambridge: MIT P, 2008. Print.

Lu, Min-Zhan. "Composing Postcolonial Studies." *Crossing Borderlands: Composition and Postcolonial Studies*. Ed. Andrea Lunsford and Lahoucine Ouzgane. Pittsburgh: U of Pittsburgh P, 2004. 9–32. Print.

Lyotard, Jean-François. *The Differend: Phrases in Dispute*. Trans. Georges Van den Abbeele. Minneapolis: U of Minnesota P, 1984. Print.

———. "The Other's Rights." *The Politics of Human Rights*. Ed. Obrad Savic and the Belgrade Circle. Trans. Chris Miller and Robert Smith. London: Verso, 1999. 181–88. Print.

Mahbubani, Kishore. *Can Asians Think? Understanding the Divide between East and West*. Singapore: Times, 2004. Print.

Malcolm X [el-Hajj Malik el-Shabazz]. "Not Just an American Problem, but a

World Problem." 16 Feb. 1965. *Malcolm X: The Last Speeches.* Ed. Bruce Perry. New York: Pathfinder, 1989. 151–81. Print.

Martinez, Jenny S. *The Slave Trade and the Origins of International Human Rights Law.* New York: Oxford UP, 2012. Print.

Massad, Joseph A. "Sexuality, Literature, and Human Rights in Translation." *Teaching World Literature.* Ed. David Damrosch. New York: MLA, 2009. 246–57. Print.

Mathieu, Paula. *Tactics of Hope: The Public Turn in English Composition.* Portsmouth: Boynton; Cook, 2005. Print.

Mayer, Ann Elizabeth. *Islam and Human Rights: Tradition and Politics.* 5th ed. Philadelphia: Perseus, 2013. Print.

McClatchy, J. D., ed. *The Vintage Book of Contemporary World Poetry.* New York: Vintage, 1996. Print.

McClennen, Sophia A. *Ariel Dorfman: An Aesthetics of Hope.* Durham: Duke UP, 2010. Print.

———. "The Humanities, Human Rights, and the Comparative Imagination." *Representing Humanity in an Age of Terror.* Ed. McClennen and Henry James Morello. Spec. issue of *CLC Web: Comparative Literature and Culture* 9.1 (2008): n. pag. Web. 21 July 2014. <http://docs.lib.purdue.edu/clcweb/vol9/iss1/>.

———. "Torture and Truth in Ariel Dorfman's *Death and the Maiden.*" *Revista Hispánica Moderna* 62.2 (2009): 177–92. Print.

McClennen, Sophia A., and Joseph R. Slaughter, eds. *Human Rights and Literary Forms.* Spec. issue of *Comparative Literature Studies* 46.1 (2009): 1–209. Print.

———. "Introducing Human Rights and Literary Forms; or, The Vehicles and Vocabularies of Human Rights." McClennen and Slaughter, *Human Rights* 1–19.

McEvoy, Kieran, and Lorna McGregor, eds. *Transitional Justice from Below: Grassroots Activism and the Struggle for Change.* Portland: Hart, 2008. Print.

McWilliams, Sally. "Tsitsi Dangarembga's *Nervous Conditions*: At the Crossroads of Feminism and Post-colonialism." *World Literature Written in English* 31.1 (1991): 103–12. Print.

Mehmedinovic, Semezdin. *Sarajevo Blues.* Trans. Ammiel Alcalay. San Francisco: City Lights, 1998. Print.

Menchú, Rigoberta. *I, Rigoberta Menchú: An Indian Woman in Guatemala.* Ed. Elisabeth Burgos-Debray. Trans. Ann Wright. London: Verso, 1991. Print.

———. *Me llamo Rigoberta Menchú y así me nació la conciencia.* Ed. Elizabeth Burgos. México: Siglo Veintiuno, 1985. Print.

Mernissi, Fatema. *Islam and Democracy: Fear of the Modern World.* New York: Basic, 1999. Print.

Merry, Sally Engle. "Human Rights Law and the Demonization of Culture (and Anthropology along the Way)." *PoLAR: Political and Legal Anthropology* 26.1 (2003): 55–76. Print.

Mignolo, Walter. "Cosmopolitanism and the De-colonial Option." *Studies in Philosophy and Education* 29 (2010): 111–27. Print.

Mikhail, Dunya. *The War Works Hard.* Trans. Elizabeth Winslow. New York: New Directions, 2005. Print.

Minnow, Martha. *Between Vengeance and Forgiveness: Facing History after Genocide and Mass Violence.* Boston: Beacon, 1998. Print.

Mitchell, W. J. T. *Picture Theory: Essays on Verbal and Visual Representation.* Chicago: U of Chicago P, 1994. Print.

Mohanty, Chandra Talpade. "Under Western Eyes: Feminist Scholarship and Colonial Discourses." Lewis and Mills, *Feminist Postcolonial Theory* 49–74.

Mollis, Kara L. "Servicing Reading: Community Work and the Revaluation of Literary Study." Danielson and Fallon 46–62.

Moolaadé. Dir. Ousmane Sembène. New Yorker Films, 2004. Film.

Morace, Robert A. "The Life and Times of *Death and the Maiden.*" *Texas Studies in Literature and Language* 42.2 (2000): 135–53. Print.

Morsink, Johannes. *Inherent Human Rights: Philosophical Roots of the Universal Declaration.* Philadelphia: U of Pennsylvania P, 2009. Print.

———. *The Universal Declaration of Human Rights: Origins, Drafting, and Intent.* Philadelphia: U of Pennsylvania P, 1999. Print.

Morson, Gary Saul, and Caryl Emerson. *Mikhail Bakhtin: Creation of a Prosaics.* Stanford: Stanford UP, 1990. Print.

Moyn, Samuel. *The Last Utopia: Human Rights in History.* Cambridge: Harvard UP, 2010. Print.

Mustafa, Fawzia. "Reading Development and Writing Africa: UNFPA, *Nervous Conditions*, and *The Book of Not.*" *Comparative Literature Studies* 46.2 (2009): 379–406. *Project Muse.* Web. 8 Feb. 2010.

Mutua, Makau. *Human Rights: A Political and Cultural Critique.* Philadelphia: U of Pennsylvania P, 2002. Print.

———. "Savages, Victims, and Saviors: The Metaphor of Human Rights." *Harvard International Law Journal* 42.1 (2001): 201–45. *Nexis.* Web. 3 June 2010.

Nance, Kimberly. *Can Literature Promote Justice? Trauma Narrative and Social Action in Latin American Testimonio.* Nashville: Vanderbilt UP, 2006. Print.

———. "*Mountains beyond Mountains*: Role Models and the 'Problem of Goodness' in Socially Engaged Teaching." *ADFL Bulletin* 37.1 (2005): 22–26. Print.

———. "Only Connect? Empathy and Exotopy in Teaching Social Justice Literature." *NOTE: Notes on Teaching English* 30 (2006): 10–14. Web. 12 June 2012.

———. "Reading Human Rights Literature in Undergraduate Literature Classes: Professional Desire, Disciplinary Culture, and the Chances of Cultivating Compassion." *Journal of Human Rights* 9.2 (2010): 161–74. Print.

———. "'Something That Might Resemble a Call': Testimonial Theory and Practice in the Twenty-First Century." *Pushing the Boundaries of Latin American Testimonio.* Ed. Louise Detwiler and Janis Breckenridge. New York: Palgrave, 2012. Print.

———. *Teaching Literature in the Languages.* Upper Saddle River: Prentice Hall, 2010. Print.

Nandy, Ashis. *The Intimate Enemy: Loss and Recovery of Self under Colonialism.* New Delhi: Oxford UP, 1983. Print.

Narayan, Uma. *Dislocating Cultures: Identities, Traditions, and Third World Feminism*. New York: Routledge, 1997. Print.

Niezen, Ronald. *The Origins of Indigenism: Human Rights and the Politics of Identity*. Berkeley: U of California P, 2003. Print.

Nitzan, Tal, and Rachel Tzvia Back. *With an Iron Pen: Twenty Years of Hebrew Protest Poetry*. Albany: State U of New York P, 2009. Print.

Nollan, Valerie, ed. *Bakhtin: Ethics and Mechanics*. Evanston: Northwestern UP, 2004. Print.

Nomani, Asra. *Standing Alone in Mecca: An American Woman's Struggle for the Soul of Islam*. New York: HarperOne, 2005. Print.

Nsehe, Mfonobong. "Obama Fights Nigerian Anti-Gay Bill 2011, Threatens to Cut Off Aid." *Forbes*. Forbes, 9 Dec. 2011. Web. 7 June 2012.

Nussbaum, Martha. "Compassion and Terror." *Daedalus* 132.1 (2003): 10–26. Print.

———. *Cultivating Humanity: A Classical Defense of Reform in Liberal Education*. Cambridge: Harvard UP, 1997. Print.

———. "Kant and Stoic Cosmpolitianism." *Journal of Political Philosophy* 5.1 (1997): 1–25. Print.

———. *Upheavals of Thought: The Intelligence of Emotions*. Cambridge: Cambridge UP, 2001. Print.

Nwelu, Onyeka. "Judging Jude." *Kwenu: Our Culture, Our Future*. Kwenu.com, 25 July 2006. Web. 5 June 2012.

Oliver, Kelly. *Witnessing: Beyond Recognition*. Minneapolis: U of Minnesota P, 2001. Print.

Olson, Lester C., and Arabella Lyon, eds. *Human Rights Rhetoric: Traditions of Testifying and Witnessing*. Spec. issue of *Rhetoric Society Quarterly* 41.3 (2011): i–vi, 1–98. Print.

Ondaatje, Michael. *Anil's Ghost*. London: Picador, 2000. Print.

———. *The English Patient*. London: Picador, 1992. Print.

Oppen, George. *New Collected Poems*. Ed. Michael Davidson. New York: New Directions, 2008. Print.

Orbinski, James. *An Imperfect Offering: Humanitarian Action in the Twenty-First Century*. Toronto: Doubleday Canada, 2008. Print.

Ostien, Philip. "Nigeria's Sharia Penal Codes." *Sharia Implementation in Northern Nigeria, 1999–2006: A Sourcebook*. Ed. Ostien. Ibadan: Spectrum, 2007. 3–21. Print.

Padmanabhan, Manjula. *Harvest*. London: Aurora Metro, 2003. Print.

Peters, Julie Stone. "'Literature,' the 'Rights of Man,' and Narratives of Atrocity: Historical Backgrounds to the Culture of Testimony." *Yale Journal of Law and the Humanities* 17.2 (2005): 249–78. Print.

Phelan, Peggy. *Unmarked: The Politics of Performance*. New York: Routledge, 1993. Print.

Pratt, Mary Louise. "*I, Rigoberta Menchú* and the 'Culture Wars.'" Arias 29–48.

"President's Statement." *University of Texas at Austin*. Office of Institutional Equity, U of Texas, Austin, n.d. Web. 22 July 2014.

Ramazani, Jehan. Introduction. *The Poetry of Mourning: The Modern Elegy from Hardy to Heaney*. Chicago: U of Chicago P, 1994. 1–31. Print.

Rancière, Jacques. "Who Is the Subject of the Rights of Man?" *South Atlantic Quarterly* 103.2–3 (2004): 297–310. Print.

Ratti, Manav. "Michael Ondaatje's *Anil's Ghost* and the Aestheticization of Human Rights." *ARIEL: A Review of International English Literature* 35.1–2 (2004): 121–41. Print.

———. *The Postsecular Imagination: Postcolonialism, Religion, and Literature.* London: Routledge, 2013. Print.

Rawls, John. "The Idea of an Overlapping Consensus." *Oxford Journal of Legal Studies* 7.1 (1987): 1–25. Print.

———. *A Theory of Justice.* Cambridge: Belknap, 1971. Print.

Razack, Sherene H. *Dark Threats and White Knights: The Somalia Affair, Peacekeeping and the New Imperialism.* Toronto: U of Toronto P, 2004. Print.

Reardon, Betty A. "Human Rights and the Global Campaign for Peace Education." *International Review of Education* 48.3–4 (2002): 283–84. Print.

Reid, Graeme. "The Traditional Courts Bill Threatens LGBT South Africans." *The Guardian.* Guardian News and Media, 26 May 2012. Web. 26 May 2102.

Rich, Adrienne. "Arts of the Possible." *Arts of the Possible.* New York: Norton, 2001. 146–67. Print.

———. "Poetry and the Forgotten Future." *A Human Eye: Essays on Art and Society, 1997–2008.* New York: Norton, 2009. 123–46. Print.

Riedner, Rachel, and Ken Mahoney. *Democracies to Come: Rhetorical Action, Neoliberalism, and Communities of Resistance.* Lanham: Lexington, 2008. Print.

Roht-Arriaza, Naomi. *The Pinochet Effect: Transitional Justice in the Age of Human Rights.* Philadelphia: U of Pennsylvania P, 2005. Print.

Ronell, Avital. "The Testamentary Whimper." *South Atlantic Quarterly* 103.2–3 (2004): 489–99. Print.

Rorty, Richard. "Human Rights, Rationality, and Sentimentality." Ishay, *Human Rights Reader* 410–14.

Ross, Michael, and Dale Miller, eds. *The Justice Motive in Everyday Life: Essays in Honor of Melvin J. Lerner.* London: Cambridge UP, 2002. Print.

Rothberg, Michael. "Pedagogy and the Politics of Memory: The Countermonument Project." *Teaching the Representation of the Holocaust.* Ed. Marianne Hirsch and Irene Kacandes. New York: MLA, 2004. 466–76. Print.

Said, Edward. *Culture and Imperialism.* New York: Knopf, 1993. Print.

———. *Orientalism.* New York: Pantheon, 1978. Print.

———. *Representations of the Intellectual.* New York: Pantheon, 1994. Print.

"Same Sex Marriage (Prohibition) Bill." SB 05. 2011. *National Assembly.* Federal Republic of Nigeria, n.d. Web. 22 May 2012.

Sarabah. Dir. Maria Luisa Gambale and Gloria Bremer. Link TV, 2011. Film.

Sassen, Saskia. "Economic Globalization and the Redrawing of Citizenship." *Moral Imperialism: A Critical Anthology.* Ed. Berta Esperanza Hernández-Truyol. New York: New York UP, 2002. 135–50. Print.

Scarry, Elaine. *The Body in Pain: The Making and Unmaking of the World.* New York: Oxford UP, 1985. Print.

———. "The Difficulty of Imagining Other Persons." *The Handbook of Interethnic Coexistence.* Ed. Eugene Weiner. New York: Continuum, 1998. 40–62. Print.

Schaffer, Kay, and Sidonie Smith. *Human Rights and Narrated Lives: The Ethics of Recognition*. New York: Palgrave Macmillan, 2004. Print.

Scheper-Hughes, Nancy. "Keeping an Eye on the Global Traffic in Human Organs." *Lancet* 361 (2003): 1645–48. Print.

———. "Postcard from Brazil: Portrait of Gaddy Tauber, Human Trafficker and Holocaust Survivor." *Anthropology News* Mar. 2007: 19–20; Apr. 2007: 23–24; May 2007: 22–23. Print.

Schimmelpfennig, Roland. *The Golden Dragon*. Trans. David Tushingham. London: Oberon, 2011. Print.

Schüssler Fiorenza, Elisabeth. "Disciplinary Matters: A Critical Rhetoric and Ethic of Inquiry." *Rhetoric, Ethics, and Moral Persuasion in Biblical Discourse: Essays from the 2002 Heidelberg Conference*. Ed. Thomas H. Olbricht. London: Continuum Intl., 2005. 9–32. Print.

Sebbar, Leïla. *The Seine Was Red: Paris, October 1961*. 1998. Trans. Mildred Mortimer. Bloomington: Indiana UP, 2008. Print.

Sedgwick, Eve Kosofsky. *Epistemology of the Closet*. Berkeley: U of California P, 1990. Print.

Senarclens, Pierre de. "Research and Teaching of Human Rights: Introductory Remarks." *Frontiers of Human Rights Education*. Ed. Asbjørn Eide and Marek Thee. Oslo: Universitetsforlaget, 1983. 7–14. Print.

Sevcenko, Liz. "What Is Being Done on . . . Memory Projects?" *World Movement for Democracy*. World Movement for Democracy, n.d. Web. 22 July 2014.

Shaw, Carolyn Martin. "'You Had a Daughter, but I Am Becoming a Woman': Sexuality, Feminism and Postcoloniality in Tsitsi Dangarembga's *Nervous Conditions* and *She No Longer Weeps*." *Research in African Literatures* 38.4 (2007): 7–27. *Project Muse*. Web. 14 Jan. 2009.

Shor, Ira. *Empowering Education: Critical Teaching for Social Change*. Chicago: U of Chicago P, 1992. Print.

Shyllon, F. O. *Black Slaves in Britain*. London: Oxford UP, 1974. Print.

Siamanto. "The Dance." *Bloody News from My Friend*. Trans. Peter Balakian and Nevat Yahjlian. Detroit: Wayne State UP, 1996. 41–43. Print.

Simon, Roger I. *The Touch of the Past: Remembrance, Learning, and Ethics*. New York: Palgrave Macmillan, 2005. Print.

Simon, Roger I., Sharon Rosenberg, and Claudia Eppert. "Introduction: Between Hope and Despair: The Pedagogical Encounter of Historical Remembrance." *Between Hope and Despair: Pedagogy and the Representation of Historical Trauma*. Ed. Simon, Rosenberg, and Eppert. Lanham: Rowman, 2001. 1–8. Print.

Slaughter, Joseph R. *Human Rights, Inc.: The World Novel, Narrative Form, and International Law*. New York: Fordham UP, 2007. Print.

———. "Narration in International Human Rights Law." *CLCWeb: Comparative Literature and Culture* 9.1 (2007): n. pag. Web. 20 Jan. 2012. <http://docs.lib.purdue.edu/clcweb/vol9/iss1/19/>.

Smith, Daniel Jordan. "Cell Phones, Social Inequality and Contemporary Culture in Nigeria." *Canadian Journal of African Studies / Revue Canadienne des*

Études Africaines 40.3 (2006): 496–523. Web. 5 June 2012. <http://www.jstor.org/stable/25433906>.

Smith, William Gardner. *The Stone Face*. New York: Farrar, 1963. Print.

"Sodomy Laws." Criminal Code ch. 42, sec. 214. 1990. *National Assembly*. Federal Republic of Nigeria, n.d. Web. 4 June 2012.

Soete, Luc. "International Diffusion of Technology, Industrial Development and Technological Leapfrogging." *World Development* 13.3 (1985): 409–22. Print.

Sommer, Doris. "Rigoberta's Secrets." *Latin American Perspectives* 18.3 (1991): 32–35. Print.

Sontag, Susan. *Regarding the Pain of Others*. New York: Picador, 2003. Print.

Sophocles. *Ajax*. Ajax, Electra, Oedipus Tyrannus. Ed. and trans. Hugh Lloyd-Jones. Cambridge: Harvard UP, 1994. 26–163. Print.

Soyinka, Wole. *The Interpreters*. London: Deutsch, 1965. Print.

Speak Truth to Power: Voices from beyond The Dark. Dir. Marc Levin. Umbrage Eds., 2000. Film.

Speck, Bruce W., and Sherry L. Hoppe. Introduction. *Service-Learning: History, Theory, and Issues*. Ed. Speck and Hoppe. Westport: Praeger, 2004. vii–xi. Print.

Speed, Shannon. "Gendered Intersections: Collective and Individual Rights in Indigenous Women's Experience." Goodale, *Human Rights* 229–45.

Spiegelman, Art. *Maus I: A Survivor's Tale: My Father Bleeds History*. New York: Pantheon, 1986. Print.

Spivak, Gayatri Chakravorty. "The Making of Americans, the Teaching of English, and the Future of Culture Studies." *New Literary History* 21.4. (1990): 781–98. Print. Papers from the Commonwealth Centre for Literary and Cultural Change.

———. *Outside in the Teaching Machine*. London: Routledge, 1993. Print.

———. "Righting Wrongs." *South Atlantic Quarterly* 103.2–3 (2004): 523–81. Print.

———. "Translator's Preface." Devi xxiii–xxix.

Stanton, Domna. "Foreword: ANDs, INs, and BUTs." *PMLA* 121.5 (2006): 1515–25. Print.

———. "Top Down, Bottom Up: Resignifying the Universal in Human Rights Discourse." Goldberg and Moore, *Theoretical Perspectives* 65–86.

"Statement on Human Rights." *American Anthropologist* 49.4 (1947): 539–43. Print.

Stevens, John Paul. Dissenting opinion. Beard, Secretary, Pennsylvania Dept. of Corrections v. Banks. No. 04-1739. Supreme Court of the US. 28 June 2006. *Lexis/Nexis*. Web. 2 Dec. 2014.

Stobo Sniderman, Andrew, and Mark Hanis. "Drones for Human Rights." *The New York Times*. New York Times, 30 Jan. 2012. Web. 28 July 2012.

Stoll, David. *Rigoberta Menchú and the Story of All Poor Guatemalans*. Boulder: Westview, 1999. Print.

Stowe, Harriet Beecher. *Uncle Tom's Cabin*. Ed. Jean Fagan Yellin. Oxford: Oxford UP, 1998. Print.

Strange, Jeffrey. "How Fictional Tales Wag Real-World Beliefs." Green, Strange, and Brock 263–86.

Strange, Jeffrey, and Cynthia Leung. "How Anecdotal Accounts in News and in Fiction Can Influence Judgments of a Social Problem's Urgency, Causes, and Cures." *Personality and Social Psychology Bulletin* 25 (1999): 436–49. Web. 12 June 2012.

Strong-Leek, Linda. "Emerging Womanism in the Works of Tsitsi Dangarembga, Barbara Mahkalisa, and J. Nozipo Maraire." *North-South Linkages and Connections in Continental and Diaspora African Literatures.* Ed. Edris Makward, Mark L. Lilleleht, and Ahmed Saber. Trenton: African World, 2004. 140–56. Print.

Sunder Rajan, Rajeswari. "The Third World Academic in Other Places; or, The Postcolonial Intellectual Revisited." *Critical Inquiry* 23.3 (1997): 596–616. Print.

Suu Kyi, Aung San. *"Freedom from Fear": And Other Writings.* New York: Penguin, 2010. Print.

Swaffar, Janet, and Katherine Arens. *Remapping the Foreign Language Curriculum: An Approach through Multiple Literacies.* New York: MLA, 2005. Print.

Sweeney, Megan. "*Beard v. Banks*: Deprivation as Rehabilitation." *PMLA* 122.3 (2007): 779–83. Print.

———. "Legal Brutality: Prisons and Punishment, the American Way." *American Literary History* 22.3 (2010): 698–713. Print.

———. "Prison Narratives, Narrative Prisons: Incarcerated Women Reading Gayl Jones's *Eva's Man*." *After the Pain: Critical Essays on Gayl Jones.* Ed. Fiona Mills and Keith Mitchell. New York: Lang, 2006. 173–202. Print.

———. *Reading Is My Window: Books and the Art of Reading in Women's Prisons.* Chapel Hill: U of North Carolina P, 2010. Print.

"Syria Crisis: The Violence Mapped by the UN." *The Guardian.* Guardian News and Media, n.d. Web. 11 May 2012.

Tate, Gary. "Notes on the Dying of a Conversation." *College English* 57.3 (1995): 303–09. Print.

———. "A Place for Literature in Freshmen Composition." *College English* 55.3 (1993): 317–21. Print.

Taylor, Low. "Image and Irony in *The Official Story*." *Literature/Film Quarterly* 17.3 (1989): 207–09. Print.

Texas Constitution. Art 1, sec. 32. *The Texas Constitution and Statutes.* N.p., 8 Nov. 2005. Web. 6 June 2012.

Thiele, Leslie Paul. *The Heart of Judgment: Practical Wisdom, Neuroscience, and Narrative.* London: Cambridge UP, 2006. Print.

Thomas, Sue. "Rewriting the Hysteric as Anorexic in Tsitsi Dangarembga's *Nervous Conditions*." *Scenes of the Apple: Food and the Female Body in Nineteenth- and Twentieth-Century Women's Writing.* Ed. Tamar Heller and Patricia Moran. Albany: State U of New York P, 2003. 183–98. Print.

Tomlinson, Emily. "Mapping the Land of 'I Don't Remember': For a Revaluation of *La historia oficial*." *Bulletin of Hispanic Studies* 81.2 (2004): 215–28. Print.

"Total U.S. Correctional Population Declined in 2012 for Fourth Year." *Bureau of Justice Statistics.* Office of Justice Programs, US Dept. of Justice, 19 Dec. 2013. Web. 9 Dec. 2014.

Tripp, Aili Mari. "The Evolution of Transnational Feminisms: Consensus, Conflict, and New Dynamics." *Global Feminism: Transnational Women's Activism, Organizing, and Human Rights.* Ed. Myra Marx Ferree and Tripp. New York: New York UP, 2006. 51–75. Print.

Tsundue, Tenzin. *Kora: Stories and Poems*. 6th ed. 2010. *Tibet Writes: Where Tibetans Write.* TibetWrites.org, 2004–10. Web. 22 July 2014.

Tuck, Richard. *The Rights of War and Peace: Political Thought and the International Order from Grotius to Kant.* Oxford: Oxford UP, 1999. Print.

Turner, Bryan. *Vulnerability and Human Rights.* University Park: Penn State UP, 2006. Print. Essays on Human Rights.

Turner, Nikki. *A Project Chick.* Columbus: Triple Crown, 2004. Print.

"United Nations Universal Declaration of Human Rights (1948): Articles 17 and 22–26." Ishay, *Human Rights Reader* 39.

"The Universal Declaration of Human Rights." 1948. *United Nations.* United Nations, n.d. Web. 14 Apr. 2011. <www.un.org/en/documents/udhr/index.shtml>.

"U.S. Reservations, Declarations, and Understandings, Convention against Torture and Other Cruel, Inhuman or Degrading Treatment or Punishment, Cong. Rec. S17486-01 (daily ed., Oct. 27, 1990)." *University of Minnesota Human Rights Library.* U of Minnesota, n.d. Web. 20 July 2012. <http://www1.umn.edu/humanrts/usdocs/tortres.html>.

Uzoatu, Uzor Maxim. Foreword. Dibia viii.

Valls, Andrew, ed. *Race and Racism in Modern Philosophy.* Ithaca: Cornell UP, 2005. Print.

Vellino, Brenda Carr. "Everything I Know about Human Rights I Learned from Literature: Human Rights Literacy in the Canadian Literature Classroom." *Home-work: Postcolonialism, Pedagogy, and Canadian Literature.* Ed. Cynthia Conchita Sugars. Ottawa: U of Ottawa P, 2004. 135–50. Print.

———. "'History's Pulse Measured with Another Hand': Precarity Archives and Translocal Citizen Witness in Dionne Brand's *Inventory.*" *University of Toronto Quarterly* 82.2 (2013): 242–60. Print.

———. "Human Rights Poetry as Ethical Tribunal: Bodies and Bystanders in Margaret Atwood's 'Footnote to the Amnesty Report on Torture.'" *Law, Mystery, and the Humanities.* Ed. Logan Atkinson and Diana Majury. Toronto: U of Toronto P, 2008. 217–46. Print.

The Visitor. Dir. Thomas McCarthy. Perf. Richard Jenkins, Haaz Sleiman, Danai Jekesai Gurira, and Marian Seldes. Groundswell Productions, 2008. Film.

Vlastos, Gregory. "Slavery in Plato's Thought." *Philosophical Review* 50.3 (1941): 289–304. *JSTOR.* Web. 18 Feb. 2011.

Vogler, Thomas A. "Poetic Witness: Writing the Real." *Witness and Memory: The Discourse of Trauma.* Ed. Ana Douglass and Vogler. New York: Routledge, 2005. 173–205. Print.

Wadud, Amina. *Qur'an and Woman: Reading the Sacred Text from a Woman's Perspective.* New York: Oxford UP, 1999. Print.

Warner, Kevin. "Against the Narrowing of Perspectives: How Do We See Learning, Prisons, and Prisoners?" *Journal of Correctional Education* 58.2 (2007): 170–84. Print.

Warner, Michael. "Uncritical Reading." *Polemic: Critical or Uncritical.* Ed. Jane Gallop. New York: Routledge, 2004. 13–38. Print.

Wideman, John Edgar. *Brothers and Keepers.* 1984. New York: Mariner, 2005. Print.

Wilkinson, Richard, and Kate Pickett. *The Spirit Level: Why Greater Equality Makes Societies Stronger.* New York: Bloomsbury, 2009. Print.

Wilson, Bruce. "Warren-Endorsed Nigerian Archbishop Backed Anti-Gay Laws Worse Than Pre-WWII Third Reich's." *Huffington Post.* Huffington Post, 24 Dec. 2008. Web. 7 June 2012.

Winter, Sarah. "The Novel and Prejudice." McClennen and Slaughter, *Human Rights* 76–102.

Wixson, Kelli Donovan. "Women and Food in Tsitsi Dangarembga's *Nervous Conditions.*" *Emerging Perspectives on Tsitsi Dangarembga: Negotiating the Postcolonial.* Ed. Ann Elizabeth Willey and Jeanette Treiber. Trenton: Africa World, 2002. 221–30. Print.

Woeser. *Tibet's True Heart.* Trans. A. E. Clark. Dobb's Ferry: Ragged Banner, 2008. Print.

Wollstonecraft, Mary. *A Vindication of the Rights of Woman.* Ed. Miriam Brody. London: Penguin, 1975. Print.

Woolley, John T., and Gerhard Peters. *The American Presidency Project.* U of California, Santa Barbara, 1999. Web. 31 Mar. 2011.

Wright, Derek. "'More Than Just a Plateful of Food': Regurgitating Colonialism in Tsitsi Dangarembga's *Nervous Conditions.*" *Commonwealth* 17.2 (1995): 8–18. Print.

Young, James E. Introduction. *At Memory's Edge: After-images of the Holocaust in Contemporary Art and Architecture.* New Haven: Yale UP, 2000. 1–11. Print.

Young, Robert. *Postcolonialism: An Historical Introduction.* Oxford: Blackwell, 2001. Print.

Zatzman, Belarie. "The Monologue Project: Drama as a Form of Witnessing." *How Theatre Educates: Convergences and Counterpoints.* Ed. Kathleen Gallagher and David Booth. Buffalo: U of Toronto P, 2003. Print.

Zlotkowski, Edward. Introduction. Danielson and Fallon xi–xiv.

Index

Modern Language Association of America

Options for Teaching

To purchase MLA publications, visit www.mla.org/bookstore.

Teaching Human Rights in Literary and Cultural Studies. Ed. Alexandra Schultheis Moore and Elizabeth Swanson Goldberg. 2015.

Teaching the Latin American Boom. Ed. Lucille Kerr and Alejandro Herrero-Olaizola. 2015.

Teaching Early Modern English Literature from the Archives. Ed. Heidi Brayman Hackel and Ian Frederick Moulton. 2015.

Teaching Anglophone Caribbean Literature. Ed. Supriya M. Nair. 2012.

Teaching Film. Ed. Lucy Fischer and Patrice Petro. 2012.

Teaching Seventeenth- and Eighteenth-Century French Women Writers. Ed. Faith E. Beasley. 2011.

Teaching French Women Writers of the Renaissance and Reformation. Ed. Colette H. Winn. 2011.

Teaching Law and Literature. Ed. Austin Sarat, Cathrine O. Frank, and Matthew Anderson. 2011.

Teaching British Women Playwrights of the Restoration and Eighteenth Century. Ed. Bonnie Nelson and Catherine Burroughs. 2010.

Teaching Narrative Theory. Ed. David Herman, Brian McHale, and James Phelan. 2010.

Teaching Early Modern English Prose. Ed. Susannah Brietz Monta and Margaret W. Ferguson. 2010.

Teaching Italian American Literature, Film, and Popular Culture. Ed. Edvige Giunta and Kathleen Zamboni McCormick. 2010.

Teaching the Graphic Novel. Ed. Stephen E. Tabachnick. 2009.

Teaching Literature and Language Online. Ed. Ian Lancashire. 2009.

Teaching the African Novel. Ed. Gaurav Desai. 2009.

Teaching World Literature. Ed. David Damrosch. 2009.

Teaching North American Environmental Literature. Ed. Laird Christensen, Mark C. Long, and Fred Waage. 2008.

Teaching Life Writing Texts. Ed. Miriam Fuchs and Craig Howes. 2007.

Teaching Nineteenth-Century American Poetry. Ed. Paula Bernat Bennett, Karen L. Kilcup, and Philipp Schweighauser. 2007.

Teaching Representations of the Spanish Civil War. Ed. Noël Valis. 2006.

Teaching the Representation of the Holocaust. Ed. Marianne Hirsch and Irene Kacandes. 2004.

Teaching Tudor and Stuart Women Writers. Ed. Susanne Woods and Margaret P. Hannay. 2000.

Teaching Literature and Medicine. Ed. Anne Hunsaker Hawkins and Marilyn Chandler McEntyre. 2000.

Teaching the Literatures of Early America. Ed. Carla Mulford. 1999.

Teaching Shakespeare through Performance. Ed. Milla C. Riggio. 1999.

Teaching Oral Traditions. Ed. John Miles Foley. 1998.

Teaching Contemporary Theory to Undergraduates. Ed. Dianne F. Sadoff and William E. Cain. 1994.

Teaching Children's Literature: Issues, Pedagogy, Resources. Ed. Glenn Edward Sadler. 1992.

Teaching Literature and Other Arts. Ed. Jean-Pierre Barricelli, Joseph Gibaldi, and Estella Lauter. 1990.

New Methods in College Writing Programs: Theories in Practice. Ed. Paul Connolly and Teresa Vilardi. 1986.

School-College Collaborative Programs in English. Ed. Ron Fortune. 1986.

Teaching Environmental Literature: Materials, Methods, Resources. Ed. Frederick O. Waage. 1985.

Part-Time Academic Employment in the Humanities: A Sourcebook for Just Policy. Ed. Elizabeth M. Wallace. 1984.

Film Study in the Undergraduate Curriculum. Ed. Barry K. Grant. 1983.

The Teaching Apprentice Program in Language and Literature. Ed. Joseph Gibaldi and James V. Mirollo. 1981.

Options for Undergraduate Foreign Language Programs: Four-Year and Two-Year Colleges. Ed. Renate A. Schulz. 1979.

Options for the Teaching of English: Freshman Composition. Ed. Jasper P. Neel. 1978.

Options for the Teaching of English: The Undergraduate Curriculum. Ed. Elizabeth Wooten Cowan. 1975.